top50resorts

ski & snowboard

in europe 2006

top50resorts
ski & snowboard
in europe 2006

pat sharples   vanessa webb

foulsham
LONDON • NEW YORK • TORONTO • SYDNEY

foulsham

The Publishing House, Bennetts Close,
Cippenham, Slough, Berkshire, SL1 5AP
England

Foulsham books can be found in all good bookshops or
direct from www.foulsham.com

ISBN 0-572-03152-1

Cover photograph by Melody Sky
(www.melodysky.com); skier: Warren Smith

A CIP record for this book is available from the British
Library.

Design and layout by Ben Cracknell Studios
Printed in Malaysia

Contents

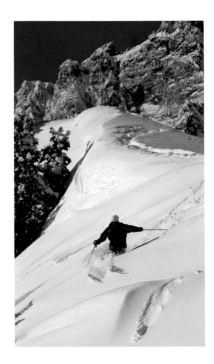

C.R. JOHNSON
NO LIMIT TO EXPRESSION

We made the Teneighty Foil for riders who wanted to have the ultimate tool everywhere: parks, backcountry and tricky terrain. Throw your tricks on the whole mountain, learn more from your mistakes, walk up again and again and try some more: the Teneighty Foil will stay with you whatever you do.

TENEIGHTY FOIL

FOOTWEAR APPAREL [EQUIPMENT]

SalomonSki.com

SALOMON

Acknowledgements

We would like to thank all the people who helped us throughout the winter, allowing us to travel to each of the Top 50 Resorts. We could not have done this without them. Thank you to tourist offices and their press and marketing departments, and to friends and family who have helped us out along our way, providing information and accommodation. In particular we would like to thank the following:

Andorra: Arinsal: Pete and Adrian. Pas de la Casa and Soldeu: Silvia Encinas and Sira Puig, Tyler Charlton.

Austria: Bad Gastein: Markus Papai. Kitzbühel: Sascha Reitsma and Tamara Prömer. Lech: Claudia Lengenfelder. Mayrhofen: Kathren Egger and Jon Weaver. St Anton: Wilma Himmelfreundpointner.

France: Les Arcs: Helen. Chamonix: Glen and Caroline. Courchevel: Laurence Bourgeois and all the regulars at the Signal. Les Deux Alpes: Elodie Lavesvre, Héléna Hospital, Pete and Lynn and Matt Sharples. La Grave: Robin and Marlene, Niels and Didier, and Jean-Charles. Meribel: Adam Johnson, The Taverne hotel/bar. Morzine: Sturan Erskine, Johnny Mclaren, Bruno Robinet. La Plagne: Giles and Claire, Marcus, Paul and Monica Sharples. St Foy: Anne Royer, Adrian Myers. Serre Chevalier: Ben Hawker aka Bungle. La Tania: Toffa. Tignes: Simi Johnson, Euan at Les Mélèzes, James Vernon. Val d'Isère: Chris Howarth, Jane Jacquemod. Val Thorens: Stefanie.

Italy: Alagna and Gressoney: Lara, Hotel Villa Tedaldi. Cervinia: Elsa and Andy North. Selva in Val Gardena: Jolanda Senoner.

Sweden: Jon Olsson, Jens H. Bond. Åre: Bengt Ullström

Switzerland: Heidi Reisz at Swiss Tourism. Arosa: Beatrice Gerber and our film crew Rachel and Simon. Champéry: Yannick Ducrot, Kina Ojdahl, John Mitchell, Paul and Rhonda. Crans Montana: Stefanie Ambuehl. Davos: Clair Southwell, Daniel Waechter, Chris Southwell, Carin Gisep-Caligari, Othmar Thomann. Klösters: Clair Southwell, Daniel Waechter, Hotel Alpina, Lukas Durr, Al Thony and Chris Southwell. Saas Fee: Robbie and Therese, Adrian Schnyder. St Moritz: Alexandra Blaha. Verbier: Warren Smith, Melody Sky, Nick Southwell, Pierre-Yves. Jamie and Kerry. Zermatt: Karin Schmid.

Photographers: Adrian Myers, Ross Woodhall, Melody Sky. Magazines: Zack Ragg and Daniel Crawford at Dark Summer.

A big shout out to all of Pat's sponsors who have supported him in his career as a professional skier and now are considered close friends. *Thank you.* Oakley Marketing Manager, Stewart Morgan. Oakley team manager, Jeremy Festa. Salomon Marketing, Sonia Prior, Richard Seymour, Andy Topping and Eric Davis. Natives.co.uk, Iain Martin, Snow and Rock, Kevin Young and Gregor Brealey, Ignite, Neil Thompson, Ortovox, Richard Want, Giro, Gregor Urquhart.

A special thanks to all at Foulsham Publishing: Barry, Roger, Wendy, Sue, Kay and the rest of the team, who believed in us and gave us the chance to write our first book.

Also, we would like to thank our families and friends, who have supported us from the start to the end of the whole project. A special thanks to David and Carol Webb, Vanessa's parents, who have let us take over their home, and provide unconditional help and support and to Paul and Monica Sharples, Pat's parents, for our European base, and for re-fuelling us when we needed a break.

We are so sorry if we have missed people out, but you know who you are and we won't forget all the support you have given us.

Many thanks, Vanessa and Pat.

Photograph acknowledgements

Photographs for the following resorts are tourist board copyright: Alagna Tourist Board. Åre Tourist Board. Arosa Tourismus. Avoriaz Tourist Board. Bad Gastein Tourist Board. Cortina Turismo. Hemsedal Tourist Board. Ischgl Tourist Board. Kitzbühel Tourist Board. La Tania Tourist Board. Lech Arlberg. Les Arcs Tourist Board. Mayrhofen Tourist Board. Meribel Tourist Board. Morzine Tourist Board. St Moritz Tourist Board. Ste Foy Tarentaise FR/A Royer. Serre Chevalier Tourist Board. Sheffield Ski Village. Val Gardenia Tourist Board. Many thanks to all the tourist boards for their help and support.

Introduction

The idea of writing a travel guide on the top locations to ski and board in Europe came to us whilst we were sitting on the ski bus from Courchevel 1650 up to 1850 in April 2004. Since then we have put this idea into reality and we are proud to have the first edition of the Top 50 Resorts out in the shops.

One of our first objectives was to make our book different from the others, so we agreed that we should travel to all 50 resorts in person, in one season, to see them for ourselves and experience what they had to offer. In this way it allows us to bring you the most up-to-date information, from a first-hand point of view, and also to compare each resort legitimately, having been to them all personally. We can guarantee that this was 100 per cent researched by the authors and, what's more, many of the photographs have been taken by us.

Our travels started in October 2004, and we were on a quest to ride and research 50 of the top spots for skiing and snowboarding in Europe. Some serious planning was required, although that soon went down

the toilet as weather conditions and such like got in the way. Luckily tourist offices and friends were very flexible and helpful and, because of them, we managed to make it work.

Each day we rode the mountain, and after a great day we got back and scribbled it all down whilst it was fresh in our minds. That done, we rushed out to check out the best restaurants, bars and clubs, and after a few days of the same we moved on to the next resort. Travelling to 50 resorts in one season was not easy, but it was the experience of a lifetime, and we enjoyed every minute. Along the way we have had the privilege of skiing and boarding with some of the world's best riders, and we have eaten some of the finest cuisine, stayed at some amazing hotels, attended some top parties, and met some of the loveliest (and craziest) people there are.

We hope that you enjoy the first edition of *Top 50 Resorts in Europe for Skiing and Snowboarding*, and that we can help you to find your Top Resort. Enjoy!

About the authors

Pat Sharples: Pat is a one of the leading names on the New School scene. He is Head Coach of the British Freeski Camps (see www.britishfreeskicamps.com) and is currently scouting new talent for Oakley and Salomon. Pat's sponsors include Oakley, Salomon, Snow and Rock, Ortovox, Giro helmets, Ignite Hats and Natives.

Formerly Pat has earned many titles such as the European Mogul Challenge Champion, and England Freestyle Champion, and he was one of the top British Big Mountain competitors. He was also the England Freestyle Team Captain for four years running.

His home resort is Courchevel, where he has lived for 12 years and the particularly detailed insider information in the Courchevel chapter probably reflects this. The

information in this book about the mountains, including parks and off-piste, was compiled by Pat, with the help of many of his contacts and friends in the industry.

Vanessa Webb: Vanessa has a passion for skiing, travelling and writing. She has skied all her life and has spent seasons in Canada and the Alps, both qualifying and working as a ski instructor and coach. Vanessa also has a first class degree in Psychology from Newcastle University.

Vanessa was responsible for writing about the resorts themselves, including the hotels, restaurants, activities and nightlife, and for the editing of Pat's dubious spelling. Vanessa has also been experimenting with photography and took a lot of the photos in the book.

How to use this book

Use this book exactly as you like, but if you want to find the best resort for you, we recommend that you start by checking out the list of 'Top 5s' (page 13). Decide which features of a resort you value the most (nightlife, lift pass price, off-piste/backcountry, parks…) and see which resorts we recommend in these categories; you might find that some overlap. Make a shortlist of three or four that you think would suit you and then refer to them in the main text of the book and decide which one you think is more your cup of tea. If you think you might like similar resorts to us you could also check out how we rank all 50 resorts.

We have tried to include piste maps for as many resorts as possible. Where one does not appear, go to the resort website or contact the tourist office (see Useful facts and phone numbers). We will do our best to add more next year.

Our top 50 resorts

1	St Anton	27	Crans Montana
2	Chamonix	28	La Plagne
3	Saas Fee	29	Meribel
4	La Grave	30	Arosa
5	Zermatt	31	Laax Murschetg
6	Verbier	32	Kitzbühel
7	Mayrhofen	33	Selva in Val
8	Courchevel 1850		Gardena
9	Courchevel 1650	34	Courmayeur
10	Champéry	35	Val Thorens
11	Morzine	36	La Rosière
12	St Moritz	37	Arinsal
13	Tignes	38	Hintertux
14	Lech	39	La Tania
15	Val d'Isère	40	Alagna
16	St Foy	41	Cervinia
17	Klösters	42	Sölden
18	Bad Gastein	43	Hemsedal
19	Ischgl	44	Davos
20	Les Deux Alpes	45	Riksgransen
21	Serre Chevalier	46	Pas de la Casa
22	Avoriaz	47	Sälen
23	Åre	48	Oppdal
24	Soldeu	49	Flims
24	Les Arcs	50	Cortina
26	Gressoney		d'Ampezzo

We want to be very clear about the fact that the following ratings are based purely on our opinion, and they are chosen specifically for us. Some people may hate our favourite resorts and others may fall in love with some that we're not so keen on. A favourite resort is a very personal choice. We even had difficulties deciding on this list between the two of us, so our top 50 should not be considered as a definitive list, it is simply our views on the best resorts, and we thought you might be interested. Amazingly, there were only a few resorts that we wouldn't go back to, most of them we rate really highly, and it was difficult to choose between them.

Our top 5s

Top 5 resorts for off-piste/backcountry
1. La Grave
2. Chamonix
3. Verbier
4. Gressoney/Alagna
5. St Foy

Top 5 resorts for parks
1. Le Crosets Park in Champéry
2. Les Deux Alpes
3. Laax Murschetg
4. Mayrhofen
5. Soldeu

Top 5 resorts favoured by the rich and famous
1. St Moritz
2. Courchevel 1850
3. Klösters
4. Kitzbühel
5. Lech

Top 5 resorts for guaranteed snow
1. Hintertux
2. Tignes
3. Sölden
4. Zermatt/Saas Fee
5. Les Deux Alpes

Top 5 most expensive 6-day lift passes
1. St Moritz tied with Zermatt
2. Flims/Laax Murschetg
3. St Anton
4. Sölden
5. Val d'Isère

Top 5 cheapest lift passes
1. St Foy
2. Morzine – Les Gets (not Portes du Soleil)
3. Arinsal
4. Serre Chevalier
5. La Rosière

Top 5 resorts to go to with a group of mates
1. St Anton
2. Soldeu
3. Mayrhofen
4. Morzine/Avoriaz
5. Val d'Isère

Top 5 resorts for a romantic weekend
1. Saas Fee
2. Bad Gastein
3. Klösters
4. Lech
5. St Moritz

Top 5 resorts for resort charm
1. Zermatt
2. Klösters
3. Saas Fee
4. Kitzbühel
5. Lech

Top 5 resorts for nightlife
1. St Anton
2. Verbier
3. Åre
4. Les Deux Alpes
5. Ischgl

Top 5 resorts that are great, but won't break the bank
1. Soldeu
2. Pas de la Casa
3. Les Deux Alpes
4. Mayrhofen
5. Arosa

OAKLEY TECHNICAL OUTERWEAR
TANNER HALL

Equipment guide

SALOMON
FuEL YOUR INSTINCT™

LOFT: *Freeride/freestyle*

This deck launches the new Lightweight Optimum Feel Technology construction, engineered with a new full wood ERA core with Nomex and honeycomb core, half the weight of aluminium honeycomb, and finished with a revolutionary patented Zeolit base technology. The result is a definitively faster, smarter, lighter and more responsive ride.

Era: *Freeride/freestyle*

The performance feel you need to push your potential to the highest level. The Era features carbon in-lays in the nose and tail, and Alium under the central ERA spine, so that you feel confident and smooth at any speed.

Pulse: *Freeride/freestyle*

The Pulse has a damp, solid feel and versatile flex, and gives you all the tools you need to progress through your first few seasons.

DB: *Freestyle*

A superior freestyle machine designed tip-to-tail by Mr Benedek. After winning Rider of the Year two years in a row, it only makes sense for the Benedek Pro model to make another run as well.

RIDE
SNOWBOARDS

LeBlanc ProModel: *Freestyle*

An aggressive board with super smooth responsiveness. This board is solid, committed, perfect for rails and the park, and adaptable for mountain riding.

Havoc: *Freestyle/freeride*

This versatile board, for the high-end rider on a budget, is great for all-mountain riding, from jibbing and sliding to backcountry steeps.

Yukon: *Freeride*

An aggressive freeride board with maximum response and handling, setting the standard for performance in variable snow conditions. It has been completely souped up for 05/06 and includes the new Thermal Sidewall Technology for even greater precision and control and Ride's signature Tapered Core technology for weight savings and better turning. Also 3D profiles create Misty Pockets for swing-weight reduction, NR Con (Noise Reduction Construction) reduces vibration and weight and the RGG (RideGlide with Gallium) Base remains waxed for a never-ending fast ride.

Timeless: *Freeride*

This is the ultimate freeride deck for the masses; responsive and full of drive. Quick and solid, the Timeless is the board of choice for the backcountry rider whose focus is turning smooth and riding fast on any snow. The Timeless has been completely redesigned for 05/06 and is built for smooth riding at its best, with the Thermal Sidewall Technology, Tapered Core, 3D profiles and NR Con as the Yukon above. Get all the latest details on Ride's boards, boots, bindings, apparel and team at www.ridesnowboards.com.

ARMADA

The Armada team is pushing the boundaries of skiing further than they have ever been pushed before, and this is reflected in the design. Athletes work side by side with engineers and artists in order to produce the most innovative and technologically advanced skis possible.

AR5: *Freestyle*

The AR5 has been completely reworked for park, pipe and urban jibbing. Armada targeted the centre and outer edge of the core with a strong, dense wood and laminated and complemented it with light wood stringers. The result is a core that provides reinforcement to the edges and sidewalls, giving the AR5 increased durability, better response, snap and weight savings. To increase edge durability further, Armada custom heat-treated a thicker edge, changed the density of the ABS and backed it with variable slant sidewalls. Combine the above with the faster, more durable Sintered 7 Series base and 8 Series top material and you have the most durable and best performing AR5 series to date.

ARV: *Freestyle/freeride*

From the backcountry to the park and groomers, the ARV provides the ultimate in versatility. Incorporating top-shelf materials, they've increased the thickness of the specially heat-treated edges for added durability and reduced weight by using less sidewall material. The sidecut profile and Torsion Triax Fabric lay-up allows the ski to be an excellent carver on the hardpack; fully capable of high-speed aggressive turns. Armada have also increased the overall dimensions of each size giving the ski more float in powder.

JP vs. Julien Signature Series: *Freeride /backcountry Freestyle*

The original backcountry freestyle ski makes its return. The JP vs. Julien Signature Model is the ultimate tool for those who want to take backcountry jumping to new levels. JP and Julien designed this model with little sidecut and a wide waist which allows you to stomp landings and makes it easier to control while skiing switch into backcountry booters – very useful for those sketchy in-runs. The progressive tip radius provides extra float in powder, while the tail sits 10mm higher than the tip for easier switch landings.

Antony Boronowski Pro Model: *Backcountry freestyle*

The ANT signature model: look no further if you crave the top of the line in Big Mountain skis. New to the signature series, ANT was developed from the inside out by team rider Anthony Boronowski. The widest ski Armada produce, it is designed for charging steep lines in all snow conditions at speeds bordering lunacy. Ideal for backcountry madness.

With only ten years under their belt, Line have shocked the industry with their forward thinking in terms of image and product.

Chronic Wide: *Freestyle/all-terrain*

The Chronic series returns, with this wider version for those with a penchant for softer snow. The Chronic's bombproof construction and stiff flex is combined with versatile all-terrain geometry to create the highest performance all-terrain freestyle ski ever conceived. These skis will turn the entire mountain into your personal terrain park, and are a favourite of Andy Bennett, one of the UK's leading skiers, and the British Slopestyle and Big Air Champion.

Prophet 100: *Freeride/big mountain*

The Prophet series represents over three years of research and development working closely with Eric Pollard to create the next generation of big mountain freeride skis. The Prophet 100 has the innovative technology, materials and design required to tackle the biggest mountains in the world. These skis are built to charge.

Mothership: *Freestyle/freeride*

Line's most popular fat freestyle ski returns, with some awesome graphics. The Mothership pioneered today's

backcountry revolution and continues to impress with its perfect blend of width, flex and lightweight agility. Line have upgraded the mounting to a Quickmount 6 pack and guaranteed it to be the lightest weight fat ski in its class by using a Poplar Macroblock wood core and Carbon Ollieband technology.

Streetracer 10 + *S921 Ti Manual heel: On-piste carving*

The revolutionary Streetracer with intuitive power steering is perfect for those who love carving clean turns. The Streetracer 10 is at the top of the range, a high-tech roadster that arcs big turns effortlessly and carves medium turns with ease.

Scrambler Hot + *S912 Ti:*

All mountain

A great all-mountain ski for carving on the piste and for freeriding. The combination of an overshaped sidecut with a wider waist, makes the Scrambler Hot tough enough to withstand the demands of multi-terrain adventuring, yet responsive enough to power through any kind of snow. Whatever you ask of the Scrambler Hot, it will deliver.

The Teneighty range – Salomon has revamped their Twin Tip range for 05/06, providing a range of skis that are adapted to all types of terrain.

Teneighty foil: *Freestyle/freeride*

The Teneighty foils are designed for riders who want the ultimate tool everywhere: parks, backcountry and tricky terrain. The foil combines Isocell complex core (smooth and dampening, with foam complex for reactivity and rebound), Monocoque composite (for lightness, manoeuvrability, rebound and reactivity) and Spaceframe technology (offering lightness, torsional flex and air balance).

Teneighty Gun: *Freeride/backcountry freestyle*

The Gun replaces the ever popular PocketRocket, a symbol of the New School freestyle culture. If you've ever jumped and crashed in the powder because your ski couldn't take it, you need to give some serious consideration to the Gun – the ski to help you fly high, throw tricks and still stomp them wherever you might try to stick them. Because New School has a classroom everywhere on the mountain, not just in parks.

Teneighty Thruster: *Freestyle*

This ski is always on the podium at any New School freestyle event. A great tool for the budding jibber; balanced, lightweight and responsive.

BODY ARMOUR

There is no doubt that skiing and snowboarding are dangerous sports. Whether you are sticking to the pisted runs, hitting the parks or venturing into the backcountry, we strongly advise the use of safety equipment. There are numerous examples of people who have seriously injured themselves, sometimes fatally, who could have protected themselves simply by wearing the basic safety equipment of a helmet, back and short protector. I hope that the loved and hugely respected professional skier and in-line skater Rich Taylor, who died from a severe head injury in August 2004, would not mind us mentioning that a helmet could have saved his life.

Helmets

In America, there are a number of resorts in which it is illegal not to wear a helmet and this attitude is spreading to Europe. You should consider a helmet as important as your skis/board, if not more so, as it could be a lifesaver. There is no excuse for not wearing one. And they make you look hardcore. We don't go anywhere without our Giro helmets. In particular we recommend…

G10, The Freestyle Boss:
This super light freestyle/freeride helmet has a skate-styled shape with progressive lines and wide-angle cut for great peripheral vision and gapless goggle fit. Its features make it a versatile helmet for a variety of weather conditions, and include EPS liner and 14 vents with Thermostat ventilation control system. In addition, the removable earpads detach for springtime sessions and are compatible with TuneUps™ (so you can hear your favourite beats in full stereo with your helmet on).

Bad Lieutenant: This is standard issue for hardcore riders. Its styling is one of a kind and it has a high-impact ABS shell with an impact-absorbing EPS (expanded polystyrene) liner. The earpads are removable and compatible with TuneUps.

For further information on Giro ski and snowboard helmets, and to find your nearest stockist contact Big Bear Sports on 020 8991 9244 or giro@bigbear.co.uk.

Back protectors

If you fill your days in the park hitting huge kickers and sketchy rail slides or going off cliff drops in the backcountry then you need a back protector. Your spine is pretty vulnerable when you crash and needs protecting; if you value the use of your limbs invest in one. Contrary to popular opinion they are perfectly comfortable and don't restrict body movement at all. We like the **Dainese Shield 8-7-6**, which has polypropylene hard plates and perforated polyethylene soft padding. The protector is tested at −20° C.

Short protectors

Not everyone feels the need to wear a short protector but it can be very handy in a crash over rocks or on a rail in the park. The **Dainese Short Protector Plus** features soft composite protection for the hipbone, sides and gluteus with rigid composite femur protectors.

Venturing into the backcountry is a risky (albeit fun) business no matter how good your knowledge of the terrain. Each year there are more reports of avalanches taking people's lives because an increasing number of skiers and boarders are exploring off-piste without the required experience or equipment. There are a few *essential* pointers. For starters, *never go alone*. No one will be there to witness your amazing Rodeo 720 off the 24m cliff and if you get caught in an avalanche – you're stuffed. Ensure that at least one person in the group has extensive experience and substantial knowledge of the local terrain. If your group does not have these qualities, hire a guide.

Additionally, it is vital to invest in the right equipment – it could save your life or someone else's...

Avalanche transceivers

This is arguably the most important piece of equipment to have when exploring off-piste. It is used to locate someone who has been enveloped in an avalanche and also allows a fellow transceiver carrier to find you. It should be worn under your jacket at all times. Remember, it is completely useless unless you know how to use it. Details on vitally important courses can be found at www.natives.co.uk.

We recommend the **Ortovox X1 avalanche transceiver**, which we carry with us religiously on the mountain. The new fully automatic X1 brings extra accuracy with greater simplicity.

Digital/analogue functions are microprocessor controlled to limit user faults. They are also safe, fast and compatible with all transceivers.

Brand new on the scene is the **S1** – the first sensor-controlled avalanche transceiver. This spectacular piece of technology can simultaneously locate up to five people within a radius of 60m. It has a large, illuminated display showing the position and distance to all buried persons. Additional features include an electronic compass, temperature, measurement of inclination and an indication of the depth of burial.

Probe pole

The probe is used to stick into the snow to find someone who has been buried. Ortovox do a wide range of probes from mega lightweight to carbon-based probes. We use the **Ortovox Carbon 280 Probe**, which is high-flex, lightweight and impact resistant with a compact length of 40cm, extending to 280cm.

Avalanche shovels

Shovels are now ultra light so you can't use weight as an excuse for not carrying one. They are designed for digging people out of an avalanche, but also come in handy for building big backcountry kickers.

The **Ortovox Professional shovel** has a light, telescopic shaft with an ergonomic left-/right-hand grip and an unbreakable, torsion-free polycarbonate blade. This is our

choice, but Ortovox's range will have something to suit your personal preferences.

Backpacks

The **Ortovox Tour Rider 30+ backpack** is the perfect backcountry companion. Avalanche shovel and probe can be attached outside, to be quickly accessible. The spacious main compartment can accommodate the hydration system and other accessories, and smaller items have a place in the front compartment or in the hip-belt pocket. All pockets have waterproof zippers. If you'd rather tote your board or skis, you can attach them with the Clip Fix buckles. An emergency signal whistle is integrated in the chest strap; the drinking tube line is on the shoulder strap. Ortovox also have a wide range of other packs.

ABS backpacks

This is one of the most recent and invaluable avalanche safety devices. It is designed to keep you above the surface during an avalanche by making the body less dense than moving snow.

Why you need it
Burial is a huge factor in avalanche fatalities (see pages 25–6) and an ABS backpack can massively increase your chances of survival, witness 30 documented cases in Europe.

How it works
The airbags are stowed in the backpack until the trigger on the shoulder strap is pulled, when the nitrogen-air cartridge is activated, releasing two 75-litre air bags within two seconds. The ABS has to be released by the user and practising this is vital.

The Warren Smith Ski Academy brings together some of the sports top professionals to create the ultimate performance coaching team.
The Academy trains Professional Freeskiers, up and coming British Athletes, Ski Instructors from Ski Schools across Europe, recreational skiers who have surpased ski school instruction and skiers who are either stuck on a plateau or wish to gain confidence.

The performance coaching develops your skill and builds your **confidence** to a level that gives you the power and technique to blast through powder, ski steep terrain, have the range of movement to master moguls, carve dynamically and become an all mountain freeskier.

WARREN SMITH SKI ACADEMY
www.warrensmith-skiacademy.com

LIFE AFTER SKI SCHOOL...
PERFORMANCE COACHING

PERFORMANCE COACHING
INSTRUCTOR TRAINING
SKI BIOMECHANICS CLINICS
FREERIDE
RACE TRAINING
NEW SCHOOL / FREESTYLE
HELI - SKIING

ALSO FOR THIS SEASON

GAP PROGRAM **VERBIER 2006**

CONTACT:
admin@snowsportsynergy.com
+44 (0)1525 374757

2005/06 COURSES

Autumn 2005 - Milton Keynes Xscape
4, 5, 6 October (daytime courses)

Winter 2005/06 - Verbier, Switzerland
26 Nov, 3 Dec, 10 Dec, 14 Jan, 4 Feb
8 April, 15 April, 22 April (5 day courses)

Winter 2005/06 - Courcheval, France
17 Dec, 14 Jan, 11 Jan (5 day camps)

Spring 2006 - Milton Keynes Xscape
4, 11, 18, 25 May (daytime courses)

Summer 2006 - Saas-Fee, Switzerland
1 July, 5 Aug, 12 Aug (5 day courses)

Photo: Melody Sky   Skier: Warren Smith

Motorola Talkabouts

The Motorola Talkabout 2-way radios are a fantastic way to keep in touch with people on the mountain, much better than using your English mobile which can be very expensive abroad. After the initial cost of about £50–100 (depending on the specification of the particular model) there is no further cost. The range tends to be up to 8km, and the different models vary in respect of the power, type of battery, number of channels and size. Well worth the investment.

Digital camera/camcorder

This is an essential item to pop into your rucksack so you can take photos of your mates hitting the big kickers in the park. If you have a camcorder, try riding by the side/in front of/behind your mate as they do a rail or kicker and film them as you're skiing/boarding. This can make for some fantastic footage if you get it right.

Suunto wristop computers

These amazing watch/computers will tell you loads of interesting stuff. Depending on the model that you choose (prices £100–500), you will be able to take advantage of an altimeter, barometer, compass, chronographic functions, logbook and on certain models, GPS (Suunto X9, £499).

The altimeter gives you an insight into your altitude, vertical speed, online cumulative descent and number of runs and altitude profile. The barometer will show you the sea-level pressure, absolute pressure, weather trend graph, temperature and has a 48-hour memory and weather alarm. The compass provides information

on bearing and bearing tracking and the ski chronograph shows the degree of the slope, maximum speed, average speed and vertical drop for individual runs. The logbook keeps a record of the total and cumulative vertical ascents and descents, as well as the number of runs. Most models also store data for later analysis – you can view, compare and analyse your riding performance through a specially designed PC interface and compare it with others over the internet.

iPod

The iPod is an easy way of transporting your entire music library with you wherever you go and can also be used as a hard drive to back up files, carry photos around, etc. It is available in 20GB, 40GB or 60GB models. The iPod mini weighs just 103g and it allows you to carry around 1000 songs. The iPod mini lasts up to 8 hours on a single battery charge and gives you up to 25 minutes of skip protection.

Oakley Thump™ MP3 player sunglasses

Oakley Thump™ is the world's first digital music eyewear. The glasses combine the high-performance optics forged with an integrated, state-of-the-art digital audio engine. They come in two sizes, 128mb (£260) or 256mb (£330), holding up to 60 tracks (4 hours of music) without a cable in sight. They weigh in at 50 grams, come in seven colour combinations, have 6 hours of battery life, and take 3 hours to

charge (80 per cent charged in 1 hour). They are, without doubt, the ultimate accessory. Find out more at www.oakley.com.

Burton clothing with built-in sound system

Burton jackets with iPod pocket: Burton has launched two men's jackets (the Ronin 2 Layer and the Burton Shield) and one women's jacket (the Radar 2 Layer) with iPod pockets and controls. The headphones plug into a socket in the collar and there are 'soft touch' buttons on the sleeve so that you don't need to faff around with gloves and opening pockets in order to skip tracks or alter the volume.
Burton headphone beanie: The Burton beanie ingeniously features a pair of removable flat headphones built in to the hat. It costs about £36 and there is one size that fits all.

Snowmobile

If you're minted and have run out of gadgets to buy, this could be the perfect toy. You can race them, whizz through trees on them or just take the muscle pain out of accessing that bit of powder you were admiring but can't be bothered hiking to. Midsize are 500–600cc and large have 700–900cc engines. The larger machine may have more horsepower, but this will also mean that it is heavier and more difficult to manoeuvre. Check them out secondhand on eBay.

For the most original beanies and hats around check out Ignite (www.ignitebeanies.com). E-mail info@ignitebeanies.com for your nearest stockist or head to your local Snow and Rock store.

Safety

Avalanche safety

For anyone who is venturing off-piste, it is vitally important to be equipped, not only with all the gear mentioned in the previous chapter, but also with the required knowledge.

Skiing and snowboarding are not without risk. Around 100 people die every year in the Alps as a result of avalanches; they do happen, so you need to be physically and mentally prepared.

Ultimately there are three key areas of knowledge in which a skier or boarder should be proficient before they step off pisted areas. These are:

1 **Avalanche avoidance:** This is by far the best method of avalanche safety!
2 **Avalanche survival:** What to do if the worst occurs.
3 **Search and rescue:** How to rescue an avalanche victim effectively.

Avalanche avoidance

While it is vitally important to carry avalanche survival equipment such as transceivers, probes and shovels, it still remains that 50 per cent of buried victims die even when they are equipped with all the gear. Therefore, the most successful way to deal with avalanches is to avoid them, and the key to this is the skier/boarder's knowledge and experience, and their ability to engage in effective risk analysis. Here are a few pointers to get you started.

Plan your route
Your route should be well considered and carefully planned, taking into account:
• **Slope aspect and gradient.** Carry an inclinometer and compass for gauging slope aspect and steepness. Remember that the majority of avalanches occur on north-west to east aspects on slopes greater than 30 degrees. Between 30 and 60 degree slopes have a potential to slide, and the gradient most likely to slide is 38 degrees.
• **Recent weather conditions.** Include new snowfall. Rain on fresh snow leads to a high risk of avalanches.
• **Evolution of the snow pack.**

• **Predominant wind direction and speed.**
• **Humidity.**

Gain experience
The better your knowledge and experience, the better able you will be to cope with problem situations. Find ways to expand your knowledge:
• **Attend courses.**
• **Read up on the subject.**
• **Go out with experienced people and listen to their advice.**
• **Study the avalanche bulletin.** Do this in great detail, especially if there is a mention of local risk factors.

Don't fall into common traps
A run is not safe just because:
• you've done it before; familiarity is dangerous and can mean that you do not assign the risk-analysis procedure that you would to an unknown slope;
• you can see other people doing it;
• you've already started so you'll finish; always be prepared to admit the danger and head back, even if it does mean a long hike;
• you've got an avalanche transceiver and all the other equipment: a transceiver is a search-and-rescue device, it should not affect the risk-analysis procedure.

Avalanche survival

In the case of an avalanche there are three main factors that will affect whether a victim survives and there are a few things you can do to enhance your chances of survival.

Depth of burial
Approximately 90 per cent of victims caught in avalanches are alive when the avalanche has stopped moving but most are buried beneath the surface and cannot free themselves. Their chances of survival decrease rapidly with time, and statistics show that two-thirds of buried avalanche victims are recovered dead.

Help yourself
If you can, try to swim in the slide, this may avoid you being entirely buried.

The ABS Airbag (a fantastic but expensive piece of equipment) has been designed to protect the victim from complete burial; airbags are triggered by the victim, making their bodies less dense than moving snow (see Equipment guide, page 21).

Air supply
Suffocation accounts for 50 per cent of all avalanche fatalities and is not easily avoided if your rescuers cannot reach you quickly.

Help yourself
If possible, clear airways to breathe. It is sometimes possible to clear an air pocket around your mouth as you feel the slide slowing down.

The Avalung is a unique piece of equipment that can be used to buy the victim valuable time. Working on the principle that avalanche debris is mostly air, it extracts air from the surrounding area and deposits exhaled air into the snow behind the victim.

Rescue time
It has been found that victims recovered during the first 15 minutes of burial have a 93 per cent chance of survival. The only fatalities tend to be those who sustained injuries as a result of the fall during the avalanche itself. Between 15 minutes and 45 minutes recovery time is a crucial half hour known as the asphyxiation phase. After 45 minutes, the chances of survival decrease to less than 30 per cent. After 45 minutes, even if you have managed to find an air pocket, the risk of death from hypothermia is high.

Help yourself
Visual clues can give rescuers an indication of your location, and speed up the rescue process. If you can push a ski pole or arm out to the surface, statistics show you have a much greater chance of being rescued.

The Avalanche Ball is another useful piece of equipment that will give a visual clue to the victim's location. By pulling a cord on the waist belt, the ball inflates and floats to the surface of the slide, whilst remaining attached to the victim via a cord. This will greatly increase the victim's chances of a swift rescue.

An effective rescue team is by far the best way to decrease rescue time. If all parties have avalanche transceivers it is vital that the rescuers start the search immediately and have prior training. The rescuer can alert the rescue services quickly if they have a phone (be aware that using a phone may interfere with the transceiver signals) but they *should not go for help*; they should start their rescue immediately as the avalanche ceases.

Search and rescue

Using transceivers
We have talked about the importance of carrying transceivers and equipping yourself with the knowledge of how to use them. However, there are a few details that are very important and not immediately obvious. For example, think about the impossibility of trying to find more than one buried body using transceivers; the signals given out by a number of transceivers will cause confusion and may render them useless. The best way to avoid this is to ensure that only one person is skiing/boarding at a time. Others should wait in safe areas, not in the way of a potential avalanche. This also provides a greater number of rescuers should the worst occur.

Help yourself
- Ensure that one person at a time is skiing or boarding.
- Ensure that transceivers are functioning and turned on.
- Practise using them in the local park, back garden or on snow; in a time of need you want use of the transceiver to be a reflex action.
- Do not carry your transceiver in your rucksack as this can be easily lost in an avalanche. Wear it as close to the body as possible to avoid it being torn from you.
- Assign a leader to ensure that every member of the group has a functioning transceiver.
- Turn your transceiver off at the end of the day and remove the batteries if it is to be stored for a long period of time. Use new batteries at the start of each season.

Park rules and etiquette

1 No snaking. Make sure you know when it is your turn to take your run up to the jump or rail; never cut people off by jumping in front of them and stealing their turn.

2 Never stand on top of the jumps unless you are marking the fact that there has been an accident, in which case you should make this obvious to those waiting at the top of the jump – make a cross sign with your arms or poles.

3 Never stand or sit on the landing of a jump for obvious reasons – the jumper can't see you, could land on you and this could lead to death.

4 If you crash on a landing, try to get out of the way of the landing area as quickly as possible, and alert those around you to indicate your crash to those at the top.

5 Never start your run in until you know the person before you has landed safely and made their way out.

6 Always stick to jumps within your ability. Don't try something that you don't feel comfortable with.

7 Wear a helmet, and back and hip protector. Landings can be hard-packed and it's easy to screw up on rails. Many people have died when a helmet could have saved them, although resorts obviously try not to advertise this fact. Helmets are not unfashionable, you can get some wicked-looking ones (see Equipment guide, page 20), and they could save you from a crushed skull.

8 Don't walk out across run-ins or landings unless you can see exactly where everyone else is and what they're doing, and they can see you.

9 Never ride down the park in a group, always go one at a time.

10 Store the resort's mountain rescue/emergency number in your phone so that you're prepared if you witness an accident. The international emergency number from a mobile phone is 112.

11 Don't intimidate people who have just started using the park – you were there once.

In your backpack should be:

- shovel
- probe
- map
- compass
- inclinometer
- first aid kit
- torch
- emergency food and water
- pocket-knife.

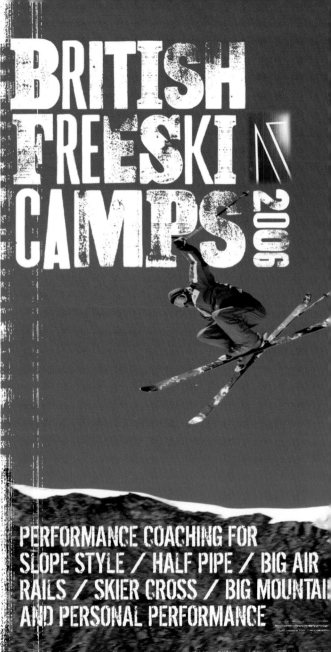

BRITISH FREESKI CAMPS 2006

PERFORMANCE COACHING FOR SLOPE STYLE / HALF PIPE / BIG AIR RAILS / SKIER CROSS / BIG MOUNTAIN AND PERSONAL PERFORMANCE

WINTER 2006 VERBIER, SWITZERLAND 18-25 MARCH. PACKAGE PRICE £499

SUMMER 2006 SAAS-FEE, SWITZERLAND 8-15, 15-22, 22-29 JULY £499

MORE INFO AT WWW.BRITISHFREESKICAMPS.COM OR CALL 01525 374757

Sheffield Ski Village

Sheffield Ski Village (www.sheffieldskivillage.co.uk) is about to have a serious, £80m facelift; in 2006 the construction of Snow Mountain will begin, a huge development that will be a godsend for the British ski industry. The huge new complex is to include a snow arena, alpine village and urban jungle, all with some impressive transport links.

The Sheffield Snow Mountain

The proposed snow arena will be 300m long (twice as long as any other UK slope) and 100m wide with a vertical drop of nearly 70m. The slopes will recreate a real-snow experience, with rock outcrops and gullies, green and red runs, fresh powder, a half pipe and rails. Perhaps most amazing is the lift system that they plan to install which includes a four-person chairlift and two high-speed drag lifts. A gondola will also be installed linking Sheffield Ski Village with Langsett Road in the city centre and on to Shirecliffe. The cable car will be linked to the bus, tram and road networks to provide seriously easy access to this incredible new complex.

To complete the experience is an ice rink and tobogganing section and eventually they will have pony trekking facilities and mountain biking. The massive glass Snow and Rock shop will also encompass a three-storey climbing wall. And when you're done, you'll be able to check out the Alpine village, with its wooden buildings, intended to reflect a real alpine resort. The street will be lined with restaurants, bars and shops and the resort will include a 4-star hotel and chalets for weekend breaks (or longer).

The Urban Jungle

Snow Mountain isn't only about snow-related activities, and the Urban Jungle is likely to grab just as much attention. It is certainly destined to get the adrenaline pumping. Urban Jungle is a high-wire adventure consisting of zip wires, vine swings, rope bridges, and slides, suspended 30m above the ground. All courses follow the same route but you will be able to choose between a children's, blue, red or black course. It should be finished by Easter 2006; check out www.urbanjunglesheffield.com for the latest updates on its construction, or just go visit.

It is anticipated that Snow Mountain will be totally completed by September 2008 (slopes will remain open throughout construction).

The freestyle scene

Sheffield has a fantastic freestyle scene, and many of the pros hang out here as well as the up-and-coming riders. Andy Bennett, this year's Big Air and Slopestyle Champion, has been riding at Sheffield for nearly 17 years and is coaching the freestyle team there (Charlie Richards, Richard Martin, Michael Nur, Will Burrows, and Joe Blackwell), and helping them in their search for sponsors. Check out **Natural Born Riders** in October 2005, one of the biggest UK freestyle events of the year (www.naturalbornriders.co.uk). Another amateur freestyle event is the **Homegrown Series**, with big-air and slopestyle comps for skiers and boarders.

EMINENT
EXCLUSIVE
INSPIRED
SKI COACHING

Coaches:
Chris Haworth
Pat Sharples
Stephan Mongellaz

Dates
Summer:
Tignes, France
Autumn:
Tignes, France
Winter:
Val d'Isere
Tignes
Courcheval
Megeve
Chamonix

Fast
High speed and
race training

Bespoke
Private coaching
tailored for you

Free
Powder, Park & Pipe,
Freeride & Big Air

www.dissent-ski.com
France: 0033 603 281 167
UK: 07973 577 671

Andorra

A friendly, fun place, full of Brits. It has a great party scene and the mountains are especially good for first-timers

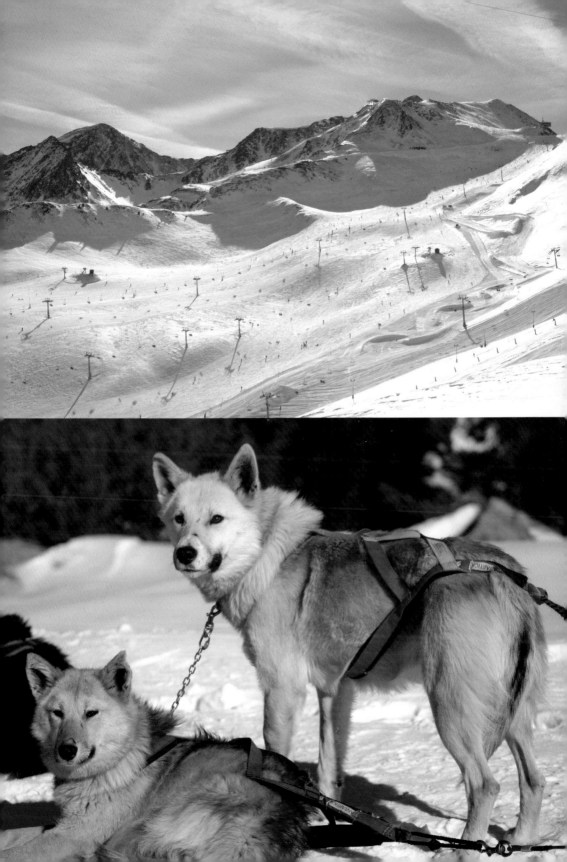

Arinsal

Friendly and fun. Ideal for big-drinking beginners on a budget

Pic de Comapedrosa 2942m

Pic Alt de la Capa 2572m

Pic Negre 2569m

Pic dels Llacs

Port de Calbes 2391m

SETURIA AREA

ARINSAL AREA

Coll de Cubil 2552m

Curtang Area

Comallempla 1950m

PAL 1550m

Xixerella 1450m

ARINSAL 1450m

Cota 1550m

PAL AREA

Els Fontanals 1700m

Pla de la Cot 2052m

Erts 1350m

LA BORDA

La Coma de la 1950m

Escas 1375m

L'Aldosa 1350m

La Massana 1300m

Sispony 1375m

On the slopes	
Snow reliability	❄ ❄ ❄ ❄
Parks	❄ ❄ ❄ ❄
Off-piste	❄ ❄ ❄
Off the slopes	
Après ski	❄ ❄ ❄ ❄
Nightlife	❄ ❄ ❄ ❄
Eating out	❄ ❄
Resort charm	❄ ❄ ❄

The resort

Arinsal might not be known as one of the great resorts in Europe, but we loved it. It's the friendliest place ever, has some wicked bars, cheap accommodation and lift passes, and the fact that 40 per cent of visitors return says it all. It's packed with Brits, which has its good and bad points and it's better for beginners than experts, although the park is pretty good.

The mountains

Height: 1550–2560m

Ability	Rating
Expert	❄ ❄
Intermediate	❄ ❄ ❄
Beginner	❄ ❄ ❄ ❄

Getting about

There are 89km of pistes in Arinsal, most of them geared for beginners and intermediates. Pal's slopes (linked to Arinsal by cable car) are less crowded and there is more to keep the keener riders happy.

The park

The Arinsal park was a big hit with us. The resort has just spent €20,000 on a massive selection of rails and the shapers are enthusiastic and friendly. The park has something to keep all standards of riders happy: a selection of kickers of all sizes, a spine, quarter pipe, ski and boardercross, and the new rails. There are a few local ski and snowboarder rippers who hang out here, like pro skier Peter Kaplansky, sponsored by Atomic, and owner of the popular snowboard, skate and freestyle ski shop in town, Loaded. He's always on hand to give tips and point you in the right direction. To add the cream on top of the cookie, there's an alluring super pipe. The walls are approximately 3.5m high and are always well maintained. Good work, boys.

Off-piste and backcountry

Arinsal seems to get its fair share of snow each year, which means you can always find a bit of fresh powder. There are a few good tree lines around and a couple of faces but nothing over-challenging. On the plus side, Arinsal attracts mostly beginners so the off-piste that there is won't get tracked out and you can find fresh powder weeks after it has dumped. We were told by a couple of the local pros that it's pretty wicked around the La Cappa area where there's a massive cornice that's great for getting huge air. Here is also, allegedly, the steepest marked run in Andorra.

Lift passes	High season	Low season
1 day	€30	€25
6 days + (price per day)	€22.50	€18.50
Children receive discounts.		

Instruction

Arinsal Ski School
T: 00376 73 70 29

Pal Ski School
T: 00376 73 70 08

Group lessons cost €18.40 for 2 hours, and €89.50 for 15 hours. Private lessons are €29. 50–€45.50 per hour depending on the time of season and the number of people. Prices are relevant to both skiing and snowboarding.

Other activities

Shopping: The main activity in Andorra is shopping on all the duty-free delights: alcohol, clothes, electronics – everything is as cheap as chips. Take care, though, as you are only allowed to take back certain quantities and values of products.

Skibikes, paragliding, hot air balloon rides, mushing: Other activities in Arinsal include skibikes (€32–47.50 per hour, depending on number of people), paragliding (€51), hot air balloon rides, and mushing in Pal. It's best to ask at the tourist office, located in La Massana, about 4km down the road.

Thermal water centre: Andorra la Vella is the best place for this, and it's only about 10–15 minutes drive from Arinsal. Also in Andorra la Vella is the Caldea Andorra (80 09 99, www.caldea.ad), Europe's biggest mountain thermal water centre. It is a massive and impressive place offering 6000m^2 of indoor and outdoor lagoons, Jacuzzis, Turkish baths, pools, waterfalls, with a variety of cultural influences – from Roman to Japanese. On top of this there is a fitness room and a variety of beauty treatments available. Entry to Caleda costs €22.80. And if you don't manage any of these things, drinking is a popular and cheap alternative!

"If you don't manage any of the activities, drinking is a popular and cheap alternative!"

Events

There are a couple of events in Arinsal including the **Arinsal Challenge** in February and the **UFO Funtime** in March.

Accommodation

There are a number of cheap options to consider if you're planning a holiday in Arinsal.

Just take care that you're not too far away from the action – there's no need to be as you can get some great deals right in the centre of town and next to the gondola. **Hostel Poblado** (00376 83 51 22, info@hotel-poblado.com) is really cheap, costing €31–40 a night and it's right next to the gondola in the centre of town. Another good budget option is the **Coma**

Pedrosa Hotel (00376 83 51 23), again bang in the centre of town and you can get a room from €50 a night. The **Micolau** (00376 83 50 52, www.arinsal.com/hmicolau) is a cosy and charming stone house, with simple, snug rooms and a relaxed restaurant, with an inviting log fire. Half-board accommodation is €45 per person per night.

"Simple, snug rooms and a relaxed restaurant, with an inviting log fire"

The 3-star **Hotel Solana** (00376 73 79 99, www.uha.ad/solana) is a large hotel with pool and sauna facilities. Half-board accommodation is €45 a night.

For ritzy accommodation, head to the 4-star **Princesa Parc** (00376 73 65 00, www.hoteldianaparc.com, hoteldianaparc@andorra.ad) with its glam feel and swish spa facilities as well as ten-pin bowling and a games area. Rooms aren't ridiculously priced either, with a choice of a standard room (€51–100 for half board), or a room with a hydromassage bath (€60–110) or a junior suite (€68–120). Price differences depend on the time of season you wish to stay. Finally the **Sant Moritz apartments** (00376 73 78 78, santmoritz@andorra.ad, www.santmoritz.com) are recently built and fully equipped, perfect for families or groups of friends with 13 apartments for two to four people and 2 for two to six people, ranging from 50 to 85m^2. Prices are available on the website.

Eating out

On the mountain

The restaurants on the mountain are mainly self-service, and usually crowded, offering the usual assortment of snack food. Panoramix, a British bar-restaurant, has a good reputation for its extensive sun terrace and Pal's main building has a decent array of options, including a large cafeteria and a proper restaurant, La Borda, serving Andorran cuisine. There are also Mexican, Chinese and Italian restaurants on the mountain!

In town

Our favourite restaurant in Arinsal is **Cisco's,** which does fab Tex-Mex food in a converted cattleshed, with a relaxed and wooden feel. The fajitas are especially tasty, as is the mango chicken. The staff are a riot, and the bar downstairs is really popular with the locals and those in the know. All in all, this is a great place for a night out. **El Moli** is a cute pizzeria in the centre of town, with great food and even better cocktails. They also do takeaway. **Surf** is a great place to munch on a plate of steak and chips. **Micolau** is open all day and serves some great snacks such as all-day breakfasts,

bacon and sausage sandwiches, and good tasty salads. At night the warming fire is very inviting and cosy. **Borda d'Erts** is a few minutes' drive down the road, and is great for a posh(er) night out away from the squalor.

Bars and clubs

The bars in Arinsal are plentiful and it's pretty difficult not to have a good night here (although that could be something to do with the size of the measures). All of the bars are open from après ski (unless they serve food at lunchtime) and stay open until 3am on weekdays and 4am on Friday and Saturday. **Cisco's** is a favourite with the locals and is a snowboarder hangout. It has a fab atmosphere, wicked staff, table football, free internet and the awesome Tex-Mex restaurant upstairs.

El **Derbi** is an Irish pub (even though its owner is from Bristol), that thankfully allows no tour operator pub crawls. It's especially heaving on karaoke night, which can be a great laugh. **El Cau** is a bar for the real locals, with a really relaxed atmosphere where you can get away with a lot! They have giant TV screens for sports too. **Quo Vadis** is famous as the longest running bar in Arinsal with a small restaurant and is very popular with tourists. The **Solana** hotel is owned by local instructors and has a big open log fire to chill out by. **Red X** is a theme bar that often has fancy dress and live music, and at the end of the day they show video analysis from the day's skiing/ boarding. **Surf** is a funky bar that has ample room for dancing and is usually the last stop of the evening before you finally collapse.

Getting there

By train

The nearest train station is at L'Hospitalet près l'Andorre, 8km away with buses to the resort.

By plane

Toulouse (190 km) Transfer to Arinsal by the novotel airport transfer service costs €39 one way and €66 return.
Barcelona (200 km) Transfer to Arinsal by the novotel airport transfer service costs €36 one way and €61 return.

> "A fab atmosphere, wicked staff, table football, free internet and awesome Tex-Mex"

Useful facts and phone numbers

Tourist office

T: 00376 73 70 20
F: 00376 83 59 04
E: palarinsal@palarinsal.com
W: www.palarinsal.com

Emergency services

- Police: 110
- Ambulance/ Fire: 118
- Emergency health care: 116
- Mountain Rescue: 112
- Hospital: 87 10 00

Taxis

- Associacion de Taxistas de Andorra (86 30 00)

Pas de la Casa

Take Blackpool, add some snow
and remove the crime and
you've got Pas de la Casa

On the slopes	
Snow reliability	❄ ❄ ❄
Parks	❄ ❄
Off-piste	❄ ❄

Off the slopes	
Après ski	❄ ❄ ❄
Nightlife	❄ ❄ ❄ ❄
Eating out	❄ ❄
Resort charm	❄

The resort

If you don't like drinking and shopping to excess, stop reading now. Pas de la Casa is the biggest, and most well known, of the six resorts in Granvalira (the others being Grau Roig, Soldeu, El Tarter, Canillo and Encamp). It is big and ugly but it does have a few things going for it. It's very friendly and it's very cheap, so the shopping is tremendous and loads of people come here to buy electrical gadgets, alcohol and perfume, etc. The nightlife could be a plus or a minus point depending on how you look at it. The comparison with Blackpool is, we feel, fairly accurate (and we're not dissing Blackpool) – it's a 'lads on stag night' kind of place and when night falls the urge comes over you to wave your hands around, shout 'Wehey' and drink until you drop. The dropping bit might not be completely your fault as Andorran drinks are as cheap as British pub prices and you get around a triple measure into the bargain. So it does tend to get a tad rowdy. We prefer to stay in Soldeu (see other chapter) – you get all the benefits of cheap drinks and there's still a great night-time scene but you're in much nicer surroundings and you can always pop over for an afternoon's shopping in Pas de la Casa or Andorra la Vella.

If you are thinking of coming to Pas de la Casa, it is worth checking out the Soldeu chapter too as the resort is only 20 minutes away by car and the mountain areas are directly accessible.

The mountains

Height: 1710–2560m

Ability	Rating
Expert	❄ ❄
Intermediate	❄ ❄ ❄ ❄
Beginner	❄ ❄ ❄ ❄

Getting about

The Grandvalira mountain contains six sectors that correspond to the six towns; Pas de la Casa, Grau Roig, Soldeu, El Tarter, Canillo and Encamp. From Pas de la Casa head up the Solana chairlift. From Grau Roig there are a number of options to take you up the hill, all directly accessible from the car park. There are 193km of runs in Grandvalira, all of which come under the same ski pass and most of which are geared towards the beginner/ intermediate skier or boarder, with lots of long 'motorway' runs. There is a bit to keep the expert happy though.

The park

If you've just got to grips with your skiing or boarding and want to start practising some tricks, the fun park here is a perfect place to learn. There are a couple of small jumps and the odd rail to practise on. It's a good place to start off and you don't get all the pros in there intimidating you. On the other hand, if you're pretty good and looking for a sick park, make your way over to the superb NCG Snow Park in El Tarter (covered in detail in the Soldeu section). There is also another small park in the Grau Roig sector with a few OK rails but not much else. If you fancy a shot on a skier/boardercross course, there's one near the bottom of the resort.

Off-piste and backcountry

Pas de la Casa doesn't have much off-piste of its own but within the Grandvalira region there are some good areas to be found. Some of the best riding can be found at the top of the mountain by Grau Roig. Here there are a few long powder fields to be had, but if you're staying in this resort and you want some decent freeriding, your best bet is to head over towards Soldeu (see Soldeu chapter, page 46).

Lift passes	High season	Low season
1 day	€35	€33.50
6 days	€168	€163.50

For seven or more days, multiply the number of days by €27 in high season or €26.50 in low season. For two days or more the only available pass covers the whole of the Grandvalira. For a half day or one day you have the option of a pass for half of Grandvalira (either Canillo–El Tarter–Soldeu or Pas de la Casa–Grau Roig–Encamp) which will cost a little less. Children (between six and 11) get a discount and a beginner's pass is also available for €20 per day giving you access to the beginners' sectors only.

Instruction

The Andorran ski and snowboard school has seven different centres with instructors that speak loads of languages. Group lessons cost from €87 per person for 15 hours. Private lessons cost €30–53 per hour depending on the time of season and number of people.

Pas de la Casa
T: 00376 87 19 20

Grau Roig
T: 00376 87 29 20/00376 87 29 27

Other activities

Adventure activities: The Grau Roig Adventure Activities Centre is the place to go to organise any activity you may want to try your hand at. They organise individual activities as well as catering for large groups of 100 or more. Here are a few of the popular choices (contact the tourist office for more details). Other activities offered by the Adventure Activities Centre include cross-country skiing, snowshoeing, igloo building, orienteering and avalanche rescue courses.

Helicopter flights: Ten- or 20-minute helicopter flights can be organised (€50 or €100 respectively), taking off from Grau Roig or Soldeu.

Husky sled trip: A romantic husky sled trip, driven by a guide costs €50 for 1.5km, €90 for 5km.

Mushing: There is a mushing circuit at Grau Roig where you can learn to ride a sled pulled by a team of huskies. Thirty minutes costs €25.

Paintball: This takes place in the battlefield in Grau Roig. All equipment is provided and participants buy the first 100 pellets for €30 and extra pellets at a price of €15 for 100.

Parapent flights: These take off from Tossa d'Espiolets (in El Tarter) and land at the bottom of El Tarter. The flights last for 20 minutes and you are accompanied by an instructor. Check prices at the Reservations Centre.

Shopping: Shopping is the main activity of choice here (unless you're too busy drinking). Shop, shop, shop. Remember to check the permitted quantities of alcohol, perfume, cigarettes, etc but take as much as you are allowed or you'll regret it. A 3-litre bottle of Jack Daniel's costs just over £20! It's worth knowing that department stores do not close at midday or on Sundays. On Sundays, most shops open in the morning and some stay open in the afternoon. Shop around before you buy as prices do differ from shop to shop.

Snowmobiling: This takes place along guided routes. Trips can last 15 minutes (€35), 30 minutes (€60), one hour (€100), or you can take a two-hour excursion (€200) to Port d'Envalira which has fantastic terrain for snowmobiling.

Snow track: The Audi snow track is located at the Pla d'Espiolets in Soldeu and you can rent 4WD cars and learn to drive on the snow. Visit www.audi.es for more info.

Sports and socio-cultural complex: Pas de la Casa sports and socio-cultural complex (85 68 30) contains a multi use court with floating floor and spectator seating, squash courts, table tennis, saunas and an indoor pool. The price of a pass covering all the sports facilities is €4.60.

Events

The **Snowgames** take place in March each year (this year will be its 7th edition) and run over consecutive weekends. The main events are a snowrunning competition (a snowshoe race) and the San Miguel Snowbike, a bike-cross for mountain bikers on snow. There is also a cross-country endurance test; 'Snowtop'. The best comps (freestyle festival and freestyle series) happen in Soldeu and El Tarter (see Soldeu, page 46).

Accommodation

Hotel **Himàlaia Pas** (00376 73 55 15) is close to the slopes and offers pretty good accommodation and facilities, including a pool, spa area, gym, games room, internet and disco. There are 98 rooms, equipped with satellite and mini bar. Prices range from €36 to €127 per person, per night, depending on the time of year and whether you require B&B or half board. **Hotel Màgic** (00376 87 55 00), is owned by the same company and is also 4 star (Andorran rating systems, however, appear to be slightly more lenient than their European equivalents). It has a similar level of comfort and price, and although there is no pool, there is a sauna, Turkish bath, gym and sunbeds.

Apartments are popular because they are often good value, and you can cook for yourself, which (personally speaking) looks more hygienic and enjoyable than eating at some of the dodgy buffets that are around. Being honest, those who don't fall into the '18–30, on a mission for carnage, the cheaper the better' category shouldn't really stay in Pas de la Casa anyway (the neighbouring Soldeu would be far better for most) and those who do fall into this category probably won't give a monkeys about the type of accommodation they're in as they won't see much of it. In fact, the grottier the better, then they won't mind as much when you throw up all over the lobby.

Eating out

On the mountain

At **Coll Blanc**, at the top of the Pas de la Casa chairlift, is an 80s-looking restaurant with pretty good views. The food comes in takeaway boxes and is OK for a quick bite but that's about it. In fact, you'll find very few places that you want to linger in Pas de la Casa and Grau Roig – apart, that is, from the restaurant at **Llac dels Pessons** (75 90 15), by far the best restaurant on the mountain. Reach it from the Comi del Pessons path running from the Llac del Cubil chair. It's sat on the edge of a frozen lake and is cosy and inviting. It's a table-service restaurant with superb food (specialising in gilled meats on their indoor wood fire) and well worth a visit.

In town

Most of the restaurants in Pas de la Casa look pretty dodgy. The street up to the car park and lift station has loads of restaurants, but most of them serve sketchy burgers and pasta that, personally, we'd prefer not to eat. If you're a junk-food addict, there are the usual **Burger King** (Pas de la Casa), **McDonald's** (Pas de la Casa) and **Pizza Hut** (Grau Roig) but we can recommend a few cool places to munch.

The funkiest places are close to the main nightlife scene (turn up the street by the Olympia Centre),

where you will find the following... firstly (and probably our favourite) is the **Perla Negra** (85 68 38, tavernapirata@hotmail.com), a funky place that you wouldn't venture into unless you knew about it, with a pirate theme. It's really good fun, especially with a group of mates, and the theme really adds to the place. They serve ribs (all you can eat for €12), meat skewers, pizzas and pasta. A main meal will cost you about €18 a head with wine. On top, they have a bar, darts and internet. El Raco is a Moroccan-style restaurant that's cosy and homely and smells of incense. A main costs around €10–14. **Vertigo** has a gorgeous, candlelit restaurant with 'Enigma'-type music. They serve all sorts, from steak and duck to foie gras and you have the very sweet choice of 'big plates' or 'little plates', depending on your appetite. It's a shame the bar isn't the same standard. For a typical, but pleasant, pizzeria, **El Marselles** has a good setup upstairs. At night they serve pizzas, meat, fondues etc and at lunchtimes they offer fish and chips, sausage egg and chips, and chilli for €8–9.

Bars and clubs

The bars and clubs are Blackpool to a T. They are cheesy, British and rowdy, and most of the 'best' clubs are down seedy backstreets where you may fear for your life (don't worry though; Andorra has one of the lowest crime rates in Europe). The most popular bars are in the same area as the best restaurants.

Milwaukee is a jam-packed bar that does good happy hours, **Surf on Inn** (next to Bilboard) is a smoky little bar that has a DJ and serves sweaty burgers and hot dogs until the early hours of the morning. **Bilboard** (85 62 36) is the most popular club, playing lots of commercial hits and attracting a mainly Dutch and British crowd. They're all tacky and packed so if that's what you're after, you'll have a whale of a time.

Useful facts and phone numbers

Ski Andorra

T: 00376 86 43 89

Grandvalira Reservation Centre

T: 00376 80 10 60/ 80 10 55

Websites to check out

- www.andorra.ad (Andorra's official website)
- www.grandvalira.com
- www.skiandorra.ad (official website of the Association of Andorran Ski Resorts)
- www.andorra.com
- www.SkiAndorra.info (unofficial – provides ratings of bars, shops, etc)

Emergency services

- Fire brigade: 118
- Police: 110
- Police station: 82 12 22
- Emergency medical service: 116
- Medical centre: 89 05 70
- Hospital: 87 10 00

Taxis

You won't find any taxi ranks out of Andorra la Vella but you can call any of the numbers below to order one. The price set by the Andorran government is €0.99 per kilometre and there are two zones: A is Andorra la Vella and Escaldes, and B is everywhere else.
- 86 30 00
- 86 10 05
- 82 80 00

Getting there

By car

From Paris, take the A6 to Nantes, the A10 to Toulouse, the A62 to Carcassone, the A61 to Foix (direction Hospitalet – RN 20).

By plane

There are no airports in Andorra due to the terrain although there are plans for one at Seu d'Urgell. Until then, the two closest airports are Toulouse and Barcelona.
Toulouse (200km) There is a daily minibus service at 10am and 6.30pm, costing around €24.
Barcelona (200km) There is a daily bus service (11.30, 13.00, 17.00, 18.00 and 21.00) with a fare of around €24.

Soldeu

Very friendly, very British, and very cheap. Slopes best for beginners and intermediates

On the slopes	
Snow reliability	✱ ✱ ✱
Parks	✱ ✱ ✱ ✱
Off-piste	✱ ✱ ✱
Off the slopes	
Après ski	✱ ✱ ✱
Nightlife	✱ ✱ ✱ ⊰
Eating out	✱ ✱ ⊰
Resort charm	✱ ✱ ⊰

The resort

The resort is set along the busy main road from Pas de la Casa through to Andorra la Vella. The buildings are far prettier than that of its neighbour, Pas de la Casa, although there are fewer amenities here. The general vibe of the resort is British, fun, friendly and cheap. There are some pretty cool pub-type bars (which are packed every Saturday with British footie fans), and good restaurants and hotels. Another great thing about the six resorts in Grandvalira (Pas de la Casa, Grau Roig, Soldeu, El Tarter, Canillo and Encamp) is that they are so close together that you can be in any one of them in half an hour. The mountains are also linked, making it one of the largest ski areas in Europe. NB If you are thinking of coming to Soldeu, it is worth checking out the Pas de la Casa chapter too as the resort is only 20 minutes away by car and the mountain areas are directly accessible.

Andorra is a mad little place. Since it only got its own constitution a few years ago they are still making the rules up as they go along. Apparently (we aren't convinced that this is gospel truth but we read it

"The general vibe of the resort is British, fun, friendly and cheap"

somewhere), divorce is illegal and wives are allowed to take their adulterous husbands outside and shout at them in public… but only for one hour! So there we have it, believe it or not. And if that's not enough, here are a few more crazy facts about Andorra: apparently, one in ten British skiers have been to Soldeu; Andorra has the lowest unemployment rate in the world (0 per cent) and if you see a farmer, they are almost certainly a millionaire! Now, go and startle your friends with this amazing knowledge. We obtained this information from Kate and James, the authors of the informative 'Inside Soldeu' booklet (that you can pick up in most bars). Cheers for telling us, guys!

The mountains

Height: 1710–2560m

Ability	Rating
Expert	✱ ✱ ⊰
Intermediate	✱ ✱ ✱ ✱
Beginner	✱ ✱ ✱ ✱ ✱

Getting about

The Grandvalira mountain contains six sectors that correspond to the six towns: Pas de la Casa, Grau Roig, Soldeu, El Tarter, Canillo and Encamp. From Soldeu, the cable car takes you up to Espiolets, where you can start your journey through Grandvalira. Alternatively you can head up the mountain from nearby El Tarter, which now has both the chairlift and a new gondola, which takes you up to the experts' snow park and general meeting place. Canillo and Encamp are slightly more inconvenient places from which to begin your journey up the mountain, being at the far end of Grandvalira, and you also have to take the gondola back down at the end of the day. From Encamp, the long Funicamp might take a while but it does set you down bang in the heart of Grandvalira.

Grandvalira tends to be geared to the beginner/ intermediate skier or boarder with 'motorway' style runs and long paths. It also caters very well for kids, and has a great Disney run (at the top of the El Tarter gondola) past pictures of Mickey, Donald, Cinderella and Buzz Lightyear. There are a few things to interest the more advanced/expert rider though, not least

Lift passes	High season	Low season
1 day	€35	€33.50
6 days	€168	€163.50

For seven or more days, multiply the number of days by €27 in high season or €26.50 in low season. For two days or more the only available pass covers the whole of the Grandvalira. For a half day or one day you have the option of a pass for half of Grandvalira (either Canillo–El Tarter–Soldeu or Pas de la Casa–Grau Roig–Encamp) which will cost a little less. Children (between six and 11) get a discount and a beginner's pass is also available which is €20 per day giving you access to the beginners' sectors only.

the superb park, sponsored by Nike ACG, in the El Tarter sector.

The park

There are three parks in Grandvalira, but the experts' park in El Tarter was the one that came as a great surprise to us, as it is far better than we could have hoped. It consists of three big kickers with a smaller side kicker by the side of each one. They range from 22m to 5m gaps, and are always perfectly shaped. There's also a 120m half pipe, a selection of rails and a massive wall ride. The quarter pipe and gigantic hip are also wicked after they've been shaped. Note to skiers: you can only enter the park in El Tarter on twin tips.

One of the guys behind the park is Jamie Phillips, a British pro snowboarder sponsored by Oakley, who always keeps it in top shape. Soldeu is also the home of Tyler Charlton (British Snowboard Champion, sponsored by Oakley and Ride), who trains here when he's not off travelling around doing comps and photo shoots. He is truly the master of this park! Big thanks to Tyler for showing us round the resort.

Off-piste and backcountry

The off-piste in Grandvalira is all really accessible and requires a minimum of hiking. It isn't over challenging but there's more than you would think and you can find fresh powder in the trees, even when it hasn't

> "One of the guys behind the park is Jamie Phillips, a British pro snowboarder, who always keeps it in top shape"

snowed for a few weeks. The big tree run back to the bottom of Soldeu is a must after a snowfall and has been nicknamed 'the land of the giants' because the trees are so huge. The hike off to the right of Riba Escorxada is amazing in the right conditions and is a favourite among the locals.

For some low-risk off-piste and an interesting experience (weather conditions permitting), there is a ratrack pistebasher that will drag you with ropes to the Pic d'Encampadana (El Tarter sector), from where there are four possible routes down. It's free, so why not give it a go?

Instruction

The Andorran ski and snowboard school has seven different centres with instructors that speak loads of languages. Group lessons cost from €87 per person for 15 hours. Private lessons cost €30–53 per hour depending on the season and number of people.

Soldeu
T: 00376 89 06 91/00376 89 06 15

El Tarter
T: 00376 89 06 41/00376 89 06 44

Canillo
T: 00376 89 06 91

Other activities

In Andorra the main activities are **shopping** for all the duty free delights (alcohol, clothes, electronics – everything is cheap as chips, take care though as you are only allowed to take back certain quantities and values of products) and **drinking**. However, for the more discerning holiday maker (of which there aren't too many), there are a fair few things to try your hand at.

Adventure Activities: The Adventure Activities Centre in Grau Roig (covered in more detail in the Pas de la Casa section) has a huge number of activities available. These include igloo building, orienteering and avalanche rescue courses, mushing, husky sled trips, snowshoeing, parapent flights, helicopter flights, snowmobile riding, paintballing and cross-country skiing.

Bowling: A two-lane bowling alley can be found in the Hotel Nòrdic in El Tarter (73 95 00).

Ice skating, go-karting and curling: In Canillo, the Palau de Gel D'Andorra contains an ice rink that is equipped for ice skating, ice go-karting, or curling. There is also a large pool, tennis and squash courts, and lots more things to do. An ice-skating pass costs €8.20 and pool pass €5.50.

Snow track: At the Pla d'Espiolets in Soldeu, Audi have designed a snow track where you can learn to drive 4WD cars on the snow. For bookings visit www.audi.es.

Sports: For €4.60 you can use all the facilities in Encamp's Sports and Socio-Cultural Complex. Facilities include badminton, basketball, volleyball, a climbing wall, tennis courts, martial arts room, squash courts, boules area, gym, solarium, saunas and indoor pool.

Thermal Leisure Centre: The Calbó Thermal Leisure Centre (87 05 00, www.sporthotelcomplex.com) is a brand spanking new complex; a huge, modern centre with 4500m² of water including Jacuzzis, Turkish baths, hammam, pools and other facilities such as beauty treatments and a hairdresser. It's connected to the Sport Hotel and only 100m from the Hotel Sport Village, all three buildings belonging to the Calbó family.

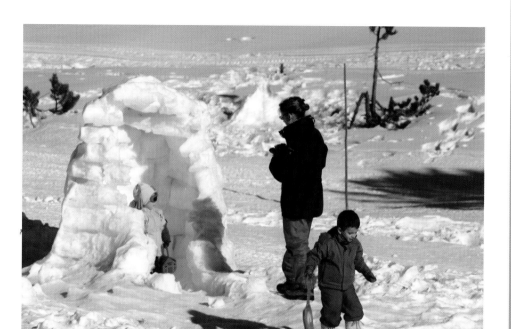

Thermal water centre: Caldea Andorra (80 09 99, www.caldea.ad) is Europe's biggest mountain thermal water centre, located in Andorra la Vella. It is a massive and impressive place offering 6000m^2 of indoor and outdoor lagoons, Jacuzzis, Turkish baths, pools, waterfalls, with a variety of cultural influences – from Roman to Japanese. On top of this there is a fitness room and a variety of beauty treatments available. Entry to Caldea costs €22.80.

Events

The ACG park hosts the **Freestyle series** which is composed of three freestyle events and is entered by a mix of pros and amateurs. At the end of the season (usually the first week in April) a **freestyle festival** takes place with ski and board comps, a live DJ in the park, equipment tests and loads of parties and concerts. The festival lasts one week. It's worth looking out for the events whilst you're there as they always have cool stuff on – we pitched up unannounced to find a wicked rail comp (Atomic Night Fever) taking place in a car park. There are also loads of freestyle comps throughout the winter, a mogul competition mid-February and a five-day touring comp at the beginning of March.

Accommodation

Be aware that accommodation ratings in Andorra may be slightly different to what you might expect. For example, two of the three 4-star hotels we visited would probably have been classed as a 3-star anywhere else in Europe although the other 4-star hotel definitely deserved its rating. For the cheapest deals, tour operators (Thompson, Crystal, etc) and the internet can have some real bargains. Just make sure your accommodation isn't too far from town. Apartments are also worth consideration; you will pay less if you self-cater and there are loads of good apartments around.

The best hotel in town (that is if you're after classy sophistication instead of a week of lairy boozing), is the **Sport Hotel Village** (with four well deserved stars, 00376 87 05 00. You walk into an immense reception area with a gorgeous bar, acres of lounge areas, all in a wooden, modern-chalet-style décor. There are 148 gorgeous rooms (25 with Jacuzzi) and the hotel has a sauna and gym. As if all this isn't enough, the hotel is in the centre of town and built over the lift system so has direct access to the slopes. Prices for half-board accommodation are €70–126 per person per night. There are supplements for Jacuzzis, lockers and rooms with slope-facing balconies. **Piolets**, also in the centre of town and classed as 4-star, is a pleasant hotel, very spacious, with a massive balcony that's in the sun all day. The pool and spa area is the best feature of the hotel with sun loungers, a huge gym, sauna, solarium, Turkish bath and massage. Prices (half board) are €66–115 per person per night depending on the season and they do special deals from Sunday to Friday for €454 per person for five nights half board and lift pass. For an extra €224 you can stay for the whole week. The 4-star **Himálaia** hotel is once again spacious and comfy with underground parking, sauna, Jacuzzi, Turkish bath and fitness area. It costs €32–97 per person per night for bed and breakfast and €42–112 for half board.

If you don't need to be near the heart of the nightlife all the time we can recommend staying in a family run, aparthotel in Canillo called **El's Meners** (00376 75 14 54, elsmeners@andorra.ad). It is a relatively new building (Dec 2003) with 15 apartments that contain a bathroom, kitchenette, dining table, lounge area (with double sofa bed) and bedroom. If there are two of you, you'll have tons of room to spread out but it definitely wouldn't be too uncomfortable with three or four people sharing. The rooms are beautifully done out with a terracotta, sunlit, Spanish feel. The service and staff are super-friendly and efficient and the hotel also has a bar and restaurant downstairs. It costs €100–215 per apartment per night depending on the time of season, which is pretty good considering that if there are two of you, you have luxury accommodation and if there are four, you have a great apartment and a great deal. For details of high/ low season etc, contact the aparthotel on the E-mail address above.

Eating out

On the mountain

In Grandvalira you don't have the best selection of mountain restaurants but they're comparatively inexpensive compared to other European countries and if you know where to look you can find some decent areas. For starters, decide whether you want a burger stand, self-service restaurant, cafeteria, table-service restaurant or a 'gastronomic' restaurant (the word 'gastronomy' seems to fly around Andorra a little looser than in the UK). Both Soldeu and El Tarter have a collection of restaurants at the top of the bubble cars from the villages which are good meeting points, especially if you have skiers and boarders of different abilities.

At the Soldeu area, **Espiolets**, you have the self-service restaurant (89 05 81) if you don't have much time, and the **Gall de Bosc** building which contains a cafeteria on the ground floor, **Fun Food** (89 06 04), selling sandwiches, burgers and salads (for about €6) and on the upper level a 'gastronomic' restaurant, **Gall de Bosc** (89 06 07). At El Tarter, at the top of the gondola, is Restaurant **Riba** (89 06 36), a self-service restaurant, and a terrace overlooking the ACG Snowpark where you can grab a burger or sandwich. There is another restaurant due to open in this area for the 05/06 season.

At **Collada d'Enradart**, at the top of the Funicamp gondola from Encamp, is a panoramic restaurant with great views and, again, a number of choices of service with a 'gastronomic' restaurant upstairs, a pretty dodgy-looking self-service restaurant on the lower floor and a burger/sandwich counter outside. The terrace is great but there are often large queues for the burger counter.

We recommend heading over to a restaurant called **Llac des Pessons** (75 90 15) in the Grau Roig area; a table-service restaurant that is by far the best in the area with cosy wooden tables, a great view over the frozen lake of the Circ del Colells mountains (so-named because they look like a circus) and superb food, where you choose anything from sandwiches to their meat specialities, grilled on their indoor wood fire.

In town

In Soldeu, there are a fair few decent eateries. For a full English breakfast head to **Slim Jims**, an English-run café where you can also check your E-mails. If you're not up the mountain at lunchtime, **Hotel Bruxelles**, right in the centre of town, has a big terrace in the sun overlooking the mountain. They serve massive sandwiches, paninis, burgers and salads. Anywhere you can get a bacon and cheeseburger for €4.20 on a terrace in the sun gets our vote. If you fancy a quick sandwich, pizza, pie or pasty in a typical British caf, take a gander at the **British Supermarket, Deli and Café** in the centre of town that also has fast internet, British newspapers, Sky news and pickled onion Monster Munch.

At night-time, there is a cosy and homely Indian, **L'Esquirol** (85 26 55 – English speaking). It's situated on the edge of the village and the food is cooked in their traditional coal-fired Tandoor. The Chicken Tikka Masala is fab. **Fat Alberts** has a restaurant in a converted barn, serving a mix of meat, fish and pasta. For some traditional cuisine, try **Borda del Rector** (85 26 06), a lovely wooden and stone, chalet-style restaurant. They have an open fire and a gorgeous bar/lounge area. It's a little out of Soldeu, closer to El Tarter, but they'll pick you up from Soldeu if you're eating. The **Red Dragon** is a Chinese restaurant that has recently changed management and has a really cosy and inviting atmosphere. It serves Chinese, Thai and Vietnamese dishes (as well as steaks and other dishes if you prefer) and has an extensive menu (a main dish costs around €9). **La Llar de l'Artesa** (known as Snails and Quails to most) used to be the best restaurant in town but has now moved to its new location: **La Cava** restaurant in the Alba Hotel in El Tarter (75 11 16) They'll even pick you up from your hotel or apartment.

Bars and clubs

Going out in Andorra is an experience. Once you've got used to the dirt-cheap booze (actually similar to British pub prices, but compared to typical European ski resorts it's pretty damn cheap), poured freely (a triple shot is the norm) until there is little room for mixer, you can join in with the other delighted Brits in causing havoc.

The **Aspen Bar** has a cool atmosphere, very much like a British pub. There are loads of TV screens for the Saturday footie matches (on Saturdays the bars are far more packed than the slopes), tons of comfy seating, and pool tables and video games to keep you

entertained. On a Thursday, don't be surprised to walk in and find two guys/ girls boxing in big kangaroo suits, and Saturday night traditionally entails a School Disco theme. From 2pm they serve good Tex Mex food (starters cost €6–8, mains €12–20). A pint will set you back €4. The **Avalanche Bar**, also full of Brits, offers live music and a local DJ, and has big plasma screens for sports. **Fat Albert's** is a really popular place, with a great après ski, an excellent restaurant downstairs and a locally renowned live band. The **T-bar** has changed hands

recently and is known by the locals for its après ski snacks and more interestingly, for the opportunity to hang upside down from the roof for a shots challenge. **Pussycat** opens from 9pm until late and is the place to be later on in Soldeu (although you can go early to make full use of the special drinks deals). They have live music, DJs and theme nights and have just introduced pole-dancing competitions to turn the heat up even more. What's even better is that it's free entry. Andorra's fab

Useful facts and phone numbers

Ski Andorra

T: 00376 86 43 89

Grandvalira Reservation Centre

T: 00376 80 10 60/ 80 10 55

Websites to check out

- www.andorra.ad (Andorra's official website)
- www.grandvalira.com
- www.skiandorra.ad (official website of the Association of Andorran Ski Resorts)
- www.andorra.com
- www.SkiAndorra.info (unofficial – provides ratings of bars, shops, etc)

Emergency services

- Fire brigade: 118
- Police: 110
- Police station: 82 12 22
- Emergency medical service: 116
- Medical centre: 89 05 70
- Hospital: 87 10 00

Taxis

You won't find any taxi ranks out of Andorra la Vella but you can call any of the numbers below to order one. The price set by the Andorran government is €0.99 per kilometre and there are two zones: A is Andorra la Vella and Escaldes, and B is everywhere else.
- 86 30 00
- 86 10 05
- 82 80 00

Getting there

By car

From Paris, take the A6 to Nantes, the A10 to Toulouse, the A62 to Carcassone, the A61 to Foix (direction Hospitalet – RN 20).

By plane

There are no airports in Andorra due to the terrain although there are plans for one at Seu d'Urgell. Until then, the two closest airports are Toulouse and Barcelona.
Toulouse (200km) There is a daily minibus service at 10am and 6.30pm, costing around €24.
Barcelona (200km) There is a daily bus service (11.30, 13.00, 17.00, 18.00 and 21.00) with a fare of around €24.

Austria

The magical charm of the resorts and the vibrant après ski are two of the main reasons why we love Austria so much

Bad Gastein

The spa facilities, and spectacular scenery, make the Gastein valley an exceptional place to visit

On the slopes	
Snow reliability	❄ ❄ ❄ ❄
Parks	❄ ❄
Off-piste	❄ ❄
Off the slopes	
Après ski	❄ ❄
Nightlife	❄ ❄ ❄
Eating out	❄
Resort charm	❄ ❄ ❄ ❄ ❄

The resort

Bad Gastein is absolutely and completely unique. The buildings are regal and majestic and the setting spectacular, with the entire resort built on the sides of what can only be described as a steep gorge, with a massive waterfall roaring through the centre of town. The Gastein valley's even greater pulling point is the extent not only of the slopes, but of the amazing spas and wellness facilities, provided by the thermal water. Gastein's 17 thermal springs produce 5 million litres of radon-enriched water every day.

If you plan to visit the Gastein valley, don't blinker yourself to the other towns that are available as Bad Gastein's neighbours Bad Hofgastein and Dorfgastein also have their own unique characters to offer. In fact, our preference is to stay in Bad Hofgastein, as Bad Gastein itself, despite its superior appearance, could do with a little facelift on the inside. Plus, the activities and nightlife aren't really up to scratch. Bad Hofgastein has many advantages such as being the location of the brand new Alpine Therme complex (see Activities), and we found it more pleasant to wander round. The Bad Hofgastein slopes are connected to the main mountain in Bad Gastein so there's no particular hassle there. A car would be a good idea here to ferry yourself around – best not to rely on the local transport system. If this isn't an option you should look into renting an electric quad bike (contact the tourist office for details).

The mountains

Height: 1080–2230m

Ability	Rating
Expert	❄ ❄ ❄
Intermediate	❄ ❄ ❄ ❄
Beginner	❄ ❄ ❄

Getting about

There are four mountains to choose from in Gastein, providing 200km of slopes, although they are not all connected by lift. The Schlossalm (2050m), above Bad Hofgastein, has a number of easier slopes for the beginner/low intermediate rider. This mountain is connected to the main area in Bad Gastein, the Stubnerkogel (2246m), from which you can ride back down to town. At the end of the valley is the small area of Graukogel (2492m), a blessing only for its tree runs, and finally you can embark on the short (15–20 minute) drive to Sportgastein's mountain, Kreuzkogel (2686m), sacred for its snow reliability when all other areas fail. Sportgastein is definitely worth a look, and not only when the snow is bad as it has some great runs on- and off-piste, even though it is only served by a two-stage gondola and one drag lift!

The park

The freestyle scene appears not to have captured the hearts of the locals in Gastein so, although they actually have a half-decent park, they aren't fussed about advertising it. You can find the park in Grossarl, above Dorfgastein. It has a half pipe, two quarter pipes, a small selection of jumps (ranging from 3 to 10m long), and a couple of fun boxes. Unfortunately, like a few other archaic Austrian resorts, the park is exclusively for boarders. Why, we do not know.

Off-piste and backcountry

Sportgastein is the highest area, and therefore has the best snow and some of the best powder runs, in the Gastein valley. There are some good spots of off-piste that are accessible and they're unlikely to be tracked out, although you should really employ the services of a local guide to make the best of the ski area (contact the ski schools/tourist office to find an available guide).

From the top of Sportgastein, at Kreuzkogel (2686m), there's a great run down the valley that is a marked route (Ski route Nord), but is not prepared or patrolled (you do need avalanche equipment and a good skill level for this run). You will come out at Heilstollen, on the road from Sportgastein back to Bad Gastein and from here you can catch the bus back into town (8am–6pm).

Lift Passes

1 day	€57
6 days	€165

There are discounts from mid to late January and at the beginning and end of the season (December and April), as well as for children and teenagers.

Instruction

Ski School Schlossalm, Bad Hofgastein

For information and pricing enquiries:

T: 0043 (0)6432 3298

E: office@schischule-schlossalm.at

Ski and Snowboard School

Group lessons cost €50 (1 day) or €125 (3 day). Private instruction costs €43 per hour for one person and €10 per hour for each additional person.

T: 0043 (0)6434 2260 (Bad Gastein)/ 0043 (0)6432 7475 (Bad Hofgastein)

E: schneesportschule@onemail.at

W: www.schneesportgastein.com

Other activities

Spas: As well as venturing to the wellness area that you are almost guaranteed to have in your hotel, visiting one of the massive spas in resort is an absolute must. Far more than just something to do on a bad weather day, these places rock.

In Bad Hofgastein is the **Alpen Therme Gastein** (06432 82930, www.alpentherme.com), Europe's most modern alpine health and leisure world covering an area of more than 32 000m². It contains six adventure and vitality worlds: leisure world, adventure world (with lazy flow river, 'black hole' slide with flashy lights, etc. and a speed slide which really

"There's also a 360-degree cinema screen in adventure world that you swim into"

is pretty speedy), sauna world, ladies wellness and beauty world, fitness world and taste world (a restaurant and bar with a 360-degree panoramic view of the mountains). There's also a 360-degree cinema screen in adventure world that you swim into. So that you don't have to faff around with money, you have a band around your wrist that records everything you buy. Clever. If you want to be extra clever, bring your own towel and dressing gown from the hotel because it's extra to hire them. Coming to the Gastein valley and not visiting the Alpen Therme would be a travesty; we didn't want to leave. Don't be shy if you're a bloke either, there are loads of men there; plus there are water slides, beer and a nudist bit.

In Bad Gastein is a similar construction, the new **Felsentherme Gastein** (06434 22230, www. felsentherme.com). This spa was re-opened in 2004 with some fantastic new features. The Felsentherme indoor area includes a pool surrounded by rocks for relaxation, a 600m² adventure area with two layered pools, massage beds, geysers and a wild water channel, a 70m water slide and a rock grotto. There is also a fitness area and a new panorama wellness area with seven different saunas, solariums, a juice bar, a nudist area and two mountain-top pools. Outdoors is a 34°C relaxation pool, a 24°C sport pool and a children's fairytale pool with interactive fairytale figures.

The **Healing Gallery** (06434 37530, office@ gasteiner-heilstollen.com, www.gsateiner-heilstollen .com) is an intensive, natural and rare spa remedy, 2.5km deep inside the Radhausberg mountain. The healing air inside the mountain was discovered by miners searching for gold, but the unique climate they revealed is far more valuable. The healing effects are due to the radon content of the air, a temperature of 37–41.5°, speleotherapy conditions (pure, dust-free, allergy-free and bacteria-free air) and a high humidity (70–100 per cent). The vast majority (80–90 per cent) of visitors have reported alleviation of medical complaints, as well as relaxed muscles and joints. The healing gallery is thought to be the most effective natural treatment of rheumatic illness and may also relieve joint infection, muscular injury, respiratory disease and allergic illness.

Snow-biking, frozen waterfall climbing, and tobogganing: All these are offered by Schneesport schule Gastein (see Instruction), if you can squeeze them in around your spa treatments.

Events

The **FIS Nokia Snowboard World Cup** in parallel slalom takes place in Gastein in mid-December but apart from that you're looking at **jazz festivals** and **ski and golf competitions**, that kind of thing.

Accommodation

Bad Gastein

In Bad Gastein you should look at location pretty carefully, especially if you're not a fan of walking with skis or board, as some hotels involve a fairly long, steep ascent. The hotel **Cordial Sanotel** (0043 (0)6434 25010, chbadgastein@cordial.co.at, www.cordial.at) is close to the lifts to the fairly small area of Graukogel but not to the others. It is a beautiful hotel though, with a fantastic wellness facility (Jacuzzi, indoor pool, sauna, steam bath, solarium and treatments), and it is right on the infamous Gastein cascades waterfall. A double room B&B will cost about €48–86 per person per night, depending on room and time of season. The **Hotel Salzbergerhof** (0043 (0)6434 20370), is in a fairly good location for the lifts, as well as containing a couple of the best bars in town (see Bars and clubs), and a good wellness area, all rooms now have plasma TV (family rooms have a DVD player) and mini bars.

The **Grüner Baum** (0043 (0)6434 25160, info@gruenerbaum.info, www.gruenerbaum.info) is in the middle of nowhere and is a beautiful and romantic retreat from the world. The décor is oldy worldy and quaint and it's not really a place for the hardcore riders as it takes about 20 minutes to get to the slopes. It is, however, the place to go for the most comprehensive list of beauty and slimming treatments, with packages such as a Shiseido beauty week or a slim and fit purification week. No matter what ailment you go in there with, you're bound to come out feeling as fit as a fiddle.

Bad Hofgastein

Bad Hofgastein is a great place to be based. It's more of an active town than the touristy Bad Gastein, with shops, bars and atmosphere. We stayed at the most beautiful hotel in Bad Hofgastein and we are already dying to return. The **Klammer's Kärten** (0043 (0)6432 67110, info@hotel-kaernten.com, www.hotel-kaernten.com) is definitely one of our favourite hotels. From the outside it doesn't appear grandiose, and it

isn't. It is friendly but luxurious, calm and classic. The wooden bar is cosy and welcoming, with new papers each day and free cakes in the afternoon. The rooms are beautiful and spacious, some even with baths in the centre of the room. Yet it is the brand new wellness area where the hotel really excels. The indoor and outdoor pools, and range of saunas, therapeutic treatments, solarium and plunge pool are set in an idyllic, serene and perfectly designed sanctuary. If you are staying in Bad Hofgastein, stay here.

Eating out

On the mountain

The best places to eat on the mountain are **Jungerstube** on the Bad Hofgastein side of Stubnerkogel (at the bottom of the Fleischleiten run and Jungeralm lift), **Treff** on Graukogel, at the mid-station of the chairlift up the mountain and **Knappenstub'n** on Sportgastein, a self-service restaurant at the first station of the gondola, with a great terrace and great views.

In town

This is one resort where we would probably opt for half-board accommodation as there isn't a great variety of restaurants to check out. **Mozart's Hotel** and **Elisabethpark Hotel** do good food and the **Weinfassl** has an old, traditional atmosphere and a good view. For a change, there's the **Sancho** Mexican – the only restaurant in town that looks genuinely cool and serves Mexican and British dishes. You will find it next to the waterfall in the centre of town. There's a kebab shop if you get desperate.

Bars and clubs

The Salzbergerhof has all the best bars, with the spirited **Silver Bullet Bar** (great live music at après ski), the **Ritz Cocktail Bar** and the **Gatz Music Club**. Of the other bars in town, the best are **Häggblom´s Bar** and the bar at **Eden**. The casino is also definitely worth a look. In Bad Hofgastein, the **Piccolo** ice bar has a great atmosphere and we loved the pool bar downstairs with three pool tables where you pay a trifling amount for an hour's play. The best club is the **Amschtadl**.

Useful facts and phone numbers

Tourist office

T: 0043 (0)6432 3393-560
F: 0043 (0)6432 3393-537
E: info@badgastein.at
W: www.badgastein.at

Emergency services

- Police: 133
- Ambulance: 144
- Fire:122
- Mountain rescue: 140
- Doctors' emergency call out: 141

Doctors

- Emergency service for drugs and medicine: 06432 85000
- Dr Foisner: 06432 8293
- Pharmacy Bad Gastein: 06434 22180
- Pharmacy Bad Hofgastein: 06432 62040

Taxis

- Taxi Rainer: 06432 3000
- Taxi Rudigier: 06432 6611

Getting there

By plane

Salzburg (90km) Transfer takes around 1 hour and costs €58 per person (book online at www.gastein.com).
Munich (290km) Transfer takes around 2 hours.
Innsbruck (200km) Transfer takes around 2 hours.

Hintertux

A tiny, charming resort and snow all year round.

On the slopes	
Snow reliability	✿ ✿ ✿ ✿ ✿
Parks	✿ ✿ ✿ ✿
Off-piste	✿ ✿
Off the slopes	
Après ski	✿ ✿ ✿
Nightlife	✿ ✿
Eating out	✿
Resort charm	✿ ✿ ✿

"They also have a perfectly shaped pipe that is used for World Cup Half Pipe events"

The resort

The major pulling point of Hintertux is that it is probably the most snowsure resort in Austria, with a peak of 3250m. Snow is guaranteed all year round and the extent of the glacier is far less confining than that of many of the glaciers in Europe. Hintertux is at the end of the Tux valley and is accessible by car or bus from Mayrhofen and from the other towns in the Tux valley: Lanersbach and Vorderlanersbach. Hintertux itself is a compact hamlet with some lovely hotels and guest houses and a few amusing bars and clubs. Though small, it has a definite charm, as all of the buildings maintain a traditional, yet new and glossy feel. The lifts are a few minutes down the road from the village centre, where there are a few more hotels and one bar with a great après ski vibe. Hintertux is most suited to those who consider guaranteed snow to be the primary requirement of a holiday, with the provision of bars and off-slope activities secondary.

The mountains

Height: 1500–3250m

Ability	Rating
Expert	✿ ✿ ✿
Intermediate	✿ ✿ ✿
Beginner	✿ ✿

Getting about

There are 225km of ski runs, which are collectively named the 'Ski and Glacier World Zillertal 3000'. Of these runs, 86km are on the glacier and to get to the rest you'll need to take a 15-minute bus journey to Lanersbach. In summer, there are 18km of pistes open, and up to ten lifts, with the longest descent being 2km long.

The park

The Hintertux park is on the large glacier, and is one of the highest in the world, so you are almost guaranteed to find good snow. It does mean that it can get windy and cold, but if you keep hiking up instead of catching the lift, you'll keep your muscles warm. They have some of the top pros up on the glacier, shaping the hits, hence their immaculate condition. They also have a perfectly shaped pipe that is used for World Cup Half Pipe events (snowboard), a choice of jumps for different standards and a mixture of rails. One of the best features of this great park, is that it is rideable practically all year round.

Off-piste and backcountry

Hintertux's snowsure glacier mountain makes it one of the best places to go when other resorts are lacking in powder; you can sometimes start exploring the backcountry from as early as October. It is, however, a place to take real care as there are huge dangers in exploring glacial areas. For starters, the weather can change totally within minutes and you could easily find yourself lost in winds and mist. It's not a good place to be in bad weather as it's too high up for trees to grow; so you're stuck in vast areas of open terrain. There are also crevasses to watch out for.

There's some good stuff though; the off-piste around the marked black runs is steep and a good place to get in some powder turns. Don't underestimate the dangers of the glacier – take a guide.

Lift passes	
1 day	€35
6 days	€165
13 days	€304
Passes bought for 4 days or more are automatically Zillertal Super Passes.	

Instruction

Luiggi's Ski and Snowbard School, Tux

Ski course (4 hours per day): 1 day €50, 6 days €122. Snowboard school (2 hours per day): 1 day €36, 3 days €73.

For further information:

T: 0043 (0)5287 86808

E: info@luiggis-schiscule.at

W: www.luiggis-schischule.at

Ski and Snowboard School Hintertux

Ski course (4 hours per day): 1 day €49, 5 days €119. Snowboard course (2 hours per day): 1 day €44, 3 days €92.

T: 0043 (0)5287 87755

E: info@skischule-hintertux.at

W: www.skiischule-hintertux.at

Ski School Tux 3000

Private instruction (4 hours per day): 1 day €170. Ski course: 5 days €135. Snowboard course: 3 days €100.

For further information:

T: 0043 (0)5287 87747

E: info@tux-3000.at

W: www.tux-3000.at

Other activities

Ice skating and curling: On the natural ice rink in Lanersbach. Open from December until the end of February 1–5pm and 7.30–10pm. Skating costs €3.70 and curling costs €8 per rink per hour. For reservations call 05287 87385.

Shooting range: Air rifle shooting takes place every Monday from 7pm at the shooting range in the Tux primary school in Lanersbach. Contact Tux riflemen's guild: 05287 87337.

Sleigh rides: Cost €90 for four people.

Sports Centre Tux: This offers bowling from 3pm. Squash at €8 per 30 min and tennis at €20 per court. Call 05287 87297.

Tandem paragliding: Take off from the Hintertux Glacier, the Sommerbergalm or the Eggalm in the double-seater glider (with qualified pilot). Contact Natursport Tirol on 05287 87287 or 0676 307 0000 or Tandem Funflights on 0676 328 1996 or 05287 86109.

Tobogganing: There are three natural toboggan runs on Bichlalm (3km run), Grieralm (5km run) and Höllensteinhütte (4km run). All runs can be accessed by taxi.

Events

In mid-October there is a **powder weekend** to celebrate the first powder of the winter. The **Snowboard World Cup Half Pipe event** also takes place in Hintertux's superb park.

Accommodation

Guesthouse Kössler (0043 (0)5287 87490, www.koessler.at, info@koessler.at) is a friendly and pretty B&B in the centre of Hintertux. The cost is approximately €42 per night per person. The Hotel Kirchler (0043 (0)5287 8570, office@badhotel-kirchler.at, www.badhotel-kirchler.at) is slightly more upmarket, with suites and apartments as well as their standard and superior rooms.

If you are looking for the utmost in quality, you're looking at the hotels next to the slopes (and therefore a 20-minute walk to the village). Of these, the smartest is probably the Neuhintertux (0043 (0)5287 85 80, hotel@neu-hintertux.com, www.neu-hintertux.com),

"If you are looking for the utmost in quality, try the hotels next to the slopes" with stunning pools and large wellness facilities. A standard room costs €75 –114 per person per day half board and a deluxe suite (50–70m²) €113 –149. **Hotel Vierjahreszeiten** (0043 (0)5287 8525, info@ vierjahreszeiten.at, www.vierjahreszeiten.at) and **Der Rinderhof** (0043 (0)5287 8558, hotel@rinderhof.at, www.rinderhof.at) are also top quality 4-star hotels by the lifts.

Staying in Lanersbach is also an option, as it is now linked to the Mayrhofen and Finkenberg slopes and is only a 15-minute drive from the glacier at Hintertux.

We'd prefer to either stay in Mayrhofen or Hintertux though.

Eating out

On the mountain
Gletscherhütte (05285 64470) at 1611m is a lovely hut at the peak of the Gletscher. It is open all year and the views are fantastic. **Spannagelhaus** (05287 87707) is popular for an après ski beer, and is a good place for a bite to eat. It is also open all year. **Tuxer**

Joch Haus (05287 87216) at the top of the Tuxerjoch chair lift is also good, but is only open December to April. Each of the latter two offer the possibility of staying over – call the restaurant for more details.

In town

There aren't too many independent restaurants, most are hotel-based. **Didi's** is a really nice pizzeria (pizza/pasta €6–9) and **Tuxersübl** has great food in a cosy atmosphere. Tasty burgers can also be picked up from the **Hohenhaus** pub by the lifts.

Bars and clubs

Après ski starts with a couple of beers at the **Spannagelhaus** and continues at the crazy **Hohenhaus Tenne** (05287 8501), just opposite the lifts back in town. Après ski is massive here, in a really atmospheric, big chalet-style bar. This really is how an après ski bar should be, with loads of drinking until around 9pm, when it closes up for the night. The Hohenhaus Tenne is also the place to pick up a good cheeseburger. Between après and dancing, there aren't too many bars to choose from, mostly hotel bars. Later on, back in Hintertux 'centre' (if you can call it that), there are a couple of amusing places to continue. **Tux 1** (05287 8501) is bizarre, but cool. The atmosphere is mixed up; it has a typical, Austrian-style chalet interior, yet mingled into the décor is an 80s style DJ box, a dance floor, disco ball, plasma TVs, a dancing pole, pool, darts and table footie. The clientele is equally bizarre, but it's really fun all the same. Look out for karaoke Wednesdays and 70s and 80s nights. At the **Batzen keller** (05287 8570), there are once again the 80s style features – smoke machine and neon – but it's really quite fun after a few pints.

"Look out for karaoke Wednesdays and 70s and 80s nights!"

Useful facts and phone numbers

Tourist office

T: 0043 (0)5287 8506
F: 0043 (0)5287 8508
E: info@tux.at
W: www.tux.at

Emergency services

- Police: 133/ 05285 622060
- Ambulance: 144
- Rescue helicopter: 0800 207 070
- Mountain rescue: 140
- Fire: 122
- Schwaz District Hospital: 05242 6000
- Innsbruck Hospital: 0512 5040

Doctors

- Dr Katharina Weber-Gredler and Dr Simon Gredler: 05285 62550
- Dr Armin Zumtobel: 05285 62054
- Dr Wilfried Schneidinger: 05285 63124
- Dr Pavel Kriz (dentist): 05285 63341

Taxis

- Siegfried's Taxi: 05287 1718
- Taxi Siebzehnwölf: 05287 1712

Getting there

By car

From the A12 take the exit for the Ziller valley. Take the Federal Highway B169 to Mayrhofen and then the Tux road to Hintertux.

By plane

Innsbruck (90km)
Salzburg (160km)
Munich (230km)

Ischgl

A mountain and resort that deserves to be recognised by the Brits

On the slopes	
Snow reliability	❄ ❄ ❄ ❄
Parks	❄ ❄ ❄ ❄
Off-piste	❄ ❄ ❄

Off the slopes	
Après ski	❄ ❄ ❄ ❄ ❄
Nightlife	❄ ❄ ❄ ❄
Eating out	❄ ❄ ❄ ❄
Resort charm	❄ ❄ ❄ ❄

"One of the first resorts to push the freestyle ski and snowboard scene"

The resort

Ischgl came as a real shock. It has characteristics that many Brits would absolutely love, yet we'd never really heard anything about it, as its clientele at present are primarily German. Firstly, there's the bling factor; Ischgl is blatantly glamorous and full of plush hotels that almost sparkle with prosperity. Secondly, the après ski is mental in true Austrian style. Thirdly, it has a fantastic terrain park. And lastly, you can ride over to the duty-free Samnaun, pack your bags with cheap booze for the evening and clink your way back to Ischgl. Those Brits who put resorts such as Val d'Isère, Courchevel, Zermatt, Verbier and St Anton on their list of places to go, should definitely give Ischgl some serious consideration.

The resort is compact and focused around one pedestrianised street, which thankfully alleviates the need for public (or private) transport. The main lift, Silvrettabahn, sets off from the centre of town, and close to here is probably the most convenient place to stay. The other two lifts, Pardatschgratbahn and Fimbabahn, are separated from the town by some high ground. Many of the après ski bars are around these lifts but the tiring walk back is eased by the moving walkway from one side of town to the other.

The mountains

Height: 2000–2872m

Ability	Rating
Expert	❄ ❄ ❄
Intermediate	❄ ❄ ❄ ❄
Beginnner	❄

Getting about

Ischgl has over 200km of snow-sure terrain to explore, as well as a superb park and some great backcountry areas.

Ischgl is good for most intermediates and for experts, but beginners should perhaps look elsewhere, partly due to the lack of decent slopes to learn on and also because many instructors speak less English than you would expect in other resorts.

The park

Ischgl claims to have one of the biggest and best parks in Europe, 'Boarders' Paradise'. They were one of the first resorts in Europe to start pushing the freestyle ski and snowboard scene, and they held the first official World Championships for snowboarders. The park has a long list of features: tons of different sized kickers (from beginner to professional), one quarter pipe, World Championship half pipe named 'the tube', rails for all levels of rider, a big fun box, a boarder/skier-cross course, a giant slalom (boarders only), wave rides (from advanced to pro), and a kindercross (boarder/skier-cross for children with waves and jumps). Though called 'Boarders' Paradise', the park welcomes skiers and boarders and it never seems to get too busy. Ischgl's park is fantastic – but perhaps not the best in Europe.

Off-piste and backcountry

Ischgl mainly attracts intermediates who stick to the pisted areas, so there are plenty of fresh untracked areas around. Like a lot of other resorts, Ischgl has marked areas for freeriding. The Palinkopf (2864m) is a favourite and not too challenging and the Greispitz (2872m) also has a freeride trail. For the more

Lift passes	VIP (Ischgl and Samnaun)	Silvretta (Ischgl, Samnaun, Galtür, Kappl and See)
1 day	€39	–
6 days	€172.50	€202
13 days	€300.50	€352.50
Flexible passes are also available for if you want to ski/board for 5 days out of 7 (€168.50/190.50) or 10 out of 14 (€269/318).		

advanced is the extreme trail on the Hollenkar face; this is one of the most challenging parts of the mountain and should be undertaken only by those in the know. Even though these runs are marked on the map, there is still the danger of avalanches so check out the avalanche danger rating and ask pisteurs if you're not sure. Also make sure you, and those you're riding with, have all the necessary avalanche equipment. Towards the bottom of the resort are some good tracks through the trees; a great place to head in flat light.

Instruction

Ischgl Ski School
Group rates (ski): 1 day €49, 3 days €114, 5 days €156.
Snowboard course: 3 half days (am or pm) €114.
Private lessons (any discipline): half day €114 (€16 per additional person), full day €193 (€21 per additional person).
For further information:
T: 0043 (0)5444 5257
E: www.schischule.ischgl.at
W: schischule@ischgl.at

Other activities

Beauty treatments: Alpenhotel Ischglerhof (05444 5330), Hotel Trofana Royal (05444 600), Hotel Madlein (05444 5226) and Hotel Seiblishof (05444 5424) offer beauty treatments to the public.
Horse-drawn sleighs: Adults pay €11 to ride to Mathon, where they have a short stop. The ride takes around 2 hours. Call 05444 5365 to book.
Ice skating and curling: The ice rink is open daily from 4–9pm (05444 526611).

"Towards the bottom of the resort are some good tracks through the trees; a great place to head in flat light"

Recreation centre: On the outskirts of Ischgl (in the direction of Mathon), the centre has four indoor and four outdoor tennis courts. The courts cost €16–20 for 55 minutes. Call 05444 5264 for court reservations. Private lessons are also available on request.
Silvertta centre: This centre (05444 606950) has an indoor pool, sauna, steam room, sunbed, massage, reflexology, internet café, bowling alley and restaurant.
Squash: At the Hotel Solaria (05444 5205). The courts are open 9am–9pm, with 50 minutes (no equipment) costing €9.50.
Tobogganing: Every Monday and Thursday, from 7pm, take the Silvrettabahn to take a ride down the huge, 7km-long, floodlit toboggan run from Idalp to Ischgl.

Events

Ischgl don't seem too fussed about attracting freestyle snowboard or ski events, but they are keen to encourage famous pop stars to play gigs here.

Accommodation

There are loads of plush hotels in Ischgl, most with a traditional luxurious feel. The minimalist **Madlein** (0043 (0)5444 5226, info@madlein.com, www.madlein.com), however, is significantly different, with vast open spaces filled only with marble, spotlights, and the occasional square pouf, or artily positioned candle. Stylish and glamorous it is, cosy and inviting it isn't. The pool and fire room are very cool, but the jury's still out on the zen garden. A double room will cost somewhere in the range of €110–235, and a design room €165–275 (per person per day, half board). If you're in the 'traditional and wealthy' category, you may be more at home in the beautifully extravagant 5-star **Trofana Royal** (0043 (0)5444 600, office@trofana.at, www.trofana.at). The 'Royal ambience' that the Thanner family aimed to create has been achieved – you will feel royal by the time you leave. There are nearly 20 styles of room, each with their own hefty price tag. The 110m² imperial suite can cost up to €300 per person per day, in the height of the season. Other good hotels are the **Yscla** (0043 (0)5444 5275, info@yscla.at), in a very central position on the main street, and the **Elisabeth** (0043 (0)5444 5585, info@ischglelisabeth.com, www. hotel-elisabeth.ischgl.com), another glamorous choice, right opposite the Pardatschgratbahn lift, with a great après ski bar.

The expensive hotels aren't the only option, there are loads of guesthouses and apartments. Call or email the reservations department of the tourist office (see Useful facts and phone numbers). They will help you find something to suit your budget; just make sure it's not out of town, or on the other side of the bypass.

"The expensive hotels aren't the only option, there are loads of guesthouses and apartments"

Bars and clubs

The two sides of town have their own après scene going on. At the base area of the Pardatschgratbahn and Fimbabahn lifts, our favourite bars are the **Ice bar** and **Schatzi** bar of the Elisabeth hotel, **Niki's Stadl** and the **Nevada Alm**, which all involve drinking, dancing and singing. There are loads more to try too and they're not hard to spot. If you ski down to the other side of town head straight to the **Fire and Ice bar**, which never stops all night, or **Trofana Alm**. When the night sets in you need to head either to the **Tenne club** at the Trofana or go Ibiza style and hit the crazy **Pacha nightclub** in hotel Madlein. If you tire of dancing and would prefer to watch some lovely ladies strut their stuff, the Hotel Madlein also has a Coyote Ugly table dancing club.

Eating out

On the mountain

Towards Fimbatal, the **Paznauner Thaya** and **Bodenalpe** are atmospheric chalet-style restaurants with busy bars. The Paznauner often has live music. On the Swiss side, the **Alp Trida Sattel** has great views and good food as does the table-service restaurant **Schmuggler Alm** in Samnaun.

In town

Ischgl's restaurants cater to most demands, from the après drinker's desire for a cheap pizza before stumbling back to the bar, to the refined palate of even the fussiest gourmand. Those in the latter category should not leave Ischgl without a visit to Trofana Royal's gourmet restaurant, **Paznauner Stube** (05444 600). For a good steak or pasta, try the **Allegra** (05444 527564) attached to the Hotel Yscla in the centre of town with a Frankie and Benny's style atmosphere and menu, and a happy pasta hour (5–6pm). For pizzas, the **Salz & Pfeffer** (05444 591956) takes some beating, with fantastic wood-fired pizzas and an open feel, reminiscent of Pizza Express. For something a little cosier, try the **Grill Alm** (05444 5293), which serves up tasty traditional treats, or the gorgeous **Tofana Alm** pizzeria (05444 602), which you will find tucked behind its 5-star hotel owner, the Trofana Royal. If your taste buds demand a change, try the top notch Eurasian food in the **Indochine** (05444 529357).

Useful facts and phone numbers

Tourist office

T: 0043 (0)5444 5266
F: 0043 (0)5444 5636
E: info@ischgl.com
W: www.ischgl.com

Direct reservations

T: 0043 (0)5444 526618
E: reservation@ischgl.com

Emergency services

- Police: 059 133 71 42
- Fire brigade: 122
- Rescue squad/Red Cross: 144
- Mountain rescue: 5234/ 140 (emergency number)
- Hospital St Vinzenz: 05442 60 00

Doctors

- Dr Walser: 52 00 (in office hours and emergency)
- Dr Treidl in Galtür: 05443 82 76

Taxis

- Alpentaxi Ischgl: 5757/ 0664 25 33 552, info@taxi-ischgl.at
- Ischgler Taxi: 5999, info@taxi-ischgl.com
- Taxi Express: 20120 or 5814, taxi@20120.com

Getting there

By car

Take the Inntal motorway towards Arlberg and exit at Pians towards Paznaun. From here it is signed tolschgl and should take 20 minutes.
Parking is free during the day, so you can pop in for a day on the mountain, but if you stay overnight you will have to pay.

By plane

Innsbruck (100km) Around an hour by road.
Friedrichshafen (170km) Around 1.5 hours by road.
Munich (300km) Around 2.5 hours by road.
Salzburg (300km) Around 3 hours by road.

Kitzbühel

A beautiful and very Old School resort

On the slopes	
Snow reliability	✲ ✲
Parks	✲ ✲
Off-piste	✲ ✲ ✲

Off the slopes	
Après ski	✲ ✲ ✲ ✲
Nightlife	✲ ✲ ✲ ✲
Eating out	✲ ✲ ✲
Resort charm	✲ ✲ ✲ ✲ ✲

The resort

Kitzbühel's distinguishing feature is its fairytale pedestrianised centre with colourful buildings, sparkly lights and exclusive cocktail bars and shops. Reflected in this cosmopolitan atmosphere are the clientele, most of whom are elegant and sophisticated. Aside from all this, however, is a great après ski scene, in which the less sophisticated Brits can revel. It's a shame that Kitzbühel's charm and character does not extend far out of the square though – you quickly reach far less attractive suburbs and congested roads.

Kitzbühel's slopes are great for cruising, although altitude is a problem and you may have to go searching for good snow on higher peaks. The resort also has a seriously Old School attitude, hiding the snowboarders away on a separate mountain wherever possible. For the typical Kitzbühel skiers, the focus is definitely more on the pit stops than the powder.

The mountains

Height: 760–2000m

Ability	Rating
Expert	✲ ✲ ✲
Intermediate	✲ ✲ ✲ ✲ ✲
Beginner	✲ ✲ ✲

Getting about

Kitzbühel's slopes are extensive, but largely disjointed. The 3S lift has alleviated this problem to an extent by connecting the Hahnenkamm/Pengelstein area to the terrain of Jochberg and Pass Thurn, but the others are still out on a limb. From Pengelstein, you can begin the Ski Safari right over to Pass Thurn, a great place to head to if conditions are bad, as it offers the highest terrain in Kitzbühel. On this route you will cover around 35km of runs. The Hahnenkamm mountain is also home to the Streif piste: the Hahnenkamm downhill run. The run's not as difficult as it may sound, confident red run riders will be fine.

The Kitzbühler Horn is home to the park (see below) and Bichalm has been left ungroomed to encourage some freeriders to make the effort to get to this inconvenient area.

The park

Kitzbühel, along with a few other Austrian resorts, should really move into the 21st century and let boarders and skiers into the same freestyle park. The snowboard-only park, on the Kitzbüheler Horn, consists of a boardercross and half pipe, and a few jumps and rails that are changed regularly according to the snow conditions. The maintenance of the park is decent, if sporadic.

Off-piste and backcountry

Some of the best off-piste is really accessible, so first-time freeriders can easily find some good spots to practise on and even the more experienced backcountry rider won't need to do massive hikes to locate some good areas. There aren't too many people looking for it either, so you should find some good, untracked spots. We weren't able to explore much of the backcountry whilst we were there as it was dumping down and the light was really flat.

Look out for the fairly steep Ehrenbachgraben bowl, or try the 'freeriding mountain' Bichalm. To explore the great backcountry areas not clearly visible from the piste, we recommend that you hire a guide. Give Alpinschule Kitzbühel a call on 05356 73323.

Lift passes	Low season	High season
1 day	€30.50	€35
6 days	€143.50	€165
13 days	€249	€287

Instruction

Hahnenkamm

Group lessons: 1 day €60, 3 days €120, 5 days €130.
Private lessons: 1 day €180, 3 days €510, 5 days €800.
Snowboard courses: 1 day €60, 3 days €130, 5 days €160.
T: 0043 (0)5356 63177
E: office@schischule-hahnenkamm.at
W: www.schischule-hahnenkamm.at

Rote Teufel (Red Devil) Kitzbühel

Group lessons (ski or board): half day €35, 1 day €60, 5 days €135.
Private lessons: half day €140, 1 day €190, 5 days €800 (€20 extra per day for each additional person).
Special snowboarding lessons: 1 day €60, 3 days €130, 5 days €165
T: 0043 (0)5356 62500
E: office@rote-teufel.at
W: www.rote-teufel.at

Other activities

Boutique shopping: Shopping and sipping wine in cafés is the usual activity of those who choose not to hit the slopes.

Bowling: This can be found in the nearby town of Reith, open 2–12pm (05356 72161).

Curling: Available at a couple of places: the Alpenhotel (05356 642540, alpenhotel-hirschhuber@tirol.com, www.alpenhotel-kitzbuehel.at) has ice stick shooting from 1 hour per person for €2. Curling at the Lebenberg (05356 62444) costs €4.

Fitness centre: This fitness centre (05356 63412, www.fitnessforfun.at) is open 9am–10pm weekdays and from 1pm at weekends.

Horse sleigh rides: These cost around €50 per hour plus €8 per additional person. Call Eberl Hubert (05356 66380) or Henntalhof (05356 64624).

Hot air ballooning: For this popular option, call Ballooning Tyrrol (05352 65666, office@ballooningtyrol.com, www.ballooningtyrol.com). Rides cost €180–360, depending on the length of ride.

Ice skating: You can also skate at the Alpenhotel (see Curling) for €5.

Paragliding: Three schools offer paragliding in Kitzbuhel: Alpin Experts (05356 72012, resl@alpin-experts.at, www.alpin-experts.at); Hermanns Flugschule (05356 67138, herm.krimbacher@tirol.com) and Tandem Flights Kitzbühel (05356 67194, tandem flights@tirol.com, www.tandemflights.at).

Tobogganing: There is a natural 5km tobogganing run at Gaisberg, above the nearby town of Kirchberg. It is free during the day (with valid lift pass) and €7.50 (single ticket) – €13 (all evening) at night. On Thursdays and Fridays there is also nightskiing at Gaisberg. The lifts are open 6.30–9.30pm but the runs stay lit until 11pm so you can stop for a drink or two on your way down. There is another, 2.5km, toboggan run at Bichalm. You can rent toboggans at the lodge and it is open in the evening but is not lit.

Water sports and spa: The Aquarena (05356 64385, aquarena@bergbahn-kitzbuehel.at, www.bergbahn-kitzbuehel.at), situated close to the Hahnenkamm lift, is pretty impressive, with a big pool, adventure slides,

sauna, hammam, massage and other treatments. It costs €8.50 for adults (€7.20 with guest card), €5.20 for kids.

Wellness facilities: You can find these in many of the smart hotels. For example, at the smart Sport Hotel Reisch you can visit the Aveda wellness facility (05356 63366 336, spothotel-reisch@kitz.net, www.sporthotelreisch.at).

Events

The **Kitzbühel Hahnenkamm Downhill** is now the most famous downhill event in the world. It's held every year in January and thousands of people flock to the resort to watch the best downhill skiers from around the globe battling it out on one of the toughest alpine courses.

Accommodation

There's a great range of accommodation, with lots of places to find 5-star luxury and equally as abundant guest houses and pensions where you can find cheaper

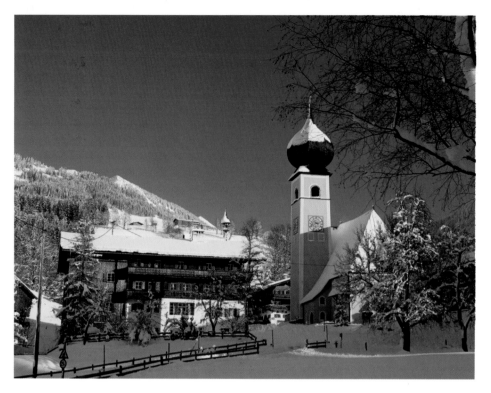

beds. Of the luxury options, we love the **Zur Tenne** (0043 (0)5356 644440, info@hotelzurtenne.com, www.hotelzurtenne,com), a stunning 4-star hotel, right in the heart of the beautiful town centre. The **Schwarzer Adler** (0043 (0)5356 6911, hotel@adlerkitz.at, www.adlerkitz.at) has superb wellness facilities and a gorgeous, traditional atmosphere. If you like the sound of a secluded alpine castle, try the imposing **Hotel Schloss Lebenberg** (0043 (0)5356 6901, schloss.lebenberg@austria-trend.at, www.austria-trend.at/leb). The location is inconvenient for the slopes and town, but there are shuttle buses to take you around.

If you are looking for B&Bs, you can get very good value places on the outskirts of town, such as pension **Thurner** (0043 (0)5356 62275), or something slightly more expensive closer to the main lifts, such as pension **Rosengarten** (0043 (0)5356 625280).

Eating out

On the mountain
The mountain restaurants in Kitzbühel have a fantastic reputation so don't be afraid to stop anywhere that looks

> "The bars that are dotted around on the snow make good pit-stops too"

nice. The bars that are dotted around on the snow make good pit-stops too. Our two favourite restaurants in the Hahnenkamm sector are the beautiful and rustic **Melkalm** (05356 62119, Melkalm@aon.at), with fantastic food and the friendliest service, and the **Sonnenbuhel** (05356 62776, schialm@tirol.com, www.schi-alm.at), that has a great terrace with deckchairs. Over towards Kirchberg, the **Ski Alm** (05357 3282) has a great little bar out on the snow.

In town
For good, traditional Tyrolean dishes, as well as the odd tasty Asian dish, the **Schwedenkapelle** (05356 65870)

is the place to go. To get into the swing of things, pop along to the dinner dancing on Saturdays. The **Neuwirt** (05356 6911), at the hotel Schwarzer Adler, provides award-winning food, with just as astonishing a price tag. For Austrian cuisine in less formal surroundings, the **Chizzo** (05356 62475) is good value and has a lovely terrace and bar outside. You will find it just outside the gated town centre entrance. Our favourite was the Mexican restaurant **La Fonda** (05356 73673), where you can enjoy some fajitas and a margarita in a cosy and well-designed restaurant/bar. The **Shanghai Chinese** (05356 62178) has great Chinese food and an extensive menu, and looks like your typical Chinese restaurant inside. If you're missing Italian food, head to the bustling **Barrique** (05356 62658) in the centre of town. If you get post-après munchies, **McDonald's** is across the street from the Londoner.

Bars and clubs

The ice bars at the bottom of the slopes (**Hahnenkamm Pavilion Bar**, for example) are good places to start the après. Most tourists head straight to the **Londoner**, which has a great atmosphere but gets really jam packed and is more expensive than other bars. The **Drop Inn**, the American themed **Highways** (with a diner area and a Cadillac convertible) and the cute **s'Lichtl** with its ceiling of fairy lights are other popular choices. New to the scene is **Brass Monkeys**, run by two English guys, with food, sport and reasonable prices (€2 a pint). The same guys have taken over the popular **Holzl Bar** and are currently turning this into **Flannigan's Irish Bar**. **Jimmy's** wine bar, in the centre of the square, is great for a more civilised glass of wine and a plate bruscetta. The Bergsinn, just at the edge of the pedestrianised area, is modern and futuristic, with a great cocktail list.

"The Bergsinn, just at the edge of the pedestrianised area, is modern and futuristic, with a great cocktail list"

Late-night dancing can be had at either **Olympia**, which has primarily German clientele, or **Take 5**, a smarter and more expensive club. The **casino** (05356 62300, http://kitzbuehel.casinos.at) has French and American roulette, black jack, poker and slot machines. For €21 you get €25 of welcome chips and for €52 you receive a glass of prosecco, €25 chips and a four-course gourmet dinner in one of the casino's partner restaurants.

Useful facts and phone numbers

Tourist office

T: 0043 (0)5356 777
F: 0043 (0)5356 77777
E: info:kitzbuehel.com
W: www.kitzbuehel.com

Emergency services

- Police: 133 or 05356 62626
- Mountain rescue squad: 140 or 05356 62265
- Mountain patrol: 05356 74544
- Rescue squad – Red Cross: 144 or 05356 691000
- Helios Hospital: 05356 6010, postmaster@ kitzbuhel.helios-kliniken.at, www.helios-kliniken.at/kitzbuehel

Taxis

- Taxi: 05356 62617
- Taxi Aufschnaiter: 05356 6969, info@kitz-tour.at, www.kitz-tour.at
- Taxi Hauser: 05356 65402

Airport transfer

- Four Season Airport transfer: 0043 (0)512 584 157, www.airport-transfer.com
- Transferbus.net: 0043 (0)820 600802, www.transferbus.net

Getting there

By car

From Munich take the E53, A9, A99 and A8, all in the direction of Salzburg. Then take the A93 to Kufstain Süd, highway 178 towards St Johann and the 161 to Kitzbühel.
From Salzburg take the highway to Walserberg, the 21 towards Bad Reichenhall, the B178 towards St Johann and the 161 to Kitzbühel.

By plane

Salzburg (80km)
Innsbruck (95km)
Munich (135km)

Lech

Everyone will find something
they love about Lech

On the slopes	
Snow reliability	❄ ❄ ❄ ❄
Parks	❄ ❄ ❄
Off-piste	❄ ❄ ❄ ❄
Off the slopes	
Après ski	❄ ❄ ❄
Nightlife	❄ ❄
Eating out	❄ ❄ ❄ ❄ ❄
Resort charm	❄ ❄ ❄ ❄

The resort

Lech gets massive thumbs up from us on almost all counts. The town itself is beautiful and the resort's planning and construction laws cleverly maintain not only the traditional look of the hotels and chalets, but also space in between buildings, providing an open feel and the convenience of being able to ski back to many hotels. The trickling stream adds to the ambience, as does the usual snow cover on the wide streets. Royalty from all countries have taken a shine to Lech, including Princess Di, whose signed painting hangs proudly from the wall of the Hotel Arlberg. However, although prosperity is abundant, the resort is by no means pretentious or elitist, and we can't imagine anyone who wouldn't love it.

Oberlech is a small, traffic-free gathering of hotels just above Lech, only accessible by cable car.

> "Oberlech is a small, traffic-free gathering of hotels just above Lech, only accessible by cable car"

The cable car does stay open until 1am so you could sample some of the nightlife in Lech and then rush back up to your hotel, but we prefer it as a lunch stop than as a base for the holiday. Families might enjoy the seclusion though, and there is the ski-in ski-out option from any of the hotels there.

You will not be allowed to forget that Lech was the location of the ski scenes in the Bridget Jones film, *The Edge of Reason*; they are obviously very proud of this fact and have decked the resort out in posters and cardboard cut outs. If you were in Lech last year and think you may have spotted Colin on the lash you may well be right, as (according to our friend Carl, the longstanding barman in the Hotel Post where the cast was staying) Colin was always out on the town having a laugh, whilst Renee stayed in her room at all times, even to eat meals.

The mountains

Height: 1450–2450m

Ability	Rating
Expert	❄ ❄ ❄ ❄
Intermediate	❄ ❄ ❄ ❄ ❄
Beginner	❄ ❄ ❄ ❄

Getting about

The main slopes of Lech and Oberlech are accessed by the Schlegelkopf chairlifts. These slopes are great for low intermediates and cruisers as they are primarily wide and flat (boarders may find the flats a tad annoying). As in many resorts now, there are a number of off-piste routes marked on the piste map. In some resorts this is a little infuriating as it can hinder your chances of fresh tracks, but in Lech there are few people to compete with.

From the Rüfikopf cable car on the main street in Lech, you can make your way over to Zurs, although this is a one-way trip; you'll have to catch the bus back. These reds and blues are geared to intermediates, but you'll also find some decent challenges.

The park
Short but sweet! The park looked perfectly shaped and groomed, despite the fact that we were in Lech fairly

late in the season. There are six kickers, ranging from 3m to 12m in length and two rails, including a superb rainbow rail. It would be a great place to learn freestyle, and get your tricks dialled, but could be a little dull for the experts – apart from the rainbow.

Off-piste and backcountry

Lech has off-piste for all levels of backcountry rider. For the less experienced freerider, there are a fair few marked ski and board routes on the map, which are not pisted or patrolled. For the fully grizzled mountain men and women, hire a guide and explore this resort's truly amazing backcountry. You will find that there is quite a bit of hiking and climbing to be done to access some of the big powder bowls, but this all adds to the adventure. On bad weather days, with high winds and flat light, the Krieferhorn area has some good off-piste spots which wind up at the bottom of Lech.

Lift passes	
1 day	€39
6 days	€184
13 days	€321
A €4 deposit is required for your electronic pass.	

Instruction

Alpin Center Lech

A private guide to show you the best backcountry areas will cost €195 for one person for one day, with a surcharge of €16 for each additional person.

T: 0043 (0)5583 39880
E: info@alpincenter-lech.at
W: www.alpin-center-lech.at

Lech Ski School (Ski and Snowboard)

Adult group lessons cost €48.50 for one day, €114 for 3 days and €164 for 6 days. There are discounts in low season. A private instructor will cost €199 for one person for one day, with a surcharge of €16 for each additional person. They can also arrange guiding.

T: 0043 (0)5583 2355-0

E: skischule-lech@aon.at

W: www.skilech.info

Other activities

Beauty treatments: The following hotels offer treatments and are open to the public: Burg-Vital-Hotel (05583 2291-930), Romantik Hotel Krone (05583 2551), and Gasthof Rote Wand (05583 34350).

Helicopter rides: For information about helicopter rides call the ski school on 05583 2355.

Horse sleigh rides: Reserve your horse sleigh rides from Haus Angelika (0664 3443 730, 4140), Pension Zugerhorn (0664 5207167, 2749) and Duftner Wilfried (0664 2841645).

Ice skating: Skating is really popular in Lech at the indoor ice skating rink at the Hotel Monzabon (05583 2104). You can also have a go at curling.

Paragliding: Ring the school on 0664 141 5166 for more information.

Tennis, squash and football: The Tenniszentrum Lech (05583 2780) offers tennis, squash and indoor football.

Therapeutic massages and remedies: Call the Physiosport Muxel (0664 1229 923).

Tobogganing: Tobogganing on the 1.2km long slope from Oberlech to Lech is open 9am–10pm. Bobsleds are available for rent from the Bergbahn Oberlech.

Accommodation

For 5-star luxury you could follow in Princess Di's footsteps and choose the central **Hotel Arlberg** (0043 (0)558321340, hotel-arlberg@lech.at, www.arlberghotel.at) with indoor and outdoor pools, sauna, beauty treatments and a gourmet restaurant. Prices are €258–306 per person per night for half-board accommodation in the main season. The **Hotel Post** (0043 (0)5583 22060, info@postlech.com, www.postlech.com), a Relais & Châteaux hotel, is also a favourite of royalty from many countries. The cosy lounge bar is the place for whisky and cigars and the numerous elaborate suites (prices on request) are exceptional. Jackets and ties are essential for meals in the dining room. This hotel was the choice of the Bridget Jones cast when they were filming *The Edge of Reason* in Lech. A night in the Post could set you back €305–450 per person per night for half-board accommodation, so get saving. The more affordable 4-star **Tannbergerhof** (0043 (0)5583 22020, info@tannbergerhof.com, www.tannbergerhof.com) costs from €80 per person per night half board. It is right in the centre of town and has a decent spa area, and one of the best bars in town.

However, you don't need to stay in the gorgeous 4- and 5-star hotels to get quality service and lovely rooms. We stayed in the charming **Hotel-Pension Felsenhof** (0043 (0)5583 2524, reservierung@felsenhof.at, www.felsenhof.at) and would recommend it to anyone. The rooms are lovely and the staff first class. It also costs a very reasonable €45–92 per person per night B&B (half board also available). Alternatively **Pension Angerhof** (0043 (0)5583 2418, www.lech-zuers.at/angerhof) is an attractive and central B&B and the cute **Pension Odo** (0043 (0)5583 2358-0, haus-odo-lech@aon.at, www.lech-zuers.at/haus-odo) is in a great, ski-in ski-out location, has only 17 beds and costs just €63–90 per person per night for half board.

Eating out

On the mountain

The **Rud-Alpe** (05583 418250), on the slopes just above town, is just how you would hope a chalet-style restaurant would look. It's big but still manages to be cosy with a nice fire. Typical Austrian food is on offer at the usual prices and spaghetti bolognese is a bargain at €6! Evening meals are also good up here. The **Panorama** restaurant at the Rüfikopf top station also serves good Austrian food, and the views from the terrace are pretty good.

The sunny terraces in car-free **Oberlech** are one of the best places for lunch. We had a great meal at the **Goldener Berg** (05583 2205), which has a huge menu, although it was a little pricey. At night the Goldener Berg restaurant is popular for its fondues.

The **Kriegeralpe** (0664 442 3697) is a cosy, romantic cabin, and a lovely lunch stop and the **Murmele** is a well-kept secret (until now), where those in the know stop for lunch.

In town

Lech/Zürs has the largest number of gourmet restaurants in Austria. Those wanting to sample such exclusive treats should try the restaurants at the **Arlberg Hotel** (05583 2134), the **Berghof** (05583 2635), the **Burg** (05583 2291) or the **Rote Wand** in Zug (05583 3435). For more information, collect a booklet from the tourist office and look for restaurants with pictures of chefs' hats next to them.

By far the most atmospheric and charming restaurant is **Haus No. 8** (05583 33220), a restored old farmhouse. The restaurant is split into sections of the old house, and you can feel the history – the owner himself was born in one of the rooms. The food is fantastic, from its traditional Austrian specialities to fondues, raclettes, salads and soups. The best thing about this restaurant is that it's not at all expensive – we each had two courses, a nice bottle of wine, and coffee for less than €90! For a romantic night, the **Älpele** (05583 3388) in Zugertal is beautiful and the evening is completed by the restaurant's seclusion – you cannot reach the restaurant by car, you must walk or take the snowcat. In Zürs, the **Flexenhäusl** (05583 4143) is another special place to dine, largely because it's so small, with only around 35 covers. Reservation is a must.

The **Schneggarei** bar (05583 39888), a little hut near the chairlifts, looks like nothing from the outside, but it's beautifully done out inside and the pizzas and ribs are great and reasonable. The **Italiener** restaurant (05583 3734) is another lovely little pizzeria, serving food from 6pm until midnight. The futuristic **FUX** restaurant and bar (05583 2992) caters for those who tire of local delicacies. Choose between an American steakhouse and the Euro-Asian option with woks, sushi and other oriental dishes. The lounge bar is great for curling up in front of the fire with a whisky and a cigar. If your taste buds ask for nachos and tortillas, head to the relaxed **Charly's Cantina** (05583 2339). The little coffee shop in the centre of town (05583 3734–23) serves great coffee and internet access (wireless and otherwise).

Bars and clubs

When après ski kicks off you have two choices. Either join the mainly local crowd at the outdoor **S'Pfefferkorndl** ice bar in the centre of town, where you can get some good snacks if you're peckish (burgers, oysters, the works), or head to the tourist favourite, the **Tannbergerhof**. This is the most popular après venue, with fab happy hours, a great atmosphere and a heaving crowd until early morning. Once you're in, it's tough to drag yourself away. The **FUX** has a bar/club and is a good place for a whisky in front of the fire, and the **Post** hotel has a cosy, upmarket bar with a comprehensive cigar menu. For seriously late-night partying you'll need to catch a taxi into Zürs, where you will find two great clubs, the **Zürserl** in the Hotel Edelweiss, and the **Vernissage** bar/club in the Robinson Club.

Useful facts and phone numbers

Tourist office

T: 0043 (0)5583 21610
F: 0043 (0)5583 3155
E: info@lech-zuers.at
W: www.lech-zuers.at

Emergency services

- Police: 05583 2203 or 0591 338 1051
- In case of emergency call 144

Doctors

- Dr Elmar Beiser: 05583 2032
- Dr Reinhard Muxel: 05583 3300
- Dr Harald Rhomberg: 05583 2234
- Dr Miomir Radovanovich: 05583 30890

Taxis

- Taxizentrale Lech: 05583 2501, info@taxi-lech.at, www.taxi-lech.at
- Taxi Zürs: 05583 3110

Getting there

By plane

Innsbruck (120km)
Friedrichshafen (130km) For bus transfers email transfer@airport-bus.at, or check out www.airport-bus.at. Expect to pay €30 per transfer.
Zurich (200km) Reserve transfer at Lech travel agency (05583 3155, reservation@lech-zuers.at) or Arlberg Express (05583 2000, www.arlbergexpress.com). One way is €45, return €75

Mayrhofen

Legendary park, lively nightlife
and good-looking town...
practically perfect

On the slopes	
Snow reliability	❄ ❄ ❄
Parks	❄ ❄ ❄ ❄ ❄
Off-piste	❄ ❄ ❄

Off the slopes	
Après ski	❄ ❄ ❄ ❄ ❄
Nightlife	❄ ❄ ❄ ❄
Eating out	❄ ❄ ❄
Resort charm	❄ ❄ ❄ ❄

The resort

We instantly fell in love with Mayrhofen and are dying to return. It simply feels like a ski resort should feel; with a charming main street, traditional architecture, bars brimming with people from 4pm onwards, great nightlife and a snow park to rival the best in Europe. Mayrhofen has so much going for it that we can forgive it for having no runs back to town, and for the resulting queues for lifts. And if you need another reason to visit, prices are far more reasonable than at most of the top resorts.

The mountains

Height: 630–2500m

Ability	Rating
Expert	❄ ❄
Intermediate	❄ ❄ ❄ ❄
Beginner	❄ ❄ ❄

Getting about

The main riding area can be reached from the Penken gondola in the middle of town. If you can be bothered, you can skip the queues by catching a bus to Finkenberg or Hippach but the resort has kindly put up a big plasma screen TV showing ski and snowboard movies, to keep you entertained as you wait. Most of the riding here is along the challenging/intermediate lines, the more daring should try the Harakiri piste, with a 78 per cent gradient. If you can't decide where to go, you can pick up a leaflet that gives you a choice of five routes. The Ahorn area is a bus ride away and is

"It starts off with a 14-metre jump and then moves on to a 16-metre, with a massive 20-metre booter to finish"

the place to go for peace and quiet; best suited to families and kids. The Hintertux glacier is only a short drive away for some sure snow and more off-piste options (see Hintertux chapter, page 64).

The park

The Burton Park (www.burton-park-mayrhofen.com) has to be one of the best in Europe in terms of kickers and rails. It has three lines of kickers; choose according to your standard. The first kicker line has three jumps, ranging from 2 to 4 metres in length. The medium kicker line has two jumps, each 8 metres long. The pro line has to be one of the best around. It starts off with a 14-metre jump and then moves on to a 16-metre, with a massive 20-metre booter to finish it off. There is also a rail line with up to five rails in a row and a pipe that can sometimes suffer, simply due to the low elevation of the park (1600m). Last year they also introduced a mini snow skate park. The park is very well maintained – it is constantly shaped and the landings are groomed each morning so that they're not too solid. This park is a favourite amongst some of the best riders around. To see the park being used to its full potential, check out the snowbombing comp (see Events) at the end of the season.

We would like to thank Jon Weaver (voted most improved rider of the year by *Document Snowboard Magazine*) for showing us around and sharing his expertise.

Lift passes	
1 day	€33.50
6 days	€168
13 days	€309.50

You can also choose more flexible passes so that you can ride for 4 days in 6 (€133.50), 5 or 6 days in 7 (€157–175) or 10 days in 14 (€270). A season pass costs €484.

Off-piste and backcountry

Mayrhofen is not known for its steep and deep, more for its lively nightlife and freestyle scene. There are, however, a few areas that are worth checking out.

After a big snow fall, head to the Zell am Ziller area which is a superb place to get freshies, and look underneath the Larchwald trees in flat light. For getting some easy powder turns in, make you're way up in the Horbergjoch area; the highest point of the mountain. Word has it, you can always find some virgin snow!

Instruction

Die Roten Profis Skischule and Snowboardschule Mayrhofen

One day in a group lesson costs €35–40 and 5 days €100–116. One day's private lesson costs €115.

T: 0043 (0)5285 63800
E: m.gager@tirol.com
W: www.skischule-mayrhofen.at

Ski Schule 3000

A great ski and board school offering lessons and guiding. Private lessons from €44 per hour. Group lessons from €34.

T: 0043 (0)5285 64015
E: skischule@mayrhofen3000.at
W: www.skischule.mayrhofen3000.at

Snowboardschule Mayrhofen Total

A great snowboard school offering a range of disciplines. Video analysis is also available. A 2-hour lesson costs €34 and a 5-day course (two hours a day) is €116.

T: 0043 (0)5285 63939
E: info@snowboard-mayrhofen.at
W: www.snowboard-mayrhofen.at

Other activities

Adventure pool: The adventure pool (05285 62559) has a water chute, saunas, crazy river, cascade, bubble pool, mountain lake and restaurant. Entry costs €3 for one hour and €5 for a day ticket. After 6pm an evening ticket is €8.

Adventure sports: Action Club Zillertal (0664 182 1898), www.action-clu-zillertal.com, info@action-club-zillertal.com) offers loads of activities such as tobogganing evenings, skidoo driving, paragliding from €75, freeriding tours and snow shoes.

Aqua centre: The Aqua Centre – Fun and Spa at Hotel Strauss (05285 6705) has sauna, solarium, massage, table tennis and squash. There are three indoor and nine outdoor tennis courts and three more squash courts at other venues. Contact the tourist office for more information.

Curling: There is an artificial ice rink with lanes for curling. Adult entry costs €3.

Nine-pin bowling: This can be found in La Fontana (05285 62578); open 4pm–1am on weekdays and 11am–1am at the weekend.

Paragliding: There are a couple of companies offering tandem paragliding flights. Stocky Air (0664 3407976/ 0664 4245580, www.fly-zillertal.com, stocky@fly-zillertal.com) has a good range of options, costing €65–130. They fly daily at 9am and can provide you with photos and film on request. **Zillertaler Flugschule** (0664 180 2483, www.zillertaler-flugschule.com) offers flights at €50–100.

Tobogganning: A natural toboggan run starts from Gasthof Wiesenhof, with a total length of 2.5km.

Events

In January a **snow and avalanche camp** is held to introduce you to freeriding (www.saac.at). In February there is a great **street festival** on the main street with live music, street performers and shows from 6pm. At the end of March, the **Ästhetiker Tour 'Wängl Tängl' Snowboard Jam** takes place. Those not invited can attend qualifiers in an attempt to compete against the top pro boarders from America, Australasia and all over Europe. **Snowbombing** is one of the main events of the season in April, and lasts a whole week, with boarding jams all day and partying all night. If you've done a whole season in Mayrhofen this could just about see you off.

Accommodation

The best place to be is as near as possible to the Penkenbahn lift, as you are close to the slopes, and most of the best bars and clubs. Right next to the lift is the good, if slightly impersonal, **Strass Hotel** (0043 (0)5285 6705, www.hotelstrass.com, info@hotelstrass.com). It has some pretty nice spa facilities with pools, saunas, solarium and all sorts, although the best facilities are the Ice Bar, the Speak Easy Bar and the Arena club (see Bars and clubs). Rooms cost €53–120 per person per night, half board. If you don't like noise, it's best to look elsewhere. Also very handy for the cable car is the very smart, friendly and welcoming **Waldheim hotel** (0043 (0)5285 62211, www.hotelwaldheim.at, hotel-waldheim@tirol.at), with prices €60–86 per person per night. In the centre of the town (a five-minute walk from the lift) is the charmingly traditional **Kramerwirt** hotel (0043 (0)5285 6700, www.kramerwirt.at, hotel@kramerwirt.at), with lovely restaurants, and staff clad in lederhosen. Prices are €53–119 per person per night. The **Hotel Rose** (0043 (0)5285 62229, www.hotel-rose.at, info@hotel-rose.at) and **Manni's**

(0043 (0)5285 633010, www.mannis.at, sporthotel@mannis.at) are also very good and central (five minutes from the lifts). If you are partial to smart surroundings, head to the beautiful **Hotel Elizabeth** (0043 (0)5285 6767, www.elisabethhotel.com, thaler familie@elisabethhotel.com) with great spa facilities. The rooms also have mini bars and balconies, and you can pay extra for whirlpool, Jacuzzi and steambath.

If you're looking for a budget option, your best bet is to check out the available apartments with the tourist

> ## "If you're looking for a budget option, your best bet is to check out the available apartments with the tourist office"

office. Alternatively, try a cheaper 'pension' (B&B). One of the best in town is the amazingly reasonable **Landhaus Thanner** (0043 (0)5285 62375, landhaus-thanner@zline.at, http://privat.zline.at/thanner), which has one of the best locations in town, only a minute's walk from the lift and very comfy rooms. Prices start at only €28 per person per night.

Eating out

On the mountain

Most of the restaurants on the mountain are self-serivce. Our favourites are the restaurant on the way down from the Tappenalm lift, just by the snow park, and renowned for its schnapps, and the **Schneekar hütte** (05285 64940), at the top of the Schneekar chairlift on Horberg, hugely cosy and traditional.

In town

Restaurants in Mayrhofen cater to most tastes. For ribs, burgers, salads, pasta, wings, and a pint or two, in Hard Rock Café-style surroundings, **Mo's bar** is definitely the way forward. Similar snack food can be found at the curvy **Randum Café**, by the tourist office, and the **Café Tirol** in the centre of town – which unfortunately has unpredictable service, but the

internet is very cheap (and they don't keep tabs on how long you've been on – they just ask you). All of these places are pretty reasonable. For pizza, the best is **Mamma Mia's** at the Elizabeth hotel, with a great atmosphere and pizzas are a snip. **Manni's** is pretty good too; both restaurants are cute and colourful. For a change, head to **Singapore Chinese**, near the tourist office. There are loads of smart restaurants in the smart hotels if you are after fancy food. For the best traditional cuisine in superb surroundings head to the **Wirtshaus zum Griena**; a 400-year-old farmhouse that has been converted into an enchanting restaurant.

"There are loads of smart restaurants in the smart hotels if you are after fancy food"

Bars and clubs

The best bars for après ski are pretty obvious as you step off the lift; right opposite you is the **Happy End Bar**, and to your left is the **Ice Bar**, which is very lively, busy and bare; so you can be as rowdy as you like. The Ice Bar is part of the Strass Hotel (see Accommodation), as is the **Speak Easy Bar**, which also gets pretty busy and the **Sports Bar and Grill**, where you can pick up some ribs or a kebab if you so desire. In the centre of town, **Mo's** is great for a pint and a bite to eat (see Eating out), and **Apropos** for a game of pool (open 8.30pm – 4am). Towards the older part of town and the tourist office, you will find the ever popular **Scotland Yard Pub** (you'll recognise it by the painted British flags and Old School English phone box). This pub has a great atmosphere and is always busy. Club-wise, you can choose between the house/techno/metal music at the **Arena**, or the more cheesy (and preferable) **Schlussel Alm**, just a minute's walk from the main lift station (away from town).

Getting there

By car

Take the A12 to Wiesing, then B169 on for another 30km.

By plane

Innsbruck (75km)
Salzburg (175km)
Munich (190km)

Useful facts and phone numbers

Tourist office

T: 0043 (0)5285 6760-0
F: 0043 (0)5285 6760-33
E: info@mayrhofen.at
W: www.mayrhofen.at

Emergency services

- Police: 133
- Ambulance: 144
- Mountain rescue service: 140

Doctors

- Dr Alois Dengg: 05285 62992-0
- Dr Simon and Katharina Gredler: 05285 62550
- Dr Jörg Ritzl: 05282 3758
- Dr Wilfried Schneidinger: 05285 63124
- Dr Armin Zumtobel: 05285 62054
- Schwaz Hospital: 05242 600
- Innsbruck Hospital: 0512 504

Taxis

- Christophorus Reisen: 05285 606
- Franky's Taxi: 0664 2500250
- Reini's Taxi: 0650 463 75 75
- Taxi Kröll: 05285 62260
- Taxi Sxhiestl: 05285 63840

St Anton

Desire to sleep seems to vanish
amidst the addictive 24-hour
atmosphere

On the slopes	
Snow reliability	�֎ �֎ �֎ �֎
Parks	�֎ ✖
Off-piste	✖ ✖ ✖ ✖ ✖
Off the slopes	
Après ski	✖ ✖ ✖ ✖ ✖
Nightlife	✖ ✖ ✖ ✖
Eating out	✖ ✖ ✖ ✖
Resort charm	✖ ✖ ✖ ✖

"You see a lot of the world's best pros filming here and making the most of natural hits"

The resort

St Anton is without a doubt one of the best resorts in Europe. For competent riders with an appetite for challenging mountains and non-stop nightlife there is no better place to be. Despite its infamous party scene, the resort retains its charm, with the long, pedestrianised main street full of attractive, traditional buildings. This street is the focus of the action; the best bars and clubs and most of the restaurants are located here, and the main lifts are only a minute's walk away.

The mountains

Height: 1300–2800m

Ability	Rating
Expert	✖ ✖ ✖ ✖ ✖
Intermediate	✖ ✖ ✖ ✖
Beginner	✖

Getting about

St Anton provides 272km of pistes and 174km of deep-snow runs to get your teeth into. What's more, the snowfall (and snow-making facilities) is sufficient to maintain the slopes up to mid/end April. The slopes don't really suit the beginner, but all others will be ecstatic with the terrain, especially the backcountry enthusiasts, who have a wide range of options from the top of the Valluga alone. The ski routes are handy to guide those who wish to venture off-piste without the aid of a guide, but don't expect fresh tracks, these routes are known to all. Make sure you have good insurance too, as the resort takes no responsibility for accidents on these routes.

The park

Given that St Anton is one of the best all-round resorts in the world, the park isn't that great, although it has improved over the last couple of winters. It has a half decent half pipe, a quarter pipe and a few kickers and rails. There is nothing that's over challenging, but it's OK for the intermediate freestyler. If you're here to push your limits, head into the backcountry and build something. You see a lot of the world's best pros filming here and making the most of natural hits; Jon Olsson, Tanner Hall and Simon Dumont filmed a lot of their movie segments in St Anton's backcountry this winter.

Off-piste and backcountry

St Anton is up there as one of the best freeriding locations in the world. We were totally blown away with what there was to offer. Like so many other resorts, especially in Austria, there are marked off-piste routes. The routes do mark good descents but they get tracked out straight away after a snowfall. The best, and most extreme, is the Pfannenköpfe, by the Valfagehr chair. It is fairly challenging, and there are some good cliff drops and gullies, a perfect place to get the heart racing. Don't think that just because it's marked on the map you don't need all the proper avalanche safety gear; it's not protected from avalanches.

To step it up a level, head to the summit of the legendary Valluga; just below is one massive bowl and here we had some of our best freeriding of the season.

"Indiana Jones types should explore over the other side of the Valluga"

This eventually leads out on to another marked ski route where you have two choices: you can either traverse left and head down the Mattun route, or keep on down the steeper face, the Schindlerkar. On a powder day this is a great place to play in the steep, deep terrain, but if it hasn't snowed for a while you will probably find black run mogul fields, which are great only if you like moguls.

Indiana Jones types should explore over the other side of the Valluga (strictly with a guide; they won't let you up the last part of the lift with skis or board without one). It's hairy in places, but a very exciting area to check out. This leads you all the way into Zürs. A mountain guide is invaluable in St Anton to take you to hidden couloirs, bowls and cliffs. We can't wait to return next year.

Lift passes	
1 day	€39.50
6 days	€189
13 days	€330

Instruction

Ski and Snowboard School St Anton

Ski courses: 1 day €54, 3 days €126, 6 days €204.
Snowboard courses: 1 day €61, 3 days €142, 6 days €220.
Private lessons cost €172 for 3 hours and €295 for 6 hours. Each additional person is €18.
One day's guiding costs €209 (€18 for each additional person).
T: 0043 (0)5446 3563
E: office@skistanton.com
W: www.skistanton.com

Ski School Arlberg

Ski courses: 1 day €54, 3 days €126, 6 days €204.
Snowboard courses: 1 day €61, 3 days €142, 6 days €220.
Private lessons cost €172 for 3 hours and €295 for 6 hours. Each additional person is €18.
One day's guiding costs €209 (€18 for each additional person).
T: 0043 (0)5446 3411
E: skischule.arlberg@st-anton.at
W: www.ski-school-arlberg.com

Other activities

Conference and sports facilities: The fairly recently built arlberg-well.com (05446 4001, www.arlberg-well.com) isn't too pretty, but has an impressive combination of conference, sporting event and wellness facilities. It contains three swimming pools: an indoor pool (with elliptical flume), a children's pool and an outdoor pool, and tons of sauna facilities (Finnish sauna, kelo sauna, samarium, steam bath, two solariums and massage showers). Additionally you will find a fitness studio and ice skating rink. Except the rink, which closes at 6pm, the facilities are open until 10pm.

Horse-drawn sleigh rides: These can take you into the Verwall valley. For reservations call Martin Tschol on 05446 2380.

Paragliding: Tandem flights and courses can be booked through Flight Connection Arlberg (0664 141 5166, www.fca.at).

Squash and tennis: These can be played at the Raiffeisen Tennis Centre (05446 2625 or 05446 4001).

Tobogganing: The 4km floodlit toboggan run from Gampenplateau down to the valley takes 10–15 minutes and covers a 500m drop in altitude. Call the Arlberger Bergbahnen on 05446 23520 for more information.

Events

Right at the beginning of December (usually the first weekend) is the official opening of the resort when there are people partying all over the place all weekend. The **Powder 8** event (mid-January) involves

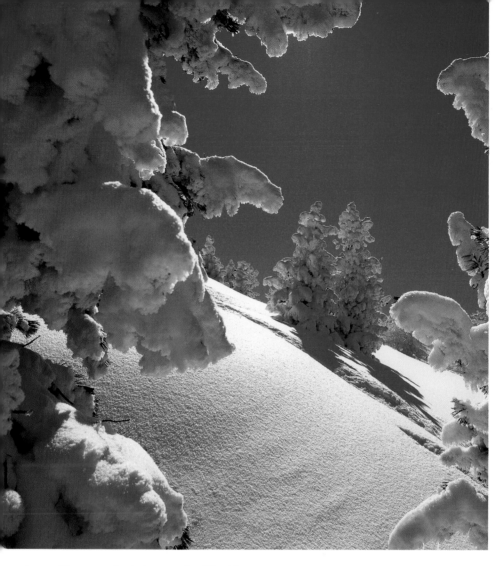

teams of two competing in deep-powder skiing. The assessment criteria are technique, style, speed, synchronisation and symmetry of turn. In April the **Weisse Rausch** is a Chinese downhill event in which all competitors (on boards, skis, telemark, anything) throw themselves from the top of the Vallugagrat (2650m) as fast as possible (1300m drop in altitude). The winning time last year was 7 minutes.

Accommodation

St Anton really does have all types of accommodation available, from low-cost B&Bs to luxurious hotels. The tourist office claims that the cheapest room (with breakfast) costs only €30 per person (low season) and the most expensive room (half board) costs €325 per person in peak season. Unless it's high season, you are usually safe just turning up in St Anton as they have a great electronic system outside the tourist office that finds all available rooms for your required dates, and lets you know the price, location, etc. The tourist office packages are also worth checking out; the Powder Snow Weeks in January allow you to take advantage of the low-season prices and more-than-likely fantastic snow conditions.

If you are looking for a comfy room in a great location, for the best value in town, we have the place for you. It is **Haus Flatscher** (0043 (0)5446 3603,

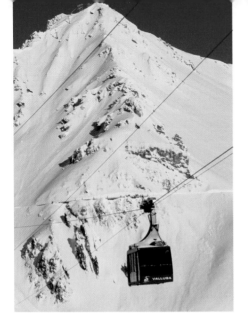

"Take advantage of the low-season prices and more-than-likely fantastic snow conditions"

haus.flatscher@st-anton.at), run by Emma Flatscher, who will do anything to make your holiday enjoyable. The rooms are excellent quality (with TV and phone), and an absolute bargain at €32–50 per person, including breakfast. We will definitely stay here next time we visit St Anton. A good 3 star is the simple but cosy **Ehrenreich** (0043 (0)5446 2353, hotel.ehrenreich@aon.at, www.arlberg.com/hotel.ehrenreich), only a minute's walk from town and lifts. A room will cost you €75–120 per person per night.

Those in search of luxury should look to either the **Hotel Alte Post** or the **Schwarzer Adler** (both are 4 star – there are two 5-star hotels but they are not particularly convenient for town or lifts). The Hotel Alte Post (0043 (0)5446 2553-0, st.anton@hotel-alte-post.at, www.hotel-alte-post.at) is absolutely stunning both outside and in, and has blended modern and traditional looks perfectly. The pool, spa and beauty facilities are incredible. Take your pick of rooms from a double (28m^2), a junior suite (39–56m^2), the Alte-Post suite (98m^2) or the Alte Post Deluxe (190m^2) that sleeps 5–10 people! You will pay anything between €133 and €265 per person per night, half board. If you want B&B, there is a €14.50 reduction per person per night. The Schwarzer Adler (0043 (0)5446 2244-0, hotel@schwarzeradler.com, www.schwarzeradler.com) is an old, traditional hotel, with very similar facilities to the Alte Post. Prices range from €82 to €306 per person per night, depending on time of season and type of room.

Eating out

On the mountain

The **Rodelalm** (05446 3745) at Gampen is one of the best restaurants on the mountain for cosiness. This original Tyrolean hut has an open fireplace, a good terrace and superb local specialities. It is also open at night when the toboggan run is open. The restaurant on Rendl (05446 2353–550) serves international cuisine, including tasty wok dishes, and the ice bar outside has live music on Tuesdays and Thursdays. The Galzig run home provides lots of opportunities to stop for a meal or, more usually, a shot or two. The **Sennhütte** (05446 2048) is popular for its huge sun terrace, and sometimes has live music. The **Krazy Kanguruh** (05446 3803) serves a great burger, and a stop here on the home run is destined to mark the beginnings of a messy après ski session. At the **Mooserwirt** (05446 3588) the fun persists, and if you get the munchies, the food's good here too.

In town

Some of the best restaurants are also the best bars. The offbeat **Hazienda** (05446 2968) has top notch steaks, fish, salads and pasta, which should always be preceded by cocktails in front of the open fire. Food is served until 11pm and then the place turns into a night-time hotspot. **Bobo's** (05446 271454) similarly turns from a busy Mexican restaurant into an even more hectic bar later on. Staff and punters are all on a mission, which creates a great atmosphere, as long as you don't mind the occasional jarring of the shoulder. Sushi, sashimi and wok dishes are rife at the **Restaurant Fiu** (05446 42692), an intimate, cosy and trendy restaurant, and also a great place to stop for a perfectly prepared cocktail at the bar. **Pomodoro** (05446 3333) and **Scotty's** are both great pizzerias. For traditional food, **Fuhrmannstube** (05446 2921) is simple but cosy, and great value for money. Traditional dishes are also superb at the rustic chalet **Alt St Anton** (05446 2432) in Nasserein.

For something a little different, the contemporary **ben.venuto** (05446 30203), at the arlberg-well.com building is worth a visit to sample its fabulous food and stylish, minimalist décor. Though 'gourmet' food (an eclectic mix from Italy and the Orient), it is not super expensive; starters cost €5–15 and a main €10–26.

Bars and clubs

The best place to celebrate a marvellous day on the mountain and kick start the evening activities is at the Krazy Kanguruh, on the slopes just above the town. The staff at Krazy's three bars (Krazy bar, Down Under bar and Ice bar) are ready to quench that thirst and encourage you to stomp on the tables to your heart's content. The **Mooserwirt** has similar activities going on next door (see Eating out).

Back in town you could stop for a drink at the **Anton** bar right at the bottom of the slopes – a modern bar with good snacks. From there it's a short walk to the ever popular **Funky Chicken**, a crowded après spot, that maintains the hordes through the evening by serving dinner (primarily roast chicken or curry), followed by the dangerous Margarita Happy Hour (11pm–midnight). The nearby **Platzl** bar is rustic, cosy, and well lit with a large open fire and live music 10pm–2am. At the centre of the main street is the **Piccadilly**, more of a British-style pub, once again with live music. **Hazienda** is a great night spot, with perfect cocktails (see Eating out) and the tireless **Bobo's** is constantly buzzing with activity (see Eating out). **Post Keller** and **Kandahar** are the clubs to head to, and they often don't chuck you out until gone 6am.

Getting there

By car

Check out www.stantonamarlberg.com and they will plan your route for you if you type in where you're coming from.

By plane

Innsbruck (100km)
Friedrichshafen (140km) Book your transfer (bus or taxi) on www.airport-bus.at
Zürich (200km) Book your transfer at www.arlbergexpress.com
Munich (250km)
At weekends there are regular bus services from the airports to St Anton.

Useful facts and phone numbers

Tourist office

T: 0043 (0)5446 22690
F: 0043 (0)5446 2532
E: info@stantonamarlberg.com
W: www.stantonamarlberg.com

Emergency services

- Police: 05446 2237 / 236 213
- Mountain rescue: 140 or 05446 2970
- Ambulance: 144
- Fire: 2237
- Report ski accidents by calling 2352 (or 2889 in Rendl)
- Hospital: 05442 600
- Avalanche warning: 0512 1588

Doctors

- Day Clinic Arlberg: 05446 42666
- Dr Sprenger: 05446 3200
- Dr Knierzinger: 05446 2828

Taxis

- Taxi Arlberg-Car/ Taxi Greisser: 05446 3730
- Taxi Harry: 05446 2315 or 2368, email taxi.harry@st-anton.at
- Taxi Isepponig: 05446 2275 or 2179
- Taxi Lami: 05446 2806, taxi.lami@netway.at

Sölden

Austria's most reliable snow, and
a raucous, Ibiza-style nightlife

On the slopes	
Snow reliability	❄ ❄ ❄ ❄ ❄
Park	❄ ❄ ❄
Off-piste	❄ ❄ ❄

Off the slopes	
Après ski	❄ ❄ ❄ ❄
Nightlife	❄ ❄ ❄ ❄
Eating out	❄
Resort charm	❄ ❄

The resort

Sölden is a sprawling town, encompassing around a mile of shops and bars. The buildings are kept traditional and are mostly pretty attractive, although the busy road is a drawback. The après ski is absolutely mad and is the reason why some people flock to the place in droves, and others flee as fast as they can. Though far prettier, the general atmosphere of Sölden's 'party mile' isn't far off that of Blackpool's 'golden mile', so make sure it's your cup of tea before you book your ticket. Personally, we prefer the après ski in St Anton and Mayrhofen. The riding is superb for both intermediates and experts, with good on- and off-piste terrain, and an excellent park.

The mountains

Height: 1350–3250m

Ability	Rating
Expert	❄ ❄ ❄
Intermediate	❄ ❄ ❄ ❄
Beginner	❄ ❄

Getting about

Sölden's mountains have far more redeeming qualities than the town itself. Sölden can happily claim to have the largest glacier terrain in Austria, and connects three 3000m peaks by lift (Gaisloachkogl (3058m), Tiefenbachkogl (3309m), and Schwarze Schneid (3370m)). It's worth taking a few hours to tour the

'Big 3 Rally', covering all the peaks. Thanks to all this, there is good snow right until the end of the season, which is usually early May.

The 150km of pistes are mostly intermediate and can be reached by two cable cars at either end of town. The experts will also be happy with the off-piste potential and great park. For those who enjoy a spot of mogul munching, Sölden has kept areas ungroomed and you can often find some great bumps here. Check out the piste map and look for the dashed red lines. Beginners will be less happy, with their learning area not being particularly convenient.

The park

The Base Boarders Park can be accessed by taking the Giggijochbahn cable car and then the Heinbachkar chair. The park has a good half pipe, three lines of kickers for all standards of rider, and a choice of rails that the shapers change throughout the season. These vary between a gondola rail, snake rail, wallride, two kinked rails, double-kinked rail, straight rail, two boxes, Y down rail, flat down rail and rainbow rail. There's also a boardercross here, although it's not always in the best of conditions. The park is especially good in the summer, when the BASE freestyle camps are held (www.base.soelden.com).

Off-piste and backcountry

Sölden has some great freeriding areas and there are loads of huge big open faces, but unfortunately a lot of areas are avalanche prone as they get the sun for most of the day, so watch out. When the conditions are right, make the most of it. Start at the top of the Gaislachkogl (3058m) and make your way down the Wasserkar valley, a great spot with a few good cliffs to hook off. It's best to do this one before lunch as it does get tracked out really quickly.

> "It's best to do this one before lunch aas it does get tracked out really quickly"

Underneath the Giggijoch bubble lift is another hot spot for some powder turns. This leads out into some decent tree runs, but be careful you don't get lost as you could end up with a long walk back to town. It's also worth checking out the unpisted ski routes marked on the map; there's a good spot from the top of Rettenbach (2684m) which takes you through the Rettenbachtal Valley and eventually leads back on to the piste.

Lift passes	
1 day	€39
6 days	€188
13 days	€311

You also have the option of buying a ticket to use 5 days out of 7 (€180), or 11 days out of 14 (€287). A deposit of €2 is required for the lift pass.

Instruction

Freeride Academy

Certified mountain guides and experienced freeriders can show you round the mountain.

T: 0043 (0)650 266 5292
E: soelden@freeride-academy.com
W: www.freeride-academy.com

Ski and Snowboard School Aktiv

Prices are available on the website or by request.

T: 0043 (0)5254 6313
E: info@skiaktiv.at
W: www.skiactiv.at

Ski and Snowboard School Sölden-Hochsölden

Group lessons (4 hours per day): 1 day €49 (ski), €51 (board), 6 days €157 (ski), €163 (board).
Private lessons for 1–2 people: 1 day: €180 (4 hours). There is a 5 per cent discount for on-line booking!

T: 0043 (0)5254 2364
E: info@ski-soelden.com
W: www.ski-soelden.com

Ski and Snowboard School Vacancia

Group lessons: 1 day €49 (ski), €53 (board), 6 days €146 (ski), €160 (board).

T: 0043 (0)5254 3100

E: vacancia@vacancia.at
W: www.vacancia.at

Ski and Snowboard School Yellow Power

Yellow powder organise off-piste guiding.

T: 0043 (0)5254 2203 500
E: info@yellowpower.at
W: www.yellowpower.at

If you want to improve your freestyle, the BASE summer camps in June and July are an ideal place to go. Check out www.base.soelden.com for more information or book a place on www.shop.soelden.com. Six nights B&B costs €289.

Other activities

Aqua dome: On a bad day it might be worth taking a trip down to the massive aqua dome in Längenfeld (about a 15-minute drive). An all day ticket costs €20.
Helicopter rides: Flights around the 'Big 3' 3000m mountain peaks cost €290 for 1–2 people, and €400 for 3–4, which seems a lot, as the flight lasts only 10 minutes. If you would like to book a flight call 0676 533 4050 (helicopter@wucher.at, www.wucher.at).
Ice skating: The skating rink, behind the sports centre, is open daily 2–9pm. Entrance for adults is €6/7 (with/without guest card) and skate rental €4.
Night skiing: This is usually Wednesdays – check with the tourist office – 5.30pm–8.30pm (last ride up). Passes cost €9.50 and can be bought at the ticket counters of the Gaislachkogl valley station.
Sledding: A 5km floodlit sledding run is open from the Gaislachalm to the Gaislachkoglbahn station.
Sports centre: The Freizeit Arena sports centre (2514, www.freizeit-soelden.com) offers a water slide, pool, samarium, sauna, steam and herb baths, fitness room, tennis, bowling, badminton and shooting.

Events

The season kicks off on 15/16 October 2005 for the **Back On Snow** parties. The **Saab Salomon Crossmax** series takes place on 24 November 2005 and the **FIS Snowboard World Cup** has its opening 21–23 December.

On 1–8 April 2006, Sölden hosts the 7th gay and lesbian ski week: **Gay Snowhappening**. Sölden claims this to be the hottest gay event of the Alps, and we're sure they're right. One of the week's highlights is the election of 'Mr Gay Ski Sölden' (€210 will get you a 6-day lift pass, free Schnapps coupons and other goodies). In mid-late April, the re-enactment of **Hannibal crossing the Alps** is pretty impressive, involving 500 actors, planes, paragliders, helicopters, bikers and fireworks. The **Winter Finale** (end April/beginning May) is a massive party weekend, with the highlight being the big air water jump, 'Queen of the Beach' contest.

Accommodation

The big and beautiful 5-star **Central Hotel** (0043 (0)5254 22600, info@central-soelden.at, www.central-soelden.at) has amazing spa facilities and beauty treatments. Prices are €105–236 per person per night. **Hotel Regina** (0043 (0)5254 23 01, info@hotel-regina .com, www.hotel-regina.com) is once again attractive and traditional and has a great pool, and beauty treatments such as wraps and special baths. The 4-star ambience may be slightly spoilt as you sip champagne on your balcony, by your full frontal view of the naked plastic mermaid on top of the Rodelhütte table-dancing club.

There are tons of good value B&Bs and pensions in and around Sölden. Your best bet is to contact the tourist office, or search online (www.soelden.com) for your specific requirements and dates of travel. If you want to be near the action, double check that the location isn't too far from the main street as they have some B&Bs a fair way from town.

Eating out

On the mountain

At the mid station of Gaislachkogl, the **Almstubn** (05254 2214) has two big self-service restaurants, a massive sunny terrace and an ice bar. It's also open

"There are tons of good value B&Bs and pensions in and around Sölden" on Wednesdays during night skiing. At the top station of the Gaislachkogl, on the second floor, is **Tre Milla** (05254 508 888), the Alps' highest pizzeria at 2058m. The views of peaks are superb from here. The quaint **Huhnersteign** (05254 2872), on the Rettenbach glacier ski route, is one of the best huts on the mountain for a good lunch in the sun.

Gampe Alm (05254 2144) and **Gampe Thaya** (0664 240 0246) on ski trail 11, between Hochsölden and Gaislachkogl, are both good rustic mountain huts with cosy atmospheres and table service. **Eugens Obstlerhütte** (05254 2186), on the run from Hochsölden to Sölden, is a great place to stop for a beer at the end of the day.

In town

The restaurants in town aren't the best selection we've ever seen, but as you'll probably be too drunk to remember them it shouldn't cause you too much heartache.

The best pizzeria in town is the **Nudeltopf** (05254 2010), and **Armin's Törggle** (05254 3535) has good-value local food. Mexican food can be found at the **Hacienda** restaurant (05254 3526), above the tourist office. The restaurant in **Hotel Dominic** (05254 3526) is one of the smarter places to dine. There's nothing we'd get too excited about.

Bars and clubs

As you ride down the mountain at the end of the day you'll have no problem spotting the après ski hangouts, with folks clomping around on tables, happily swinging their beers. If you come down the slopes into Ausserwald, stop at **Philipp's** for a few beverages.

Back in town, the atmosphere continues in many bars along Sölden's sprawling streets. **Fire and Ice**, **Bierhimml** and the glass-housed **Bla Bla** at the Dominic hotel are three of the best bars to start at. **Hinterher**, **Ötzi Keller** and **Lawine**, under hotel Tyrolerhof, are all good bar/clubs to move on to and are open late. To see some naked ladies strutting their stuff, head to the classy-looking Rodelhütte – if you can't spot it just look out for the naked plastic mermaids on the roof.

Getting there

By car

Sölden's website (www.soelden.com) has a very user-friendly route planner to help you find your way there by car.

By plane

Innsbruck (85km) Transfer time is just 1 hour.
Munich, Zurich, Salzberg and Bozen (all 210–280km) Transfer time is 2.5–3.5 hours.

Useful facts and phone numbers

Tourist office

T: 0043 (0)5254 508
F: 0043 (0)5254 508 120
E: bergbahnen@soelden.com
W: www.soelden.com

Emergency services

- Police: 05254 30399
- Ambulance (Rotes Kreuz): 05254 2360
- In the case of an accident on the mountain: 05254 508 825

Doctors

- Dr Gerhard Leys: 05254 2040
- Dr Gerhard Wutscher: 05254 2207
- Dr Wolfgang Drapela: 05254 30399

Taxis

- Funktaxizentrale: 05254 2626
- Joe's Funktaxi: 05254 3232
- Taxi mit Herz: 05254 2030
- Taxi Quaxi: 05254 3737
- Taxi Lenz: 05254 2133

France

The home of many of the big commercial resorts,
with a few hidden gems

Les Arcs

Versatile mountain and the resort has its plus points

On the slopes	
Snow reliability	❄ ❄ ❄ ❄
Parks	❄ ❄ ❄
Off-piste	❄ ❄ ❄ ❄
Off the slopes	
Après ski	❄ ❄ ❄
Nightlife	❄ ❄ ❄
Eating out	❄ ❄ ❄
Resort charm	❄ ❄ ❄ ❄ for 1950
	❄ ❄ for 1800

The resort

Les Arcs has four resorts at different levels; Arc 1600, Arc 1800 (which itself is split into Charvet, Villards and Charmettoger), the beautiful new Arc 1950 and Arc 2000. We didn't like Arc 1600 or Arc 2000 as, to put it bluntly, they're ugly and dull. Arc 2000 has good access to the slopes but that's about it. However, we liked the rest of Les Arcs and we don't want the dull parts to cloud our vision so we're going to ignore them and refer to only Arc 1800 and Arc 1950.

Arc 1800 isn't beautiful, but it's not ugly either and there's lots going on. Charvet and Villards are centred round slightly claustrophobic open-air shopping centres and Charmettoger is prettier in the trees but it's a 10–15 minute walk to the bars in Villards.

The brand new Arc 1950 is stunning. It's still in the process of being built (due to be completely finished in 2008) by the Canadian company Intrawest, and it has a certain Canadian feel to it. The apartments are spacious and modern and the buildings are colourful. There are a few good bars and restaurants popping up but it'll be a couple of years before there's a load going on.

The mountains

Height: 1200–3326m

Ability	Rating
Expert	❄ ❄ ❄ ❄
Intermediate	❄ ❄ ❄ ❄
Beginner	❄ ❄ ❄ ❄

Getting about

In Les Arcs there are 200km of pistes (105 pistes in total) and within the whole Paradiski area (combining Les Arcs and La Plagne) there is a massive 425km. The terrain is fabulously varied, with slopes for all levels, good backcountry areas, and woodland runs for bad-weather days. Les Arcs is one of the few resorts in the world which has its own speed skiing area: the Flying Kilometre. See how fast you can go; the world record at the moment is 256kph. As a final point, make sure you behave well on the slopes; there is a team of people out there apparently looking to reward good behaviour. There are prizes to be won including a holiday for four in Les Arcs!

The park

The Les Arcs park, named Apocalypse (www.apocalypse-parc.com), has always been popular amongst the ski and board bums who live in the resort or travel up from Bourg St Maurice, although we feel that there's some room for improvement. This year the park has gained some good sponsorship and they now have three shapers keeping it in tip-top condition. Apocalypse park now consists of one hip, four rails, ten table tops and one pipe. We always find that this park has a great, friendly atmosphere and it's good for all standards. Pat got his first front cover shot for the *Daily Mail Ski and Board* magazine here in the pipe! There's also a good flood-lit half pipe in Arc 2000.

"Les Arcs is one of the few resorts in the world which has its own speed skiing area: the Flying Kilometre"

Off-piste and backcountry

Les Arcs is a tremendous place for freeriding as so much terrain is available now that it is linked with La Plagne. If the conditions are good and the lifts are open, it's worth heading up the Aiguille Rouge cable car. Underneath there are loads of steeps and couloirs and it's here that they hold the famous North Face Freeride competition, which attracts the best big mountain freeriders in the world. The cable car is often closed due to high winds, but on a perfect powder day, you will love it. It's an area for the experts as it is quite challenging. If the weather's not so great, it doesn't matter as there are loads of tree lines above 1600m that can be fun. Also the Trans Arc cable car gives you easy access to some wicked riding that always seems to be in good condition. For more off-piste exploits in the Paradiski area, check out the La Plagne chapter (see page 188). To make the most of this amazing mountain, it's worth hiring a guide to show you all the secret backcountry hide-out spots.

Instruction

Arc Aventure (1800)

Thirty instructors offer group lessons (€25 for a 2.5-hour lesson, €121 for 6 half days) or private skiing and snowboarding lessons (€35 per hour, €300 for a full day), off-piste excursions (€60 for one day, €300 for private guide) as well as other, non-skiing activities.
T: 0033 (0)4 79 07 41 28
E: arcs-adventures@wanadoo.fr
W: www.arcs-aventures.com

Lift passes	Les Arcs only	Les Arcs + one day in Paradiski	Paradiski
1 day	€38	N/A	€45
6 days	€181	€205	€225

You can also get an extension for one day's Paradiski pass with a valid Les Arcs pass (€25 or €18 on Saturday or Sunday). There is also a discount in early or late season.

ESF Arc 1800

There are 90 qualified instructors in Arc 1800. Six half-day ski or snowboarding lessons will cost €121. Off-piste skiing/boarding costs €60 per person per day, and heliskiing is €185 for a full day.
T: 0033 (0)4 79 07 40 31
E: esf-arcs-1800@wanadoo.fr
W: www.esflesarcs.com

Privilege (1800)

Private lessons in skiing or snowboarding cost €40 for 1 hour, €75 for 2 hours, €169 for half a day or €295 for a whole day. They also offer an all-day Paradiski discovery (€65) and off-piste guiding (€60). For snowboarders, Privilege offer freestyle coaching (€75 for 2 hours) and an introduction to jumping in the park (€110 for 3 hours).
T: 0033 (0)4 79 07 23 38
E: contact@ecoledeskiprivilege.com
W: www.ecoledeskiprivilege.com

Spirit 1950

Spirit 1950 offers heliskiing and freeriding as well as group and private lessons for skiing and snowboarding. Group lessons cost €30 (half day), €60 (full day), €270 (6 full days), €150 (6 half days). A day's freeride or Paradiski discovery will cost €80 for a full day and private lessons cost €90–145 for 2 hours.
T: 0033 (0)4 79 04 25 72
E: contact@spirit1950.com
W: www.spirit1950.com

Other activities

Helicopter trips: Take a trip over Mt Blanc (30 minutes for €153) or the Paradiski area (15 minutes for €78). Call Heli Mountains (06 11 74 38 83, mikeb@helimountains.com, www.helimountains.com).

Hot air balloon rides, overnight igloo stays, dog sled trips: You can do any of these with Nordic Adventures (06 09 49 32 07, nordicaventures@free.fr).

Ice drive: Drive on ice with Ecole de Pilotage (06 08 06 67 22 or 06 07 06 34 42).

Massage: Be soothed and re-energised by 1950 (04 79 04 1950). A 45-minute massage costs €70, or pay €200 for five days (30 minutes per day).

Paragliding: Arc Adventures (details above) offer paragliding.

Skidoo: With Arc Adventures (details above) you can take out a skidoo after the lifts have shut, either as a passenger or driver (€75 per hour), led by a guide. You have to ride round a selected track and follow speed limits and safety guidelines so you won't be able to go crazy.

Events

The **North Face Freeride** takes place in Les Arcs in late February/early March, a hugely acclaimed event that attracts the world's professionals.

Accommodation

Most accommodation is in the form of apartments although there are one or two hotels.

1800

In 1800 a four-person studio apartment will cost €166–355 per person per week based on occupancy of the studio. This includes 7 night's accommodation and a 6-day ski pass with certain packages. A booking handling charge of €10 will be additional, as will tourist tax (€0.80 per day), damage deposit and a charge for linen (about €10 per week).

The best of the hotels is the smart **Grand Hotel Mercure** in Charmettoger (0033 (0)4 79 07 65 00, H1669@accor-hotels.com, www.mercure.com; the hotel code is 1669). (For information or reservation from the UK you can also call 0870 609 09 65.) The hotel is about a ten-minute walk from the nearby Villards, which has more bars and restaurants than Charmettoger. Half-board accommodation costs €110–158 per person, B&B €90–140 per person per day based on a double room. The **Golf Hotel** in Charvet has a good location but is in desperate need of a facelift as it looks pretty 70s. Inside are two restaurants: the Petit Zinc restaurant is massive and impersonal but the Restaurant du Golf is pretty good. The hotel also contains the Bar Le Swing jazz bar, which again needs a revamp, and the Mont Blanc Bar, which is pretty cool. Half board costs €513–1000 per person per week depending on season and type of room; per night the cost is €95–159 (minus €11 for B&B).

1950

In 1950, all the accommodation (apartments) is owned by HMC hotels (www.hmc-hotels.com). At present there are three 4-star apartment blocks containing fewer than 300 apartments; by 2008 there will be 750. Apartments can sleep from 2–10 people and you have the choice of paying extra for more space. For example, standard four-person apartments are 33–41m² (€630 in low season, €1659 in high season) and the spacious apartment is 42–56m² (€693–1799). The apartments are comfortable and well-fitted, some with open fires and all with balconies. In addition there is a health spa with a swimming pool, sauna and Turkish bath, fitness training and solarium as well as an open-air heated swimming pool and Jacuzzi and the apart-hotel has underground parking and WiFi internet connection. The tour operators Erna Low and Neilson do packages to 1950.

"The apartments are comfortable and well-fitted, some with open fires and all with balconies"

Eating out

On the mountain

The mountain restaurants in Les Arcs aren't amazing on the whole. One that is outstanding is **Chalets de l'Arc**, above Arc 2000. It is really cosy with a wood and stone décor and fantastic service and it's also open in the evenings. For good views, try **The Solliet**, above Le Pré, or the restaurant at the Col de la Chal. The **Chalet de Luigi** (04 79 00 15 36), in 1950 town, has a large, south-facing terrace alongside Marmottes piste. This smart restaurant offers a welcome break from Savoyard food and burgers, with homemade pastas and proscuitto its speciality. It's not cheap but not ridiculous either. Inside, the high ceilings and wooden beams complete the luxurious European/American chalet feel.

In town

Charvet (1800)

In Charvet (1800), the **Mountain Café** is a popular Tex-Mex restaurant with long wooden tables. A main meal (fajitas, burgers, etc.) costs €12–15, and you can get a massive €16 dish of nachos. **L'Hedoniste** wine bar and eatery (lhedoniste@tiscali.fr) is a tiny restaurant (14 covers) and really cute. They serve soups, oysters and a number of different boards of food such as the gormet board (including duck and homemade foie gras), a Savoyard board or a butcher's board. A number of wines and sparkling wines are served by the glass. **Chez Les Filles** has fantastic views and is really friendly. They serve pancakes, local specialities and salads at lunchtime and traditional Savoyard fare in the evenings. The Italian-run **Casa Mia** (04 79 07 05 75) is a fantastic and charming restaurant. At lunchtimes it serves the usual pizzas, etc. and at night the gastronomic Italian and Savoyard specialities are brought out. **Chez Boubou** serves English breakfast for €9 and good value burgers and chips.

Villards (1800)

In Villards (1800), **Le Triangle** is really cute and the service is good. They serve omelettes at lunch and local specialities at night (€13–25 for a main). **Chalet Bouvier** is an attractive restaurant serving the usual fondues, etc. There are loads of places serving Brit-friendly foods (pure grease!) including the **Jungle Café** and **Red Hot Saloon**. On a similar note is one of our favourites, **Benji Bar**. Here they serve a massive range of food until 4pm, including Indian dishes, fajitas, ribs, salads and burgers (around €13 a piece) followed by a 3-hour happy hour (4–7pm).

1950

In 1950 the lovely, spacious and smart **Chalet de Luigi** (see On the mountain) serves fresh, homemade pasta and other delights at lunchtimes and in the evenings. **Café Hemmingway** is a nice café serving fish, meat dishes and local specialities for around €14–19.

Bars and clubs

Charvet (1800)

In Charvet (1800), the **Gabotte** is popular with the locals for a cheeky après beer. **L'Equipe** is a funky big bar, with a semi-pirate theme (barrels and the odd net). It serves good-value sandwiches, chicken wings and burgers (€4.50–6) and salads and meats (€10–15) as well as offering a takeaway option. You can also check your E-mails.

Villards (1800)

The largest selection of bars is to be found in Villards (1800). **Ambiente** is a cool après bar with darts, sports on TV and extortionate €11 cocktails. **Benji Bar** gets full points for the longest happy hour (4–7pm, see Eating out). **The Jungle Café** serves steaks, pastas and omelettes (€8–18) and not-cheap burgers (€12.50). A cocktail can also cost you €7–12. However, it does have a very funky jungle interior with cool murals on the walls and lots of leafy decoration. The tables can be folded up to allow dancing to the eclectic tunes. The Jungle Café opens at 9.30am and shuts at 2am. In the massive **Red Hot Saloon** there's a lot to keep punters entertained: live music, theme nights, pool, and sports on big TVs. They serve salads and sarnies 12–4pm and a full menu 4–10pm, which includes steaks, burgers and smaller snacks such as wedges and garlic bread. Happy hour is 5–6pm.

1950

In 1950 **Les Belles Pintes** (04 79 07 35 42) is an 'Irish pub' (as perceived by Canadians, not the Irish) open 11.30–1am. Happy hour is 5.30–6.30pm. They serve hot dogs and sandwiches (€5), burgers and chips (€10), croque monsieurs and bruschetta (€5–10) 12–2.30pm. **Le Chalet de Luigi**, as well as having a top restaurant, has a bar (04 79 00 05 17) and a nightclub, **Le Bachal** (04 79 01 16 94). The bar is open every day from early morning until 2am. It has satellite TV, happy hours and theme nights.

This information was gathered in the 04–05 season so by 05–06 this rapidly expanding resort is likely to have far more to offer.

Useful facts and phone numbers

Tourist office

T: 0033 (0)4 79 07 12 57 (1950) / 0033 (0)4 79 07 61 11 (1800)
E: lesarcs@lesarcs.com
W: www.lesarcs.com

Direct reservations 1800

T: 0033 (0)4 79 07 68 00
F: 0033 (0)4 79 07 68 99
E: reservation@lesarcs.com
W: www.lesarcs.com

Direct reservations 1950

T: 0033 (0)4 79 04 1950
W: arc1950@hmc-hotels.com, www.hmc-hotels.com

Emergency services

• Slopes rescue: 04 79 07 85 66
• Fire: 18

Doctors

• Centre Médical du Charvet: 04 79 07 40 60
• Centre Médical des Villards: 04 79 07 49 99
• Cabinet Médical Arc 2000: 04 79 07 30 01
• Cabinet Médical Arc 1600: 04 79 07 78 57
• Hospital in Bourg St. Maurice: 04 79 41 79 79

Taxis and airport transfers

• Allo lolo: 06 79 07 04 49
• Taxi Boirat: 06 13 61 63 10
• Borne taxis à Bourg St Maurice: 04 79 04 04 20
• Airport transfers: 04 79 07 04 49

Getting there

By car

You will need to park in the underground car park in 1950 if you drive there. Seven days will cost €73. Call 0033 (0)4 79 04 12 37 or e-mail eric.chevalier@sceta-parc.fr.

By train

The Eurostar takes you straight from London to Bourg St Maurice on Saturdays and the trip will take you 8 hours. Contact SNCF on 0033 (0)8 92 35 35 35, www.sncf.fr. From Bourg you can take the 7-minute funicular train to Arc 1600. Get your tickets at the funicular train station (call 0033 (0)4 79 04 24 00 for information). By coach you can transfer to resort by Autocars Martin (0033 (0)4 79 07 04 49, www.autocars-martin.com). You could also get a taxi from the Bourg St Maurice taxi stand (0033 (0)4 79 07 03 94).

By plane

Lyon (200km) Transfers can be booked through Satobus (0033 (0)4 37 255 255, www.satobus-alps.com.
Geneva (145km) Transfers can be booked through www.alpski-bus.com or www.altibus.com (0041 (0)22 798 20 00).
Heliport transfers can also be booked on 0033 (0)6 11 74 38 83.

Avoriaz

Far more charming than first-appearances suggest, and a superb mountain to explore

NTS DU MIDI
3257 m

DENTS BLANCHES
2756 m

MONT BLANC
4807 m

Les Hauts Forts
2466 m

Col du
Fornet

Pointe de
Ripaille
1937 m

Pointe de
Mossette
2277 m

Avoriaz
1800-2466 m

Col des Portes
du Soleil

Pointe de
l'Au
2157 m

Pointe de
Chésery
2249 m

Les Prodains

Les Crosets

Tête du
Géant
2236 m

Les Lindarets

Morzine
1000-2460 m

Grand Paradis

Champéry
1050-2300 m

Tête de
Linga
1536 m

Ardent

Champoussin
1580-2200 m

Montriond
900-2200 m

La Corbeau
1991 m

Mont de Grange
2432 m

Pic de la C...
2084 m

Morgins

Troistorrents

Le Rochat

Monthey

Châtel
1200-2100 m

La Combe
1700 m

Crêt Béni
1650 m

On the slopes	
Snow reliability	✳ ✳ ✳
Parks	✳ ✳ ✳ ✳
Off-piste	✳ ✳ ✳

Off the slopes	
Après ski	✳ ✳ ✳
Nightlife	✳ ✳ ✳
Eating out	✳ ✳
Resort charm	✳ ✳ ⟨

The resort

Avoriaz is a completely unique resort for a number of reasons. The design and architecture of the town is very 60s and a little dated, but it was nevertheless well thought out. Although not beautiful to look at, there is something spectacular and charming about its crazily angled structure, enhanced by its impressive setting on the edge of a cliff. One of the really exceptional features is that practically all the accommodation is ski-in ski-out. As the village is car-free and very wide, everyone whacks on their equipment outside their apartment and cruises down to the lift – a much preferable way to start the day than cumbersome bus journeys and long walks. The mountains are unquestionably superb, with Avoriaz being bang in the centre of the massive Portes de Soleil circuit that unites the slopes of France and Switzerland.

If you are looking for luxurious accommodation think again – there is only one hotel that could be described as such, Les Dromonts (see Accommodation); most of the apartments are pretty cramped.

The mountains

Height: 975–2275m

Ability	Rating
Expert	✳ ✳ ✳
Intermediate	✳ ✳ ✳ ✳
Beginner	✳ ✳ ✳

Getting about

This resort is great for mixed ability groups; beginners have some good areas on which to learn, intermediates can cruise around the 650km of pistes in the Portes de Soleil cicuit quite happily (might be an idea to ditch the unhelpful piste map and follow the little pictures of animals – pick one depending on your ability) and experts have challenging pistes, great off-piste and superb parks to choose from.

Transportation within Avoriaz

Within Avoriaz you can get about in sledges or shuttles. You have three options when it comes to transporting you, your mates/family and your luggage to your accommodation:

You can use baggage sledges yourself for only €1. This should be fine if you are staying in the Falaise area (chalets de la Falaise, Chapka, Douchka, Elinka, Kouria, Malinka, Néve, Saskia, Tilia) as it's really close to the car park/dropping-off point.

Between 8am and 7pm you can hire a sledge to transport you from €5–13, depending on the length of journey.

Between 7pm and 8am you will need a shuttle at a cost of €8.

If you are travelling on a Saturday as most people are you don't need to worry about organising or calling up for transportation, as there are assistants all over the place and they'll call a sledge for you. At any other time you will need to call 04 50 74 01 55.

The park

Avoriaz definitely knows how to build and look after its three parks. They have some big sponsors like Burton and Forum putting money behind them so they can now afford to have six full-time shapers working hard to keep it sweet! In Arare there are four decent sized kickers, two spines, seven rails, a step up and a pipe. In La Chapelle, there are six kickers of all different dimensions, five rails, a skier and boardercross and a super pipe where they hold the O'Neill freestyle pro event. The Avoriaz parks are among some of the most respected in Europe, so if parks are your thing, you should give Avoriaz a try. Check out the website www. snowparkavoriaz.com.

You also have access to one of the best parks in Europe in Champéry, Switzerland (see Champéry chapter, page 330).

Off-piste and backcountry

Avoriaz has a fair bit to offer in terms of off-piste, and if you get bored with this you have the whole of the Portes de Soleil to explore (see Morzine and Champéry chapters, pages 182 and 330). The top of the Combe du Machon chairlift is a great place to start. From here, you can explore either the terrain off the back of the Coupe de Monde run (with a guide/local) or the more accessible powder on the Crozets side. From the Fornet lift you can traverse to a cornice and bowl that winds up at the Valée de la Manche (Mindor lake). You can then commence the 45-minute hike down the road to Morzine, or you could arrange for someone to pick you up. The foolhardy riders can take the Cubore lift and attempt the sketchy hike to a big, fun, and untracked bowl.

"From the Fornet lift you can transverse to a cornice and bowl that winds up at the Valée de la Manche (Mindor lake)"

Instruction

Alpine Ski and Snowboard School

Group lessons cost from €100 for 6 hours or €120 for 10 hours (beginners and improvement). Private lessons cost €100 per person for 2 hours.

T: 0033 (0)4 50 74 12 64
E: info@avoriazalpineskischool.com
W: www.avoriazalpineskischool.com

ESF

The ESF teach skiing, boarding and free ride. Six half days will cost €85–110 depending on discipline and time of year.

T: 0033 (0)4 50 74 05 65
E: info@esf-avoriaz.com
W: www.esf-avoriaz.com

International Ski and Snowboard School

Six half days will cost €120, and a 3-day discovery course with 3–6 people in a group will cost €115. Private lessons cost €64–75 for 2 hours depending on the number of people. The international ski school also offer tandem paragliding from €60.

T: 0033 (0)4 50 74 02 18
E: info@ecoledeglisse.com
W: www.ecoledeglisse.com

Other activities

Bowling, pool, table footie, video games: These activities can all be found in a bar in the Place des Dromonts (see Bars and clubs).

Diving under ice: Try the amazing experience of diving under the ice. For €60 you get your first dive, equipment and training. E-mail cameleon@cameleon-organisation.com or call 04 5074 94 00 for more details.

Hammam and squash: Both of these can be found in the Fontaines Blanches building, open 3.30–9pm, Sunday to Friday. Squash or hammam session costs €5.30 per person for 30 minutes.

Lift passes	Avoriaz only	Portes de Soleil
1 day	€30	€36
6 days	–	€176
13 days	–	€298

Hang-gliding, paragliding and parasailing: These are arranged by the International Ski School (04 50 74 02 18). Flights start at €50.

Hot air balloons: A one-hour hot air balloon flight costs €245 per person (04 50 75 94 00).

Ice skating: You can skate for just €5 (04 50 74 08 52).

Jacuzzis, sauna, therapies and sports hall: Check out the Altiform fitness centre (04 50 74 18 48).

Mountain biking on the snow: This involves riding down the hill to Prodains. Bike, helmet and ski pass are provided for €35.

Night sledging: This takes place every day from 6pm (except Sunday) on the Crôt slope. The cost is €17 (06 07 75 92 48).

Sledge rides: Riding in a sled pulled by dogs costs €15 for the sledge for 3 people, €80 per person for half a day and €125 for the whole day. Call 04 50 73 15 17 to book.

Events

Avoriaz hosts some of the biggest freestyle comps in Europe and attracts the biggest names on the circuit. Events include **O'Neill freestyle Pro, PlayStation Air Games** and the **Billabong Pro**. The comp focus is more to boarders than skiers.

Accommodation

Most of the accommodation is in the form of self-catering apartments. **Pierre and Vacances** is one of the largest rental companies (0033 (0)4 50 74 35 35), but don't expect a spacious apartment, they are usually on the cosy side. The service you will receive is also minimal – expect to make your own beds, etc. If you wind up in an apartment in Crozats with views of people passing on the chairlift up from the centre of Avoriaz bear in mind that it is a popular game with the locals to collect snow on their skis/board to hurl at unfortunate people like yourselves from the chair lift. Your best bet is to get yourself out on the chair and try this childish, but great, game on your neighbours.

There are just three hotels in Avoriaz. One is down in Les Prodains so not ideal if you would like to sample the Avoriaz nightlife. In Avoriaz centre you have **Hotel de la Falaise** (0033 (0)4 50 74 26 00, avoriaz@pierre-vacances.fr), owned by the Pierre and Vacances group. With absolutely no atmosphere or character you are far better to get an apartment rather than stay here. The final hotel, **Hotel les Dromonts** (0033 (0)4 50 79 03 21, www.christophe-leroy.com/dromont.htm, leroych83@aol.com) is an incredible contrast to the others. From the outside it is a deceptively dull building, camouflaging itself perfectly in the less-than-stunning surroundings. However, once inside those dreary doors the innovative architecture is captivating. All rooms have something to gawp at, with crazy lines and unexpected angles fashioning fantastic spaces.

N.B. You can leave your luggage at the luggage room at the ice rink office (which also has showers) on your arrival or departure day if you have to move out of your room or apartment and don't want to lug it round everywhere. It costs €1.60 per item of luggage and €2.50 for a shower.

Eating out

On the mountain

The **Yeti** on the slopes near Avoriaz is a great place to stop for a crêpe, with deckchairs, a good terrace and great après ski. There are a bunch of great restaurants under the half pipe, at the top of the cable car from Les Prodains. Our favourite is **Changabang** (04 50 74 06 39), with fantastically cheap and tasty burgers. **La Tanière** (04 50 74 13 10) and **Les Trappeurs** brasserie (04 50 74 17 33) are also really good. There's another good bunch of restaurants at Lindarets – try **Pomme de Pin** and **Cremaillare** (04 50 74 11 68). On the Super Morzine side of town, **Les Cretes de Zorre** (04 50 79 24 73) is by far the best.

In town

If you are in desperate need of a hangover cure before you take to the slopes, the **Tavaillon** bar serves English breakfasts. The **Cabane** (04 50 74 20 60) is a popular and informal bar/restaurant that is great for food and beers. **La Falaise** (04 50 74 10 48) is the best pizzeria, with really friendly and helpful staff who are more than willing to cater for large groups. **Intrets** (04 50 74 15 45) is also good for pizza and pasta – the service wasn't as good as the food when we stopped, but we hope that was a one off. **Fontaines Blanches** (04 50 74 10 48) has a lovely alpine feel and serves all the usual French fare. The staff are a bit odd though. **Duchess Anne** (04 50 74 12 50) has a really nice terrace for lunch and serves good pizzas, local specialities and steak haché. **Le Chalet D'Avoriaz** (04 50 74 01 30) is a really cute alpine restaurant up by the slopes, near the car park with great pierrades. For gourmet fodder, the uniquely designed **Dromonts** hotel (see Accommodation) has a fantastic restaurant. You can even attend one of Mr Leroy's three-hour cookery courses.

Bars and clubs

For après ski on the slopes the **Yeti** is good (see Eating out). In town, **Shooters** is the place to go, populated with Brits, Deutsch and Danish, bopping away to the live music 4.30–6pm and the disco beats until 2am. There are theme nights every week and on Saturdays the bar is usually dominated by seasonaires. **The Place**

"There are theme nights every week"

also has live music for après. The **Wild Horse Saloon** is open 4pm–2am and has a great atmosphere. You can also grab some greasy foods – burgers, ribs, nachos, that kind of thing. For dancing until 5am, you have the choice of **Festival** or the **Choucas**, which has great live music and is our favourite place to hit the dance floor. All the best bars and clubs are around the same area so it's pretty easy to check them all out without getting too chilly.

If you fancy a change from the usual bars and clubs there is a cool and atmospheric **bowling bar** with two lanes, pool, darts, air hockey and arcade games.

Useful facts and phone numbers

Tourist office

T: 0033 (0)4 50 74 02 11
F: 0033 (0)4 50 74 18 25
E: info@avoriaz.com
W: www.avoriaz.com

Emergency services

- In an emergency call 18 or 112 from a mobile phone.
- Police: 17
- Medical Centre: 04 50 74 05 42 (for emergencies, general medical care, physiotherapy etc.)

Taxis (for transfers)

- Hubert Buttet: 04 50 79 64 54
- Momo Cheraiet: 04 50 79 03 40/ 06 07 94 58 35
- Richard Gourvil: 04 50 75 97 12
- Laurys France Taxi: 04 50 79 06 10
- Sarl Evason: 04 50 26 29 29

Getting there

By car

When you arrive in Haute-Savoie, follow the signposts to Chamonix by the A40. Take the Cluses Exit n° 18, head towards Taninges by the D90, then follow les Gets, Morzine and finally Avoriaz. Avoriaz is only an hour or so away from Geneva. If you drive, you will be required to leave your car at the car park at the entrance of Avoriaz. The indoor car park (800 places) will cost €12.50 a day or €76 for a week. The outdoor car park (1600 places) will cost €6.50 for a day or €40 for a week. If you want to save that extra few euros and park outdoors be prepared to dig your car out of the snow when you leave. Reserve your spot on www.avoriazparkings.com.

By plane

Geneva (80km) Taxi transfer will cost around €140 (see numbers above). To find out about buses from Geneva to Avoriaz call 0041 (0)22 732 02 30. For a more 'bling' entrance into resort, a helicopter will pick you up from Geneva and drop you in Avoriaz for €993 (0033 (0)4 50 74 22 44).

Chamonix

A base for the serious extreme
community, this town has
everything. Bring a car
if you can

On the slopes

Snow reliability	✳✳✳✳
Parks	✳
Off-piste	✳✳✳✳✳

Off the slopes

Après ski	✳✳✳✳
Nightlife	✳✳✳✳
Eating out	✳✳✳✳
Resort charm	✳✳✳✳

The resort

The first thing that hits you about Chamonix is the scenery; you can't possibly drive into Cham without being impressed. Being at the foot of Mont Blanc, Chamonix was destined to be a popular resort from the start, nearly a century ago. Amazingly, Chamonix seems to have developed and matured into the perfect town, rather than being destroyed by ugly buildings and tourists like so many resorts. It has plenty of olde worlde charm, streets that you could wander round for days, a diversity of nationalities and more facilities than anyone could need. On top of the beautiful town, the mountains are the best without a shadow of a doubt and the nightlife is incredible. The commute between the town and the mountains isn't ideal but it's this fact that lets Chamonix maintain the feel of a real town, as opposed to a purpose-built resort, so we'll forgive this slight inconvenience.

The mountains

Height: 1035–3840m

Ability	Rating
Expert	✳✳✳✳✳
Intermediate	✳✳
Beginner	✳✳✳

Getting about

On one side of the valley are Flégère and Brévent, both perfect for panoramic views in the sun. Brévent can be accessed close to Cham centre and Flégère a little further down in Les Praz, although the two are linked. The Aiguille du Midi and Les Grands Montets, home of the steep and deep, are on the opposite side of the valley and Le Tour, at the far end, has some great tree runs. In total there are 155km of runs with the longest downhill run coming in at 7km.

Learning to ski/ board in Chamonix

When you think Chamonix, you might not think it would be a great place to learn how to ski and snowboard and in some respects you might be right as it is geared towards the more extreme market. However, once you have been wiped out a few times by speedy riders hurtling through the beginners' slope to get to the bottom of the mountain you might appreciate the fact that Chamonix has four beginners' slopes (one attached to each of the mountains except Flégère) with no other runs going through them. Progression is difficult though, and for intermediates it's not all that great; Chamonix really comes into its own for the experts and pros.

The park

There is a park at Les Bossons but it's completely separate from the main mountain and your pass won't cover it – you have to pay for it separately. It's open at night. For more information call 04 50 53 12 39 or visit www.glaciermontblanc.com.

Off-piste and backcountry

When Pat thinks of Chamonix, he thinks of Glen Plake and Scott Schmitt in the infamous ski movie – *The Blizzard of Arzhh*. This film changed the lives of every professional big-mountain skier out there today and it was mainly filmed in Chamonix on the Grands Montets. There is so much off-piste and backcountry terrain in Chamonix that we can hardly do it justice. The **Grands Montets** is a good place to start. The drop is around 2000m and you don't even need to hike. Just drop over the back at the top of the gondola and you're off. One of the routes from here is actually marked on the piste map but it's completely ungroomed and gets bumped up at the bottom (you have the option of trees rather than bumps at the other side if you prefer). From the **Brévent** lift you can hike for about ten minutes to the face (marked as a black on the map). You start on a couloir that's pretty steep and has the tendency to avalanche but they do bomb it. A great run. From the **Aiguille de Midi,** the popular Valley Blanche is a 22km descent. The run isn't too difficult, but you could probably do with a guide, especially if you want to go down some steeps. Off the back of the **Tête de Balme** are some steep and dangerous couloirs if you fancy a challenge.

Further information
The Vamos edition of *Chamonix* is a good off-piste guide book written by two mountain guides based in Cham. It's written in good English and sold in Snow and Rock.

Avalanche risk
The avalanche risks in Chamonix are less than you might think. There is a huge potential for avalanche but a fairly small chance of being caught in one. Because all and sundry want to hit the off-piste when they head to Chamonix, the local officials are very paranoid and keep everything shut unless it's safe.

Lift passes	
1 day	€43
6 days	€181
14 days	€397

The Cham ski pass allows you two free ascents of the Grands Montets cable car (with a 6-day pass; €5 per extra lift), one day in Courmayeur (with a 4-day pass or more) and the resort bus. If you're buying a 5-, 10- or 15-day pass you can pay more (€208/ 330/ 480 respectively) to avoid the queues!

Instruction

The tourist office will provide you with a list of guides and schools to choose from but these are the two that we were recommended by local experts.

Chamonix Experience
They also have a good reputation but are pretty expensive; a guide for one day costs about €350 (EV2 costs around €310 and ESF €290).
T: 0033 (0)4 50 54 09 36
E: info@chamex.com
W: www.chamex.com

Evolution 2
EV2 have a good reputation with the locals and can provide you with any kind of instruction or guide.
T: 0033 (0)4 50 53 22 57
E: chamonix@evolution2.com
W: www.evolution2.com

"Some really steep and dangerous couloirs if you fancy a challenge"

Other activities

Bowling: Open 5pm–2am (earlier in bad weather), the bowling alley is situated on the Avenue de Courmayeur in Chamonix Sud (04 50 53 74 37).

Casino: Situated on the Place de Saussure, the casino (04 50 53 07 65) has slots open from noon and French and English roulette, black-jack, and poker from 9pm. The restaurant is open from 7.30pm until midnight.

Cinema: Bang in the centre of town, the cinema (04 50 55 89 98) has three screens and has several shows per day. Films are shown in French and English (with French subtitles).

Paint ball: This costs €16 per person including all the equipment necessary. Extra bullets cost €1 for 20 bullets. There are discounts for groups over five people. Call 06 07 36 01 51.

Panoramic flights: These are pretty popular around Chamonix. Chamonix Mont Blanc Hélicoptères (04 50 54 13 82, www.helico.fr) organise trips from €60 per person (on the Aiguille Verte) to €190 per person (for a flight over the Massive). SAF Chamonix Hélicoptères (04 79 38 48 29) organise 30-minute flights for five people.

Paragliding: This can be done on Aguille du Midi, Brévent, and Les Grands Montets. Contact Alpine Flying Centre (04 50 54 59 63, info@flyers-lodge.com, www.flyers-lodge.com; Centre Ecole Parapente Mt Blanc (04 50 56 85 14, info@parapente-ecole.com) or Summits (04 50 53 50 14, summits@summits.fr, www.summits.fr).

Richard Bozen Sports Centre: Situated at 214 Av. De la Plage (centre.sportif@chamonix.com), this centre contains a swimming pool, sauna and hammam (04 50 53 23 70 – €4.20 pool entry, €10.55 for sauna, pool and hammam), tennis and squash (04 50 53 28 40 – €13.55 for 1 hour of tennis, €6,75 for 45 minutes of squash), skating rink (04 50 53 12 36 – €4.20 entrance; night sessions on Wednesday), weights and fitness room (04 50 53 23 70 – €8.30 inc. pool) and climbing hall (04 50 53 23 70 – entry €3.40).

Shopping: With 400 shops to choose from, shopping in Chamonix is an absolute pleasure. If you want to try on every pair of designer sunglasses available, Chamonix's your place.

WiFi for free! The tourist office has wireless connections and if you have the right equipment you can use it for free during your stay!

Events

The **Bosses de Boss** is a mogul competition without many rules; anything goes. It began 16 years ago when all the Chamonix ski bums challenged the Val d'Isère ski bums to a mogul challenge. Since then a number of the major ski resorts have become involved and enter their own teams. A resort's team must consist of five male skiers, two female skiers, two snowboarders and one telemarker. Pat has entered for the last 12 years and has captained the Courchevel team (when they won, he would like to add!) and it's always one of the highlights of his year. It's a really fun day (around mid-March) and a legendary competition. We love it. The **Red Bull Snow Thrill**, a big-mountain, extreme skiing contest has been held in Chamonix for many years. It is an invitational event, open only to the world's best big-mountain skiers.

Accommodation

High Mountain Holidays (www.highmountain.co.uk) have a number of catered and self-catered accommodations in locations across Chamonix, from dead in the centre, to quieter areas near the ski lifts. The service is superb; Glen and Caroline will bend over backwards to make sure your stay is enjoyable. The main catered chalet is **Kosciusko Lodge** in Les Praz, with eight en-suite rooms, located at the bottom of the Flégère cable car. This chalet has tons of regular guests

and you can certainly see why they return. The cosy rooms, TV lounge (that has a great selection of games and movies), snug bar and dining room make this chalet really welcoming. Additionally, they always employ a qualified chef and the food is served to an incredibly high standard. Kosciusko Lodge also has the benefits of a chauffeured minibus to take you to all the lifts and into town at night, and a ski host to show you the highlights of Chamonix's mountains. If you prefer self-catered accommodation or have a specific location in mind just call up Glen and he will tailor your holiday specifically – they even book alternative accommodation for you if it's more suitable for your requirements. Basically they take all the hassle out of organising your holiday. What more can you ask for?

The **Hotel Swisse** (0033 (0)4 50 53 07 58, www.chamonix-park-hotel.com) is a good 3-star hotel opposite the tourist office. A modern, new 3-star is **Oustlat** (0033 (0)4 50 55 54 99, www.hotel-oustalet .com), near the Aguille de Midi. The **Valley Blanche** (0033 (0)4 50 53 04 50, www.lasavoyade.com) (technically a 3 star), is great value although slightly 'olde worlde'. The staff are great. You can't get a more central location than the new 4-star **Hotel des Alpes** (0033 (0)4 50 55 37 80, www.grandhoteldesalpes .com, info@grandhoteldesalpes.com) that is right smack in the centre, next to the Chanel shop. It's an excellent hotel, with swimming pool, sauna and Jacuzzi although the parking's a tad difficult.

Eating out

On the mountain

There are 14 restaurants on the mountain, and pretty much the lot have incredible views over the Mont-Blanc mountain range. In the Brevent/ Flégère region, **La Flégère** (04 50 53 06 13) and **Le Panoramic** (04 50 54 05 77) have amazing terraces and views, and not-so-bad food. **La Bergerie** (04 50 53 05 42) has a beautiful atmosphere with both table and self-service options and **Altitude 2000** (04 50 53 15 58), at the top of the gondola in Planpraz, has great food and service and a superb terrace. On the Grands Montets, the **Plan Joran** (04 50 54 05 77) offers quick snacks, a pizzeria, a picnic area, a terrace and a smart restaurant. The **Lognan** (04 50 54 10 21) is pretty smart and has a good 'pasta corner' and the

Refuge de Lognan (04 50 54 10 21) is rustic and off the beaten track. The food is fantastic. At the summit of the Aiguille du Midi is **Le 3842**, a café with salads, sandwiches, pies and remarkable views. Over on Le Tour, the **Charamillon** (04 50 54 09 05) is a good self-service eatery.

In town

Munchies on the Rue du Moulin has some of the best food in Cham. It's mid range, fresh and tasty. **Mason Career,** just out of town, is pretty smart (wear a shirt) but relaxed too. The chef has a Michelin-starred reputation and for the food and service you get it's not too expensive. **Chez Valereo** is a great Italian with tasty pizzas and a renowned wine list. A three-course meal can cost only €20 but the wines that are sold range from €20 to €1100! It's a popular place with the locals. The **Bistro des Sports** (04 50 53 00 46, www.bistrodessports.com) is a very French restaurant/ bar right in the centre of town on the main street. Savoyard food is the speciality and the bar is legendary, and frequented by hardcore locals as well as passing tourists. The **Caleche** (04 50 55 94 68, www.restaurant-caleche.com), in the town centre (just past the cinema) is atmospheric and also serves a large selection of good traditional Savoyard food. It's a little touristy and mid price range, probably €15–50 per head before wine. For Tex Mex, the **Cantina** (04 50 53 64 20) is great. It can be found down a little back alley just off the main street and does good food at a good price. For top quality pub food, go to **Goophy's** by the station or **CyBar** in town. For a tasty takeaway sandwich and chips you can't go wrong with the **Midnight Express** in the centre of town that is open most hours of the day and night.

Bars and clubs

Since Chamonix has loads of permanent residents (about 10,000) and 180 licences, there are loads of good bars, pubs and clubs to pick from.

L'M is a hotel and restaurant in the centre of town that has a great Austrian-style après ski bar outside with big outdoor heaters and a large outdoor screen for footie and other sports.

Just opposite the station are a few cool bars. **Chambre Neuf** is a classic après ski bar, popular with the locals and the Scandinavians. **Goophy's** is a real snowboarder hangout with a funky vibe and it's pretty cheap too. It's popular with the après ski crowd and has great pub grub. **Elevation** is next to Goophy's and does really good food during the day, including healthy snacks.

MBC (about 5 minutes' walk from the centre of town) has a good reputation for homemade beer and a year-round clientele, both English and French. **South Bar**, right at the end of town is a hip and full-on après ski bar.

The **Rue du Moulin** is a street in the centre of town, just off the main street, packed with funky bars. **Cy Bar** (www.dicksteabar.com) is massive and has a great atmosphere, open 8.30am–2.30am. The bar is on three levels: the middle floor is huge, with long wooden tables, a pool table and big comfy leather chairs that you could curl up in all day. On the top floor are a host of computers with internet access (€1 for 10 mins). Food is available 2–10pm: traditional pub fare as well as paninis, salads and nachos. During Happy Hour (6–9pm) a pint drops from €5 to €3. The bar shows all major sporting events on a massive projector screen and for the footie matches and Six Nations they tend to do some really good offers such as burger and a pint for €8. Bargain! There is live music three nights a week: Freestylers, Scratch Perverts, that kind of thing, and every other Thursday they run comedy nights with three comedians and a compere. The comedy nights start around 10pm and there is no entry charge. Connected to the CyBar is **Bar du Moulin**. It's a pretty cool little bar, with a cosy, dark kind of vibe. It opens 7pm–2am and sometimes has live music or DJs playing. **Dick's Tea Bar**, next to the Cy Bar, is a popular and busy club open 10pm–4am. They do all sorts of theme nights, often have live music and always have a decent DJ playing. On special nights, CyBar, Bar du Moulin and Dicks can all be connected up for one massive party. **Bar'd Up** attracts a more British crowd.

Useful facts and phone numbers

Tourist office

T: 0033 (0)4 50 53 00 24
F: 0033 (0)4 50 53 58 90
E: info@chamonix.com
W: www.chamonix.com

Emergency services

- In a medical emergency dial 15, for the fire
  brigade call 18, or 112 for either from a
  mobile
- Mountain Rescue: 04 50 53 16 89
- Ambulance: 04 50 53 46 20
- Hospital: 04 50 53 84 00
- Weather information: 08 92 68 02 74

Doctors

In Chamonix
- Drs Dartigue-Peyrou, Dehlinger and Plumerault,
  125 rue Straton:
  04 50 54 08 55
- Dr Roncin, 10 av. du Mont-Blanc: 04 50 55 85
  74
- Drs Cadot and Richard, 275 rue des Allobroges:
  04 50 55 80 55
- Doctor on call (nights, Sundays and bank
  holidays): 15

Taxis

- ABAC Taxi Gopée: 06 07 02 22 13,
  abactaxigopee@aol.com
- Cham Taxi: 04 50 53 19 14
- Taxi Monard: 04 50 55 86 28
- Taxi Rousseau: 06 07 67 88 85,
  www.taxichamonix.net

Getting there

By car

Chamonix is really easy to access by road. From
Paris take the A6 towards Lyon then the A40
towards Lyon/ Geneva then N205.

By plane

Geneva (88km) is only an hour's transfer away.
There is a daily coach transfer three times daily.
Contact the tourist office/ www.chamonix.com for
timetables or call 0033 (0)4 50 53 01 15.
Lyon (220km) Bus connections are via Satobus
(0033 (0)4 37 255 255)
Annecy (90km)
For taxi transfers contact the airport transfer
services:
ATS: 0033 (0)4 50 53 63 97, www.a-t-s.net
Chamonix Transfer Service: 0033 (0)6 62 05 57
38, www.chamonix-transfer.com.

Courchevel 1650

Pat's lived here for 12 years
and wouldn't live anywhere else

On the slopes	
Snow reliability	❅ ❅ ❅ ❅
Parks	–
Off-piste	❅ ❅ ❅ ❅ ❅
Off the slopes	
Après ski	❅ ❅ ❅
Nightlife	❅ ❅ ❅
Eating out	❅ ❅
Resort charm	❅ ❅ ❅

The resort

We are biased – we'll tell you that now. Pat has lived here for 12 years and Vanessa has been coming here on holiday since before she could speak in sentences. We will try to be as impartial as possible but it is tough. It's a great place to be; less cosmopolitan than 1850 but more friendly and more of a community, and the mountains are fantastic, with huge off-piste potential. It's the sort of place you go year after year. The reason Vanessa's family have come here for so long is primarily due to the convenience of the place: stumble out of bed and you can be on the slopes, in restaurants or shops in matters of seconds with no need for buses or trekking you equipment miles through town. Come and have a look for yourself, you'll love it too.

The mountains

Height: 1850–2740m

Ability	Rating
Expert	❅ ❅ ❅ ❅
Intermediate	❅ ❅ ❅ ❅
Beginner	❅ ❅ ❅ ❅

Getting about

Courchevel has something for everyone. Beginners and intermediates will enjoy the skiing on-piste in 1650 as it is filled with beautiful long, open blue runs, as long as you are confident on drag lifts as they tend to be the only way up. Experts should find plenty to keep them entertained with loads of off-piste and the whole of the Trois Vallées to play with.

The park

There's no park in 1650 and the one in 1850 is nothing to rave about. You can always extend your lift pass and go to Meribel moon park, which is great, or you can build your own backcountry kickers around the pyramid area, which has some wicked natural terrain and is great for building big-gap jumps. The Matchstick production filming crew shot a big part of *Ski Movie 2* here, which starred Pep Fujas, CR Johnson and Mike Douglas. Since then you often see groups building and filming the kickers here. Note to Courchevel: this area would be perfect for a park!

Off-piste and backcountry

Courchevel 1650 has to have some of the best off-piste in the Trois Vallées area. It never gets as busy as 1850, so there are less people to share the powder with. The **Chapelets** area has some wicked spots just off to the side of the piste and you can always find something decent to do whatever the conditions are. In the heart of the mountain, there is the **hidden valley** – a favourite of the locals, including ourselves. The hidden valley is a huge funnel of a bowl leading down to the bottom of the Roc Mugnier chairlift and there are loads of different lines that can be fairly challenging in parts. It's normally better to do this run in the morning before it gets too much sun, otherwise the snow can get heavy and has been known to slide. Another popular face can be found at the top of 1650, the **Equinox**, nicknamed after it was shown avalanching and taking three skiers out on the documentary programme *Equinox*. This is only recommended in the right conditions. There's a pisteurs' hut at the top of the Chanrossa chair where you would start your 10–15 minute hike to the top of the face and we recommend you ask if it's safe before you try it.

For an exhilarating adventure, try a firm favourite of ours, **Les Avals Valley**. This valley can be accessed by hiking up from the top of the Chanrossa chairlift. Once you have entered the valley you will be astounded by the breathtaking scenery and wide sections of untracked snow. If you wish you can turn this into an overnight escapade. Equipped with a warm sleeping bag and food for the evening, you can catch the last lifts up the Chanrossa, stop halfway down at a mountain refuge and spend the evening there. Early in the morning head back down towards 1650. The only drawback to this awesome trip is a fair amount of flat terrain that you have to push and walk out of. Snowboarders will find this a little harder than skiers. However, it is well worth all the effort and yields sufficient respect when you recount your adventures in the bars later. It is also essential to research snow conditions and weather fully before you attempt the Les Avals valley.

Instruction and equipment

New Generation
New Gen teaches all levels of skier and boarder.
T: 0033 (0)4 79 01 03 18
W: www.skinewgen.com

RTM
The name is made up of the initials of the three directors: Rob, Tom and Mark, or Ride The Mountain. Up to you.

The way forward when it comes to snowboard instructors, RTM have a group of passionate and professional snowboarders. They employ the best instructors, provide the best service and by the end of the day or week they will be more of a friend than an instructor. They'll also be more than happy to join you for a beer at the end of the day.
T: 0033 (0)6 15 48 59 04
E: info@rtmsnowboarding.com
W: www.rtmsnowboarding.com

Rob Sewell
Rob is a private ski instructor who has lived in Courchevel for many years and is now one of the most respected instructors in the Trois Vallées. He is known for teaching the unteachable and also tuning up

> "It is well worth all the effort and yields sufficient respect when you recount your adventures in the bars later"

advanced skiers. If you want top results with your skiing, Rob's your man.
T: 0033 (0)4 79 08 04 17
Mobile: 0033 (0)6 10 144 762

Ski Supreme
The reputation of Ski Supreme is superb. They are the longest-serving British ski instructors in Courchevel and have led the way for those that followed (the directors are the parents of Alan Baxter, Britain's most successful alpine racer). The ski supreme team are extremely friendly and provide first-rate instruction.
T: 0033 (0)4 79 08 27 87
E: info@skisupremeski.com
W: www.supremeski.com

Equipment
For renting or buying, the best shops are **Francis Blanc Sports** (see Roger, the most respected boot technician around) and the **Freeride** shop with its

Lift passes	Trois Vallées	Courchevel
1 day	€41	€35
6 days	€204	€166
13 days	€372	€305

Trois Vallées extension passes are available for €20 a day, which is good if you only want to do the full tour for one day. Children up to 13 years and adults over 60 receive a discount. Family passes are also available. It's worth getting the insurance for an extra €2.50 a day as the emergency services on the mountain can cost an absolute fortune and if they see an insurance card the whole thing runs a lot more smoothly.

enthusiastic bunch of staff. Ask for Big Ewan! Both are located opposite the Bubble Bar in town.

Other activities

Massage: Pamper Off-piste provides a large range of massage and beauty treatments. (06 17 60 89 02, enquiry@pamperoffpiste.com, www.pamperoffpiste.com). They visit you in the comfort of your chalet to relieve tired, aching bones.

Parapenting: This involves skiing off one of the top peaks with an instructor, gliding for around 15 minutes and landing in Le Praz where you catch the lift back up. There are a number of schools offering parapenting. Craig's Paragliding (04 79 08 43 65) is run by the only British pilot in the Trois Vallées.

Skidoos: These can be hired for an afternoon of fun from Chardon Loisirs (04 79 08 39 60) or Ski Vol (06 83 97 53 26). A guide will take you along the marked tracks from €75. Great fun but they won't let you go wild.

More options close by

There are lots more options very close by (see Courchevel 1850 on page 146).

Bowling: There are 8 bowling lanes at the Forum in 1850 (04 79 08 23 83), which are open every day 11am–2am.

Cinema: The cinema in 1850 often shows films in English.

Ice go-karting: Literally go-karting on ice, you can do this in 1550 (06 08 73 70 58, www.kartinglace, asp@kartinglace.com). Really good fun but fairly expensive at €30 for only 10 minutes.

Ice skating: The rink at the Forum in 1850 is open every day 3–7pm and until 11pm on Wednesdays and Fridays. Adults pay €4.80.

Luging: Grab a sledge, available at most ski shops, and head down the specially made luge track in front of the Kalico in 1850 to the bottom of 1550. Accidents are not uncommon. Take your ski pass for the ride back up.

Raft on the Olympic ski jump: In Le Praz (04 79 08 39 60), this costs from €30 per person.

Sky diving: Available through the whole of March, all reports of this have been fantastic. If you're in Courchevel in March, do it.

Events

In 1650 is the legendary **Derby** that takes place at the end of March; contestants start at the top of the pyramids run and have to race to the bottom to claim their prize. It can turn into carnage! The Derby was an institutional event a few years back, was then cancelled and has now been reinstated. In 1850 events such as the Courchevel Freeride and Playstation Big Air are great to watch and worth a visit (see 1850, page 146).

Accommodation

Most of the accommodation in 1650 is in chalets, run by tour operators. For some of the best chalets in town, check out **Cordon Rouge** (www.frenchskiholidays.com) that has chalets for all sizes of group, all in excellent locations. Others include chalets and chalet hotels run by **Ski Olympic** and **Le Ski**, which are worth checking out. There is a beautiful new 3-star hotel bang in the centre of 1650, **Le Seizena** (the old signal, 0033 (0)4 79 01 46 46, welcome@leseizena.com) that looks stunning. It has 20 rooms, a hot tub, fitness and internet terminals. B&B accommodation costs from €180 per day for 3 people.

The **Golf Hotel** (0033 (0)4 79 00 92 92, www.hotel dugolf-courchevel.com, info-reservation@hoteldu golf-courchevel.fr) is another good-looking 3-star building and has the best position in 1650; you can ski to the door and you're right in the centre of town. It has 47 rooms and half board costs €237–500 per day for 2 people depending on the type of room and time of season. The 2-star **Edelweiss Hotel** (0033 (0)4 79 08 26 58, www.courchevel-edelweiss.com) is good for those on a budget (from €86 for 2 people B&B) and also well positioned.

Eating out

On the mountain

In 1650, try the very popular **Bel Air** (04 79 08 00 93) restaurant, which serves omelettes, salads, pasta and snails. The menu is fairly limited but the food is fantastic. Between two of you, we recommend sharing an omelette, chips and the Bel Air salad. It is advisable to book. There's a terrace on three levels with deckchairs on the bottom level and it's a great place to chill and watch the world ski and board by. **La Casserole** (04 79 08 06 35), at the bottom of the Signal chair, is all right and has a fantastic terrace but it has got a bit too expensive now for what it is and there are better places to go. The **Bubble Bar**, just off the slopes, serves panini at lunch time and is popular but if you get there after about midday it's a gamble as to whether they'll have any left.

In 1850 there are some great restaurants and some ridiculously expensive ones too. Check out the Courchevel 1850 chapter for more details (page 146).

In town

Petit Savoyard (04 79 08 27 44) is the best restaurant in 1650 with a cosy atmosphere, traditional food, and the best menu, food and service. It is always busy and you should really book, especially on the chalet staff's night off. **L'Eterlou** (04 79 08 25 45) is another great, traditional restaurant with superb pizzas and the friendliest staff. **La Montagne** (04 79 08 09 85), between the two mentioned above, has two parts: one smart restaurant with fish and meat dishes and a simpler, brasserie-style restaurant. These restaurants are all in a row opposite the Bubble Bar and you can't really go wrong. **L'Alberon** (04 79 08 24 87) has to be

"These restaurants are all in a row opposite the Bubble Bar and you can't really go wrong" mentioned. It has a great selection of salads, meats and Savoyard specialities and the setting is lovely. There is also an added bonus that the English translations are the funniest things we've ever seen (we're not being mean, we genuinely love it). For example, the ingredients of a goats' cheese salad are 'green salad, tomato, let's lard (lardons), let's eat (croûtons) and hot goat'. Now guess the following dishes: 'Plate of ham of country', 'Muffs of duck', 'Tartar of built boeuf to the knife', 'Scallop of poultry to the Norman', 'Mouse of lamb roasted to the thyme', 'Marmitte of Fish to the Bouillabaisse', 'Net of Milling Perch', 'Mixture of three melted cheeses to the white wine, green salad and butcher's shop', 'Mount of gold, Butcher's shop of country and potatoes' and 'An ice two balls'. Mmmm, tempting. You have to go there and the food is really good once you've figured out what it is. For a really smart meal or just for a change, get the

bus up to 1850 where there is a superb Asian restaurant, **Le Grand Café** (pricey), a very smart pizzeria, **Via Ferrata**, and loads more great places to try (see 1850 chapter, page 146).

Bars and clubs

There are a few bars in 1650, but even we – who love it so much – can see that it really needs somewhere new or a bit of a revamp. The **Signal** bar has recently changed although Deni, who has been there for years, is still at the helm. It is a real locals' bar and where we hang out in Courchevel, mainly due to the provision of Mutzig, the strongest beer in town that is guaranteed to get you leathered. It opens at 6am and closes at 9pm. Many of the locals go for après ski, stay until they're hammered, pass out at 9 and still feel good for the next day. **Rocky's** is still a really popular one even though it hasn't changed for years. It has a great location and internet terminals. Twice a week there is live music, which is really popular, and it's one of the cheapest places to drink in 1650. **The Bubble** is the other bar and it's not a bad hang-out spot. It does good panini at lunch time and is a good meeting point (also with internet terminals). You can have a good night there although they have had warnings from the local police to keep the noise down so it's a bit more chilled

out now. The best place in 1650 is **The Space Bar**, at the far end of town, open 4pm–4am. It gets really busy when everywhere else closes and is great for a good dance but it's also good for après as there's a pool table, table football and games room. They have loads of big screens showing extreme sports and always have something going on: live music, theme nights, that kind of thing. Carnage is always to be found here!

Useful facts and phone numbers

Tourist office

T: 0033 (0)4 79 08 04 10
F: 0033 (0)4 79 08 15 63
E: info@courchevel.com
W: www.courchevel.com
Direct reservations (1850)
T: 0033 (0)4 79 08 14 44
E: info@courchevel-reservation.com
W: www.courchevel-reservation.com

Emergency services

- In a medical emergency dial 15, for the fire brigade call 18, or 112 for either from a mobile.
- Police: 04 79 08 34 69/ 04 79 08 26 07

Doctors

In 1650, there is one doctor (04 79 08 04 45). We recommend those in 1850.
- Blanc Alexandre: 04 79 08 26 40
- Cabinet Médical du Forum: 04 79 08 32 13
- Chedal Marc: 04 79 08 20 14
- Physiotherapy Clinic: 06 68 57 00 99 (Siân and Chris are definitely the best in town)

Taxis

- Courchevel Taxi Association: 04 79 08 23 46
- Abatrans Taxi: 04 79 00 3000 (www.courchevel-taxi.com)
- Taxi Jack: 06 12 45 11 17

Getting there

By car

From Calais, the drive will take you about 10 hours. Car parking for the week will cost you €60–70.

By train

You can get the train from London Waterloo to Moutiers (25km/15miles away). Bus transfers are available from here and cost €11 for the 1 hour journey. A taxi costs €60.

By plane

Geneva (145km) From here there are a number of different options to get to Courchevel. The bus costs €109 for a return trip and takes about 3.5 hours. Contact Touriscar on 0033 (0)4 50 43 60 or visit www.touriscar.net. Best to book in advance. A taxi (1–4 people) will cost €285 and a helicopter (up to 5 people) €1450.
Lyon (180km) is also 3.5 hours away by bus. Contact Satobus on 0033 (0)4 37 25 52 55, www.satobus-alps.com. A taxi costs €330 and a helicopter €1700.
Chambery (115km) is closer, transfer by bus costs €75 and takes 1.5 hours, a taxi is €220 and a helicopter €1000.

Courchevel 1850

The depiction of Courchevel as 'St Tropez on ice, a magnet to the rich and famous' isn't far from the truth

On the slopes	
Snow reliability	✽ ✽ ✽ ✽
Parks	✽ ✽
Off-piste	✽ ✽ ✽ ✽

Off the slopes	
Après ski	✽ ✽ ✽
Nightlife	✽ ✽ ✽ ✽
Eating out	✽ ✽ ✽ ✽
Resort charm	✽ ✽ ✽

The resort

Courchevel is one of our favourite places. Four different resorts come under the name of Courchevel: Courchevel 1850 is the highest and most cosmopolitan, 1650 is Pat's home and is described in detail in its own chapter (see page 138), 1550 is less expensive than the above and is often used as a base for those who work in other resorts and the last is Courchevel 1300, also known as Le Praz, a traditional Savoyard village where the Olympic ski jump dominates the town. There is a bubble lift in Le Praz that takes you right into 1850, which has a reputation for attracting the rich and famous and many a celeb has been spotted on the slopes. This brings with it inflated prices, Michelin-starred restaurants, exclusive and well-hidden cocktail bars and plush chalets. If you have a fat wallet you'll love it here, but if not, don't stop reading yet as there is another side to the resort that isn't as elitist and the mountains have so much to offer it's worth spending an extra bob or two.

The mountains

Height: 1850–2740m

Ability	Rating
Expert	✽ ✽ ✽ ✽
Intermediate	✽ ✽ ✽ ✽ ✽
Beginner	✽ ✽ ✽ ✽

Getting about

The skiing in Courchevel appears almost endless, with access to the massive area of Les Trois Vallées. Due to this vast expanse of pisted runs, there's plenty to keep everyone happy. No matter how experienced the skier or boarder, you would struggle to cover all the runs in a week. For most, there is more than enough terrain in Courchevel alone, so many people would be advised to buy a lift pass for Courchevel and buy extensions where necessary.

The park

The park is located at the bottom of Courchevel 1850 by the Plantry chairlift. Two quick drag lifts allow easy access to the park. There are a variety of jumps and rails, a half pipe and a spine jump. Unfortunately, the park is not maintained very well and is at a relatively low altitude so the snow easily becomes slushy. If hitting the park is your thing, perhaps you should head over to the Meribel moon park, which is very well looked after and usually in good condition.

Off-piste and backcountry

The couloirs are at the top of the Saulire cable car. Directly under the cable car is the easily accessible Telepherique couloir; perhaps slightly less challenging than the rest although there are a number of shoots and drop-offs to the side of the run. Further along the path from the Telepherique is the Grand Couloir, which is marked as a black run on the piste map but is far more difficult than the average black. It is wider than most couloirs but has the tendency to transform into a mogul field in the absence of fresh powder. A short (5 minute) hike up from the Grand Couloir is the Petit Couloir, where incredible conditions can be unearthed as the short hike, though fairly easy, puts a lot of people off. Don't be discouraged by this couloir's name as the narrower width limits the sun's access to the slope, thereby preserving the snow's condition. If you fancy a slightly longer hike (around 30 minutes) head to the next couloir over, Croidex la Verdons. This has the advantages of a wide, open face, very few tracks and a long run down. Be aware of the drop-off on the right-hand side (from the riders' point of view) as it's a long fall to the rocks below. All the couloirs arrive at the Saulire piste, which leads you straight back to the cable car so you can head back up and try another.

It is this ease of accessibility that makes the couloirs a great playground for the adventurous.

For some more easily accessible powder, take the Creux chairlift and traverse left to reach a vast open powder bowl (the **Creux bowl**). Cross right to the end of the bowl to a huge, pointed rock, known as the Needle. The first face you come to (left of the needle from the riders' viewpoint) is usually tracked out by mid-day as it is so easy to get to. Climb around the Needle to experience fresh powder that usually takes a good week to be tracked out after a snowfall and provides a long run down to the bottom of the Chanrossa chairlift.

Arguably some of the finest powder in Courchevel can be found on the **Roche de Loze**. From the bottom of 1850 take the Chenus gondola and the two-man chair to the top of Col de la Loze. Turn towards your left and look straight ahead of you, where you will see the Roche de Loze. This is the site of the classic Courchevel Freeride competition that attracts the best skiers from around the world. It is not for the leisurely skier/boarder as it takes a good 45 minutes to hike to, but the ride down is well worth it and your mum will appreciate the pictures from the top. There are a number of couloirs that you can drop in from, depending on your ability, and plenty of shoots and cliffs to hook off. It's a 'safe' run to do as it rarely slides and has become popular with the locals. Manu Gaidet, the 2004 world champion freeskier, declares it to be his favourite place to train in Courchevel.

"The site of the classic Courchevel Freeride competition that attracts the best skiers from around the world"

Over the back of the Freeride is a huge face known to residents of Courchevel as the butcher's run. This was named after a local butcher who climbed to the top of the face before the lifts opened each day, leaving perfect tracks. It is imperative that, should you wish to re-enact this legendary story, you follow the butcher's lead and hike up first thing in the morning as it faces the sun all day, resulting in a potential avalanche risk later in the afternoon.

Lift passes	Trois Vallées	Courchevel
1 day	€41	€35
6 days	€204	€166
13 days	€372	€305

Three Valley extension passes are also for sale for €20 a day, which is good if you only want to do the full tour for one day. Children up to 13 years and adults over 60 receive a discount. Family passes are also available. It's worth getting the insurance for an extra €2.50 a day as the emergency services on the mountain can cost an absolute fortune and if they see an insurance card the whole thing runs a lot more smoothly.

Instruction

ESF

The ESF have around 190 instructors in Courchevel alone. They are a well respected association. Group lessons (for skiing or snowboarding) cost €95–254, depending on whether you require 5 or 6 days' instruction and whether you choose morning, afternoon or all day lessons. Private lessons are €250 for the day.
T: 0033 (0)4 79 08 07 72
E: ski@esfcourchevel.com
W: www.esfcourchevel.com

Magic in Motion

Magic has both French and British instructors but all are English speaking. They have dodgy jackets and a big mouse mascot who skis around to entertain the kids. No matter what, these guys always look as if they're enjoying themselves and they employ lots of fun and charismatic instructors. Group lessons cost from €240 for 2 hours a day and private lessons (ski and board) are €350 for one day.

T: 0033 (0)4 79 01 01 81
E: courchevel@magicinmotion.co.uk
W: www.magicinmotion.co.uk

RTM

The name stands for the initials of the three directors, Rob, Tom and Mark, or Ride The Mountain. Up to you.

The way forward when it comes to snowboard instructors, RTM have a group of passionate and professional snowboarders; they employ the best instructors, provide the best service and by the end of the day or week they will be more of a friend than an instructor. They'll also be more than happy to join you for a beer at the end of the day. Group sessions can be booked for five days (€195) or four days (€165), and private lessons are 2 hours (€120) or 3 hours (€165).

T: 0033 (0)6 15 48 59 04
E: info@rtmsnowboarding.com
W: www.rtmsnowboarding.com

Ski Academy

Ski Academy offer skiing and boarding lessons for all abilities. One of their best ideas is to offer semi-private tuition, where you will be placed in a group of between three and five people so you get lots of attention and can still make friends. Prices range from €250 to €330 depending on the time of season and a 15-hour or 18-hour course. They are also good for kids and supply helmets for free.

T: 0033 (0)4 79 08 11 99
E: courchevel@ski-academy.com
W: www.ski-academy.com

Ski Supreme

Ski Supreme are the longest-serving British ski instructors in Courchevel and have led the way for those that followed (the directors are the parents of Alan Baxter, Britain's most successful Alpine racer). The Ski Supreme team are extremely friendly and provide first-rate instruction. Ski courses cost from €160 for 10 hours and a private lessons costs €80 per hour.

T: 0033 (0)4 79 08 27 87
E: info@skisupremeski.com
W: www.supremeski.com

Other activities

Artificial climbing wall: At the Forum (04 79 08 19 50), this is a 13m high wall with seven ways up. A session costs €8.

Bowling: There are eight bowling lanes in the Forum (04 79 08 23 83) which are open every day 11am–2am.

Ice climbing: This takes place on the ice tower in between 1850 and 1650. It can be quite challenging and is dependent on conditions and temperatures.

Ice go-karting: Literally go-karting on ice in 1550 (06 08 73 70 58, www.kartinglace.com, asp@kartinglace.com). Really good fun but fairly expensive for the short time you spend on the ice at €30 for 10 minutes.

Ice skating: The ice skating rink at the Forum is open every day 3–7pm and until 11pm on Wednesdays and Fridays. Adults pay €4.80.

Luging: Grab a sledge, available at most ski shops,

and head down the specially made luge track in front of the Kalico to the bottom of 1550. Accidents are not uncommon. Take your ski pass for the ride back up.

Massage: After you have indulged in all these activities, get Pamper Off Piste (06 17 60 89 02, enquiry@ pamperoffpiste.com, www.pamperoffpiste.com) to visit you in the comfort of your chalet to relieve those tired, aching bones. They provide a large range of massage and beauty treatments and come highly recommended.

Paraponting: This involves skiing off one of the top peaks with an instructor, gliding for around 15 minutes and landing in Le Praz where you catch the lift back up. There are a number of schools offering parapenting. The best are the legendary Pascal Piazzalunga (06 09 76 50 40) and Craig's Paragliding (04 79 08 43 65), the only British pilot in Les Trois Vallées.

Plane trips: These are on hand for extravagant spenders to splash some cash to see the mountains from above. The Trois Vallées circuit costs €70 per person (04 79 08 31 23, www.areoclub-courchevel .com). In our opinion, if you're going up in a plane you should really jump out of it...

Raft on the Olympic ski jump: In Le Praz (04 79 08 39 60), this costs from €30 per person.

Shopping: The shopping is great (Prends tu luge is our favourite shop).

Skidoos: These can be hired for an afternoon of fun from Chardon Loisirs (04 79 08 39 60) or Ski Vol (06 83 97 53 26). A guide will take you along the marked tracks from €75. Great fun but they won't let you go wild.

Sky diving: Available through the whole of March, all reports of this have been fantastic. If you're in Courchevel in March, do it.

Events

The **Courchevel Freeride** (March) is one of the best big-mountain freeride events in Europe. People come from all over the world to compete for big cash prizes, and it attracts some of the biggest names in the business. The freeride competition takes place on the Col de la Loze and is great for spectators as you can see it really clearly from the piste and it's pretty impressive. The **PlayStation Big Air** usually takes place in February. It's an open competition so anyone who fancies a pop can sign themselves up. There are loads of wicked prizes so it's worth a shot. Again, it's a good

one to watch as it takes place at the bottom of 1850 on a specially built jump and always attracts a big crowd. **Ice hockey matches** take place on the ice rink at the Forum throughout the season and are good to watch. Courchevel vs. Meribel is a popular event with the locals and workers. **New Year's Eve Party on the Piste** is a great event in the centre of 1850. Hundreds and thousands turn up to boogie on the snow to the live music and wonder at the fireworks. All the bars serve drinks in plastic cups so you can wander round with them and most places stay open until the last people fall over.

Accommodation

Luxury accommodation is provided by Flexiski, Kaluma and Ski Scott Dunn, so why not bankrupt yourself for a week of sheer indulgence. In similar fashion, there are some amazing, top-of-the-range hotels that have to be seen to be believed, as do the prices. **Le Kilimandjaro** (00 33 (0)4 79 01 46 46, www.hotelkilimandjaro.com, welcome@hotelkilimandjaro.com) is a stunning, grandiose building with a piano bar, beauty salon, spa and pool. It's right at the top of 1850 and not too handy for the town although there is a good shuttle service. If you can afford to stay here, you can afford taxis. Half-board accommodation costs €670–5830 per day for two people depending on the season and how super-posh you want your room to be. The **Lana** (0033 (0)4 79 08 01 10, www.lelana.com, info@lelana.com) is a similar level of luxury, with great service, a cosy feel and it's closer to the town centre. The Lana will set you back €370–1010 per day for half board for two people.

If you've not quite made the rich list just yet, there are a few other places to try. **Hotel de la Croisette** (003 (0)4 79 08 09 00, www.hoteldelacroisette.com, hotel.croisette@wanadoo.fr) is well placed for the main lifts and town centre and contains the popular Bar le Jump. It's a good, 3-star hotel and rooms on the first floor tend to be slightly cheaper because of the noise from the bar so why not take advantage of the good rate and go out and join in the fun. Bed and breakfast costs €150–230 for two people per night. **Courcheneige** (0033 (0)4 79 08 02 59) is a 2 star on the Bellecotte piste, very handy for the slopes but not so much for going out at night. There is a huge terrace that is busy at lunch, and reports of the staff and food

are superb. Rooms cost from €248 per day for half board for two people. **Hotel Olympic** (0033 (0)4 79 65 07 65) has competitive rates and contains a small bar, popular at happy hour. It's handy for town and generally good value but not much to look at. Rooms cost €70–178 per day for two people for B&B.

Eating out

On the mountain
The **Cap Horn** (04 79 08 33 10), next to the Altiport, is a favourite of the rich and famous and the ultimate exclusive lunch. You'd never believe you were in the mountains. It has a cosy but luxurious feel and fabulous food. Don't stumble in, thinking you'll just grab a quick sandwich – reservations are essential. The beautiful **Panoramic** (04 79 08 00 88) restaurant is at the top of the Saulire cable car and is highly recommended, again, if your wallet can handle it. The **Bouc Blanc** (04 79 08 80 26) just below the Col de Loz chair has fantastic views, a huge open deck and a great Beaufort cheese tart. It's fantastic value compared to most of the restaurants on the mountain and the food and service is excellent. The **Jump** (04 79 08 09 00) at the bottom of the slopes in 1850 serves lunch 12am–3pm and the chilli and chips is highly recommended. The **New solarium** (04 79 08 02 01) serves a more economical panini or suchlike at the first stop of the Jardin Alpin lift.

In town
Firstly come the posh places – if you've forgotten your gold card, skip to the next paragraph. The **Chapelle** (04 79 08 19 48) has a fabulous, cosy, candlelit atmosphere, focused around an open wood fire on which all the meat is cooked. If you are not a big fan of red meat this may not be the place for you as there are few vegetarian options. The **Via Ferrata** (04 79 08 02 07) is impressive and whilst you can pay top dollar for some dishes and for drinks, the pizzas are surprisingly reasonable. They may have loud music but this somehow manages to remain unobtrusive and adds to the stylish, cosmopolitan environment. The **Grand Café** (04 79 08 42 97) is one of our favourite restaurants and serves Oriental cuisine to the highest standards in beautiful surroundings. Try the chicken supreme with mango and curry sauces. The **Mangoire** is a restaurant/bar (see Bars and clubs) with an ambiance second to none. Those with a poor sense of humour need not apply as it is not unknown for the barmen to open up the fancy dress box and pop a hat on your head. They will also set the bar on fire, and provide jovial entertainment, despite any language barriers. Also be prepared for two guys/girls on stilts that surfaced whilst we were there; they are scarily amusing and fling themselves in your face with no sense of personal boundaries. The **Bergerie** (04 79 08 24 70) serves some of the best food we have tasted in the mountains and often offers live music and theme nights. It is just by the side of the piste so you can stop in for lunch or book dinner, in which case a car will come and pick you up.

> "It is not unknown for the barmen to open up the fancy dress box and pop a hat on your head"

Getting cheaper (but not necessarily cheap cheap)...
If you fancy some good Savoyard food, head to the **Saulire** (04 79 08 07 52), which has good local specialities and the **Fromagerie** (04 79 08 27 47) which serves one of the best fondues in town. You will find many restaurants offering Savoyard food such as fondues and pierres chaudes (hot stones on which you cook your own food) and, whilst scrumptious, the novelty will wear off. When it does, we recommend the **Refuge**, which offers a range of dishes from steak and ale pie and chips to a delectable Thai curry. The **Plante du Baton** (04 79 08 02 10) also offers curries and burgers at a great price in a great atmosphere. **Kalico** (04 79 08 20 28), the nightclub, serves good food at lunch and at night. It is less expensive than its counterparts and serves massive portions of great food (burgers, salads, fajitas, etc.). For a tasty, good value

take-out pizza try the **End Café. Vache Qui Ski** is open from 10pm until the early hours of the morning and offers great burgers and baguettes for late-night clubbers. We recommend the American baguette, which contains steak and chips and tastes amazing (under the influence of a pint or two).

Bars and clubs

Make sure your wallet's looking healthy if you're after a big night in 1850 – the nightlife reflects its cosmopolitan reputation meaning that (in certain places) drinks can be pricey and dress codes may apply. The **Jump** has a great atmosphere and is busy all day; for mid-morning stops, lively après ski and 10.30pm–1am, when people are getting going for the evening. It's an English-run bar that attracts both holiday-makers and season workers, all mainly English. The Jump's excellent reputation is due primarily to the staff who, year after year, engage and entertain the crowds and keep them coming back for more. If you want to save your pennies slightly and mingle with the season workers, try **TJ's** (town centre) or **Gringo's** (at the far end of town). They have cosy, fun atmospheres and relatively cheap drinks. Flavoured vodkas are popular and can be bought by the tray and if you're lucky you might turn up on a theme night – not for the faint hearted.

For the high society, here are a couple to try. For a luxurious, calm atmosphere, try **Piggy's** bar (04 79 08 00 71) in the heart of 1850. While you may enjoy the thought of sipping cocktails in this 'Old English library' style atmosphere, be prepared for the bill – half a lager costs around £6. The **Mangoire** is a fantastic bar, slightly off the beaten track. Prices are high but not unjustified – a £25 cocktail may sound extortionate but, when you catch a glimpse of the size of the glass and the artwork involved, you can only be amazed. It serves as a fine dining restaurant in the early evening (if you don't intend buying champagne you won't fit in) but when dinner is over you are, surprisingly, actively encouraged to jump on to chairs, tables and any other surfaces available.

After the bars have shut, **Kalico** (04 79 08 20 28) is the only place to be for most. DJs play every night, as well as top quality bands twice a week and every night is guaranteed to be jam packed with hedonistic young people. All in all an exceptionally successful recipe for a club, provided you don't mind the crowds. For exclusivity, there are two places to go: **La Grange** (04 79 08 14 61), right behind the Jump bar, and **Les Caves** at the edge of 1850. These clubs attract a similar clientele – those who won't bat an eyelid at splashing out hundreds of pounds for bottles of vodka or champagne (few people drink by the glass) which are lit by sparklers and brought to your table. For neon strip lighting and a funky, dance atmosphere hit Les Caves; for a slightly more laid back, classic club, try La Grange.

Useful facts and phone numbers

Tourist office

T: 0033 (0)4 79 08 00 29
F: 0033 (0)4 79 08 15 63
E: info@courchevel.com
W: www.courchevel.com

Direct reservations

T: 0033 (0)4 79 08 14 44
F: 0033 (0)4 79 08 33 54
E: info@courchevel-reservation.com
W: www.courchevel-reservation.com

Emergency services

• In a medical emergency dial 15, for the fire brigade call 18, or 112 for either from a mobile.
• Police: 04 79 08 34 69/ 04 79 08 26 07

Doctors

• Blanc Alexandre: 04 79 08 26 40
• Cabinet Médical du Forum: 04 79 08 32 13
• Chedal Marc: 04 79 08 20 14
• Physiotherapy Clinic: 06 68 57 00 99 (Siân and Chris are definitely the best in town)

Taxis

• Courchevel Taxi Association: 04 79 08 23 46
• Abatrans Taxi: 04 79 00 3000 (www.courchevel-taxi.com)
• Taxi Jack: 06 12 45 11 17
• Luxury Taxi Service: Poirel Thibaut, 06 09 40 19 10 (www.snowtaxis.com, thibaut@snowtaxis.com)
• Helicopter-Taxi: 04 79 08 00 91 (www.saf-helico.com, saf@saf-helico.com)

Getting there

By car

From Calais, the drive will take you about 10 hours. Car parking for the week will cost you €60–70.

By train

You can get the train from London Waterloo to Moutiers (25km/15miles away). Bus transfers are available from here and cost €11 for the 1 hour journey. A taxi costs €60.

By plane

Geneva (145km) From here there are a number of different options to get to Courchevel. The bus costs €109 for a return trip and takes about 3.5 hours. Contact Touriscar on 0033 (0)4 50 43 60 02 or visit www.touriscar.net. Best to book in advance. A taxi (1–4 people) will cost €285 and a helicopter (up to 5 people) €1450.
Lyon (180km) is also 3.5 hours away by bus. Contact Satobus on 0033 (0)4 37 25 52 55, www.satobus-alps.com. A taxi costs €330 and a helicopter €1700.
Chambery (115km) is closer. The transfer by bus costs €75 and takes 1.5 hours, a taxi is €220 and a helicopter €1000.

Les Deux Alpes

The heart of the European freestyle community

ES ALPES 3600

On the slopes	
Snow reliability	✳ ✳ ✳ ✳
Parks	✳ ✳ ✳ ✳ ✳
Off-piste	✳ ✳ ✳
Off the slopes	
Après ski	✳ ✳ ✳ ✳
Nightlife	✳ ✳ ✳ ✳
Eating out	✳ ✳ ✳
Resort charm	✳ ✳

The resort

Les Deux Alpes is situated where the Northern and Southern Alps meet, in the heart of the Oisans. The nearest town is Grenoble, 79km away. It seems more like a regular town than a resort, partly due to the fact that the resort is open year round and therefore has far more permanent residents (mainly British and French). The town centre is focused along the main street, about a mile long. It's not exceptionally beautiful but the mountains, slopes and the flawless snow park more than make up for it. The town also has its own charisma within the warmth of the community and the diversity of year-round activities that are available. Les Deux Alpes was built on a marshy plateau between two villages: Mont de Lans (Les Deux Alpes 1300) and Venosc, a more traditional craft village at the far end of the resort. We will be referring to the Mont de Lans and Venosc sides of town throughout this chapter. There is also the 'Village' area (Les Deux Alpes 1800), known to the locals as the 'ghetto'. This area has been known to attract some dubious characters and isn't particularly close to the lifts or local amenities but if you're looking for a bargain it could be worth checking out.

The mountains

Height: 1650–3600m

Ability	Rating
Expert	✳ ✳ ✳ ✳
Intermediate	✳ ✳ ✳ ✳
Beginner	✳ ✳ ✳ ✳

Getting about

There are 200km of marked runs in Les Deux Alpes, 59 ski lifts, a superb snow park, and an abundance of alternatives for the budding freestyler or freerider. There are a little more than 700 hectares of off-piste. Sixty per cent of on-piste runs are designated for beginners and intermediate skiers and boarders and 40 per cent for the more competent and experienced riders. In total there are 73 runs: 14 black, 15 red, 29 blue and 15 green. Les Deux Alpes also has the advantage of guaranteed snow year round due to high altitude and the use of 105 snow canons.

The Jandri Express cable car takes you up to 3200m and then the funicular up to 3425m. At the top you are greeted with a 360-degree panoramic view of the French and Italian Alps: la Meije, le Mont Blanc and many others.

The Diable gondola heads up to the Tête Moute at 2800m and gives access to steep on-piste runs, including a challenging 1200m vertical mogul field.

The magnificent park

Les Deux Alpes was one of the first resorts passionately to adopt the newborn wave of New School riding. Evidence of this can be seen throughout the resort in the personality of the locals, the beginning of season festival 'The Mondial du Snow' and, essentially, in the outstanding quality of the snow park. It costs €726,690 (around half a million pounds sterling) per winter to maintain the New School riding zones, including 28 hours of piste grooming per day. In winter the resort's snowpark is situated at 2600m, on the Toura area which can be reached by the Jandri cable car. In the summer, the park is shifted up to the glacier.

The snow park consists of:
- an area of 10 hectares
- a beginner's zone, created for freestyle debutantes, and containing six small kickers
- a half pipe zone 120m long and 4m high
- a slopestyle zone with a series of hips, gaps and quarters leading to rail zones of almost 400m
- BBQ, music, DJ's turntable and deckchairs.

There is also a boardercross area at 2600m where official boardercross competitions are held. The length of the boardercross is 1000–1230m and there is also a new, smaller boardercross for beginners, which is situated parallel to the old one.

Unique to Les Deux Alpes is the **JTS (Jumping Training System)** or the 'snow air bag' which Les Deux Alpes ESF snowboarding school set up. The air bag is 14m by 28m and allows both beginners and experienced freestylers to up the level of their tricks in complete confidence as there is less chance of injuries if you land badly. It's only €6 for half an hour and definitely worth a try. Each week there is a JTS competition where competitors battle for the biggest air.

Off-piste and backcountry

Les Deux Alpes benefits from significant heights, guaranteeing good snow. Therefore, although the resort is not known for its off-piste terrain, there are many excellent spots for off-piste freeriding, such as Chalance, La Fee, Les Vallons du Diable, Les Posettes, Bellecombes and La Selle. There are also the legendary descents to La Grave.

In the centre of the mountain is the Clot de Chalance, a big playground of open powder fields, small couloirs and cliffs. Word has it that you need to be there first thing in the morning after a fresh snow fall to get first tracks – by the afternoon it's tracked out. It is often blasted by the pisteurs and is relatively safe from avalanching, but there are stories of a couple of fatal slides. If you're feeling slightly more daring, it is possible to carry on all the way down to the Lac du

Chambon, located below the base of the resort. It concludes with a lengthy tree run, but this should only be done with a guide and in the right conditions.

The Diable (at 2400m) also has some top quality runs after a big powder storm. Starting from the top of the Télécabine du Diable (the ones that look like red eggs), you can ride all the way back to town. The terrain isn't too challenging but great for getting freshies.

For couloirs, make your way to the Lac du Plan, which can be seen as you're heading up the mountain in the Telepheriques Debrayables and can be reached by taking the Télésiège de la Fee chair lift. Just below the lake is a variety of options, including a long, narrow, challenging couloir that is held in high regard amongst the top riders in the resort.

For guaranteed, amazing snow, make your way to the top of the glacier by catching the Funiculaire Dome Express. The Dome, nicknamed the Ice Wall, is ideal for getting fresh powder and a perfect place for building backcountry kickers. From here you can see all the terrain leading to La Grave, which has some of the best off-piste riding in the world (see the chapter on La Grave, page 166). A guide is highly recommended if you fancy attempting this terrain.

> "In the centre of the mountain is the Clot de Chalance, a big playground of open powder fields, small couloirs and cliffs"

Lift passes

1 day (21 lifts)	€16.50
1 day (54 lifts)	€34
6 days	€161.50

If you are under 5 or over 72, lifts are free.
There is a discount on passes in early December.

Instruction

Burton Connexion

The Burton Connexion is a Burton snowboarding programme offering courses for all levels and freestyle.
T: 0033 (0)6 76 74 05 44
W: www.oisans.com/burtonconnexion

ESF

Ecole du Ski Français and Ecole du Snowboard. Group lessons for 6 half days costs €113–144.
T: 0033 (0)4 76 79 21 21
W: www.2alpes-esf.com

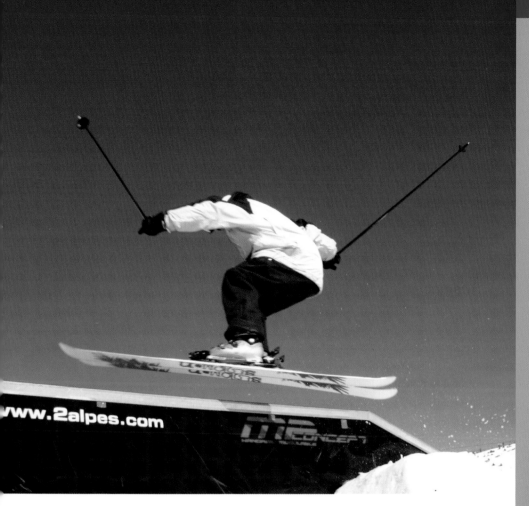

European Ski School

This ski school comes highly recommended by the locals due to the quality of instruction. They limit the size of groups to eight or nine maximum and all speak good English. They also offer a 'Natural Born Skiers' course with a maximum of four per group, lift-queue priority and video analysis. This costs €170 for 2 hours a day for 5 days.

T: 0033 (0)4 76 79 74 55
W: www.europeanskischool.co.uk

Salomon Station

This company offers you the chance to get off the beaten track and discover some beautiful spots.

T: 0033 (0)4 76 79 04 71
E: Salomonstation-2alpes@wanadoo.fr

St Christophe International Ski and Snowboard School

Six half-day ski lessons cost €123, while six half-day snowboard lessons cost €137. To improve your New School riding techniques, private lessons in the park are offered from €33 per hour.

T: 0033 (0)4 76 79 04 21
E: ecole.ski.internationale@wanadoo.fr
W: www.oisans.com/ecoleski.2alpes

Ski Privilège

This school offers group and private ski or snowboard lessons by the hour or half day. Anne Millet is an ex-member of the French Ski Team and offers competitive prices with group lessons from €65 per person per week (five 2-hour sessions).

T: 0033 (0)4 76 79 23 44
W: www.anne.millet.free.fr

Stages Damien Albert

This school teaches only freeride, off-piste and 'bump' courses. They require that students can ski black runs. A 6-day course costs €250.

T: 0033 (0)4 76 79 50 38
W: www.abc-skifreeride.com

Mountain Guides Bureau

The bureau offers training in avalanche rescue and snow awareness. There is also the weekly Free Respect event, which aims to heighten awareness of the risks and dangers of the mountain for off-piste enthusiasts.

E: guides2alpes@yahoo.fr

Other activities

On the mountain

Unless otherwise stated, contact the tourist office (see Useful facts and phone numbers) for more information.
Full moon parties: Combining night riding and drinking

sounds pretty dangerous but, by all accounts, is great fun. Take the last lifts up the mountain at around 4.30pm, ski/ board as the sun sets on the glacier and enjoy a lively meal in a mountain restaurant. Then, after nightfall, ski back down towards the resort, over a drop in altitude of 1300 m with only the moon to see by (€40 includes your ski pass, meal, ice cave and mulled wine on return).

Ice Cave: Found at 3400 metres, this is the longest and highest in the world. The grotto was dug entirely by pickaxe, there was no use of machines, and it now contains many ice sculptures. Open winter and summer.

Night in an igloo: In the Pied Moutet area, at 1700m, in a wild mountain setting, the Kanata igloo village offers the chance to spend a night in an igloo (€60 for an adult). Access is on snowshoes in the evening or on skis during the day.

Night skiing and boarding: This takes place three times a week on the Piste de Lutins in the middle of the resort – and it's free! For more information call Deux Alpes Loisirs (04 76 79 75 01, 2alpesloisirs@2alpes.com, www.2alpes.com).

Paragliding, hang-gliding or helicopter rides: All these are options so you can take in the beauty of the mountains from the sky.

Snowmobiles and quad bikes: Try an evening excursion on the piste. Don't expect to go crazy – there will be a guide to keep you under control.

In the town

Bowling: There are two bowling alleys and lots of games arcades.

Cinema: The local cinema has two screens.

Fitness activities: Health and fitness activities available include squash, jacuzzi, hammam, sauna, tanking, fitness circuits, slimming courses, massages, relaxation, gym, body building, cardio-training, aqua gym, solarium, UVA, spa and shiatsu.

Ice skating: There's an open-air Olympic ice rink (04 76 79 22 73). You can either ice skate or try out the dodgem cars on ice.

Pool, spa and treatments: Aquaflorès wellbeing centre (04 76 80 56 90) has an indoor pool plus spa days from €97: physiotherapy, massages, diet advice, seaweed treatments, aromatherapy, etc.

Swimming: Try the heated outdoor pool (04 76 79 25 64).

Events

The Mondial Du Snow (October/ November) is one of the most popular and highly anticipated events of the year as it marks the beginning of the winter season and celebrates the New School wave of riding. The Mondial du Snowboard is held at the end of October (the 16th edition). The Mondial du Ski takes place a week later (the 8th edition). There are many events during these two weekends. On the glacier, you have the chance to test an incredible number of skis and snowboards: over six days, roughly 85 brand names will be ready to give advice and loan the latest equipment, accessories and clothing from the new collections. A giant rail, more than 50m in length, will also be set up on the glacier. In the town, marquees premier the latest snow-riding films and a massive skate ramp (12m long, 3.5m high) is set up for demos from the world's best skateboarders.

The **Saab Salomon Crossmax Series** reunites the best international skiers. They will be jostling for a qualifying place in the American X Games.

Other events include the **Snowzone event** (mid-March) which combines snow-riding and music. The day starts with sounds on the slopes which gradually make their way down to the resort, and then carry on into the bars and clubs. Popular DJs will be playing house, techno and electronic sounds in an extraordinary atmosphere at the bottom of the Deux Alpes slopes. The **Taravana event** (April) is another freestyle event, closing the winter season in the snowpark.

Accommodation

Hotel prices range from €672 to €980 (based on a week for two people at half board) and apartment prices from €264 to €686 (for four to six people).

There are two 4-star hotels in resort. **Bérangère** (0033 (0)4 76 79 24 11, www.berangerehotel.free.fr) has a piste-side position by the Belle Etoile chairlift. There's a pool, sauna, Jacuzzi and high-quality restaurant. **Farandole** (0033 (0)4 76 80 50 45, www.utaf.com/lafarandole) is a traditional chalet, with 60 bedrooms and apartments. There is a smart restaurant, fitness club, indoor pool, sauna and Jacuzzi.

There are eight 3-star hotels, one of the most highly recommended being **Chalet Mounier.** This has a great atmosphere in an authentic chalet. It is handy for the Diable gondola and the main bar scene. Prices ranged from €77 to €114 in 2004.

There is also an enormous choice of **apartments** but it is very important to check their location as Les Deux Alpes sprawls over a large area.

One company that is definitely worth checking out is **Scuba-Ski** (www.scuba-ski.com), owned by Pete and Lynn Foreman (0033 (0)476 11 03 14/0033 (0)6 03 32 33 00), which offers both catered and self-catered apartments, for between two and ten guests.

> "All their accommodation benefits from a great location, right in the middle of the action"

All their accommodation benefits from a great location, right in the middle of the action (just a few minutes' walk from the ski lifts) and is priced at a very competitive rate (expect to pay around £300 per person per week depending on the time of season). They have one 10-bed chalet (comfortably fits 7), which really is home away from home with hundreds of classic videos to watch, and board games to play. We were lucky enough to sample Pete and Lynn's cooking and the whole experience was superb. It's more homely than luxurious but highly recommended.

They will even arrange for your lift passes, ski/ board hire and/or ski/board school to be booked and ready for you on arrival if you wish, with a 10 per cent discount! If you're looking for luxury, the new **Le Prince des Ecrins** residence is situated 500m from the nearest shops and within immediate proximity of the slopes. It contains 28 luxury apartments for between four and ten people that have a magnificent view over the Veneon valley and the Venosc and Muzelle peaks.

Eating out

On the mountain

There are nine mountain restaurants in Les Deux Alpes. Le **Panoramic** (04 76 79 06 75) is a popular meeting point, at the heart of the action at 2600m. **Chalet La Fee** (04 76 80 24 13) has a friendly atmosphere and good views from the terrace.

In town

There are more than 60 restaurants in Les Deux Alpes with a wide variety of cuisines. Fast food joints and crêperies can be found all through town and offer decent burgers, kebabs, paninis and steak sandwiches. Don't expect a bargain though, it will still cost you around €8 a piece.

Most of the restaurants in the area serve traditional French cuisine – fondues, raclettes, tartiflette, pierres chaudes, etc. – of these the locals recommend the following. **Cellier** (04 76 79 08 79) has a charming wooden interior with a roaring fire. It is located at the end of town; follow the main road to the Place de Venosc and it's just opposite. **Crepes a GoGo** (04 76 79 29 61) is a stunning restaurant, a real treat and not bad prices for such a gorgeous place. It also has a huge fire, cushioned benches and a very cosy and traditional atmosphere. Le **P'tit Polyte** at the Chalet Mounier (04 76 80 50 45) has a strong reputation for serving traditional Savoyard dishes.

For a change to the local fare, try these recommendations. **La Spaghetteria** (04 76 79 05 77) has good value pasta dishes at €7–8 each. **Thai Alloi** is a cosy restaurant run by a local man and his Thai wife. The atmosphere is café-like but the food is first class. **Smokey Joes** and **The Red Frog** (see Bars and clubs) serve good, classic bar food all day until 11pm.

Bars and clubs

There are 30 bars, open until 2am and three clubs that are open until about 5am.

Smokey Joes (04 76 79 28 97) is right in the heart of Les Deux Alpes, a second's walk from the lifts and town centre. It is British run and is open 8am–2am every day. The food has a fantastic, and well-deserved, reputation and it is served all day until 11pm. Choose from full English breakfasts until midday, bacon sandwiches, paninis, fajitas, wraps, and many more tasty morsels. While you're there, why not check your E-mails on the brand new computers with broadband connections. The most popular nights are theme nights (Tuesdays and Thursdays) and it is also a top quality après ski joint to soothe the aching bones with a few vodka shots while DJs play live music. Smokey Joes

is a place much-loved by locals and tourists alike, and everyone is welcomed as a friend. The Red Frog (04 76 79 23 28) is truly a meeting place for the locals and seasonaires. It is run by the interesting combination of a Englishman, Irishman and Scotsman and always has a good busy atmosphere. Located at the Venosc end of town, it is open 7am–2am, serving

"The food has a fantastic, and well-deserved, reputation"

food until 11pm. The Frog offers a legendary, all day, full English breakfast as well as burgers, pasta, steaks and salads. They show all the footie on new plasma TVs and have also opened a sitting room at the back of the bar with comfy sofas to chill and watch the matches. The Frog also has a pool room and wireless laptops at broadband speed that they rent out for a bargain of 10 cents per minute.

Smithy's (04 76 11 36 79, www.smithystavern.com) is open 5pm–2am and is located next to the Avalanche club at the Venosc end of town. It's a huge, open plan pub on two floors, the ground floor being the pub and the top floor the restaurant. The bar has a good reputation, predominantly due to the weekly DJs and live bands. It allegedly contains the longest vodka bar (over 20 flavours of vodka shots) in the Alps. The music is an eclectic mix (anywhere from cheesy pop to hip hop, rap and house), and is usually adapted to suit the

crowds. Pool and table football tables also help to entertain the masses. The restaurant (open 5–11.30pm) serves steaks, fresh fish and vegi dishes and, in the summer, BBQs are held on the outside terrace, which is used as an après ski terrace during the winter.

The Boardroom (previously Bôum Bôum) changed hands in 2004. It benefits from a very central location on the main street and a terrace that receives the sun 1–6pm. It opens 11am–2am and serves food (that they fetch from a local take-out) all day. At happy hour, usually 7–9pm, free tapas is available. Its plasma TVs show videos during the day as well as all the major sporting events. Amongst the variety of drinks and cocktails available, they also have an interesting range of absinth cocktails for the more courageous drinkers. Mezzanine (www.mezzaninebar.com) is a small bar, towards the Mont de Lans end of town, that does great cocktails and is the only place in town to serve the lethal 'Mutzig' beer.

There are a few clubs that are open until 5am, the best being the **Bresilien** and the **Avalanche**. The Avalanche, towards the Venosc end of town, isn't huge but has plenty of atmosphere and regularly has DJs playing to keep the crowds entertained. It's a funky club and is right next door to Smithy's, so there's no need to get cold – just stumble on over.

Useful facts and phone numbers

Tourist office

T: 00 33 (0)4 76 79 22 00
F: 00 33 (0)4 76 79 01 38
E: les2alps@les2alpes.com
W: www.les2alpes.com
     www.2alpesexperience.com will also give you more information on the resort

Direct reservations

T: 0033 (0)4 76 79 24 38
F: 0033 (0)4 76 79 51 13
E: Res2alp@les2alpes.com
• Weather information:
     00 33 (0)8 92 68 02 38

Emergency services

• In a medical emergency dial 15, for the fire brigade call 18, or 112 for either from a mobile.
• Police: 04 76 79 24 24/ 04 76 79 26 11

Doctors

• Centre Clinique des 2 Alpes:
  04 76 79 20 03
• Centre Médical du Lauvitel:
  04 76 80 52 48
• Doctor Labalette, Rue des Perrons:
  04 76 80 51 40

Taxis

• Trans'Oisans Taxis: 04 76 80 06 97/ 06 82 58 08 46

Getting there

By car

Take the motorway direct from Paris (643km) or Lyon (170km/2-hour drive approximately) to Grenoble (turn off n8 Briançon, Vizelle, stations de l'Oisans), then RN 91 in the direction of Briançon via Bourg d'Oisans. Turn right at Barrage du Chambon (Chambon dam) and take the D213. If you are driving from the UK, it's about 950–1130km from the channel ports.

By coach

Eurolines run a bus from London to Grenoble, where you can pick up the VFD/ Satobus connection to Les Deux Alpes.

By plane

Geneva (220km) Connect to Les Deux Alpes by VDF coaches via Grenoble – 3-hour drive.
Lyon St Exupery (170km) Connect to Les Deux Alpes by Satobus – 2-hour drive.
Grenoble St Genoir (110km) is closer but is no longer serviced by a schedule airline, although charter flights still operate – 1.5-hour drive. N.B. Bear in mind that car hire from the airport can be reasonable if you book far enough in advance and can be a lot less hassle than bus transfers.

By train

Take the TGV direct from Paris to Grenoble (3 hours). Connect from Grenoble to Les Deux Alpes by VDF coaches.
VDF coaches reservations: 00 33 (0)4 76 60 47 08, www.vfd.fr. Single from Geneva to Grenoble €25.50. Single from Grenoble to Les Deux Alpes €4.90.
Satobus: 0033 (0)4 72 35 94 96, www.satobus-alps.com
SNCF: 0033 (0)8 92 35 35 35

La Grave

There is nowhere like it in Europe,

it's simply incredible

On the slopes	
Snow reliability	✽ ✽ ✽ ✽
Parks	–
Off-piste	✽ ✽ ✽ ✽ ✽
Off the slopes	
Après ski	✽ ✽
Nightlife	✽ ✽
Eating out	✽ ✽
Resort charm	✽ ✽ ✽ ✽

The resort

You shouldn't come here if…

- you like cruising round between mountain restaurants.
- the idea of a steep red run sets you panicking.
- you place great importance on a resort's provision of late-night drinking holes.
- you won't stay in hotels that have less than 4 stars.
- you are a snow-park junkie.
- you couldn't fathom the thought of skiing (if applicable) on skis that are anything less than about 195cm – they'd call you a pussy.

And, to be honest, we hope that this includes most people because if you all came, you'd spoil it. However, if you are still interested, you'll have the most amazing time of your life on this mountain. It really has to be seen, you can't do it justice on paper. It takes the mountains back to how they used to be, and how they should be, completely opposite to the crowded, motorway-style runs that now shroud most resorts. You will not see lifts (apart from the one old-school bubble that takes you to 3200m), you will not see coloured poles marking nicely groomed runs (as there aren't any), you will not see ski patrols (there is only the great Jean-Charles who starts the morning at the bottom of the lift to provide you with invaluable info about the avalanche risk, etc. – then he's off skiing), you won't see anything to warn you about rocks, cliff drops or crevasses (of which there are many), you probably even won't see other skiers or boarders; you will simply see the majestic, imposing and commanding mountains – and they're all yours. With a vertical drop of 2150m from top to bottom, the devoted freerider will be in heaven.

If you do come to La Grave you will need, without question, all the avalanche-safety gear (probe, shovel and transceiver) and enough money to invest in a guide, or know someone who knows the mountain well. It's not that it's not safe to be without one – it's no different to anywhere else, you just won't have a clue where you're going and you will, for definite, get completely lost, which would be a shame as no one's there to come and find you. You also need to be in pretty good physical condition.

The mountains

Height: 1400–3550m

Ability	Rating
Expert	✽ ✽ ✽ ✽ ✽
Intermediate	✽ ✽
Beginner	✽

Getting about

The whole mountain is available to ride, depending on your ability. They do have some set itineraries but they are pretty much impossible to follow without a guide, never mind if you want to explore the couloirs and hidden areas. If, for some unknown reason, you do want to leave this beautiful mountain, La Grave is also connected with Les Deux Alpes, although there is a walk involved. If you are a beginner and you somehow end up in La Grave, La Chazelet is nearby and a good place to learn. (If you need lessons contact the ESF: 0033 (0)4 76 79 92 86.)

"You'll have the most amazing time of your life on this mountain"

The one and only cable car takes you right to the top of the mountain and takes around 30 minutes in total. There are a few stops, and the usual course of action is to take the lift right to 3200m first thing and then ride down to P1 (the first stop) and take the lift back up. You'll probably manage this three to four times in one day. At first you may think the cable car is too slow but after a couple of runs you'll welcome the break and, if you think about it, if it went any quicker it would allow more people to be on the mountain at once which is against the philosophy of La Grave.

Be sure that you prepare yourself with sufficient safety equipment and knowledge. For example, for some couloirs you need ropes and climbing equipment to lower yourself in – do your homework before you set off. If you have any questions, make sure you seek out the patrouilleur (not ski patrol, we hasten to add), Jean-Charles, as he is the best person to help you. He usually resides in the wooden chalet by the lift pass office.

The park

The mountain is your park. Having anything man-made in La Grave would be an insult and is unnecessary. We bet that you completely forget about parks when you get up here; it's a mountain for the true soul riders.

Backcountry

For years one of Pat's closest friends and favourite ski buddies, Andy Bowern (ex big-mountain competitor), has been raving about La Grave and telling us we have to check it out. When we did, we were still unprepared for the experience. From the moment you step on the lift you know that you're about to start an amazing adventure. We were lucky enough to have Jean-Charles (top patrouilleur) and Nials (a fantastic skier who works for the tourist office), to show us around the mountain. As you step off the lift at the top of the mountain (3200m), you can tell in an instant that you are somewhere special and unique. As we have already mentioned (and can't stop raving about), there are no marked pistes, no ski/ board schools and no ski patrol. Therefore, it is 100 per cent certain that you need a guide, especially if you have not been here before. We bumped into a couple of people who ventured up without a guide and they looked very confused, lost,

and, if we're not mistaken, a little scared. Without a guide, you will also miss out on some of the best areas.

One of the first places to check out for your warm-up run is the classic itinery: les Vallons (turn left as you exit the lift). If you get to do this after a snow storm, you'll be in heaven. If not, you'll still be amazed by the challenging and fun terrain and you can really let yourself go. It's a long-lasting run and the likelihood is that you won't bump into a single person on your way down. Your guide can also show you some great couloirs if you're up for it. On this run, our favourites were the Triffides couloirs; we checked out Triffide 1 which is at the top of Les Ruilliains. The chances are that your guide will rope you in and then it opens up into one nice shoot. You need to make sure the snow's in good condition as you wouldn't want to attempt this when it's icy or windy.

> ## "The likelihood is that you won't bump into a single person on your way down"

If you turn right on exiting the lift, you can set out along the Chancel, another classic itinery, with some exciting deviations. One such digression was over to English Man Valley (nicknamed by the locals) where we skied a couloir called the Banane, approximately 150m long. It's quite steep at the top but it's easily accessible and a wicked ride down to a beautiful lake called Lac de Puyvachier (it was Vanessa's first big couloir and she loved it!). If the conditions are bad, and there's too much wind for them to open the top lift, panic ye not, as there are some of the best tree runs at the bottom of the mountain. If there's not much snow, you can still ride some sick mogul lines through the trees.

What we mention above is just what we managed to ski in one day, so imagine what you could be shown in a few days with a good guide. There are some amazing riders in La Grave and all have a great deal of knowledge about the mountains. La Grave, we salute you!

Lift passes	
1 day	€30

Guiding

There are 28 guides in La Grave, ranging from former ski champions to locals who've lived here forever.

Bureau des Guides

On a one-day tour you will discover the classic off-piste descents of Vallons de al Meije and Chancel in a group of 1–8 people. They can also take you to couloirs and the steeper, secret spots, depending on the level of the group. Other courses include off-piste awareness courses, ice climbing, winter mountaineering, heliskiing, ski touring and paragliding (€130 per person). A private guide costs from €270 per day and a day's skiing within a group at a similar level costs €70.

T: 0033 (0)4 76 79 90 21

E: meijenet@aol.com

W: www.guidelagrave.com

Safari Grand Oisans

The Safari Grand Oisans is for skilled skiers or snowboarders who will be shown the secret spots of La Grave, Les Deux Alpes, L'Alpe d'Huez and Serre Chevalier by a local mountain guide with seven nights' accommodation in a gite (€610–1050) or half board in a 2-star hotel (€820–1265). Prices depend on the number of people booking; two people pay top price per person and five people the lowest.

Other activities

All the activities in La Grave are pretty extreme; serious mountaineers will be in their element. Apart from that there isn't much; this resort is not purpose built to suit the demanding tourist, and thank God for that. Plus, you'll be too knackered to do anything – hitting the mountain, eating, sleeping and having a few quiet drinks seems to suit most.

Events

Derby de la Meije (www.derbydelameije.com) takes place around the end of March/ beginning of April. It comprises the longest vertical drop of any race in the world: 2150m. There are over a thousand participants, on snowboard, skis or telemarks, dressed up or not, alone or in a team and each one chooses their own line down the mountain. For a few days La Grave really kicks off with loads of music, partying, drinking and riding, after which it returns to its idyllic state.

Accommodation

There aren't many places to stay in La Grave but there are some great ones, and nothing's too expensive. L'Edelweiss (0033 (0)4 76 79 90 93, info@hotel-edelweiss.com, www.hotel-edelweiss .com) is a lovely, 2-star hotel offering a great standard of accommodation and in a beautiful location. There are 23 rooms that are all en suite and can house two to four people. The atmosphere is cosy, friendly and homely with loads of facilities: a TV room, Jacuzzi, sauna, library, games and videos. Robin and Marlan, the Scottish/Dutch couple that run the hotel, will make sure you are very well looked after and, don't worry, you are in good hands. Robin can provide you with good advice about the mountain, he's had many years of experience and we also managed to drag it out of him that he was the British freestyle champion (in the days of hotdogging).They offer flexible accommodation so you can book for long weekends, a week, whatever you like. Half board accommodation (including buffet breakfast and excellent four-course evening meal) will cost you €246–52 per person depending on how many in a room. B&B costs €273 for a double room. The food's great (even the bread's

Eating out

On the mountain

There are three good restaurants up the mountain. At 3200m is a self-service restaurant that serves excellent pizzas, steaks, pork and all sorts. The staff are all really friendly. At full moon, there has been known to be the occasional party after everyone else has gone down the mountain. The locals congregate at 3200m, have a fair few shots and ride down the mountain in the bright moonlight. It's probably not recommended unless you know the mountain like the back of your hand. The **Evarist Chancel** (04 76 79 92 32, www.refuge-chancel.com) at 2508m, just off the Chancel route, is a great restaurant and, for an

> "Just off the Chancel route, is a great restaurant …
> for an experience not to be missed"

homemade), there's a good bar, they have free internet and often have live music events – all the staff play instruments as do loads of the locals!

The **Castillan** (0033 (0)4 76 79 90 04, castillan.hotel@wanadoo.fr) is another 2-star in the centre of town. It costs €56 for a double with bathroom, and €36 without. If you're looking for self-catering accommodation, the 3-star **Les Enfetchores** (0033 (0)4 38 37 13 60, www.les-enfetchores.com, mail@les-enfetchores.com) offer good apartments with dishwasher, washing machine and TV. You can book accommodation through the central reservation office, **Meije Tours** (0033 (0)4 76 79 97 72, meije.tours@wanadoo.fr, www.meijetours.com), who will advise you on accommodation for your budget and requirements, and put you in contact with private apartment owners if necessary. They will also offer you good prices for mountain guides.

experience not to be missed, try staying there overnight. Half-board accommodation costs from €35. The other restaurant, at the middle station, also serves good quality food. There's nothing you'll be disappointed with in La Grave.

In town

There are two restaurants in town that are fantastic. The **Edelweiss** hotel (see Accommodation), serves a delicious, homemade four-course set menu at a very good price and, if you don't fancy what's on the menu, they also have an à la carte selection with a great three-cheese fondue. If you go here, we definitely recommend chilling out in the bar afterwards with a genepi and chatting to the locals, who are fascinating and very proud of their town. The other restaurant is the **Au Vieux Guide** (04 76 79 90 75), down a small alleyway, which is fabulously cosy and serves

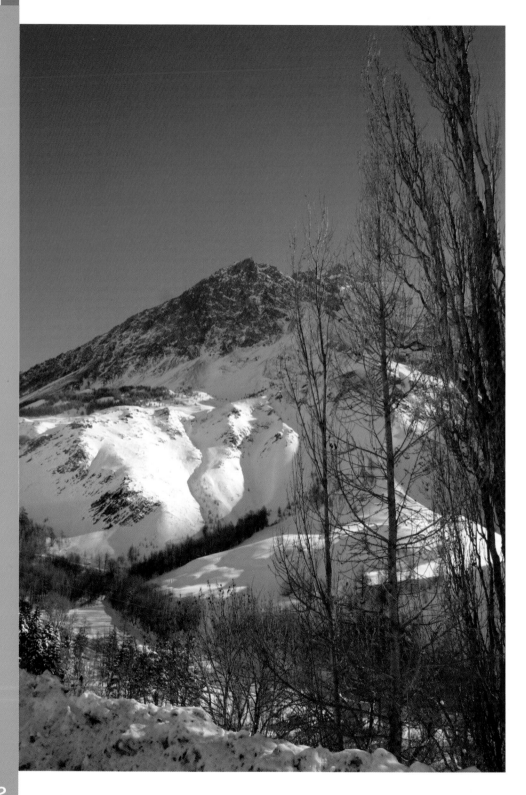

fantastic, traditional Savoyard food. We loved the raclette and left feeling very content; it's a real treat. The **Bois de Fées** bar also serves superb food if you fancy a simple but tasty pizza or gratin. It is themed in a kind of Midsummer Night's Dream fashion. If you fancy a snack after skiing you can warm yourself up with a sweet or savoury crêpe from the huge selection at the **Alp bar** (04 76 79 96 67) in the centre of town. They do all sorts of food and have good hot chocolate.

Useful facts and phone numbers

Tourist office

T: 00 33 (0)4 76 79 98 32
F: 00 33 (0)4 76 79 91 65
E: ot@lagrave-lameije.com
W: www.lagrave-lameije.com

Direct reservations

T: 00 33 (0)4 76 79 97 72
• **Snow and avalanche bulletin:** 08 92 68 10 20

Emergency services

• In a medical emergency dial 15, for the fire brigade call 18, or 112 for either from a mobile.
• Police: 04 76 79 91 02
• Mountain rescue: 04 92 22 22 22

Doctors

• 04 76 79 98 03

Bars and Clubs

There isn't much in the way of bars in La Grave. The **Bois de Fées** is one of the most popular bars with a pool table and good food (see Eating out). Apart from that there is the **Glacier Bar** which is more of a bar/café that's good for a coffee in the morning or a cheeky après ski beer. The bar under the Hotel des Alpes is known as the **Swedish** bar and is quite popular although not as busy as it used to be. The **Edelweiss** bar is a popular choice with the locals and a really friendly place. It stays open as long as Robin and Marlon feel they want to keep it open and they often arrange music nights; the locals all seem to be top musicians as well as exceptional riders.

N.B. Don't try and brag about the 30m cliff you dropped off or the couloir you straight-lined – the 80-year-old local sat next to you probably went ten times faster yesterday and wouldn't even bother to mention it.

Getting there

By car

It will take nearly 10 hours to drive from Calais. Head towards Grenoble and then take the RN91 towards Briançon. La Grave is around 80km from the motorway exit and is easily accessible.

By plane

Lyon (150km) Transfer takes around 2 hours.
Geneva (220km) Transfer takes around 3 hours.
Grenoble (100km) Transfer takes just under 2 hours.

Meribel

Trendy, with a great atmosphere (and great parks), if you don't mind feeling like you are in a pub on the King's Road

On the slopes	
Snow reliability	❄ ❄ ❄
Parks	❄ ❄ ❄ ❄
Off-piste	❄ ❄ ❄ ❄
Off the slopes	
Après ski	❄ ❄ ❄ ❄
Nightlife	❄ ❄ ❄ ❄
Eating out	❄ ❄ ❄
Resort charm	❄ ❄ ❄

The resort

Meribel is a friendly place, dominated by the Brits. It's a purpose-built resort but much more attractive than others such as Tignes, Les Arcs and Val Thorens as everything has been built in chalet style. Meribel prides itself on being funky and trendy, with some really smart bars and a good atmosphere. Many bars are smartening up to fit in with this hip and chic vibe. It can feel like you're in a bar in London, so your perception of Meribel will relate to whether you think this is good or bad thing. Either way, you can't doubt that the riding is fantastic, and Meribel should be especially praised for its two superb parks. Mottaret is not as charming (i.e. it's ugly), and has only a minimum of services (i.e. it's dull). However, it does have good access to the slopes.

The mountains

Height: 1450m

Ability	Rating
Expert	❄ ❄ ❄ ❄
Intermediate	❄ ❄ ❄ ❄
Beginner	❄ ❄ ❄

Getting about

There are 150km of trails in Meribel; 74 runs in total. Of these, nine are black, 23 red, 34 blue, and eight green. There are also 650 snow guns which assure snow coverage for 37 per cent of the ski area. This is a great help in Meribel as the resort is pretty low so the snow at the bottom is often fairly poor. The lift system is very quick and efficient.

The park

At 1800m is the Meribel **Moonpark**, which has it all. It has ten table-top jumps, ten rails, two pipes (one competition level pipe, 145m long and a 125m pipe for novices), a massive hip and a 1000m boarder/skier cross course. It is always kept in tiptop condition and is the main meeting point in Les Trois Vallées. There's a group of enthusiastic shapers taking care of the park every day and experimenting with different ideas. This park rocks. Check out www.moonpark.net for pictures and videos.

Meribel's little brother Mottaret, also has a kick ass park at 2400m; the **Plattières Park**. It has five table tops, one hip, three rails, two pipes and a skier/boardercross. Having all this in the same area has to make Meribel one of the best places for freestyle in Europe. We love it!

Off-piste and backcountry

From the top of Saulire, which is famous for having amazing couloirs leading to Courchevel, you have the couloirs to Meribel. There is the central Meribel couloir, and just along from this is death couloir which is great when the snow's right, and first thing in the morning before the sun does too much damage.

The locals don't like to say too much about the favourite areas as they want to keep it for themselves but look out for the following areas that have been nicknamed by the citizens of Meribel as Super Mario Land, Rock Garden and the Spot. They are all around the Bartavelle area which you can get to by going up the Roc de tougne drag lift. The Bartavelle also has one of the best mogul fields in Les Trois Vallées, which has hosted events like the Meribel Shaker Bump

"A favourite adventure of one of our sources is the Gébroulaz"

"The Magic team consists of both British and French instructors who are a fantastic choice for all"

British and French instructors who are a fantastic choice for all, from beginners to those who want to hook back flips in the park. Disciplines taught include skiing, snowboarding, monoski, telemarking and ski-touring. There are a lot of characters within the team! Some of France's top freestyle skiers work for Magic in Motion and have set up their own 'Team Magic' who now do the freeride and freestyle competition circuit as well as doing demos. Don't be surprised if you see a big orange bunny doing a massive trick off a kicker – it'll be one of the Magic team.

T: 0033 (0)4 79 08 53 36
E: meribel@magicinmotion.co.uk
W: www.magicinmotion.co.uk

New Generation
T: 0033 (0)4 79 01 03 18
E: info@skinewgen.com
W: www.skinewgen.com

Ski Academy
Ski Academy offer skiing and boarding lessons for all abilities. One of their best ideas is to offer semi-private tuition, where you will be placed in a group of 3–5 people so you get lots of attention and can still make friends. Prices range €250–330 depending on the time of season and a 15- or 18-hour course. They are also good for kids and supply helmets for free.

T: 0033 (0)4 79 08 11 99
E: meribel@ski-academy.com
W: www.ski-academy.com

competition. A favourite adventure of one of our sources is the Gébroulaz. It's best to take a guide or you might not find it. It's a good 1-hour hike via Val Thorens and has to be done early in the morning. Once you're at the top you can look forward to a 14-km run across a stunning glacier untouched by the masses.

Lift passes	Meribel Valley	Les Trois Vallées
1 day	€35	€41
6 days	€166	€204

Instruction

ESF
The ESF offer freeride, freestyle and off-piste tuition as well as the usual private and group lessons.
T: 0033 (0)4 79 08 60 31
E: esf.meribel@wanadoo.fr
W: www.esf-meribel.com

Magic in Motion
Magic in Motion are well respected and loved in the local community. The Magic team consists of both

Other activities

Cinema: Check out what's on at the cinema (0892 687 333, www.cinealpes.fr).

Climbing: The Bureau des Guides (04 79 00 30 38, guides.meribel@laposte.net, www.guides-courchevel-meribel.com) offers climbing classes – either on a frozen waterfall or on a climbing wall.

Dogsledding: This costs €50 per person for an hour

(06 80 63 15 72/ 04 79 08 81 55, trianeauevasion@ wanadoo.fr).

Go-karting: On a Monday night you can have a go at driving go-karts on ice, at €20 for a 10-minute round (06 11 27 76 72, pasgirard@wanadoo.fr).

Hot air ballooning: Take a 1- or 2-hour flight for €220 (Ski Vol on 04 79 08 41 72).

Ice skating, swimming and bowling: The Parc Olympique (04 79 00 58 21, m.e.l@wanadoo.fr) is home to a number of amenities such as an ice skating rink (€4.60 plus €3.10 for skate hire), a climbing wall (free for experienced climbers), a huge swimming pool (€4.30) with spa facilities (sauna, Jacuzzi for €13) and a six-lane bowling alley (04 79 00 36 44).

Massage: For massages and beauty care contact the Ludicur health centre (04 79 08 89 08) at La Chaudanne Hotel (www.chaudanne.com, infos@chaudanne.com).

Mountain flying: Courses in mountain flying are available with coaching for the mountain pilot qualification from the Méribel Air Club (04 79 08 61 33, www.aeroclub-meribel.com, a.c.meribel@tiscali.fr).

Paintballing: There are special enclosures at Les Ravines for 'one on one' and 'eight against eight' games. A package of 100 paintballs and necessary equipment costs €20. Call Vincent (06 75 48 76 30, www.ampire.fr, contact@ampire.fr).

Paragliding: From the top of Saulire or La Loze pass. Contact either A-Érodynamique (06 09 92 25 80, www.parapentemeribailes.com), A Parapente (06 80 11 86 77, c.jaud@free.fr) or Tandem Top Saulire (04

79 00 45 67, astro@montagneparapente.com).

Skidoos: These can be rented in Meribel-Mottaret from Snow Biker (04 79 00 40 01, info@snow-biker.com, www.snow-biker.com).

Snowshoeing: This is offered by the ESF (see Instruction), costing €20–45. Overnight expeditions with mountain-hut accommodation are available from €62 from Raquette Passion (04 79 24 10 40, www.raquettevasion.com, info@raquettevaison.com).

Events

Magic in Motion (see Instruction) hold a competition dedicated to one of their friends who died in an avalanche in Courchevel a few years back. It's called the **Magic Dedern competition**, consists of a big air and a quarterpipe and is open to anyone. If you're around Meribel in April, check it out. Contact adam@adamj.net for more details.

It's also worth looking out for the ice hockey battles in Meribel at the **Parc Olympique** (04 79 00 58 21, m.e.l@wanadoo.fr).

Accommodation

Meribel has 36,420 beds, mostly in apartments. There is only one 4-star hotel in Meribel (another in Mottaret): **Le Grand Coeur** (0033 (0)4 79 08 60 03, www.legrandcoeur.com, grandcoeur@relaischateaux.com) which will cost €160–307.50 per person for half-board accommodation, depending on the time of the season. This impressive hotel manages to be very welcoming and grandiose at the same time.

Most tourists arrive on package holidays and there are tons of luxury chalet companies to cater for them, for example **Meriski** (www.meriski.co.uk) and **Kaluma** (0870 442 8044 (UK number), enquiries@kaluma travel.co.uk, www.kalumatravel.co.uk). They tend to be either 'ski in, ski out' or they will provide minibuses to shuttle you about so not too much room for concern. Look out for chalets with outdoor hot tubs.

Le Roc, above the lively Taverne bar and restaurant (see Bars and clubs), is one of the only really good value hotels with a fantastic location in the centre of town. The 12 rooms are comfy and homely and the staff are friendly and helpful. B&B will cost €80–110 per night for two people. Call 04 79 08 64 16, F 04 79 00 48 29 or E-mail taverne.meribel@wanadoo.fr.

Eating out

On the mountain

The **Rond Point** is a great place for lunch and *the* place for après ski, with loads of live bands. If you want to chill on a good sun terrace, head to the **Chardonnet** (04 79 00 44 81), at the mid-station of the Pas du Lac gondola. In Mottaret there are loads of fast food joints that have

> "In Mottaret there are loads of fast food joints that have easy access from the slopes"

easy access from the slopes. Cruises to Courchevel for lunch are pretty good if you've got a few quid in your pocket. Check out the Courchevel chapter for more info (see page 138).

In town

The smart hotels, such as **Le Grand Coeur** mentioned above, all tend to have smart restaurants attached. Apart from this, the **Fromagerie**, next to the 'boarder brains shop', is highly recommended, especially for its superb fondues, and the **Refuge** is a cosy, central restaurant serving great pizzas. There is a **Pizza Express** if you're missing home. The menu hasn't even changed and, surprisingly, the prices aren't much different either. It's just above Dick's Tea Bar. The also completely British **Cactus Café** or **The Taverne** in town both offer simple food such as sandwiches, cheesy chips, etc. and are often really busy as they are popular with the locals.

Bars and clubs

For apres ski, the **Rond Point** is the place to be. It's packed from 4pm with live music and lots of dancing. **Jack's Bar** is also hugely popular at après ski as it's close to the slopes and also kicks off later on, until 2am. It has 'pitcher hours' 4–5pm and 7–8pm and then cocktail hour 10–11pm. It's just had a makeover and looks great. As well as TVs they have a 42-inch plasma screen for showing all the big sporting events and have DJs or live music each evening. Funky, fresh and generally a great place to drink. Next door, **Evolution**, also owned by Jack's Bar, is a new bar on the scene. They serve food all day (with a variety of culinary influences), including a great full English brekkie in the mornings. The ingenious bit about this bar is the entertainment: for starters you have the usual broadband internet terminals which double up as sports TVs for crucial matches. On top of this is a massive plasma for movies and you can even while away a few hours on the X-box. A great new addition to Meribel.

Le Pub has pool tables and is a good place to watch sports. It's a bit big and characterless though, and they don't provide much in the way of seating in order to try and cram in as many people as possible. **The Barometer** is on the main street and also has a number of pool tables and a good ambience. The

Taverne, right in the centre of town is the hub of the local (British) community. It's a really cool bar with a good atmosphere and does decent food too. It also has a few internet terminals downstairs.

If you want to escape the drunken Brits and head for a more sophisticated climate, Le Poste is the one. It is very trendy and stylish with big leather chairs and a DJ. They sell numerous cocktails (for about €12 a pop) and a huge variety of bottles of champers, with prices from €60 to €1100 (a glass is a mere snip at €9). A pint and a glass of wine and you'll get change from a €10 note if you want 'chic-on-a-budget'. Definitely the place to impress a potential mate.

Dick's Tea Bar (04 79 08 60 19) is the place to go later on. It's always got a good line up of DJs, and it's jam packed full of Brits up for a good laugh, although this can result in a bit of trouble now and again. There's sometimes cheesy music, or there can be house/trancey sort of stuff. Just depends on the night. Le Loft nightclub (04 79 00 36 58) is the alternative.

Useful facts and phone numbers

Tourist office

T: 0033 (0)4 79 08 60 01
F: 0033 (0)4 79 00 59 61
E: info@meribel.net
W: www.meribel.net

Direct reservations

T: 0033 (0)4 79 00 50 00
E: infos@meribel-reservations.com
W: www.meribel-reservations.com
Weather information: 0892 68 02 73/32 50
     (www.meteo.fr)

Emergency services

- In a medical emergency dial 15, for the fire brigade call 18, or 112 for either from a mobile.
- Police station: 04 79 53 00 17
- Moûtiers Hospital: 04 79 09 60 60

Doctors

- Cabinet medical – Mottaret: 04 79 00 40 88
- Dr Schamash: 04 79 08 60 41
- Dr Mabboux: 04 79 08 60 41
- Dr Vabre: 04 79 08 65 40

Taxis

- Meribel 04 79 08 65 10
- Meribel-Mottaret 04 79 00 44 29

Getting there

By car

Take the autoroute A43 to Albertville, then the N90 to Moutiers, then follow the D90 for 18km. Meribel is 665miles from London.

By train

Moutiers (18km) is the closest station. The TGV (from Paris, Bruxelles and London with Eurostar and many more cities) runs to Moutiers and you can get bus transfers to the resort (0033 (0)4 79 24 21 58, www.altibus.com). For train ticket booking call the SNCF (0033 (0)8 92 35 35 35).

By plane

Lyon (185km) Transfers take 3.5 hours by Satobus (0033 (0)4 37 255 2555, www.satobus-alps.com, mail@satobus-alps.com). One way costs €57 and a return costs €86.
Chambéry/ Aix les Bains (95km) Transfers take 1.5 hours by Cars Transavoie (0033 (0)4 79 54 49 66, www.altibus.com). One way costs €42.69 and return costs €70.13.
Geneva (135km) Transfers are by Touriscar bus and should be booked in advance (0033 (0)4 50 43 60 02, www.alpski-bus.com).
Helicopter and plane transfers are also available with SAF (0033 (0)4 79 08 00 91 (www.saf-helico.com, saf@saf-helico.com).

Morzine

Extensive riding and easy
accessibility from Geneva are just
a couple of the reasons why
Morzine is so popular with the
British pros

On the slopes	
Snow reliability	✽ ✽ ✽
Parks	✽ ✽
Off-piste	✽ ✽ ✽ ✽

Off the slopes	
Après ski	✽ ✽ ✽
Nightlife	✽ ✽ ✽ ✽
Eating out	✽ ✽ ✽
Resort charm	✽ ✽ ✽

The resort

Morzine is a fantastic example of how a French resort should be. You can certainly see why Morzine attracts so many of Britain's leading boarders and skiers; you have access to the impressive Portes de Soleil circuit, including some of Europe's best parks (see Champéry and Avoriaz chapters, pages 330 and 122), a great night scene, a picturesque village, and easy accessibility from Geneva.

The mountains

Height: 975–2275m

Ability	Rating
Expert	✽ ✽ ✽ ✽
Intermediate	✽ ✽ ✽ ✽
Beginner	✽ ✽ ✽ ✽

Getting about

From Morzine town centre you can access two very different areas. The official Morzine slopes are on the Le Pléney side of town and from here you can ride over to Les Gets, etc. This area has a park and some good off-piste of its own, although many of the more proficient riders will probably head to the Super Morzine lift on the other side of town to gain easy access to the superb terrain of Avoriaz and Champéry (see below and relevant chapters, pages 122 and 330).

The park

On the Le Pléney side of Morzine is a beginners' park with a selection of rails (one box, one rail and one

> "There is a legendary rail by the outdoor pool in Morzine, that was conquered last year by only one snowboarder – Scott McMorris, British Slopestyle Champion. Are you up to the challenge?"

down-rail) and intermediate kickers. Some fantastic parks are accessible via the Portes de Soleil circuit including those in Avoriaz (see Avoriaz chapter, page 122), and arguably the best park in Europe at Crozets (see Champéry chapter, page 330). There is a legendary rail by the outdoor pool in Morzine, that was conquered last year by only one snowboarder – Scott McMorris, British Slopestyle Champion. Are you up to the challenge?

Off-piste and backcountry

The best off-piste on the Le Pléney side of town can be found off the back of the Pointe de Neon – you really need a guide to be able to explore this area properly. Alternatively head to the top of the Chamosa, from which you will find a pretty accessible bowl on the left. There is some good tree skiing around the Le Pléney area too so it's a good place to head towards in bad weather.

As mentioned above, the Portes de Soleil circuit is extremely easily accessible and has some fantastic terrain to unearth (see the Avoriaz and Champéry chapters , pages 122 and 330 for more ideas).

Lift passes	Morzine-Avoriaz	Portes du Soleil
1 day	€26.30	€36
6 days	€131.80	€176

Instruction

ESF

Individual classes cost €33.50 per hour (1–3 people of the same level), and €48.50 for a 1-hour group class. To hire an instructor (max. 6 people) costs €252 a day.

T: 0033 (0)4 50 79 13 13
E: info@esf-morzine.com (reservations)/
administration@esf-morzine.com (admin)
W: www.esf-morzine.com

E2SA

This ski, snowboard and adventure school take freeride, freestyle and backcountry lessons, as well as the usual.

T: 0033 (0)4 50 79 05 16
E: info@morzineski.fr
W: www.morzineski.fr

The Guidance Office

Off-piste, helicopter trips and skiing the Vallée Blanche can be arranged through the Guidance Office.

T: 0033 (0)4 50 74 72 23
E: marcobaya@wanadoo.fr

Traces Direct – Mountain Activities Guidance Office

Contact Traces Direct for information about off-piste, heliskiing, paragliding and nights in mountain huts.

T: 0033 (0)4 50 74 70 40
E: agence@tracesdirects.com
W: www.tracesdirects.com

The best shop in town for ski and board stuff, the internet and great bagels is **Slopestyle**.

Other activities

Unless otherwise stated, contact the tourist office (see Useful facts and phone numbers) for more information.
Horse-drawn sleigh: You can take a short tour of Morzine or a longer tour of Montriond (€15–70).

Hot air balloon: Flights cost €245 (04 50 75 94 00, www.cameleon-organisation.com).
Ice diving: This takes place under the ice of Lake Montriond for €60. Contact Indiana ventures (04 50 74 01 88).
Night skiing: This popular activity takes place on Le Pléney.
Parapente: Try a tandem flight, with an instructor (€60–115), a discovery lesson (€120) or a course to take you from a beginner to a proficient flier, with pilot licence (€400–500). Morzine has a well-established parapenting scene. Contact Ecole de Parapente des Portes de Soleil (04 50 75 76 39/06 12 55 51 31, www. morzineparapente.com) or L'Ecole Buissonnière (04 50 90 96/06 07 63 16 25, www.aireole.com).
Snowmobiles: Guided tours are available for either half an hour (10km) or 1 hour (20km).
Sports centre: Facilities include a skating rink ice hockey, climbing wall and fitness centre (04 50 79 08 43).
Tobogganing: This can be organised from 6pm onwards. Contact Indiana ventures (04 50 74 01 88).

Events

The main events are in Avoriaz (see Avoriaz chapter, page 122).

Accommodation

When choosing your accommodation in Morzine it is advisable to take into account the slopes on which you will spend most of your time, as cable cars set off from opposite sides of Morzine and the slopes are not connected by lifts. On one side of the valley the Le Pléney cable car takes you up to the Morzine and Les Gets slopes and on the other side of the valley the Super Morzine cable car takes you to Avoriaz and the Portes de Soleil. The street of bars is pretty much midway between the two cable cars.

At the Le Pléney side, you couldn't get closer to the lifts than the logis L'Equipe (0033 (0)4 50 79 11 43, www.hotelequipe.fr, morzine@hotelequipe.fr), that costs from €62 per person per night for half board, or the 3-star **Tremplin** (0033 (0)4 50 79 12 31, www.hotel-tremplin.com, info@hotel-tremplin.com).

The Tremplin's dining room is basic but the lounge is comfortable with books, chess and a piano. It also has a large outdoor terrace at the bottom of the slopes that's great in good weather. Prices start at €100 per person per night, with additional costs for breakfast or half board. The **Hotel Sporting** (0033 (0)4 50 79 15 03, info@hotelsporting-morzine.com), a minute or so's walk from the lift to Le Pléney, is a gorgeous and great value hotel (with homely rooms from €64 per night). In the centre of town, one of the friendliest and cosiest hotels is **La Bergerie** (0033 (0)4 50 79 13 69, www.hotel-bergerie.com, info@hotel-bergerie.com). Rooms cost from €450 per week, rooms with kitchens €600–1200 and suites with kitchens €1000–1550.

Eating out

On the mountain
On the Le Pléney slopes **Chez Nannon** is definitely one of the best restaurants. It has a beautiful chalet atmosphere, excellent food and a good terrace. At Super Morzine, les **Cretes des Zorre** is one of the best mountain restaurants on the way back to Morzine from Avoriaz. Both food and service are fantastic. Our other favourites are elsewhere in the Portes de Soleil circuit – these are detailed in the Avoriaz and Champéry chapters, pages 122 and 330.

In town
Restaurant **la Chamade** (04 50 79 13 91, restaurant@ lachamade.com, www.lachamade.com), in the centre of Morzine, is a gourmet restaurant, but also does basic pizzas from €9. It's really cute and cosy inside, with loads of cow-bells and other paraphernalia. The **Farmhouse** (04 50 79 08 26) is a famous chalet above the Dixie bar, down the hill. It is possible to call up and book in for dinner – the chalet can accommodate 15/16 guests, but they usually cook for around 40 people. The best pizzeria in town is **L'Etoile,** on the strip of bars. It has great staff and serves fantastic food; massive salads and good meat dishes, as well as the wood-fired pizzas. At the other end of town is the very pleasant **Tyrolien** pizzeria; a decent restaurant with a good terrace and also a wood-fired oven.

For a good panini or hot dog before you hit the slopes, check out the little hut, **L'Anka**, just in front of the Super Morzine telecabine. If you get the munchies in town you'll want to head to the **Burger Place** at the end of the row of bars (the strip), near the Le Pléney

cable car. They do great burgers, hot dogs and bacon sandwiches. It's a little wooden hut with a good terrace.

In our opinion, although the restaurants in Morzine are great, the resort could do with a larger diversity of cuisine; a Tex-Mex or Chinese restaurant would go down a treat here.

Bars and clubs

For après ski you will want to be hitting one of two bars down the hill. **Bar Robertson**, a local-looking bar, that is a favourite with all Morzine residents, is one of the most popular après venues – largely due to the supply of Mutzig (very strong beer). The other hangout spot for après, and later on, is **Dixie bar**; an atmospheric and big pub (though still cosy) with a sizeable games room. If you are staying on the other side of the river to Morzine town centre you should check out the **Ridge bar** (500m from the bridge; part of the Ridge hotel), with big TVs for sports, friendly staff, hip hop nights and a games room with free table footie. As the night moves on, you will no doubt find yourself on 'the strip': a great row of bars and clubs that always end up packed. The best are the **Cavern**, an atmospheric bar full of seasonaires and great for a drunken dance, and **Buddha Bar**, with some superb interior design going on (the owner makes his own furniture and it is for sale at his shop in town). As far as clubs go, you have a choice between **L'Opera** (cheesy, with cages) and **Paradis**, a proper porno palace, with a dancefloor that lights up, black and pink zebra print chairs and neon lighting. If you're drunk, it could be hilarious. If not, we wouldn't recommend it.

Getting there

By car

On the Autoroute Blanche motorway, take the Bonneville or Cluses exit.

By plane

Geneva (75km) Transfer takes only an hour. Helicopter transfers can be arranged for €993 (0033 (0)4 50 92 78 21).

Useful facts and phone numbers

Tourist office

T: 0033 (0)450 747 272
F: 0033 (0)450 790 348
E: touristoffice@morzine-avoriaz.com
W: www.morzine-avoriaz.com/ www.morzine
     .com

Direct reservations

T: 0033 (0)4 50 791 157
F: 0033 (0)4 50 747 318
E: reservation@morzine-avoriaz.com
W: www.resa-morzine.com

Emergency services

• Police: 04 50 79 13 12
• Ambulance: 04 50 75 91 00/ 04 50 75 93 09
• Thonon Hospital: 04 50 83 20 00

Taxis

A full list of taxis is available from the tourist office/website. An example of price for 1–4 people transfer from Geneva is €115–120. Luggage and waiting time is extra.
• Cheraiet Momo: 0033 (0)4 50 79 03 40
• Heritier Eric: 0033 (0)6 11 95 02 26
• Laury's France Taxi: 0033 (0)4 50 79 06 10

La Plagne

If you do your research and
stay and ski in the right place
you'll have a good holiday

On the slopes	
Snow reliability	�֎ �֎ �֎ ֎
Parks	�֎ ✷ ✷ ✷
Off-piste	✷ ✷ ✷

Off the slopes	
Après ski	✷ ✷
Nightlife	✷ ✷ ✷
Eating out	✷ ✷ ֎
Resort charm	✷ ✷

The resort

La Plagne consists of about ten villages, all of varying degrees of attractiveness, from the sleepy, quiet beauty of the small village resorts of Montchavin and Les Coches to the ugly, but functional and well-placed Bellecôte and Aime-la-Plagne. The resorts also have varying number of services (bars, restaurants, facilities, etc.). Plagne-Centre is a functional resort that has great access to the slopes (you'll be at the top of Grand Rochette in minutes) and attractive on-piste restaurants that have tons of deckchairs with fab views. It is let down, however, by the run-down indoor centre that contains the bars (all two of them), restaurants and shops, which is pretty rough round the edges and needs a good face lift. Bellecôte is excellently placed for the half pipe but it is not aesthetically pleasing to say the least. After visiting them all we decided that, if we were staying in La Plagne, we would choose to stay in Belle-Plagne as it is very central in the Paradiski area (that consists of La Plagne and Les Arcs), it's attractive and has a few good bars and the best club. Therefore, whilst we might refer to other areas, Belle-Plagne is being referred to if we don't specifically say otherwise.

The mountains

Height: 1250–3250m

Ability	Rating
Expert	✷ ✷ ✷
Intermediate	✷ ✷ ✷ ✷
Beginner	✷ ✷ ✷ ✷

Getting about

The Paradiski area (combining La Plagne with Les Arcs) is one of the largest in Europe with a total of 293 pistes over 425km (225km in La Plagne). Most of the runs are pretty cruisy (well over half the pistes are blue runs) although, with two accessible peaks over 3000m, there is a lot to keep the fervent backcountry rider happy.

The park

There are three parks in the La Plagne area. One is in the Champagny valley, and consists of two hips, four rails, ten table tops and a skier/ boardercross. This is by the Télesiège de la rossa at 2300m so the snow is always pretty good and there is no excuse for them not to keep it well maintained. Montchavin also has a respectable park, which has its own skier/ boardercross, six rails, two hips and six kickers. The main park is Snowpark Pro, in which you may spot the likes of Julien Regnier, Marie Martinod and Matthieu Crepel hanging out. This is the place to really push yourself. It contains three skier/boardercross courses, five rails, three hips, eight table tops, one pipe and a step up and quarter pipe! You can find this in the Bellecôte 1800 area. Definitely worth checking out.

Off-piste and backcountry

There are loads of good faces and couloirs in La Plagne if you know where to look. Although you may think you can see loads of powder bowls from Plagne Centre, some can seem a bit flat and boring for the advanced freerider – they can be good to practise a few powder turns for the free-riding newcomers though. From the top of the Bellecôte, the highest point of Paradiski at 3417m, there are exploits in all directions. For a good long powder run, take the glacier chair from the top of the Bellecôte bubble and hike for 20 minutes straight up to the backside of the glacier. From here you can ride right down the back to Champagny, which should take between an hour and an hour and a half. There is a lot of flat terrain at the end, so probably not a great one for boarders – skiers will be poling for about half an hour. You should take a guide, or someone who knows the mountain well, as there is a 20m drop into a river at one point, which you may not see if you don't know where it is. From the Bellecôte bubble you can also take the Trevasse chair from which you can either hike up to tackle the challenging terrain from the

Glacier de Bellecôte and end up in Nancroix (from where you will have to take a bus to Peisey and catch the Vanoise express), or you can come down to the Pointe de Friolin and ride down to the Bauches chair. Alternatively, the North face of the Bellecôte has some good lines but it is prone to sliding. From the Roche de Mio cable car, come back on yourself and you will find a few great couloirs off to the right, just below the Roche de Mio restaurant. This will bring you back down to the Bauches chair. Couloir fanatics can also head up the Funiplagne cable car from Plagne Centre, go straight ahead (under the barriers) and there are loads to choose from. You even have an easy out – you

> "From the Roche de Mio cable car, come back on yourself and you will find a few great couloirs off to the right"

will come to a blue run that brings you down to the Versant Sud chair. Take care though as this is prone to avalanches. A 45-minute hike from the Fornalet lift above Montalbert leads you to a number of faces although this area can get a bit sun trapped.

From Aime La Plagne you can set off on a momentous quest – head up the Becoin chair and the Crêtes poma, where a traverse followed by an hour and a half hike will allow you to ride all the way down to the sleepy little village of Notre Dame du Pre. You might have to place your car there strategically before you do it though – not much passes through N.D. du Pre and the locals don't look kindly on wandering skiers and boarders.

Lift passes	La Plagne only	Paradiski
1 day	€38	–
6 days	€181	€225
13 days	€333	–

There are discounts for seniors and children. You can also pay €205 for 6 days which would include skiing in either La Plagne or Les Arcs and a one-day Paradiski extension during the period of validity.

Instruction

El Pro Belle Plagne

Multi-Snowsports Groups (one session: €40, 6 half days: €180, 6 days: €250). Snowboard (one session: €50, 6 half days: €185). Private lessons are €55 per hour and a half, €135 for half a day and €270 for a full day. They also organise guiding, bobsleigh, snowmobiling, quads on ice and parapenting (see Other activities).
T: 0033 (0)4 79 09 11 62
E: contact@elpro.fr
W: www.elpro.fr

ESF

Skiing (6 half days: €133, 6 days: €163). Snowboarding (6 half days: €142). Private lessons are €33 per hour, €134 for half a day and €249 for a full day. They also have mountain guides that offer a mix between ski touring and off-piste skiing – an all day activity (€65).
T: 0033 (0)4 79 09 06 68 (Belle Plagne)
W: www.esf-belleplagne.com

Evolution 2 (Monchavin-Les Coches)

Skiing (5 half days: €88). Snowboarding (5 sessions: €80+, depending on ability). Private lessons are from €34 for one hour, from €140 for half a day and from €260 for a full day.
T: 0033 (0)4 79 07 81 85
W: www.evolution2.com

Oxygéne (Plagne Centre)

Skiing (6 half days: €152, 6 full days: €164). Snowboarding (6 half days: €158). Private lessons are €39 for one hour, €188 for half a day and €285 for a full day.
T: 0033 (0)4 79 09 03 99
W: www.oxygene-ski.com

Other activities

Unless otherwise stated, contact the tourist office (see Useful facts and phone numbers) for more information.

Bobsleigh: Between the beginning of December and mid-March you can ride the bobsleigh course built for the Albertville Winter Olympics. Choose from a Bob Raft (a self-steering bobsleigh with automatic braking, at about 80km/hour: €33 per person), a Taxi Bob (a four-man sleigh, driven at 100km/hour by a professional driver: €100 per person) or a Mono Bob (on your own in a self-steering bobsleigh at almost 90km/hour: €95 per person). Book at the ESF schools in resort or in advance (www.bobsleigh.net, contact@bobsleigh.net, 04 79 09 12 73).

Bowling alley: This is located in Belle Plagne.

Cinema: Aime La Plagne, Plagne Centre, Plagne Bellecôte, Champagny en Vanoise and Montchavin-Les Coches all have local cinemas that often show films in English.

Dog sledding: In the nearby resort of Montalbert you can sign yourself up to dog sledding – call Mathias Bernal on 06 12 78 50 05.

Ice climbing wall: You can climb on the 22m high artificial wall (with or without supervision) in Champagny. There are three levels of difficulty and you will be given equipment as part of the package. It is also the venue of the Gorzderette tournament (see Events). Call the Bureau des guides (06 63 18 40 27) in Champagny-le-Haut for more details.

Ice rink: Bellecôte has a natural outdoor ice rink.

Library: The library in Plagne Centre stocks books in English.

Paintball: This can be played in Bellecôte.

Paragliding: From the top of the Grande Rochette, the Roche de Mio and Les Verdons, tandem paragliding flights can be booked. There are a number of schools to contact. For take off from Grande Rochette call Plagn'Air on 06 12 73 66 56, or the ESF on 04 79 09 00 40. For take off from Les Verdons call Planet Air on 06 12 73 66 56 or Fly Light Parapente on 06 20 64 49 61. For take off from the Roche de Mio call Ecole El Pro on 04 79 09 06 68, or Fly Light Parapente (see above).

Relaxation centres: These can be found in Belle Plagne (04 79 09 26 88), Plagne Centre (04 79 09 03

45) or Plagne Bellecôte (04 79 09 22 48) and have a variety of facilities such as relaxation, spa treatments, beauty care, massage, multi-treatment courses, physiotherapy, saunas and Jacuzzis.

Snow bike circuit: Biking can be booked at Belle Plagne from the Ecole El Pro (04 79 09 11 62).

Snow quad biking, adventure trail, snowmobiling: To zip round the circuit in Belle Plagne call Ecole El Pro (see above). El Pro can also book you on to the adventure trail in Belle Plagne and organise snowmobiling.

Snowshoeing and cross-country skiing: These can be booked through the ESF schools (see above).

Sports hall, weight training, snow skating: These are all available in Plagne Centre.

Swimming pool: Bellecôte has a heated, open air swimming pool.

If you want to try an activity in another resort, the shuttle bus or gondola lift will take you between most of the resorts.

Events

A **World Cup Mogul** event takes place in late December in Plagne Centre, where they also hold **World Cup Slalom and Telemark** events throughout the season. Champagny le Haut village is host to the **Gorzderette Trophy** that brings together big air freestyle, cross country skiing, the Mont de la Guerre derby and an ice climbing contest. The **PlayStation Air Games** take place in La Plagne high level resorts in mid–late February. The **Urban Style** competition is a relatively new event on the scene and attracts many of the top, French New School riders including Julien Lopez and Julien Régnier. It's in mid February and costs €15 to enter.

Accommodation

There is loads of ski-in, ski-out accommodation in La Plagne, some of which is not too far from the bars and restaurants either, although you should check your location carefully to be sure. Apartments take up most of the visitor beds in La Plagne (17,210 beds available in apartments as opposed to only 1,024 in hotels) although there are some good hotels to check out if you prefer. If you wish to take an apartment it's best to go

to the direct reservations office (see Useful facts and phone numbers) and let them know your specific requirements.

In Belle Plagne there are two main hotels. **Les Balcons de Belle Plagne** (0033 (0)3 84 86 15 51/ 33 (0)4 79 55 76 55, contact@les-balcons.com) is by far the best, in a good location with authentic wooden-chalet-style charm, great views, a cosy restaurant and bar with comfy seats and games to play. There is also a pool, sauna and gym as well as underground car parking (for €60 per week). Half-board accommodation (in double/triple rooms) costs €475–908 per person per week depending on the time of season. Single rooms are also available, and bed and breakfast can be requested. There are also apartments in the same building if you prefer. **Mercure Belle Plagne** (0033 (0)4 79 09 12 09, H5627@accor-hotels.com, www.accorvacances .com) is also pretty good but bigger and less personal. However, Mercure have only just taken over the hotel and could make some good changes in the next year. It's in a great position to ski to the door. Prices are €112–185 per person per day depending on the time of season.

In Plagne Centre, the **Hotel Terra Nova** is the only one in town, pretty new and not a bad looking place. It has a fairly smart but simple restaurant serving a basic menu and plat du jour (steak and chips, that kind of thing). There is also a bar, fitness and sauna rooms, sunny terrace and a good location for riding to the door and for the town 'centre'. A double room will cost €92–152 per room per day with breakfast. Triple (€122–182) and quadruple (€152–232) rooms are also available and if you want the evening meal, there is a supplement of €23.

In Plagne Montalbert, a small friendly resort, at the far end of the Paradiski area, there are some great chalets to stay in. One chalet (04 Le Genepy, Montalbert, 0033 (0)4 79 09 80 50 – or 01937 5181287 (UK number) during the summer – www.cgski.co.uk, cgski@cgski.co.uk), run by a British couple, Giles and Claire, would be a fab place for either families or a group of friends (there are only a few bars and one club in Montalbert but it's a giggle if you've got a good group). The chalet sleeps 12 and costs £360–540 per person for half-board accommodation with afternoon tea. There is a cosy lounge area with a bar (the monkey bar) in which you could happily chill out all night.

In the tiny village of Montvilliers, less than 10 minutes' drive from Montalbert (which gives access to the Paradiski area), is Maison Astier (0033 (0)4 79 09 26 03, p.sharples@tiscali.fr); a huge family-run guest house and the home of the lovely Paul and Monica Sharples. The Sharples family spent three years renovating this derelict farm house, which now accommodates 12 guests, and the open plan living/dining area has a large fireplace and a cosy, homely atmosphere. This is a fantastic place for families and those looking for the seclusion of a genuine, tiny, French village, yet still with easy access to one of the best and largest ski/board areas in Europe. You will need to bring/rent a car to stay here as you will need to drive to the lifts in Montalbert. The price is €55 per night (half board). There are discounts for week-long packages.

Eating out

On the mountain

On the mountain itself there are some great options. If you head towards Champagny you will find a beautiful restaurant at the bottom of the Versant Sud chairlift, called **Versant Sud**, which can be accessed from the hara-kiri or kamikaze runs. This restaurant, built for the 2004/5 season, had a lot of money ploughed into it – it has a great terrace, deckchairs in which to soak up the sun and, most importantly, the best toilets on the mountain! **Le Forperet**, at the bottom of the Fornelet lift, above Montalbert, is an excellent, traditional log-cabin-style restaurant with a log fire, nice terrace and lovely views. **Le Vieux Bon Temp**, next to the Golf lift, just below Aime La Plagne, is a cute little chalet-style restaurant with lots of character. They have two open log fires and do a superb 'chocolat verte': hot chocolate with green chartreuse in it. Finally, in the middle of the Paradiski area, just above Les

Coches by the Pierres Blanches lift is **Le Sauget**, a traditional Savoyard restaurant with an open fire and lots of atmosphere.

There are also some great restaurants on the piste in the town centres. In Plagne Centre, there are three big restaurants, **Croq-neige, Chaudron** and **Le Vega**, with massive terraces and loads of deckchairs, all serving the usual pizzas, pasta and steaks. If you fancy just grabbing a sandwich, pop inside the indoor shopping bit to **Bar La Cheminee** on the left for a panini, sandwich or hot dog that will cost you only a few euros. In Belle Plagne, **Le Matafan** is on the piste and serves delicious food and great portions. You can also eat at **Papagonne** or **Face Nord** which are really popular and equally good. These restaurants turn into good bars at night.

In town

In Belle Plagne, the restaurants mentioned above: **Le Matafan, Papagonne** and **Face Nord** are open at night and all have a great atmosphere. The **Cheyenne** serves great Tex Mex (see Bars and clubs).

In Plagne Centre the **Métairie** is cosy and traditional with chequered table mats, Savoyard bits and pieces on the walls and tables, and serves pizzas, salads, meat and the traditional fondues, raclettes, and pierres chauds (average main course €14–21, pizza around €10). It's just a shame that after a lovely meal you have to walk back though the battered indoor centre. **L'Étalle**, opposite, is another cosy, traditional Savoyard restaurant serving similar fare with tables tucked into alcoves. For a quick pizza or take out, **Blu Noir**, at the end of the corridor, is open at night and pizzas cost €8–11. **Le Vega** and **Chaudron** (see above), are also popular in the evenings, serve great food and have a great atmosphere. Le Vega has fantastic fish. Also in Plagne Centre is **La Galerue**, a wooden restaurant with a range of tasty crêpes as well as the usual, and it has a nice, small terrace to sit on at lunchtime.

In Bellecôte, the best restaurant is **Colosses**, offering unusual cuisine for a resort – the chicken curry, for example, is fantastic. You can't miss it – there's a red phone box outside.

Bars and clubs

In Belle Plagne, the **Tête Inn** (also referred to as Mat's bar) has loads of character and is atmospheric and wooden. There are big barrels to sit on and a good happy hour 4–6pm every day and live music from 5.30pm. They serve a few sandwiches at lunchtime. The **Cheyenne** is a cool, unassuming bar with memorabilia hung up all over the place and fantastic Tex-Mex food. The **Saloon** is a funky club that everyone goes to later on and is definitely worth checking out. It's open 4pm–4am and often has live music and a great atmosphere. Out of the centre of town, next to the Balcons de Belle Plagne hotel is another bar/restaurant, **Maitre Kanter** that has a big and slightly impersonal bar but has a few cocktails

for €6 and the restaurant is great for big groups. If you're staying nearby it'd be worth popping in at happy hour (4–6pm).

In Plagne Centre, **No Bl'm Café** is the only real bar, open from 4pm onwards and is massive, has internet access and you sit round big beer barrels. It's wooden, atmospheric and pretty cool. After this, the only place to go is the **Luna Bar,** open from 7pm, which is funky, but might get a little monotonous after a few days.

In La Plagne 1800, there is one (and only one) bar, the **Mine,** but it is very cool, and has bar tables set out like a train.

Useful facts and phone numbers

Tourist office

T: 0033 (0)4 79 09 02 01
F: 0033 (0)4 79 09 27 00
E: stations.altitude@la-plagne.com
W: www.la-plagne.com

Direct reservations

T: 0033 (0)4 79 09 79 79
F: 0033 (0)4 79 09 70 10
E: reservation@la-plagne.com

Emergency services

In a medical emergency dial 15, for the fire brigade call 18, or 112 for either from a mobile.
- Police: 04 79 09 22 10
- Medical surgery, Belle-Plagne: 04 79 06 93

Doctors

- Belle Plagne: 04 79 09 06 93
- Plagne Centre: 04 79 09 04 66

Taxis

Christian Bouzon (Plagne Centre) has a number of minibuses (0033 (0)4 79 09 03 41, www.taxi-bouzon.com, transport.bouzon@wanadoo.fr) and will transfer between stations in La Plagne, as well as to stations and airports. They even speak English.

Getting there

By car

La Plagne is 645km from Paris and will take around 10 hours from Calais. Head towards Lyon/Alberville on the A43 and A430 then follow signs to Moûtiers, Aime, Macot and La Plagne. If you are driving from Geneva take the N201 (Cruseilles) then A41 to Chambéry, then A43 and A130 to Albertville then N90 to Moûtiers and head towards Aime, Macot and La Plagne.

By plane

Geneva (149km) Take the bus with Transports Berard (0033 (0)4 79 09 72 27) or go by taxi. *Lyon (200km)* Take the Satobus (0033 (0)4 72 22 71 27, www.satobus-alps.com) or taxi or the A43 autoroute if you're in a hired car.

By train

There are daily, direct trains from Paris with sleeper carriages and you can get from Paris to Aime in 4 hours and 15 minutes. On Saturdays, the Eurostar will take you directly to Aime from the UK. Contact the SNCF for more details on 0033 (0)8 92 35 35 35.

La Rosière

A charming village with good access to Italy's pistes, great beginners' slopes and some excellent heliskiing

espace
San Bernardo
FRANCE - ITALIA
LA ROSIERE   LA THUILE

On the slopes	
Snow reliability	❄ ❄ ❄
Parks	❄
Off-piste	❄ ❄

Off the slopes	
Après ski	❄
Nightlife	❄
Eating out	❄ ❄
Resort charm	❄ ❄ ❄

The resort

La Rosière is a small, attractive, purpose-built resort in the Savoie region. It's quiet and friendly, and the main attraction is the connection with La Thuile in Italy. This appeals to intermediates who enjoy cruising over the border for an authentic pizza, but more importantly draws those wishing to take advantage of the heliskiing opportunities that the connection with Italy brings (as it is banned in France). The views of Mont Blanc, the Matterhorn and Monte Rosa are pretty good too.

The mountains

Height: 1175–2610m

Ability	Rating
Expert	❄ ❄
Intermediate	❄ ❄ ❄ ❄
Beginner	❄ ❄ ❄ ❄ ❄

Getting about

There are 150km of runs in the whole of the Espace San Bernardo (La Rosière and La Thuile). The snow's pretty good and the slopes are sunny. Beginners and low-intermediates will want to stick mainly to the greens and blues at the bottom of the mountain and everyone else can head up to the reds at the top and over to Italy. It's also really easy to drive to Tignes and Val d'Isère (about 45 mins) or St Foy (30 mins) – check out these chapters (pages 222, 232 and 202) and to see if it's worth the trip.

"If you are an expert you should definitely splash out on a heli-trip"

The park

La Rosière do keep playing with the idea of a park; they have built jumps and were planning to build a half pipe. Hopefully we will see more happening this winter.

Off-piste and backcountry

There are some good open powder bowls, couloirs and tree riding, although the terrain is relatively flat. It's not going to get the adrenalin pumping but it's fun to play on. If you are an expert you should definitely splash out on a heli-trip (usually from mid-January).

Instruction

Ecole de Ski et Snowboard Internationale

Heliski or surf costs €120 per person for one drop on Mt Ouille or Miravidi. Two drops is €220 per person. There must be at least 4 people in the helicopter. A 2-hour ski or board lesson costs €53.

T: 0033 (0)4 79 06 88 46
E: ecoleduski@shop-esi.com
W: www.shop-esi.com

Lift passes	Espace San Bernardo	La Rosière
1 day	€31	€27
6 days	€146	–
13 days	€270	–

ESF

Not a bad establishment, and the longest running school in France.

T: 0033 (0)4 79 06 81 26
E: info@esflarosiere.com
W: www.esflarosiere.com

Evolution 2

EV2 is a superb school that we would definitely recommend. Instructors are friendly and encouraging

"Instructors are friendly and encouraging and all reports are good"

and all reports are good. One day's off-piste skiing costs €270, and a half day €150. For heliskiing, one drop on Miravidi (3066m) costs €145 per person, one drop on Freduaz (2900m) costs €150, one drop on Ruitor (3300m) costs €160, 2 drops (Miravidi or Ouille, and Ruitor) costs €240 and 3 drops (Miravidi or Ouille then Freduaz or Ouille Miavidi Sud) is €220. All prices are on the basis of a minimum of 4 people. A 1-hour private lesson costs €33 and a day with a private instructor €245.

T: 0033 (0)4 79 40 19 80
E: larosiere@evolution2.com
W: www.evolution2.com

Other activities

Evolution 2: This school (details above) organises loads of activities including driving packs of dogs (€35 for 30 mins, €110 for 3 hours), helicopter flights (€95 for 20 mins), ice diving in Tignes (€75 for 1 hour),

Paragliding (€80 for 30 mins), ice climbing in Val d'Isère (€60 for 3 hours) or snowmobiling (prices on request).

Cinema: The cinema (04 79 06 86 04) shows films in English. In bad weather there are extra showings in the afternoons.

Fitness centre, jacuzzi and gym: The fitness centre (04 79 06 86 95, fitness73@aol.com) has a sauna, hammam, Jacuzzi and a gym and weight training room.

Accommodation

Le Relais du Petit St Bernard (0033 (0)4 79 06 80 48, info@petit-saint-bernard.com) is right at the foot of the slopes. It's only a 2 star, but it's comfortable and the prices reflect its category at only €46–60 per night (B&B). Half board and full board prices are also available on request. Le Plein Soleil (0033 (0)4 79 06 80 43) is centrally located too. All hotels in town are 2 stars, but as long as you're not expecting anything too special you shouldn't be disappointed. There are loads of apartments available which can be booked on the tourist office website and www.ifyouski.com is the best place to book chalet accommodation – they have a huge range.

Eating out

On the mountain

The **Traversette** (06 11 70 51 07), at the bottom of the Fort chair is one of the best places to stop in La Rosière. The **San Bernado** (01 65 84 14 44) at the border is another good choice, and the **Riondet** (01 65 88 40 06) over on the La Thuile side does tasty raclette.

In town

The **Yeti** (04 79 06 83 17) is one of the friendliest restaurants in town and they serve some great cocktails and shots into the bargain. They do great pasta, pizza, meat, fish and Savoyard specialities. The **Chalet** (04 79 06 80 79) and **Le Turia** (04 79 06 13 65) are the two smartest restaurants in town. Le Turia serves Lebonese dishes, meat and fish skewers to cook at the table and gourmet menus.

Bars and clubs

There aren't a great many bars in town. The **Yeti** is a good little hangout as well as restaurant, and they have the odd live music night. **Le Petit Relais** isn't bad for après and **Arpin's** has karaoke and a pool table. **Le Pub** is one of the most popular places to go and it's the only real club in town. The **Roc Noir** is where most of the season workers go; it has a good happy hour and it's the best place to be later on at night.

Useful facts and phone numbers

Tourist office

T: 0033 (0)4 79 068 051
F: 0033 (0)4 79 068 320
E: info@larosiere.net
W: www.larosiere.net

Direct reservations

T: 0033 (0)4 79 06 83 92
E: reservation@larosiere.net
W: www.larosiere.net/uk/reservation.html

Emergency services

- Local Police: 04 79 06 86 60
- Police, Bourg St Maurice (23km): 04 79 07 04 25
- Ambulance, Bourg St Maurice: 04 79 07 23 60

Doctors

- Chemist: 04 79 06 86 00
- Dr Nawi: 04 79 06 89 09
- Nurses, Bourg St Maurice: 04 79 07 10 95
- Hospital, Bourg St Maurice: 04 79 41 79 79

Taxis

- Bontoux Michel Taxi: 04 79 41 02 05
- Jean-Pierre Taxi: 06 26 45 94 16
- Minibus hire with chauffeur, Mr Prud-homme: 04 79 06 84 55

Getting there

By car

Take the motorway to Albertville and then the dual carriageway N90 to Moutiers. Continue on the N90 to Bourg St Maurice and then to La Rosière, in the direction of the Petit St Bernard Pass (this pass is closed in the winter; you can access La Rosière but you will not be able to drive this way into Italy).

By plane

Geneva (170km) From the airport you can transfer by bus (0041 (0)22 798 20 00, www.alpski-bus .com).
Lyon (225km) From the airport you can transfer by bus (0033 (0)4 37 25 52 55, www.satobus-alps .com).

St Foy

An unspoilt gem, with almost endless powder - it probably won't stay undiscovered for much longer, so hurry

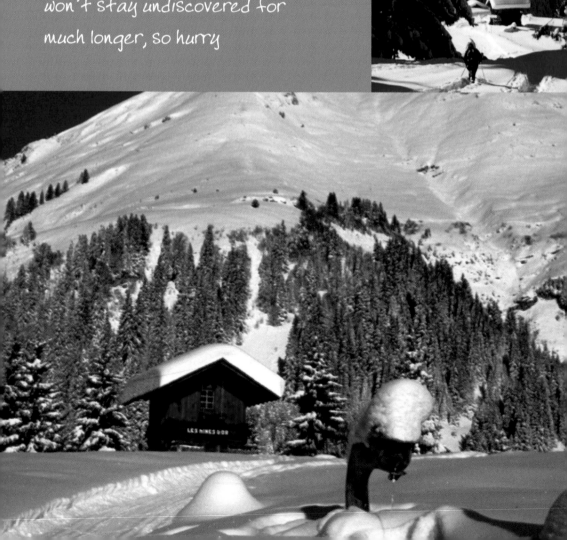

On the slopes	
Snow reliability	✱ ✱ ✱
Parks	–
Off-piste	✱ ✱ ✱ ✱ ✱
Off the slopes	
Après ski	✱
Nightlife	✱
Eating out	✱ ✱
Resort charm	✱ ✱ ✱ ✱

The resort

St Foy is a beautiful, traditional and authentic alpine resort. There are none of the big, ugly buildings that plague many of the big European resorts; all of the buildings are nestled amongst the trees, and built in the traditional chalet-style, using local wood and stone. Don't come here if you are looking for crazy nights out though, as it won't happen. If you take your riding seriously and want to explore, St Foy is the place to be, as it has some of the best freeriding terrain around.

The mountains

Height: 1550–2620m

Ability	Rating
Expert	✱ ✱ ✱ ✱
Intermediate	✱ ✱ ✱
Beginner	✱ ✱ ✱

Getting about

Unless you're staying right by the lifts, you'll need to get the free shuttle bus from the main village to the slopes. St Foy only has three chairlifts, and just 25km of slopes, adding to its character and charm, so getting about the slopes shouldn't be too much of a mind-bender (unless you are exploring the backcountry, in which case you will need a guide). These three chairlifts will eventually take you to the top of the Col de l'Aiguille at 2612m and from here the backcountry adventures begin. St Foy is also on the road to Val d'Isère and Tignes, so day trips are possible if you want to explore some different terrain.

The park

A few years ago St Foy decided to make a half-decent park, but they have now stopped maintaining it. There is far too much amazing terrain for this to worry you though and there are loads of great areas for building backcountry kickers if your heart is set on freestyle.

Off-piste and backcountry

St Foy is one of our favourite places for venturing out into the backcountry or off-piste. The resort is still fairly unheard of, which the regulars love as there are never any lift queues. It does, however, attract the powder hounds from Val, Tignes and La Rosière on a blue bird powder day.

As you are slowly making your way up the chairlifts, it's fairly easy to see the area's potential and spot some good lines. Further exploration of this backcountry playground will unearth some sweet faces and a few decent size cliffs. A guide can take you from the top of the Col de l'Aiguille through lots of little derelict villages, coming out on the main road between Val d'Isère/Tignes and St Foy (you can come back to the bottom of the resort if you know where you're going).One of the most spectacular

> ## "One of the most spectacular routes takes you though the deserted farming hamlet of Le Monal"

routes takes you though the deserted farming hamlet of Le Monal, with amazing views of Mont Pourri. It is also worth employing the services of a guide in order to explore the infamous 1700m vertical descent of the north face of Fogliettaz, which retains a good quality of snow long after other routes have been skied out. Lower down there are some superb tree runs to be had.

Generally, the terrain is challenging so you should make sure that you know what you're doing. It's also advisable to hire a guide to make the most of this area. We are very lucky to have been shown the area over the years by top British photographers such as St Foy locals Mark and Holly Junak and Adrian Myers.

N.B. There have been many reports of avalanching in St Foy so be careful, be aware of the conditions and check with the pisteurs before attempting anything you're not sure about.

Lift passes	
1 day	€14.50
6 days	€79
Season pass	Just €130!

If you buy a lift pass for 6 days or more, you can get a discount for a day's riding in the Espace Killy (Val d'Isère and Tignes).

Instruction

ESF
Group lessons: 2.5 hours €22, 6 half days €120.
Private lessons: €30 per hour for 1 person, €35 for 2 people and €45 for 3/4 people.
Off-piste to Le Monal (€120, 6 people max.) or to Fogliettaz (€200, 4 people max.).
T: 0033 (0)4 79 06 96 76
E: esfsaintefoy@tiscali.fr
W: www.esf-saintefoy.com

Mountain Guides
The local mountain guides in St Foy organise off-piste trips and heliskiing.
T: 0033 (0)6 14 62 90 24
E: bureauguides.stefoy@wanadoo.fr

Other activities

Dog sledding: Drive your own sled pulled by a team of dogs, under the leadership of a professional guide. Trips are available for half a day, a whole day, or over

> "Trips are available for half a day, a whole day, or over 2 days, with a night in a refuge"

2 days, with a night in a refuge. For more information contact Stéphane and Véronique Lépine (06 16 48 60 47, stephanemush@aol.com).

Heliskiing: As St Foy is so close to Italy, it is one of the few places in France where heliskiing is possible, with the potential for virgin descents from 3400m right back to St Foy. Contact the tourist office for more details.

Parapente: This can be booked with Laurent Ottobon, a paragliding instructor (06 09 89 65 46, ottolaurent@yahoo.fr).

Ski biking: An initiation lesson (2 hours) costs €30 per person (ski bikes provided). Subsequent hire is €25 per day. Contact Alistair Platt: 04 79 40 11 61, info@skibike.net, www.skibike.net.

Accommodation

Accommodation is available at the ski resort itself, in the main village, and in many of the surrounding small farming hamlets. The chalets are often the most attractive and cosy places to stay and there are loads to choose from. Check out the list of chalets on the tourist office website (www.saintefoy.net).

We particularly like **Gite de Sainte Foy Station** (0033 (0)4 79 06 97 18, www.ste-foy.fr, gites.foy@wanadoo.fr) with Jacuzzi, sauna, heated ski room and DVD home cinema and **Chalet Chevalier** (0033 (0)4 79 06 51 69, chaletchevalier@free.fr, www.chaletchevalier.com) for a peaceful location and spectacular views. In the small village of Villaroger, is a beautiful and cosy chalet, **Tarentaise** (08702 406 198, info@optimumski.com, www.optimumski.com), owned by the lovely Martin and Deirdre Rowe. There are nine bedrooms, all done out beautifully and all with en-suite facilities, and a sauna and in-house masseur. From Villaroger you have direct access to the slopes of Paradiski (Les Arcs and La Plagne), as well as easy access to St Foy, Val d'Isère and Tignes.

The **Auberge** (0033 (0)4 79 06 95 83, mail@ auberge-montagne.co.uk) is a lovely wood-beamed chalet/hotel in the small hamlet of La Thuile, run by a really friendly British couple. The chalet has a cosy lounge with big fire, and an outdoor hot tub and sauna. Half-board accommodation for one week costs €288–497, depending on the time of season. If you completely book out the hotel (eight rooms), they will run it as a private chalet for you. **Hotel Le Monal** (0033 (0)4 79 06 90 07, www.le-monal.com, le.monal@ wanadoo.fr) has 24 rooms, that cost €55–60 per

person per night. **Auberge Le Cret Folliet** (0033 (0)4 79 06 97 47, lecretfolliet@wanadoo.fr) is a traditional inn with only three rooms.

Eating out

On the mountain

The mountain restaurants in St Foy are superb and we would quite happily, and do, stop anywhere that takes our fancy, in the knowledge that we are unlikely to be disappointed. All of the huts are in true, rustic, alpine style. Two of our favourites are at Plan Bois at the top of the first chair lift: **Chez Leon** (04 79 06 90 83, chez.leon@free.fr) and **Les Brevettes**. Both have excellent Savoyard food and sunny, south-facing

terraces. At the top of the Arpettaz chair is **Chalet La Foglietta** (06 17 36 10 88), a little hut where you can pick up a hot drink and a tasty panini to munch on the lifts.

In town

There are few restaurants in St Foy, so here we would recommend staying in a catered chalet, and choosing a restaurant to sample on their day off. **Le Be de L'ane** (04 79 06 92 45) is a pizzeria open day and night, with a good sun terrace for lunches. Takeaway pizzas are also available. **La Grange** (04 79 06 90 07) is a good typical Savoyard restaurant/wine bar, popular for its wood-fired grills and **La Maison a Colonnes** (04 79 06 94 80), at the base of the first lift, is another excellent traditional farmhouse restaurant (see Bars and clubs).

La Bergerie (04 79 06 25 51, www.LaBergerie.tv) is a stunning, wood-beamed and candle-lit restaurant with a warm and cosy fireplace by which to sip a glass of champagne. You could also book the private room for a group of family or friends (16 people max.). **Chez Marie** (04 79 06 90 16), in the nearby village of Miroir,

is one of the best restaurants in the area. Reservation is absolutely essential.

Bars and clubs

As après ski goes, there's not too much going on in St Foy. There are a couple of local bars that are cosy and relaxed, but that's about it. **La Maison a Colonnes**, at the base of the first lift, is a cool little bar for a beer at the end of the day. It's also a good restaurant (see Eating out). **La Pitchouli** is the liveliest bar around, with live music several times a week. There's table football, and the drinks are a good price.

Getting there

By car

Take the motorway A43 (dir. Lyon/Albertville) and then the main road N90 to Bourg St Maurice. From here there are signs to Tignes and Val d'Isère and on this road you will soon come to St Foy.

By plane

Lyon (215km)
Geneva (160km) Both Geneva and Lyon are approximately 2.5 hours away from St Foy.

Useful facts and phone numbers

Tourist office

T: 0033 (0)4 79 06 95 19
F: 0033 (0)4 79 06 95 09
E: stefoy@wanadoo.fr
W: www.saintefoy.net

Central reservations service

T: 0033 (0)4 79 06 95 22
F: 0033 (0)4 79 06 95 09
E: saintefoy@wanadoo.fr

Emergency services

• Police: 17 or 04 79 06 91 03
• Fire: 18 or 04 79 06 91 03

Doctors

• Dr Régis Gobert: 04 79 06 92 22

Taxis

• Altitude Espace Taxi: 06 07 41 11 53

Serre Chevalier

A good mountain
for cruising and for freeride

On the slopes

Snow reliability	✳ ✳ ✳
Parks	✳
Off-piste	✳ ✳ ✳ ✳

Off the slopes

Après ski	✳ ✳ ✳
Nightlife	✳ ✳ ✳
Eating out	✳ ✳ ✳
Resort charm	✳ ✳ ✳

The resort

Serre Chevalier, more affectionately known as 'Serre Che', comprises four main areas/towns, on the main road from Gap to Grenoble, all of which have access to the massive ski area of Grand Serre Che. These towns combine traditional rustic French town and ambience, with new, purpose-built (and sometimes ugly) buildings. There are nine other smaller villages too but, whilst charming and pretty to look at, there's not much going on in most of them.

From Grenoble, the first town you will get to is Le Monêtier, which is more beautiful, charming and quiet than the others, but far less convenient. Next are the two main towns, Villeneuve and Chantemerle, collectively referred to as 'Le Serre Che'. Villeneuve is the hub, with some purpose-built architecture by the slopes, and a much more charming village centre. Chantemerle is a popular town and a good place

"Briançon is a very large town and the highest in France"

to look for a cheap apartment. Briançon is a very large town and the highest in France. The old town isn't convenient for the slopes, but it's traditional and pleasant to walk around. The resorts are really spread out; the closest are the 'Serre Che' resorts but these are still a half hour walk from each other.

There is a free bus service within the resorts for those with a valid lift pass, but they stop running at night. A car is not essential but we think it's worth it; there are some fantastic resorts nearby and the strange climate in this area means that if there is bad weather in Serre Che, it is more than possible that you will find decent snow within an hour of the resort. Les Deux Alpes is a good start or La Grave, one of our favourite spots in Europe for freeriding (check out these chapters for more information, pages 156 and 166). Sestriere in Italy and Risoul are also under an hour away.

The mountains

Height: 1200–2850m

Ability	Rating
Expert	✳ ✳ ✳
Intermediate	✳ ✳ ✳ ✳
Beginner	✳ ✳ ✳ ✳

Getting about

The massive 250km of pistes covers 4445 hectares and comprises 104 runs: 19 green, 28 blue, 43 red and 14 black. These slopes provide well for all levels of skier and boarder; there are good slopes for learning, travelling through the various sectors will please the cruisy intermediates and the experts can pick from some good challenging black runs, especially the steep run back to Chantemerle, which is great fun when it's quiet. Freeriders will also be more than satisfied.

The park
There is a 'park' marked on the piste map but Serre Che has no park shaper so when you get there, as Bungle, our knowledgeable local predicted, the most you could hope to find is a couple of large moguls. Bungle's exact words were that a marmot could build bigger jumps. There is also a 'half pipe', next to the beginners' slop in Villeneuve (The Mickey), but this is also very rarely groomed and the walls are only 1.5m high.

Off-piste and backcountry
Riding through the trees is Serre Che's speciality, although it's not that steep if that's what you're after. One of the best off-piste tree runs is under the Prorel

chair above Chantemerle, where there are some good lines. The trees next to the piste in Briançon are worth checking out too. You have to be careful when you are riding through the trees in Serre Che as it's pretty easy to get stuck or end up at the main road with a long walk home. Stick by the piste, or make sure you're with someone who knows where they're going.

Villeneuve and Monêtier are home to the best big mountain runs. There is a great open powder field in between the two, under the Cucumelle peak. Head up the Cucumelle chair and go for a ride. The best powder is on Monêtier, on La Montagnole. If you are very nice to the locals and buy them a beer or two, they might show you where to go within this area; it's a big secret. Our source told us he would get shot if he told us, and we don't want that to happen. Avalanching is a problem here too, so you really do need a guide.

Instruction

ESF
Six half-day lessons cost €85–91 for an adult skier and €117–150 for a snowboarder. Private lessons cost €31–42 per hour.
T: 0033 (0)4 92 24 17 41 (1350), 0033 (0)4 92 24 71 99 (1400), 0033 (0)4 92 24 42 66 (1500)
E: esf-serre-che-1350@wanadoo.fr (Chantemerle), esfserreche@wanadoo.fr (Villeneuve), esf1500@esf-serrechevalier.com (Monêtier)
W: www.esf-serrechevalier.com

Instruction in Chantemerle

Génération Snow
Six half-day lessons in ski or board cost €116. Private lessons cost €48 for 1.5 hours and €64 for 2 hours. Sessions in freestyle and freeride cost €23 for half a day.
T: 0033 (0)4 92 24 21 51
E: generation-snow@freesbee.fr

Montagne Aventure
Phone or E-mail for information.
T: 0033 (0)4 92 24 05 51
E: montagne@aol.com

Instruction in Villeneuve

Axesse
Heliskiing and freeride, from 2 hours to a full day. Prices start at €80.
T: 0033 (0)4 92 24 27 11
E: info@axesse.com

Ecole de Ski Buissonnière
This school consists of both British and French instructors and mountain guides. Advanced and off-piste groups are limited to 6 people. Individual lessons start at €30 per hour and group lessons from €79.
T: 0033 (0)4 92 24 78 66
E: info@ecole-ski-buissonniere.com

Montagne à la Carte
Off-piste and touring (in a group) costs €50 for a half day and €80 for a full day. Heliskiing starts at €290.
T: 0033 (0)4 92 24 73 20
E: montagnealacarte@free.fr

Instruction in Monêtier

Ecole de Ski et de Snowboard Internationale
Group lessons in ski or snowboard for 6 days (2 hours per day) costs €108–118. A day's freeride costs €50, and a private lesson €35.
T: 0033 (0)6 83 67 06 42
E: info@esi-monetier.com

Montagne et Ski
Ski touring costs €46, heliskiing €130. They also organise a snowmobiling tour with a meal in Italy.
T: 0033 (0)4 92 24 46 81
E: tallaron@online.fr

Lift passes	The Grand Serre Che	Le Serre Che	Monêtier	Briançon
1 day	€33	€29	€25	€21
6 days	€160	€137	€122	€104

It's really worth getting the Grand Serre Che pass unless you're a beginner – exploring is the best bit. There are discounts for children.

Other activities

Unless otherwise specified, contact the tourist office for more details.

Cinemas: There are cinemas in each resort.

Drive on ice: Learn how to drive on ice using a quad or a kart; costs €12–18 for 10 minutes. Contact 04 92 24 78 44, www.slide-world.com for more information.

Horse-drawn carriage/ sleigh rides: These take place on the roads or in the snow, from €5 for a half-hour excursion.

Ice climbing: Climb on gorges, chutes and waterfalls. Contact 04 92 24 75 90, www.guide-serrechevalier .com for more information.

Natural hot pools: These can be found in Monêtier.

Paragliding: Introductory flights are available from €60.

Ski jöring: Get a horse to pull you on skis. One session costs €18. Contact 06 08 93 52 87, www. clubhippique-serreche.com for more information.

Snowmobiling: Sun Scoot (04 92 24 21 79) offer snowmobile trips in which you can either be a passenger (€20) or a pilot (€65).

Events

There aren't any major on-slope activities, but there are some funny ones. The **Miss Chantemerle** contest at the end of February isn't as sexy as it sounds; it involves men dressing up as women in the Extreme Bar in Chantemerle on one of the local's birthdays. Towards the end of the season there is a **mountain bar crawl**, with only one day to visit 15 bars. It finishes in the Grotto du Yeti and you should expect some seriously drunken behaviour on the slopes. Few, if any, make all 15 bars.

"Enjoy a mountain bar crawl … to visit 15 bars"

Accommodation

Chantemerle

The **Plein Sud** (0033 (0)4 92 24 17 01, www. hotelpleinsud.com) is one of the best bets, well placed for the centre of town and 250m from the lifts and pistes. They have mini bars and dressing gowns in the rooms and a heated swimming pool open both summer and winter. There is also a steam room and parking if necessary. The rooms are lovely and the restaurants good too. B&B for one week, based on two people sharing a double room starts at €670.

Villeneuve

The **Christiana** (0033 (0)4 92 24 76 33, www.le-christiana.com) is a really cute and cosy hotel, recognised by the dependable 'Logis de France'. Prices are €68–79 per person per day half board.

"The Christiana is a really cute and cosy hotel"

Hotel du Mont Thabor (0033 (0)4 92 24 74 41, www.mont-thabor.com) is a great and attractive hotel in the centre of town, with minibars and TVs in rooms, and a solarium, sauna and hammam. It is also home to the Baïta nightclub. There are 24 standard rooms and three luxury suites; prices are €70–140.

Monêtier

Those looking for exclusivity and expensive rooms should look to the **Auberge du Choucas** (0033 (0)4 92 24 42 73, www.aubergeduchoucas.com). You can explore the charming and quiet town of Monêiter from here, but you won't be having any crazy parties.

It's pretty easy to find apartments in any town, the Serre Che tourist office will help you out and you can book on the website.

Eating out

On the mountain

Café Soleil (04 92 24 17 39), in the middle of Serre Che, doesn't look very pretty but is good value and serves great food. **Bachas** (04 92 24 50 66) above Monêtier (at the top of the Bachas chair) has good sandwiches and hotdogs, but it's not the place for a long relaxing lunch; for this you should head to **Peyra Juana** (06 81 11 40 26). This restaurant is on the blue slope Rochamout and has table service inside or on the lovely terrace. For a mega-smart meal, with full-on main courses, book a table at **L'Echaillon** (04 92 24 05 15, www.perso.wanadoo.fr/echaillon/) on the Fangeas piste from the summit of the Casse du Bœuf chairlift. Sit on the sunny terrace or inside by the fire.

In town

In Chantemerle, the **Triptyque** (04 92 24 14 94) is a small French restaurant where you can get a fantastic three-course meal for €22. Who can argue with that? For a smart, and extremely expensive meal, look out for **Crystal** (04 92 24 03 09).

In Villeneuve the **Refuge** (04 92 24 78 08) has the best French specialities such as fondues and pierrades (cooking meat at your table on a hot stone). **Marotte** (04 92 24 77 23) is a gorgeous and tiny place, that has the best atmosphere in town and the **Vielle Ferme** (04 92 24 76 44) is the most stylish. If you're desperate for a **McDonald's**, there's one in Briançon.

Bars and clubs

It's a bit of a nightmare going out in Serre Che because everything is so far apart. If you are in Briançon or Monêtier you are pretty much stuck there as buses don't run at night, and taxis are pretty expensive. Travelling between the Serre Che resorts Villeneuve and Chantemerle is half an hour walk or a €10 taxi ride.

The best place to go is the **Grotte du Yeti** in Villeneuve, unless you don't like being stuck with all the other Brits. There are advantages of this, however; they serve a great English breakfast, or pie, chips and gravy, until 8pm every day. There's usually a live band playing – look out for the Harper Brothers, a really good English rock band. Also in Villeneuve is a good **Swedish bar** where the beautiful

people hang out. They also often have a live band playing. The French clubs are pretty easy to see on the main street, but the main parting happens in the bars. The **Baïta** nightclub is open 5.30pm–5am and has themed evenings every Wednesday.

In Chantemerle, the **Yeti** and the **Underground** bars appeal to most Brits. They have the odd fancy dress night and that kind of thing. For a late night boogie you could head to the French club **QG** on the main street.

If you do happen to end up in Monêtier, the **Rif Blanc** is the place to be, especially to watch sports, and in Briançon the **Rosbif** bar is a lively après ski bar at the bottom of the lifts and the **Gotcha** bar is good for a cheep beer.

A massive thank you is due here to our great guide and friend, Ben Hawker (a.k.a. Bungle), sponsored by Faction skis, Animal and Dragon.

Useful facts and phone numbers

Tourist office

T: 0033 (0)4 92 24 98 98
F: 0033 (0)4 92 24 98 84
E: contact@ot-serrechevalier.fr
W: www.serre-chevalier.com
Unofficial website: www.skiserreche.com

Emergency services

- Police: 04 92 24 00 56
- Mountain Rescue: 04 92 22 22 22
- Briançon Hospital: 04 92 25 34 56

Doctors

- Dr Assor (1500): 04 92 24 42 54
- Dr Cuvilliez (1400): 04 92 24 71 02
- Dr Varziniak (1400): 04 92 24 71 37
- Dr Levy (1350): 04 92 24 18 56
- Dr Revalor (1350): 04 92 24 18 13

Taxis

Villeneuve
- Jacques Caillaud: 06 13 51 17 66
- M. Turco: 06 08 61 20 63
Chantemerle
- Allo Taxi Serre Chevalier: 06 09 32 22 81
- Blanchard Phillippe Taxi: 06 87 82 21 21
- Taxi Rank: 04 92 21 18 94
Monêtier
- M. Bonnardel: 04 92 24 41 40
Briançon
- Allo Taxi Marion: 06 09 32 22 81
- Caillaud: 06 07 69 35 19

Getting there

By car

From Paris, Lyon, Turin or Nice take the A43 motorway (via the Frejus tunnel from the north) and exit at Oulx, Montgenèvre, 35km from Serre Che. From Marseille, and Montpellier, take the A51 motorway via Aix en Provence, and Sisteron. Exit at 'La Saulce', 90km from Serre Che. From Grenoble, Lyon or Paris, take the A51, and exit at Pont de Claix, 80km from the resort via the Lautaret Pass.

By plane

Turin (108km) Transfer takes just 1 hour. BA, Easy Jet and RyanAir all fly to Turin from London airports.
Grenoble (110km) Transfer takes 1.5 hours. Buses and trains regularly run to Serre Che. Buzz fly to Grenoble from London Stansted.
Lyon (200km) Transfer by bus (www.satobus-alps.com).

La Tania

A small, friendly resort,
with a big mountain

On the slopes

Snow reliability	✽ ✽ ✽
Parks	–
Off-piste	✽ ✽ ✽ ✽

Off the slopes

Après ski	✽ ✽ ✽
Nightlife	✽ ✽ ✤
Eating out	✽ ✽ ✤
Resort charm	✽ ✽ ✽

"La Tania primarily appeals to those looking for a less expensive way"

The resort

La Tania is a small, mega-friendly resort set in the middle of a pine forest, with access to the massive Trois Vallées. It was purpose built in the early 90s for the Albertville Olympics, and is far more attractive than other French purpose-built resorts. The small, traffic-free centre doesn't contain huge numbers of bars and restaurants, but it still manages to have a lively après ski scene and season workers from much larger resorts in the Trois Vallées come here for a night out now and again. La Tania primarily appeals to those looking for a less expensive way (in comparison to Courchevel and Meribel) to enjoy the delights of the Trois Vallées mountains.

The community feel of La Tania is obvious, and the locals are keen to spread the love, by organising events such as the Charity Day (see Events). The unofficial website, www.latania.co.uk, was also started to share the community feel, and contains an absolute wealth of information about La Tania, and the whole of the Trois Vallées area. The website was started for a laugh in December 1999 when a bunch of the locals came down with flu and couldn't ski for a few days. We'd like to thank Toffa (Chris Brown) and all the crew for pulling the community together, and letting us join in too, through the website.

The mountains

Height: 1260–2740m

Ability	Rating
Expert	✽ ✽ ✽ ✽
Intermediate	✽ ✽ ✽ ✽ ✽
Beginner	✽ ✽ ✽

Getting about

There's a mass of terrain within Les Trois Vallées (600km of pistes in total); some people spend the whole season trying to cover it all. The area caters well for all levels of skiers and boarders, from first timers through to the pros.

The run back down into La Tania is a refreshingly beautiful track through the trees, and a great run on which to end the day.

The park

There is no park in La Tania itself but you can head over to Courchevel 1850 by the La Plantrey chair and check out the park there (see Courchevel 1850 chapter, page 146). This park isn't the greatest though; if you want to check out the best parks in Les Trois Vallées head over to Meribel and Motteret – the moon park is one of our favourites (see Meribel chapter, page 174).

Off-piste and backcountry

You are spoilt for choice in this massive playground of a mountain. You have Courchevel 1850 at your feet, which has some of the best freeriding in Europe, or Meribel just over the other side of the Saulire, and you can easily venture over to Val Thorens (see Courchevel 1650 and 1850, Meribel and Val Thorens Off-piste and backcountry sections, pages 138, 146, 174 and 242).

The local slopes shouldn't be underrated though and the off-piste in the trees down to the bottom of La Tania comes into its own on a powdery, stormy day when the light is flat. In better conditions, the best local area is underneath the Dou des Lanches chair. It has a good bit of steepish terrain with some sweet cliff drops and is a perfect place to show off to everyone coming back up on the chairlift.

Instruction

ESF
Group lessons cost €150 for 6 mornings, and €130 for 6 afternoons. Private lessons cost €120/140 for 2 hours (pm/am) or €295 for the whole day.
T: 0033 (0)4 79 08 80 39
E: info@esf-latania.com
W: www.esf-latania.com

Magic in Motion
Group lessons for the week (ski or board) cost €140–170, depending on your level. A private lesson (any discipline), costs €120 for 2 hours, €230 for 4 hours and €350 for the whole day.
We think Magic is one of the best ski and snowboard schools around.
T: 0033 (0)4 79 01 07 85
W: www.magicinmotion.co.uk (online booking available)

Other activities

Cinema: The cinema shows films in French and English.
Husky dog sledding: A musher will teach you the basics of driving a dog team in the forest of La Tania – call 04 79 08 81 55 for more details or for bookings.
Paragliding: This is available from the Col de la Loze; call Pascal Piazzalunga (06 09 76 50 40) or Craig's Paragliding (04 79 08 43 65), both based within the Trois Vallées area.
Skidoos: Skidoos are available for evening trips and you can cover up to 25km of terrain. You will be guided though, so you can't completely let rip. Contact Chardon Loisirs for more information (04 79 08 39 60, chardon.loisirs@aol.com).

Check out the activities in Courchevel and Meribel too, as they are only a short taxi ride/drive away.

Events

La Tania goes to town on massive snow parties at **Christmas and New Year**, with concerts and firework displays and there is always a great atmosphere. The **Trois Vallées Challenge** in April is another popular occasion, with events for everyone, including a derby, mini freeride, giant slalom, and a skier and boardercross. These aren't taken all that seriously and the events are for both holiday makers and seasonaires. Contact the tourist office for details, or to enter. Also, each year at the end of the season is the **La Tania Charity Day** in aid of Cancer Research, a great example of how the local community of La Tania comes together. This was inspired by Dan Provost in 2002 and since then it has gone on to raise over €30,000! This is one of the most fun, all-day events of the season. For more information, check out La Tania's unofficial website, www.latania.co.uk.

Accommodation

The **Mountain Centres** (0044 (0)1202 653 456, www.themountaincentre.com) are situated in the forest at the top of La Tania. This is one of the few resorts catering for people on a tight budget and they are great, fun places to stay. Prices are as cheap as £21 a night in a dorm or £27–31 for ensuite facilities. A simple brekkie is included, bacon butties are a little extra. There are two buildings: **TMC A** has 32 beds consisting mainly of twin and triple rooms with ensuite shower and toilet. **TMC B** has 40 beds consisting mainly of bunk rooms – this is perfect for groups who want to rent the entire chalet for a week or long weekend.

Hotel Télémark/Chalet du Sud (0044 (0)1202 653 456, info@hoteltelemark.com, www.hoteltelemark.com) is owned by the same company, but is more of a chalet/hotel than backpacker accommodation. It has

Lift passes	Courchevel-La Tania	Les Trois Vallées
1 day	€35.50	€42
6 days	€170	€210

12 spacious rooms, all with ensuite facilities; three are twin rooms, two are doubles, and the others have between four and seven beds. The bistro and bar (open until 1am) at the hotel are good too. The mountain centre and hotel have the advantage of offering flexible breaks; ski weekends or mid-week breaks, not simply Saturday to Saturday trade.

More luxurious accommodation is available from various tour operators and chalet companies. We recommend checking out **Icicles** (0033 (0)4 79 08 81 54, info@icicles.org, www.icicles.org), who have a lovely catered chalet, **Chalet Helene**. All rooms (communal and private) are at a very high standard and five of the six double bedrooms have good en suite facilities.

Eating out

On the mountain
The **Bouc Blanc** (04 79 08 80 26) is one of the best mountain restaurants in the area, just below the Col de Loz chair. The huge open deck has fantastic views, and they do a great beaufort cheese tart. It is fantastic value compared to most of the restaurants on the mountain and the food and service is excellent. Back in La Tania town, the **Ski Lodge** (04 79 08 81 49) is right at the bottom of the Folyères piste, and loads of people come over to La Tania for a massive lunch here (see Eating out). Under the same ownership is **Lodge du Village** (04 79 01 03 55, www.lodgeduvillage.com), an Italian restaurant (pizzas from €9, and tasty salads and pastas) with a large sunny terrace and balcony. The lodge is located in between Meribel and La Tania, and can be accessed via the blue Lapin piste below the Meribel altiport. The bar upstairs is a good place to pop in during happy hour (4–5pm).

In town
The food at the **Ski Lodge** (04 79 08 81 49) is absolutely superb – the ribs are Pat's favourite, and the burgers and legendary chilli burger are mouth-wateringly huge. A bonus for the lunch crowd is when

Tim, the owner, comes out and plays a little tune on his bugle. **La Taiga** (04 79 088 033, www.easytaiga .com) has a great menu, mingling traditional and modern Savoyard cuisine. A main meal will cost you €12–22. New management have created a great new décor and extended the mezzanine level.

The bistro at **Hotel Télémark** (0044 (0)1202 653 456) has some fixed price three-course menus that are great value and the **Hotel Montana** has a varied and international menu. If a fondue takes your fancy, head to **La Ferme** (04 79 08 23 25). Whole-hearted Savoyard cuisine can also be found at **Les Chantarelles** (04 79 08 23 25), **Le Farçon** (04 79 08 80 34) or **Les Marmottons** (0479 08 81 63). Takeaway pizza and sandwiches are available at **Snow Food** (04 79 08 48 99) or the **Bakery**.

Bars and clubs

Pub le Ski Lodge (04 79 08 81 49), open 10am–1.30am, is the main bar and the social centre of La Tania, with the friendliest staff in town. The food is superb (see Eating out), the prices are good (especially during happy hour: 4–6pm), and the big party nights are fantastic. Tuesdays are the biggest nights with some great live bands, and the regular theme nights are worth looking out for. All the sports events are shown on a massive TV and you can watch the footie results coming in each Saturday. The Ski Lodge is the place to be for lunch and at night, and seasonaires from all over the Trois Vallées love coming. **La Taiga**, just across the main road from the Troika beginners' piste in the centre of the resort, has a new modern cocktail bar; 2 for 1 cocktails are on offer during happy hour, 4–6pm.

Le Farcon (Pub L'Arbatt) is the place to go for a game of pool or a go on the pinball machine. **Hotel Montana** has a piano bar, which is a good place to get away from the crowds and **Hotel Télémark** also has a bar. The nightlife focuses around these bars and, whilst these are fantastic, if variety is important you might be best looking to La Tania's neighbouring resorts: Courchevel and Meribel.

Useful facts and phone numbers

Tourist office

T: 0033 (0)4 79 08 40 40
F: 0033 (0)4 79 08 45 71
E: info:latania.com
W: www.latania.com (official), www.latania.co.uk (unofficial, and far more informative)

Emergency services

- Police: 04 79 08 60 17
- First aid and piste rescue: 04 79 08 04 09
- Hospital (Moûtiers): 04 79 09 60 60

Doctors

- Dr Maalej (Courchevel 1650): 04 79 08 40 45
- Meribel Medical Centre: 04 79 08 60 41

Taxis

- Taxi La Tania: 04 79 00 47 37

Getting there

By plane

Geneva (130km)
Lyon (190km)
Transfer from each airport is 2 hours on a good day, but can double or even treble on a busy Saturday or during bad weather.
There are regular airport buses (€83/€109 return – Lyon/Geneva) or you could call the Trois Vallées Transfers (ww.3vt.co.uk) who charge a minimum of £350 for a return journey to Geneva (extra for 4 people or more). Fill out an enquiry form online, email info@3vt.co.uk or call 0044 (0)1782 644420.

Tignes

Best skiing and boarding in
Europe, with stunning mountains,
that are only slightly spoilt by
the ugly town

On the slopes	
Snow reliability	❄ ❄ ❄ ❄ ❄
Parks	❄ ❄ ❄
Off-piste	❄ ❄ ❄ ❄ ❄
Off the slopes	
Après ski	❄ ❄ ❄
Nightlife	❄ ❄ ❄
Eating out	❄ ❄ ❄
Resort charm	❄

The resort

It has to be said that Tignes is pretty damn ugly. In 1952 the original village was swallowed up with the opening of the Chevril dam and in 1954 the Tignes we now know, and kind of love, was founded. It's pretty obvious that the majority of the buildings were erected in the 60s and the architecture leaves a little to be desired. The squad in charge of Tignes Development are doing a pretty good job of improving it considering the state of the raw material they had to work with. In short, if you choose a resort almost purely for the quality of the snow and riding potential, you can't go far wrong with Tignes. If, on the other hand, you rate a resort's charm as a necessary quality, maybe Tignes isn't for you.

There are a number of areas to Tignes which can be confusing at first. Initially you will see Tignes Le Brevieres (at 1550m), a traditional and peaceful town with a beautiful Baroque church.

You will then arrive in Tignes Le Boisses (at 1850m). This area is quiet at present but it has the advantage of having a few pretty chalets (comparatively speaking) and you can ski to and from it fairly easily on some nice runs. If you fancy some peace and quiet and maybe only one or two nights out up the hill, this may be worth a look. It's also worth keeping an eye on this area as there is some major redevelopment planned in the coming years, which could really make Le Boisses a very tempting option.

The hub of Tignes is focused at 2100m, which is split into another three areas: Lavachet, Le Lac and Val Claret. Lavachet and Le Lac are next to each other and it's easy to walk between them. Val Claret is a bus/car journey away from the other two. Both areas have quite a lot going on although Val Claret has better access to the slopes and good parking next to the pistes.

The mountains

Height: 1550–3455m

Ability	Rating
Expert	❄ ❄ ❄ ❄
Intermediate	❄ ❄ ❄ ❄
Beginner	❄ ❄ ❄

Getting about

There are 150km of pistes in Tignes alone. If you add this to the accessible area of Val d'Isère, the whole of the Espace Killy has 300km of pistes. There are 90 lifts and 131 pistes: 16 blacks, 35 reds, 60 blues and

> "Access to this area is pretty swift considering its height"

20 greens. With the height of the resort at 2100m you can almost guarantee good snow all the way down to the resort. If there isn't good snow in Tignes, you will struggle to find good snow anywhere in Europe.

To get your bearings, you have the Grande Motte Glacier at a height of 3656m, from which you can ski a number of really good red runs, in summer (mid-June to Sept) as well as winter (Oct to May).

Access to this area is pretty swift considering its height; the underground funicular from Val Claret takes only 7 minutes. The Tovière area is the way to head over to Val d'Isère, and there are some good cruisy runs back to Val Claret from here. Le Palet and Pramecou are in the shade of the Grande Casse mountain and the freeriding potential here is huge. Finally, there are the quieter, east-facing slopes on L'Aiguille Percée, from which you can ride all the way down to Les Boisses or Le Brévières.

The park

The park at Val Claret has two pipes and a number of rails. One of the pipes is a 120m expert half pipe that complies with FIS standards and the other a 70m beginners' pipe. There are also the necessary deckchairs and sound system without which no park is complete. There are hardly any jumps, and the park isn't the best, but there is logic behind the madness. Val d'Isère has a good park that is easily accessible from Tignes so, rather than compete with this, Tignes have decided to focus on a brand new concept called Le SPOT where you can build your own kickers in a massive area designated for freeriding (see Off-piste and backcountry).

Off-piste and backcountry

In Tignes, safety is an extremely important consideration because the avalanche risk here and in Val d'Isère is one of the highest in Europe. It is advisable to ski or board with a guide or very knowledgeable local if you fancy testing the off-piste. Having found your guide, however, you have access to some awesome backcountry exploits.

> "It can be reached by the Col des Ves chair and is a fantastic place to learn how to read the mountain"

For backcountry beginners, Le SPOT (Skiing the Powder of Tignes) is a new concept for raising awareness of exactly what is involved in going off-piste. It can be reached by the Col des Ves chair and is a fantastic place to learn how to read the mountain. There are seven different zones. The Arva zone on the lower section of the SPOT is for avalanche transceiver training, where you can recreate an avalanche situation and attempt to locate buried beacons using a transceiver, a probe and a shovel, in the allotted time. This vitally important zone can be utilised by anyone, from novices to pros, as you can search for up to eight transmitters. The piste patrol 'mentors' will be on hand all the time to help you, teach you how to read the Avalanche Hazard Bulletin, understand the evolution of the snowpack and have a go at terrain reading. There is also a black run left ungroomed to practise some tough (and more than likely mogully) off-piste and two freeride zones for different abilities. Additionally there is a boardercross course, and a backcountry freestyle zone for building your own kickers.

Tignes also has excellent and extensive backcountry for the experienced freerider. As you drive into Tignes you will see the lake to your left. Overlooking this is a massive face named the Tignes Fingers due to the appearance of the rocks and couloirs. Some of the couloirs are a lot more challenging than others, so do your research. Tignes Fingers are popular amongst the locals and seasonaires, and you can pretty much stick to the area all day long and not get bored. Remember to check out the conditions though, as there have been rumours of slides taking riders right down into the lake.

Just above Le SPOT is the Pramecou. The 45-minute hike up to Dôme de Pramecou will give you access to some challenging off-piste and this will lead you to the Grande Balme just below; another area with some superb powder. Chardonnet can be hiked to from the Col du Palet in which you are faced with a range of couloirs to choose from. There is one that is always tracked out so shop around. If you are after tree runs, the Brévière is definitely worth a look. Alternatively, from the top of the Chaudannes, you can ride off-piste all the way back to Les Boisses through some great trees. It might be an idea to go with someone who knows the way if you don't want to get lost.

Lift passes	Tignes	Espace Killy
1 day	€33	€39
6 days	€160	€187

Passes are free for children under 5 and adults over 75 and children aged 5–12 get a discount. If you keep hold of your lift pass you will also get a discount off next year's for your loyalty!

Instruction

ESF

The ESF offer instruction and off-piste guiding.
Tignes Le Lac T: 0033 (0)4 79 06 30 28
Tignes Le Lac W: www.esftignes.com
Tignes Val Claret T: 0033 (0)4 79 06 31 28
Tignes Val Claret W: www.esfvalclaret.com

Evolution 2

Ask anyone in Tignes, these guys are definitely the best. They offer any kind of instruction/ coaching for skiers and boarders, including the bumps, race training, freestyle, avalanche awareness, off-piste training or they can simply provide a guide to help you explore on- and off-piste (as well as loads of other things – see Other activities). With no more than eight in a group, video feedback presentation on all adult group lessons and lift queue priority, these guys are heads above the rest. You can even opt to test next years skis! Prices are competitive and there

are too many options to go into detail here. Contact Evolution 2 with your specific requirements or check out their website.
Tignes Le Lac T: 0033 (0)4 79 06 43 78
Tignes Val Claret T: 0033 (0)4 79 40 09 04
E: reservationstignes@evolution2.com
W: www.evolution2.com

Other activities

For all the activities mentioned below (unless otherwise stated), **Evolution 2** are the people to call (04 79 06 43 78). They also organise corporate events.

Winter

The Aquatonic Centre: Situated in Val Claret, the centre provides relaxation which will also seemingly promote blood circulation and good skin tone. It costs from €27 (04 79 40 25 56).

Gastronomic Espace Killy Tour: This usually takes place on a Friday (9am–4.30pm) so that you can treat yourselves at the end of the week. Ski the best pistes in the Espace Killy and eat in a beautiful and traditional Savoyard farm restaurant (€75).

Helicopter flights: These cost between €30 (for a 5-minute discovery flight) and €195 (for a 35-minute flight over Mont Blanc).

Horse riding. An hour and a half riding excursion with a vin chaud break costs €40.

Husky driving and rides: These take place on 2 days a week (book as far in advance as you can). It costs €30 to be a passenger, €60 for a family package, €50 to drive the pack or €130 for a half day Ste Foy Husky Experience.

Ice climbing: The keen mountaineers can use ice axes and crampons to scale a frozen waterfall (€50). You can even do it floodlit at night if you so desire.

Ice diving: This basically involves dropping through a hole cut into the ice and swimming under the ice to check out the ice formations. It is available from mid-December until early April and you don't need any prior experience (€70).

Paragliding: Longer flights are available in the summer when you can also learn to fly solo (check out www.parapente-tignes.com). Costs €65/70.

Skidoo trips: There are a variety of different options, at night or during the day, where you can be a passenger or the driver, with prices ranging €16–79.

Ski jörring: Here the skier is pulled along the snow by a riderless horse – looks kind of dangerous, but lots of fun (€32 for 30 mins).

Snowshoe expeditions: Half a day of sheer fun – apparently (€50/70). On the more expensive tour you return by helicopter, which sounds preferable.

Summer

Adventure assault course: Contact Evolution 2 for more information.

Canyoning: This combines abseiling, swimming, jumping and sliding through rivers and waterfalls. It costs €55–100 and a canyon weekend in Italy costs from €200.

Climbing the Via Ferrata: This will cost €50.

4x4 driving: You can either be driven by a pro for 1.5 hours (€90/ 125), or drive yourself with the advice of a pro (€133). You can even have a lesson with your own vehicle (€42)!

Mountain biking: This costs €30–80.

Mountaineering: Enjoy the beauty of the mountains on foot.

Quad biking: An adult will pay €46 for 1 hour and €72 for 2 hours.

Rafting or riding river rapids: These activities cost €46–67.

Trial biking: For experienced or beginner motorcyclists. Private lessons cost €50, a 2-hour advanced trip costs €60 and a technique trial course €230 (hiring the bike will cost you another €220).

Events

The **Free Games** was new for 2005, aimed at attracting the world's top riders to compete in one of Europe's biggest events. The intention is that it becomes the European equivalent to the renowned American X-games. Tignes is a logical place for such an event as the snow is almost guaranteed. It takes place mid-January and looks like it might become pretty big. Qualifiers will be held in December and the three top amateurs will be allowed to compete against the top eight pros in each of the six disciplines: skiing and snowboarding with big air, slope style, half pipe (on a purpose-built Big Air Park), freeride and skiiercross events, kiteboarding, base jumping, motocross and snowmobiling.

A special package is offered for those who wish to watch the games: a 6-day holiday will cost €233 per person for studio accommodation (4 sharing) and a 6-day pass for all of Espace Killy. Contact the tourist office for more details (see Useful facts and phone numbers).

"Attracting the world's top riders to compete in one of Europe's biggest events"

Le Grand Raid is a long-standing event organised by Evolution 2. The idea is that, in teams of two (any combination of boarder/skier, male/female and pro/amateur), you hike to the chosen face to compete against other teams for the fastest times. The competition takes place at the weekend, and the competitors sleep in a mountain refuge. Around 60 teams compete (it is advisable to book around a month in advance) and the price (unconfirmed) includes all food and the non-luxury refuge accommodation! Contact simijohnson@evolution2 .com for more information or to book yourself on! Recently Le Grand Raid has expanded and now involves the Grand Raid Tour, which is held on six separate days throughout the season in different resorts. One day will always be held somewhere within the Espace Killy. It costs €30 per person to enter and there are usually around 50 teams competing. There is also the newly introduced **Grand Raid Master** in which all the winners of the Grand Raid since 1992 are invited to compete.

If you are in Tignes in the summer don't miss the **beach soccer** event in which Eric Cantona is the guest star!

Accommodation

Tignes has 28,000 beds on offer, so there should be something for most people. It is a good idea to shop around, according to the region of Tignes in which you would like to reside. You have the choice of peace and quiet, easiest access to the lifts, the centre of the night-time action or budget.

For a really friendly and cosy South African/ Scottish run hotel in a peaceful location with good slope access, look no further than **Les Mélèzes** in Les Boisses (0033 (0)4 79 06 31 49, euan@topnotchtours.org, www.top notchtours.org). The 20 rooms in the hotel (8 with balconies) are fairly basic with no TV, phone or anything – but who needs it? The hotel really excels in its other provisions. There is a TV room and a big residents' bar (open until midnight) that has Monopoly, chess and other classic games to keep you entertained. The dining room is very comfortable, and the food is terrific. Unusually for a resort hotel and to ensure that the staff really care about your stay, not just about when they can finish to get on the mountain, the owner does not recruit the typical seasonaires. Prices for a week's half board (per person) costs €351–541 depending on the

time of season (one night costs €59–90). Another option is to book on one of the **development centre courses** in which you stay at the hotel and develop your off-piste skiing during the week with video analysis held at night. With everything included (ski pass, half-board accommodation and coaching – not flights though) it will cost £740–1075. Contact Euan at Les Mélèzes for more details (see above).

Les Campanules 3-star Hotel (0033 (0)4 79 06 34 36, www.campanules.com) in Tignes Le Lac is another good option with a good restaurant and a new feature – the Altitude Spa, which is open only to hotel guests. It includes a sauna, a Turkish bath, a Jacuzzi and a heated outdoor swimming pool with a clear view of the Grande Motte Glacier. There are also a number of specialised treatments such as hydromassage baths and chromotherapy.

Eating out

On the mountain

There are a couple of decent restaurants on the pistes such as the **Alpage** (self service) and **Lo Soli** (table service) at the top of the Chaudannes which both have really good views. Generally though we would recommend coming down the mountain for a burger, salad, or panini that can be found close to the slopes.

In town

The best variety of restaurants can be found in Val Claret. The **Petit Savoyard** has a great atmosphere and range of food, from meat dishes to salads and pizzas and it's all very good. **Daffy's Tex Mex** in the centre also has some good fajitas and burritos at fairly good prices (although you do have to pay €2 for extra tortillas with your fajitas – you only get three!). A typical main dish at either of the above will cost €10–15. For a fairly smart night, try **Le Caveau**, a highly recommended French restaurant with live music.

In **Le Lac** we recommend eating at the highly rated **Loop Bar**; they have a great menu and a good reputation. A main meal will cost about €12. **Le Clin d'Oeil** is a tiny restaurant that seats about 20 people, and the menu is displayed outside. There isn't much choice but it's all very fresh and very good. **Le Bagus**

Café, above the Angels bar, is a funky eatery serving traditional Moroccan dishes.

Bars and clubs

There are more than 50 bars in Tignes. Here is a selection of the best in each area.

In Lavachet go to **Harris** (re-named Censored but everyone still calls it Harris), a cosy, sometimes so crammed it's a bit too cosy, wooden bar in the centre. **TC's bar** (04 79 06 46 46, www.tcsbar.com) is a small, English-run bar, open around 3pm–1am. They serve snacks such as paninis and hot dogs, and at weekends they offer full English brekkies all day long. They host a number of parties including fetish nights and the night of 1000 shots (in which TC will give away the first 100 shots, then sell the next 500, then give away 100, etc.) It gets messy.

In Le Lac one of our favourites is **Angels Bar**, a cosy and funky place owned by three lovely English girls, open midday–1am. It serves tasty English food such as jacket potatoes, nachos, paninis and hot dogs all day and night. Babyfoot, a pool table, internet (€5.50/hour) and a TV provide all the entertainment one needs in a bar. On a bad weather day, pop in and watch a film or sports on the weekends. On a Friday

> "A cosy and funky place owned by three lovely English girls"

night there is a raffle where a €1 ticket might well win you a snowboard. They also have various fancy dress theme nights. The **Loop Bar** (alistair@theloopbar.com) is a very popular bar for a game of pool and a bite to eat at lunch (12–2.30pm) or at night (7–9.30pm). During happy hour (4–6pm) all wine and draft beers are 2 for 1. A speciality cocktail is also brewed each weekend. For a chilled out night, with masses of cocktails, try the **Alpaka Lodge**. It has a big cosy fire and a massive Irish Wolfhound to make you feel at home.

In Val Claret, the British-run bars **Crowded House** and **Fish Tank** are the bars of choice. **Crowded House,** run by Paul and Jaffa, is very popular. It's open 4.30pm–1.30am and happy hour is 4.30–6.30pm. Until 10pm the bar is fairly chilled out and then after that is really heats up, with DJs every other Saturday and a mix of hip hop, cheesy classics and chart music. They also hold regular theme nights with a

school disco, and a doctors and nurses night. The **Fish Tank** is the place to be when the sports are on.

For a late night boogie, **Le Lac** (in Le Lac obviously) has just been revamped. It wasn't open when we visited but it looked potentially very funky. The **Blue Girl** in Val Claret is a French club, with a dodgy mirrored ceiling, zebra skin upholstery and a dancing cage to accompany the long-standing pole. The **Melting Pot** is the seasonaire hangout with good DJs. **Yorin** is a fairly hardcore techno club, quite in your face and you'll either love it or hate it. This club is owned by a massive Dutch company, who own the equivalent of Radio One, so they have the budget for some crazy laser lights, decent DJs, massive giveaways and TVs in the urinals!

Useful facts and phone numbers

Tourist office

T: 0033 (0)4 79 40 04 40
F: 0033 (0)4 79 40 03 15
E: information@tignes.net
W: www.tignes.net

Direct reservations

T: 0033 (0)4 79 40 03 03
W: www.tignesreservation.net

Emergency services

In a medical emergency dial 15, for the fire brigade call 18, or 112 for either from a mobile.
• Police: 17 (Emergency)
    04 79 06 32 06 (Gendarmerie)
    04 79 40 04 93 (Municipal police)
• Piste safety: 04 79 06 32 00
• **Doctor's surgery**: 04 79 06 50 07

Taxis

• 06 07 05 84 85
• 06 09 41 01 46
• 06 09 51 90 99

Getting there

By car

Bourg Saint Maurice is accessible by Eurostar and the snow train. From Bourg drive up the road towards Val d'Isère and Tignes (takes about 30 minutes). Look out for the painting of Hercules holding back the water as you cross over the spectacular dam. Under the water in the dam is the old village of Tignes which can actually be seen when the dam is drained.
From Calais it will take you around 12 hours (995km).

By train

Paris is only 5 hours away by TGV.

By plane

Lyon (235km) Transfer takes 2.5–3 hours by car.
Geneva (179km) Transfer takes around 2.5 hours.

Val d'Isère

Val gets top marks for snow,
off-piste, shopping and bars;
we love it

On the mountain	
Snow reliability	✳✳✳✳
Parks	✳✳✳✳
Off-piste	✳✳✳✳✳
Off the slopes	
Après ski	✳✳✳
Nightlife	✳✳✳✳
Eating out	✳✳✳
Resort charm	✳✳✳

The resort

We love Val d'Isère; it definitely lives up to its hyped up reputation and we get excited every time we come here. For a big, busy resort it's really quite attractive and full of sparkly fairy lights. The few not-so-pretty buildings are well hidden. The only slight niggle we have with this resort is us rowdy Brits. You can easily go a week without hearing a word of French and every night you are guaranteed to see a load of drunken Brits swearing as they fall out of bars. In our opinion it's an awesome place to come with your mates for a week of hedonistic riding and partying (if you've got enough cash), but if you are after a romantic getaway or with your family there may be better places to go.

The mountains

Height: 1785–3300m

Ability	Rating
Expert	✳✳✳✳✳
Intermediate	✳✳✳✳✳
Beginner	✳✳✳

Getting about

Val has 300km of marked runs: 20 green, 60 blue, 35 red and 16 black. There are 90 ski lifts that are a credit to Val d'Isère.

There are three main sectors:

Bellevarde is easily accessed by the funicular at La Daille or L'Olympique gondola in town and is the route over to Tignes. The Bellevarde area contains the legendary Face run, often completely bumped up and it's also home to the famous downhill course.

Solaise is a sunny area that's really good for intermediates although there are some challenging runs back to the village.

Col de l'Iseran can be accessed from Solaise or from Le Fornet in the main valley. The runs are pretty easy and the views beautiful. From here you can also access some of the best off-piste terrain.

The park

The Val d'Isère park has always been a favourite amongst some of the top pro boarders and skiers and all the locals are at such a high level that they have to make sure this park rocks. Last winter the legendary

"Last winter the legendary pro snowboarder Gumby, who's behind the Xbox Big Day Out, took over maintenance of the park"

pro snowboarder Gumby, who's behind the Xbox Big Day Out, took over maintenance of the park – a massive bonus to all who ride there. The park is regularly changed so nobody gets bored doing the same stuff, but it always consists of a big mixture of rails, a huge hip and a quarter pipe and two massive hits at the bottom of the park that would put a shiver down the spine of even the top riders. There are a few smaller table tops so you don't have to damage yourself on big ones at first. You will often see photographers and cameramen around here, as the park's featured in loads of movies. This is a place to really push yourself.

Off-piste and backcountry

La Fornet is the backcountry mecca, with access to huge areas of off-piste. The trees are fantastic and there are loads of shoots, gullies and cliffs; a great playground, especially when there's too much wind on top. The Grand Vallons, Col Pers and Pointe Pers are awesome but take care on Pointe Pers as it's steep – approaching 50° at the top. Grand Vallons is easily accessible from the Signal drag lift; for the others a guide is recommended.

> "This run has some of the best back drops, especially if you keep left under the epic cliff face"

From Solaise, take the Cugnai 'antique' chairlift and, rather than taking the St Jacques red run down, head over the back of the mountain to the Cugnai off-piste run. This run has some of the best back drops, especially if you keep left under the epic cliff face. This can warm you up for L'Auress, some of the best off-piste in Val. For this though, do take a guide as it can be dangerous. To reach it, once you have skied the first half of Cugnai, hang a left and ski tour up to the Refuge des Fours. From here it's about an hour's walk to L'Auress ridge, where you can chill and check out the stunning views and then head down the best powder field you'll find in Val. The Bellevarde is another huge playground with countless couloirs and bowls. Couloir des Pisteurs is a firm favourite. When looking from the top of the funicular, you are faced with a flat-topped mountain which forks into three halfway

down. You can take any route, but the left fork (from the rider's point of view) has some of the best powder. Another great run is the Face du Charvet; there are many routes down but it is often best in treacherous snow conditions so be warned and take a guide. To the rider's right is the most adventurous and encompasses great mini-bowls and couloirs, just don't get stuck or go over any cliffs!

Lift passes	
half day	€28
1 day	€39
6 days	€187
14 days	€315.50

The lift pass for Val d'Isère seems fairly expensive but it does cover the whole Espace Killy area. Your lift pass will also give you bad weather insurance and free access to the swimming pool. You can buy your lift pass on-line or by post and it will be delivered to your holiday home in Val. Reserve your pass at www.stvi-valdisere.com or write to STVI, Gare Centrale, 73 150 Val d'Isère. There are also 'loyal customer' discounts, so save your lift pass and you'll get a discount off next year's pass.

Instruction

There are tons of ski and snowboard schools to choose from, so you'll easily be able to find something to suit you. Here are a few that have been recommended to us.

Billabong Ski and Snowboard School

This school has a good name around town, especially for boarding. It also has qualified mountain guides.
T: 0033 (0)4 79 06 09 54
E: billabong@snowboardfrance.com
W: www.snowboardfrance.com

ESF

This is the largest and oldest school in town with over 400 instructors. Some of the best skiers in town work for the ESF, but you'd be lucky to get one. It can be great, but it's a bit of a lottery.
T: 0033 (0)4 79 06 02 34
E: esf.valdisere@wanadoo.fr
W: www.esfvaldisere.com

Evolution 2

A wealth of variety and programmes are available on and off your skis.

T: 0033 (0)4 79 41 16 72

E: valdisere@evolution2.com, reservationsval@evolution2.com

W: www.evolution2.com

Misty Fly

This snowboard school has a great reputation for all aspects of boarding, including off-piste and freestyle. The shop is also pretty cool.

T: 0033 (0)4 79 40 08 74

E: lionel.surf@infonie.fr

Mountain Masters

The French and British ski instructors and guides have a great depth of experience. They are extremely popular and perhaps the best guarantee of quality coaching whether for on-piste cruising, heliskiing or racing, etc.

T: 0033 (0)4 79 06 05 14

E: info@mountain-masters.com

W: www.mountain-masters.com

Snow Fun

Best for kids and intermediates. The first school to insist on small group sizes: max. 8 people.

T: 0033 (0)4 79 06 16 79

E: info@valfun.fr

W: www.valfun.com

Top Ski

Pat Zimmer, an ex-French-team skier, heads up a team of around 20 excellent guides and instructors, many of whom have a strong background as competitive skiers. Eric Berthan, the ex-World-Champion mogul skier is based with Top Ski.

T: 0033 (0)4 79 06 14 80
E: top.ski.val.isere@wanadoo.fr
W: www.topskival.com

Dissent

Chris Haworth, sponsored by Salomon, is a well respected and liked face in the British Ski Industry (especially with the ladies). He takes race training camps all year round and he's the boy to coach you if you are a training ski instructor, or a race competitor in slalom, GS or Super GS. Chris also runs freeride, freestyle and mogul camps with Pat Sharples (i.e. me) throughout the winter season. The feedback from these courses has been fantastic and everyone improves substantially. People particularly benefit from the quality of the video analysis, which takes place with a few beers after a day's coaching. These camps are always popular and get booked up quickly, so get hold of Chris or Pat as soon as possible if you fancy joining them.

T: Chris Haworth on 0033 (0)6 03 28 11 67 or Pat on 0044 (0)79742 05852 (English mobile) or 0033 (0)6 80 23 95 76

E: christopherhaworth@hotmail.com or patsharples@hotmail.com

"The feedback from these courses has been fantastic and everyone improves substantially"

Other activities

Driving on ice: Fancy this? You can have a go using karts, quads, snowmobiles or a Fiat Panda (04 79 06 21 40).

Health and relaxation spa: Hotel Christiania (04 79 06 02 90) has a health and relaxation spa that offers massages, whirlpool baths and a very expensive slimming treatment. **Yoga** lessons are available in English and French (06 03 10 63 95, charlotte@snowrental.net).

Husky driving: If you've got a spare evening you could always have a go at driving a team of huskies (06 16 48 60 47, stephanemush@aol.com).

Ice skating: The rink (04 79 06 05 90) has one late night session per week.

Scenic flights: If you fancy it, take a scenic flight over the Espace Killy (06 07 22 43 97, www.marine-air-sport.com).

Shop shop shop: The shops are far better than the usual resort rubbish, and form a great way to while away a bad weather day. If you're broke, don't risk looking.

Sports hall: Located at the foot of the Bellevarde Face, the sports hall is open 9am–midday and 3–7pm. It has basketball, ping-pong, volleyball, hand-ball, badminton, trampoline, gymnastics, football, weights room and a rock climbing wall. Call 04 79 06 03 49 for more information.

Swimming pool: The indoor swimming pool is at the foot of the Bellevarde Face (04 79 06 05 90) and is free with your lift pass. It's open every day 2–7pm and there is one late night session per week.

Events

The **Xbox Big Day Out** brings together the world's best professional skiers and snowboarders and 50 amateur riders. Val also hosts the **World Cup Downhill, Super Giant Slalom and Giant Slalom** at the beginning of the season and has now secured the **2009 World Alpine Skiing Championships**.

Accommodation

Val has 15,152 beds. The main lift stations are linked by efficient, free shuttle buses. During the day they are up and down all the time but at night you might get a bit nippy waiting at the bus stop. There are ski-in, ski-out hotels but going out at night will be a bit of a mission. It's worth looking around to find the best location for you. There is a huge range of accommodation available from budget to luxury.

The 4-star, luxury **Balme de l'Ours** (0033 (0)4 79 41 37 10, www.hotel-les-balmes.com, welcome@hotel-les-barmes.com) is super expensive – rooms cost €325–700 per night and suites €560–4000. If you are lucky enough to be minted, the bar and restaurant are awesome. The **Blizzard** (0033 (0)4 79 06 02 07, www.hotelblizzard.com, information@hotelblizzard.com), also 4 star, is cosy and civilised with a great bar but has prices to match. It has a swimming pool, Turkish bath and Jacuzzi. The restaurant is good quality but expensive and lacks inspiration for the price.

Hotel Kandahar (0033 (0)4 79 06 02 39, www.hotel-kandahar.com, hotel.kandahar@wanadoo.fr) has 3 stars, is mid ranged and has a great location, smack in the centre of town. It has a comfortable modern alpine décor, a great bar and a tavern downstairs that is a favourite with the locals.

Hotel Moris (0033 (0)4 79 06 22 11) is a favourite of the Brits. The food and accommodation are pretty good and the pub below is a well-liked watering hole. A popular choice, especially for those who don't place pampering high up on their priority list.

Eating out

On the mountain
One thing that amazed us about the mountain restaurants in Val is that they are all pretty good value.

Obviously we're not talking cheap but, compared to other resorts of a similar standard, Val scores very highly for value for money on the mountain.

La Fornet

Le Signal (04 79 06 03 38), at the summit of the Signal cable car, is on the top floor of the building with a cheap and cheerful self-service below. The staff are attentive and friendly and the hearty portions have an excellent reputation. The **Edelweiss** (06 10 28 70 64) is a beautiful chalet, recently constructed halfway down the Mongard blue run, and has had great reviews for food, ambience and service.

Solaise

Le Bar de l'Ouillette (04 79 41 94 74) is a bustling little self-service restaurant that is a huge sun trap. It is popular with instructors and has very friendly staff.

Bellevarde

La Folie Douce (04 79 06 01 47, lafoliedouce@ wanadoo.fr) and **La Fruitière** (04 79 06 07 17, lafoliedouce@wanadoo.fr) are at the top of the La Daille bubble. The self-service Follie is OK for food,

"If you want a good table it's best to reserve and the upper terrace is fantastic in the spring"

but better for après beers. La Fruitière, set in a restored cheese and cream farm, is *the* place to be seen on the hill in Val d'Isère. It's often over crowded and fully booked but worth it. The best tables and service are on the upper tier inside; reservations are a must. **Marmottes** (04 79 06 05 08) is a well positioned meeting place by the lift of the same name, overlooking the park. It is a great self-service restaurant with good portions and good value for money. Outside is a fab hot dog stand and a couple of rows of deckchairs. **Le Trifollet** (04 79 41 96 99) serves the best pizzas on the hill. If you want a good table it's best to reserve and the upper terrace is fantastic in the spring.

In town
Reservations are essential, especially in high season. The **Lodge** (04 79 06 02 01), up by Dick's Tea Bar, is a funky and cosy little restaurant that is fantastic for groups of mates, families and also for romantic dates. Great food at good prices; a pizza will cost you about €10–12 and a steak or speciality dish will cost €18–25. The **Perdrix Blanche** (04 79 06 12 09), right in the centre of town, is popular with the locals. It's atmospheric and serves good food. **Taverne d'Alsace** (04 79 06 48 49) has good rustic food, a great atmosphere and good service, but it's pricey. **Le Grand Ourse** (04 79 06 00 19) is expensive, kitsch and has an entertaining interior! **Chez Paolo** (04 79 06 28 04) has the tastiest pizzas and Italian fare in town. It can get really busy though, so it's best to pick your times. **Bar Jacques** (04 79 06 03 89) combines great quality, service and price. It's the only non-smoking restaurant in town and everyone is greeted with a smile. The pizzas and lemon meringue pie are pretty tasty. **Sur La Montagne** is mid-expensive and serves fab French cuisine in gorgeous surroundings. **Bananas** (04 79 06 04 23), just by the slopes, is a Tex-Mex restaurant upstairs that is really busy when people come in from the slopes and has a great bar downstairs.

Bars and clubs

The **Folie Douce** (04 79 06 01 47, lafoliedouce@ wanadoo.fr) is the place to be for après ski. From lunch onwards you will often find people dancing on the tables and/or roof. There's always loud music, and sometimes a DJ, that you can hear from the top of the mountain. When you're suitably hammered you can ski/board back down (which we obviously don't condone) or take the lift. **Café Face**, opposite Dick's Tea Bar, is a packed après ski bar with a fab atmosphere and an inspired happy hour (from about 4pm) during which the beers are amazingly cheap; the prices get steadily more expensive as time passes. **Pacific Bar** (04 79 06 29 19) is the

place to watch sports as it has plasma screens pretty much in front of every table. The **Moris Pub** (04 79 06 22 11), at the end of town, is a massive pub that has great live music, happy hours and theme nights.

Victor's bar (04 79 06 67 00), near to Dick's Tea Bar, does a huge range of great cocktails and is a bit more classy and international than a lot of the bars around. It's our favourite bar in town. The **Saloon Bar** (04 79 06 01 58) has a fab atmosphere, loads of seating and is great at any time of day or night. The

> "It has a fab atmosphere, loads of seating and is great at any time of day or night"

2 for 1 cocktail hours are a plus point too! Later on, the bar has a funky vibe and a dance floor on which to strut your stuff. **Bananas** (04 79 06 04 23) is a funky small bar with a good atmosphere and good cocktails. It has a wicked group of staff too, who are all very handy bumps skiers! Upstairs is a popular Tex-Mex restaurant (see Eating out). **Petit Danois** (04 79 06 27 97) is a cool late-night bar that has some good DJs and is often hectic and crowded but fun.

Dick's Tea Bar (04 79 06 14 87) is the main club and gets absolutely packed. Despite Val's reputation for being a hive of late-night entertainment, if you want a boogie this is pretty much the only place to go (or at least where all the Brits go). It's worth a visit, but it is ridiculously expensive to get in (about €12) and the queues are often massive. Once inside, it's full of little alcoves and can be fun but it's nothing particularly special and the drinks aren't cheap – a round of four sambucas cost us €36! Val really needs a new club to give Dick's some competition. Luckily two clubs are due to open for the 05/06 season. Fingers crossed.

Useful facts and phone numbers

Tourist office

T: 0033 (0)4 79 06 06 60
F: 0033 (0)4 79 06 04 56
E: info@valdisere.com
W: www.valdisere.com

Direct reservations

T: 0033 (0)4 79 06 18 90/ 0033 (0)4 79 06 06
     60
E: valhotel@valdisere.com/ vallocation@
     valdisere.com

Emergency services

In a medical emergency dial 15, for the fire
     brigade call 18, or 112 for either from a
     mobile.
• Police: 17 or 04 79 06 03 41
• Ambulance: 04 79 06 43 00
• Slope rescue/ Ski patrol: 04 79 06 02 10

Doctors

• Médival Medical Centre: 04 79 40 26 80
• Centre Medical Centre: 04 79 06 06 11
• Val Village Medical Centre: 04 79 06 13 70
• Hospital in Bourg St Maurice: 04 79 41 79 79

Taxis

• Bozzetto: 04 79 06 02 50
• ABC taxis: 06 22 73 05 31 (abctaxi@
     wanadoo.fr)
• Taxi Nicholas: 04 79 41 01 25 (www.taxi-
     nicholas.com/ info@taxi-nicholas.com)
• Altitude Espace Taxi: 06 07 41 11 53
• Taxi Papillon: 06 08 99 93 96
• AA Taxi: 06 09 51 90 99/ 04 79 06 02 95
     (www.taxi-valdisere-tignes.com/ taxiaa@
     wanadoo.fr)

Getting there

By car

Drive via Bourg St Maurice and take the N90
towards Tignes and then Val d'Isère. Around 10.5
hours from Calais.

By train

Trains go to Bourg St Maurice, 20 minutes away.

By plane

Geneva (180km) Transfer 3–3.5 hours.

Val Thorens

If you're looking for a good nightlife and great snow and can ignore the concrete jungle, you're sorted

On the slopes	
Snow reliability	✸✸✸✸
Parks	✸✸✸
Off-piste	✸✸✸

Off the slopes	
Après ski	✸✸✸
Nightlife	✸✸✸◖
Eating out	✸✸
Resort charm	✸

The resort

Val Thorens is the highest resort in Europe at 2300m. This makes the snow as reliable as it can be, but it sure doesn't make it pretty! There are lots of blocks of ugly flats which seriously damage the 'resort charm' factor. Our first impression wasn't great but we were persuaded by a trustworthy source to give it a break and it turns out to have some pretty good points. For starters, it's not all ugly. The cluster of newer developments at the top of the resort contains much prettier, traditional chalets, and there is a lively night scene. Additionally, Val Thorens is very compact so many hotels and residences have the ski-in, ski-out facility and you are never too far from the bars and restaurants. It's mid/expensive – if you want somewhere cheaper you could try Les Menuires, although this place is even less attractive.

The mountains

Height: 2300–3200m

Ability	Rating
Expert	✸✸✸✸
Intermediate	✸✸✸
Beginner	✸✸✸

Getting about

Val Thorens' mountains are far more appealing than the town. There are 170km of pistes (66 pistes), with access to the 600km of Les Trois Vallées (328 pistes). Of the 66 pistes in VT, five are black, 28 red, 25 blue and 8 green. It is therefore more suited to intermediates and experts than beginners. The more challenging pistes are towards the top of the glacier with some motorway pistes that are great for intermediates. There is also plenty to keep the backcountry explorer entertained. The snow is virtually guaranteed and the lift systems are pretty modern and quick. The disadvantages are that there is nowhere to escape to in bad weather as the trees are non existent, and the runs can get busy due to people coming over from Courchevel and Meribel. If you fancy a pretty view, head up to the Cime de Caron (at 3200m) for a panoramic view of hundreds of French, Swiss and Italian summits.

The park

Just above the 2 Lacs piste, at the bottom of the resort and accessible from the 2 Lacs chairlift, is the snow park. The park is always kept in really good condition. The jumps are not the most fierce in Europe, but are perfect for practising your latest tricks. There are lots of rails to jib on which are changed throughout the winter so the locals don't get bored and a 115m half pipe which can be pretty good after it's been shaped. This park has been used for the X-games qualifiers in the past, so it does attract some of the top pro riders.

Off-piste and backcountry

VT has a huge quantity of off-piste, and the snow stays in good condition as the mountain is one of the highest in the Alps, so you can pretty much always find some tempting powder. The Cime de Caron is one of the most popular places to go and has one of the best views in Les Trois Vallées. Some of the riding on the glaciers of Peclet and Chaviere can be totally mind blowing, and this has to be the place to go after a snow storm (with someone who knows the place). If steeps and couloirs are your bag, head to le Plein Sud; these get tracked out pretty quickly but the snow's always wicked and they don't get boring. Our favourite place is the long ride over the Gébroulaz glacier down towards Meribel. You can get to this by hiking up from the top of the Col chair lift. One of the locals guided us here and we don't recommend that you do this without a guide or a knowledgeable local. The off-piste and backcountry terrain in VT is certainly exciting but there are places that can be sketchy, so watch out.

Lift passes	Val Thorens	Les Trois Vallées
1 day	€33	€41
6 days	€156	€204

There is a discount for children under 13 years and adults over 60. There are discounts on the normal tariff 1 November–17 December and 16 April–8 May, You can book your ski passes online at www.valthorens.com and they will be delivered to your hotel or apartment.

Instruction

ESF

The ESF provides a variety of courses, including group, private, freeride, freestyle and heliriding. As an example of price, a 6 half-days course costs from €99, while private lessons are from €32 for 1 hour.

T: 0033 (0)4 79 00 02 86
E: info@esf-valthorens
W: www.esf-valthorens.com

International Ski School

The international instructors each speak at least three of ten languages. They limit groups to 6 people and offer a number of different programmes, including some with hi-tech tuition and video analysis at €35 per hour.

T: 0033 (0)4 79 00 01 96
E: esi@intl-skischool.com
W: www.esivalthorens.com

Prosneige

Prosneige offers all-inclusive packages (lessons plus ski pass and equipment) as well as private tuition, guiding and heliskiing on Italian summits.

T: 0033 (0)4 79 01 07 00
E: info@prosneige.fr
W: www.prosneige.fr

Ski Cool

Ski Cool offers carving and freestyle courses for both boarders and skiers. They also offer skiing lessons for the blind. Three-hour ice-climbing courses are available from €45. You can choose between private and group lessons or a mini group, limited to 4 people, halfway between a group and private lesson.

T: 0033 (0)4 79 00 04 92

E: mail@ski-cool.com
W: www.ski-cool.com

Thomas Diet

This X-Games freestyle competitor (in 2003), on the Dynastar Team, takes a 5 half-days course for €99.

T: 0033 (0)6 80 88 41 75

Other activities

Unless other contact details are given, call the tourist office for more information (04 79 00 08 08).

Beauty and well being: L'Isba chalet (04 79 01 04 81) uses Decléor methods. Well being packages are available for 2-hour long sessions up to 5 days!

Flying: Take an ultra light aircraft over Les Trois Vallées for a real thrill.

Ice climbing: You can take a 3-hour introduction or improvers' lesson on a natural waterfall. Equipment is provided and it costs from €45. Contact Ski Cool (04 79 00 04 92).

Ice driving: The Val Thorens Ice Driving School (06 79 41 35 26) gives lessons on general ice driving through to competition level. Beginners use cross cars and quads and can then progress to use the Mitsubishi Evo 6.

Osteopathic treatments, sauna and steam room: These can be booked at L'Espace Yin Yang in the Montana 4-star residence (04 79 00 29 00). Check out www.beauty-valthorens.com for more information.

Paragliding: Tandem paraglides are available over Les Trois Vallées from €65 (06 81 55 74 94).

Snowmobiling: This is a fairly popular activity in Val Thorens. Val Tho Motoneige (04 79 00 21 46) have 42 snowmobiles and you can rent one for an hour from €70.

Sports centre: This freshly revamped centre (04 79 00 00 76) combines fitness, sport and relaxation. The Aquaclub is made up of a swimming pool, with quirky facilities such as swimming against the currents and some massaging jets. There are also several saunas, Jacuzzis and a heated solarium. The fitness centre contains a 170m² weight/circuit training room and a 110m² fitness room. Leisure activities include tennis, volleyball, football, squash, ping pong, badminton, roller skating, hockey, and a kids' play room with trampolines and ball pools. Bizarrely, the sports centre also organises fitness and aqua gym lessons for couples. Apparently these lessons are done in pairs and 'will be full of surprises for loving couples' – interesting! If you dare to check it out, let us know.

Tobogganing: The highest toboggan run in Europe is situated in the Tête Ronde sector. At the foot of the Péclet glacier, this run drops 700m during its 6km descent. It costs from €8.50 (with ski pass) and is accessible during the day via the Funitel of Péclet in just 8 minutes.

Events

There aren't many major events in Val Thorens, except for a few slalom races. A popular, beginning of season party is **Boarderweek** which takes place every year, around the second week in December. It is a ski and snowboarding freestyle party with equipment testing

"A ski and snowboarding freestyle party with equipment testing and lots of fun parties and concerts"

and lots of fun parties and concerts. Check out www.boarderweek.com.

Accommodation

There are 24,500 beds in Val Thorens, all in pretty good locations, either near town and/or the slopes. There are 11 hotels; one 4-star, six 3-star, two 2-star, and two club hotels/holiday villages. There are also 15 residence chalets and almost 100 private renters (list available at the tourist office).

For exclusive, self catering accommodation try the 4-star **Oxalys** chalet complex (0033 (0)4 79 00 20 51, www.montagnettes.com, which will set you back €1850–4805 for a 6-person chalet depending on time of season and whether you require a VIP chalet (contains whirlpool bath, video recorders, slippers…). The other glam option is the 4-star **Fitzroy** (0033 (0)4 79 00 04 78, www.fitzroyhotel.com, €1260–1820 per person per week for half board) which is very posh and beautiful. For slightly less expensive beautiful apartments in a big, cosy, wooden chalet, try **Les Chalets du Soleil** (0033 (0)4 75 40 80 25, www.chalet dusoleil.com, €704–2164 per apartment per week depending on time of season and size of apartment). If you fancy a catered chalet holiday in Chalet du Soleil, contact Cordon Rouge (www.frenchskiholidays.com).

If you are looking for a less expensive visit, try the **Novotel hotel** (0033 (0)4 79 00 04 04, H0457-GM@ accor-hotels.com, www.novotelvalthorens.com). There are 104 rooms (half smoking, half non), with prices €65–145 per person per night (half board), depending on the time of season. There are loads of benefits to this hotel. For starters, it's right on the slopes and you can literally ski from the door. If you don't want to, you need never leave the hotel as it offers a ski shop

> "It's right on the slopes and you can literally ski from the door"

and hire centre (where you can even rent ski/board clothing), a good bar and restaurant and loads of entertainment such as piano players and guitarists in the bar, black jack parties and magic at the dinner table. However, if you wish to explore Val Thorens you can take your half-board meal at lunchtime (on the huge terrace on the slopes) instead of dinner so that you are free to roam in the evenings. The Novotel attracts a large range of clients, but mostly families, attracted by the nightly entertainment for children, and family rooms with no supplement for children up to 16 years; and corporate clients, who can take advantage of the 500m^2 of conference and meeting facilities that the hotel offers. The hotel also offers a WiFi internet connection so you can access the net from your room if your laptop supports it.

If you would prefer an inexpensive apartment, rather than a hotel, try **Le Chamois D'Or** (0033 (0)4 79 01 34 34, www.residchamoisdor.com) in the centre of town, offering studios or apartments for 2 to 8 people. A 4-person studio will cost €398–864 per apartment per week, depending on time of season.

Eating out

On the mountain

There are many restaurants overlooking the mountains on the slopes by the town centre. **Le Galoubet brasserie** (04 79 00 00 48) is one of the best traditional restaurants on the mountain; it has a big terrace and you can either have a quick €5 panini or opt for a fancy main meal (€12–30). We didn't find the staff particularly efficient or friendly but we hope this was a one-off. **Le Scapin**, just behind Le Galoubet, has very friendly service and more simple food such as pizzas, pastas and steak.

On the slopes, **Chalet des 2 Lacs** has a snack bar outside for hot dogs, chips and crêpes to enjoy on deckchairs in the sun (hopefully). It also has a very cute, wooden restaurant with an open fire and serves good pizzas and big chunky chips. **Chalet du Génépi** (04 79 00 03 28) is another cosy chalet with a big fire that is worth a look.

In town

There are lots of places to eat in town, including a number of fast-food options and kebab houses. For British pub grub (fish and chips, burgers and

"El Gringos serves absolutely fab Tex-Mex food and the staff are a hoot"

the like), try the **Frog and Roast Beef** (04 79 00 07 17). **El Gringos** serves absolutely fab Tex-Mex food and the staff are a hoot. There are long wooden benches, perfect for large groups to settle in. This is the place in which to have some quality banter and line the stomach before a night on the town. For a pizza, or traditional Savoyard cuisine, **La Paillotte** (04 79 00 01 02) in the town centre is very cosy and serves excellent food. Pizzas and salads are also available at **Le Scapin** (see above) with a good atmosphere and affordable prices. If you want something less affordable but definitely memorable, try **L'Oxalys** (see Accommodation – 04 79 00 20 51). The restaurant is run by Jean Sulpice, with three knives and forks in the Michelin guide. It is unsurprisingly expensive, and supposedly out of this world. Unfortunately we couldn't tell you what it's like first hand – there's no way we could afford it. Make sure you book well in advance.

Bars and clubs

The row of bars at the top of the resort is where your night should begin. Pick an end and work your way along, picking your way through bars such as the **Frog and Roast Beef**, **Friends**, **O'Connells** and **Le Viking** (which also has internet). All of them have various happy hours and some offer tasty meals too. O'Connells happens to be the highest Irish pub in the world and was the fastest built in France – it took just four weeks to build it, ship it to the Alps and install it. **Le Chantaco** in the centre of town is another option with a table football table and somewhere you can usually sit for a chat.

Later on the place to be is the **Malaysia** cellar bar. It's right by the piste and looks like it's just a little wooden hut but, once inside, you walk down into a really funky, large club which has live bands all the time, and at about 1.30am the second part of the club opens up. For a very cheesy option, which is good for a laugh if you're in the mood, try the underground nightclub in **Place de Péclet**.

Getting there

By car

From Calais (209km), drive time is around 11 hours. You can't park your car in town, so either make sure your hotel/apartment has a car park or book into one (0033 (0)4 79 00 02 49, www.valthoparc.com); it's cheaper than paying on arrival. One week's parking will cost € 50–62.50 depending on the height of your vehicle, whether you want indoor or outdoor and whether you have booked in advance.

By train

Trains go to Moûtiers. There are regular buses from the station but you should book at least 48 hours beforehand (0033 (0)4 79 00 06 83, www.altibus.com).

By plane

Lyon (193km) Transfer time is around 3 hours. For bus transfers contact Satobus on 0033 (0)4 37 25 52 55.
Geneva (160km) Transfer takes about 3 hours. For bus transfers contact Touriscar on 0033 (0)4 50 43 60 02.

Useful facts and phone numbers

Tourist office

T: 0033 (0)4 79 00 08 08
F: 0033 (0)4 79 00 00 04
E: valtho@valthorens.com
W: www.valthorens.com

Direct reservations

T: 0033 (0)4 79 00 01 06
F: 0033 (0)4 79 00 06 49
E: reserver@valthorens.com

Emergency services

- In a medical emergency dial 15, for the fire brigade call 18, or 112 for either from a mobile.
- Police station: 04 79 00 08 50
- Medical centres: 04 79 00 00 37/04 79 00 74 39 (Rue du Soleil)

Taxis

- Station de taxis: 04 79 00 69 54
- Favre, Pascal: 04 79 00 64 59
- Legay, Eric: 04 79 00 28 74

Italy

Italy is one of the few countries in the world that allows heliskiing, and it also has some of the most incredible scenery in Europe

Alagna

A sleepy, undiscovered town with access to Freeriding Paradise

On the slopes	
Snow reliability	❄ ❄ ❄ ❄
Parks	❄ ❄
Off-piste	❄ ❄ ❄ ❄ ❄

Off the slopes	
Après ski	❄
Nightlife	❄
Eating out	❄ ❄
Resort charm	❄ ❄ ❄ ❄

The resort

'Freeriding Paradise' is written all over the lifts and town of Alagna, and for good reason. Alagna is one of the three valleys in the Monterosa area (others are Champoluc and Gressoney – see Gressoney chapter, page 274), which encompasses a massive range of

"The jagged, striking mountains provide a stunning backdrop to your explorations of the surrounding peaks"

backcountry escapades. The jagged, striking mountains provide a stunning backdrop to your explorations of the surrounding peaks. If you should ever get bored of this magnificent area you can turn your hand to heliskiing or a backcountry quest to Zermatt. Alagna's town is beautiful, centred round a prominent and eye-catching church. Beauty aside, there's not too much going on, although you can find a good glass of wine or bite to eat if you know where to look. Like its neighbouring Gressoney, Alagna is probably more suited for a weekend of intense riding, followed by a couple of relaxing evenings, rather than a week-long holiday.

The mountains

Height: 1200–3550m

Ability	Rating
Expert	❄ ❄ ❄ ❄
Intermediate	❄ ❄ ❄
Beginner	❄

The Monterosa area is best-known for its off-piste and this extends throughout the three valleys. Now that the connecting lift between Gressoney and Alagna is completed, it makes no sense to separate them, as the Gressoney lifts lead to the Alagna off-piste and vice versa. Therefore, for information on the Alagna mountains (including lift pass prices, the park, off-piste and general info), please refer to the Gressoney chapter, page 274.

Instruction

Corpo Guide Alagna (Scuola di Alpinismo)
T: 0039 0163 913 10
E: info@guidealagna.com

Guide Monterosa
Guide Monterosa comprises 25 guides who can take you on heliskiing trips or just guide you round the mountain. They also offer a service of organising your accommodation, taxis, the works. For more information refer to the Gressoney chapter (page 274) as the company is based there.
T: 0039 0125 366 139
E: info@guidemonterosa.com
W: www.guidemonterosa.com

The Lyskamm Group
This adventure travel group can offer heliskiing, freeriding, winter mountaineering, ski mountaineering and other adventure excursions as well as organising hotels and taxis if required.
T: 0039 0163 922 993
E: lyskamm@alagna.it
W: www.lyksammviaggi.com

Scuola Sci and Snowboard Alagna

A 1-hour private lesson costs €35–40 and a group lesson €25 for half a day, €45 for a full day and €110 for 5 half-days.
T: 0039 0163 922 961

Other activities

Apart from heliskiing and guiding, the only other activity is to stroll around town.

Events

In mid-February, Alagna is home to the **Telemar Karnival** (www.telemark.it) to which many budding telemarkers will flutter. Gressoney hosts the **Red Bull Snow Thrill** (www.redbullsnowthrill.com) freeride event in mid-March which attracts a number of the world's leading pros.

Accommodation

There is a stunning 4-star hotel in Alagna called the **Hotel Cristallo** (0039 0163 922 822, info@ hotelcristalloalagna.com, www.hotelcristalloalagna .com), with top notch service and a luxurious feel. You have the choice of the lovely and colourful classic room (€160–200 per room B&B), the more roomy Prestige room (€200–250 per room B&B) or the ultimate, multi-level suite (€300–350 per room B&B). Half-board accommodation is also available. The Wellness suite, lounge and restaurant are also divine. This hotel would be a wonderful place for a romantic weekend.

The 3-star hotel **Monterosa** (0039 0163 923 209, hotelmonterosa@liberto.it, www.alagna.it) was the first to be opened in Alagna in 1865. It is bang in the centre of the village, opposite the church and 100m from the cable car. There are 14 rooms with en-suite facilities, and an old restaurant (La Stube) with magnificent high ceilings and chandelier, although there is a feeling of eating in an archaic school dining room. Per person per day, the hotel costs €52–72 for half-board and €42–62 for B&B.

Indren Hus (0039 0163 911 52, info@indrenhus.it, www.indrenhus.it) has rooms or apartments on offer, as well as some 'panoramic attics' which boast spectacular views. All rooms have satellite TV and most have a deck or balcony. The bar and restaurant are friendly and great and there is a small fitness centre as well as a sauna and whirlpool shower. Rooms cost €35–52 for B&B and €45–62 for half-board accommodation, eating at the Dir und Don Brasserie (see Eating out). The hotel is also in association with the local wine bar (see Bars and clubs) and guests are occasionally invited to wine tastings.

Eating out

On the mountain

Most of the restaurants can be found as you head towards Gressoney. The **Alpenhütte Lys** (0125 366 057), by the side of the chair from Gabiet to Passo Salati, has a stunning terrace with hand-built wooden loungers looking out on to the pistes and the mountains. In Gressoney, the smart **Morgenrot** just below the Bedemie looks like a rowdy bar but inside it is a beautiful restaurant with great food (homemade pastas, and chunky chips), lots of character and it's pretty good value too (dishes cost €8–12). The **Gabiet** is a good, simple establishment with a terrace overlooking the snow park and the **Rifugio Guglielmina** (0163 914 44/ 0163 915 47,rifugioguglielmina@libero.it, www.rifugioguglielmina.it) has a traditional restaurant as well as accommodation, which can only be accessed off-piste.

In town

Most of the hotels have restaurants attached, for example **La Stube** at the Monterosa is the place to go if you fancy a fondue or raclette. **Indren** also has a good restaurant. There is also a surprisingly stylish bistro in the centre of town called the **Dir und Don Brasserie**. This has a terrace with outside heaters and

bar, and a cosy wooden interior. They serve meat, pasta, risotto and pizzas (a bargain, at €3–8). **Unione** is a friendly, informal restaurant that's not bad inside and has a good terrace. A main dish will cost €8–13.50.

Bars and clubs

As you will have guessed there's not too much going on and most people are tucked up in bed early preparing themselves for the next day. The best bar in town is the **Bacher Wine Bar** that's really cosy and has wine bottles covering the walls. Apart from this, the best bet is to infiltrate a local crowd and suggest that they throw a party.

Getting there

By car

From Milan or Turin, take the motoway or A26 and turn off at Biandrate for Gravellona Toce and Romagnano-Ghemme. Then take the main road ss299 to Alagna.

By train

The nearest train station is Varello from where it will take an hour by bus (regular bus service 9am–6.30pm). The connection can also be made by taxi.

By plane

Milan Linate (137km)
Milan Malpensa (98km)
Turin Caselle (170km)
All information about buses linking Alagna with Milan and Turin can be obtained by calling 0039 0163 922 988.

Useful facts and phone numbers

Tourist office

T: 0039 0163 922 988
F: 0039 0163 912 02
E: iatalagnavalsesia@libero.it

Emergency services

• Call 118

Cervinia

Compact town, perfect slopes
for beginners and low
intermediates

On the slopes	
Snow reliability	✳✳✳✳
Parks	✳✳✳
Off-piste	✳
Off the slopes	
Après ski	✳✳⅊
Nightlife	✳✳⅊
Eating out	✳✳⅊
Resort charm	✳✳

The resort

Cervina is a strange resort but regular visitors love it. The pedestrian centre is great; everything's really handy and within a few minutes' walk, there are some top bars, decent restaurants and you can ride over to Zermatt without paying Zermatt prices. On the other hand, the buildings outside of the centre are mostly pretty ugly, and the slopes aren't challenging for anyone above an intermediate level. But if you're not an expert, it will probably do you just fine.

The mountains

Height: 1525–3480m

Ability	Rating
Expert	✳
Intermediate	✳✳✳✳
Beginner	✳✳✳✳

Getting about

Cervinia has 200km of pistes of its own, and connects to the lower valley, Valtournenche, and over the Swiss border to Zermatt; in total providing 350km of accessible terrain. Most of this area is great for cruisy intermediates, but can be dull for gutsy intermediates and experts. Even though the link to Zermatt opens up some more challenging areas and good off-piste, it is really only the Schwarzsee area that is easily accessible; for the Rothorn and Stockhorn areas you have to ride down into the centre of Zermatt and then travel across town.

The park

Cervinia's park was well shaped and there was a fairly good variety of kickers. The jumps were graded, with two blues, four reds, and one black that was a good 12m table with perfect transition. At the bottom of the park was a hip that you can hit from either side. Jibbers would be happy with the few rails and fun boxes. We had heard that it was only for boarders, but there were just as many skiers and it had a great atmosphere. Sometimes there's a mediocre pipe, if the conditions are right. A great park for all, from learning your first jumps to pulling crowd pleasers off the big bertha.

> "At the bottom of the park was a hip that you can hit from either side"

Off-piste and backcountry

Cervinia is not the place to come if all you want to do is ride off-piste. The resort gets loads of snow due to its high altitude, but also gets a lot of strong wind which can wreck the fresh powder. There are not that many easily accessible areas, but if you're determined, your best bet is to get a guide, and maybe head over towards Zermatt, where you will find some of the best riding in Europe. There's also some amazing heliskiing and boarding that can be done with a guide (details on page 258) and check out the Zermatt chapter (page 400) for the backcountry terrain on the Swiss side of the glacier.

Instruction

Breuil Ski School

Skiing and boarding lessons are available. Private lessons cost €30–50 per hour, depending on the number of people. Three mornings group lessons cost €100, 5 mornings €145.

T: 0039 0166 940 960
E: info@scuolascibreuil.com
W: www.scuolascibreuil.com

Lift passes	Breuil Cervinia – Valtournenche	Inc. Zermatt
1 day	€32	€42
6 days	€170	€206
13 days	€277	€361

Discounts are made for early and late season and for children. An international daily supplement costs €27 on presentation of a multi-day pass or seasonal pass (and allows you to ski the slopes in Zermatt). There is a pass that can only be used in the snowpark and one for those who only use the mountains in the mornings or in the afternoons.

Cervinia Ski School

Skiing and boarding lessons are available. Private lessons cost €32–50 per hour, depending on the number of people. Group ski lessons cost €145 for 5 mornings. The school also organises heliskiing on the Monte Rosa and on the downhill from Château des Dames on the Grandes Murailles mountains.
T: 0039 0166 949 034/0166 948 744
E: info@scuolacervino.com
W: www.scuolacervino.com

Heliski Company

A drop on the Monte Rosa costs €190–235 per person and 1 day's heliskiing €300–360. Two days is €420–570 and a 3-day heliski tour of the Matterhorn and Monte Rosa costs €650–840, with a total of 8000 vertical metres of riding. The cost for a guide of the best freeriding areas is €55–65 per person.
T: 0039 0166 949 267
E: info@heliskicervinia.com
W: www.heliskicervinia.com

Other activities

Horse riding: Bepe, at the Hotel Hermitage, can take you out horse riding on the slopes (0166 948 998).
Ice skating: The natural ice skating rink is open day and night, and hockey matches are also organised here.
Night skiing: Every week guides organise a night trip in a snow-cat followed by skiing/boarding down by torchlight.
Paragliding: A half-hour paragliding flight can be organised by Fans de Sport (0347 995 018 – mobile, info@fansdesport.it). They also arrange **quad biking** on specially laid track, **kite-skiing** and **airboarding**.
Skidoos: These can be driven across the snow at night

(contact Motoslitte on 0166 940 127 or 0335 565 0635).
Sports centre: Situated in Valtournenche, the Centro Polivalente has a gym, swimming pool, volleyball, tennis, 5-a-side football, a climbing wall, a sauna and a Turkish bath.

Accommodation

Cervinia doesn't come across as an upper-class place, but there are a load of 4-star hotels to choose from. For the ultimate in luxury, head to the **Hotel Hermitage** (0039 0166 948 998, www.hotelhermitage.com, info@hotelhermitage.com), an elegant and beautiful hotel that also manages to be welcoming and friendly. The 34 luxurious rooms and suites have fireplaces and spa baths. Facilities include a transfer service to the lifts that are 300m away, a beauty spa and swimming pool. Prices are €1190–1820 for a standard room and €1400–2240 for a luxury suite (per person per week for half-board accommodation). Another 4-star treat is the **Hotel Europa** (0039 0166 948 660, infohtl@ europa.com, www.htl-europa.com), a central hotel positioned just 600m from the minibuses to the lifts. There's a beautiful bar and a luxurious hotel lounge. Half-board accommodation costs €468–1365 per person per week depending on time of season and type of room (standard or suite).

"There's a beautiful bar and a luxurious hotel lounge"

The **Excelsior Planet** (0039 0166 949 426, info@ excelsiorplanet.com, www.excelsiorplanet.com) is a lovely hotel with 35 suites and 11 rooms and is a decent price for a 4 star (€450–1085 per person per week, half-board). They also offer short breaks. The **Sertorelli Sport Hotel** (0039 0166 949 797, info@ sertorelli-cervinia.it, www.sertorelli-cervinia.it) is a 4 star that is undergoing renovations for the 05/06 season. The junior suites will have balconies, living rooms and whirlpools and the rooms will all be made much bigger. There will also be a sauna, Jacuzzi, fitness centre and beauty spa. The prices are set to change so it's best to consult the website.

For a 3-star option, check out the **Hotel Edelweiss** (0039 0166 949 078, info@matterhorn.it, www. matterhorn.it), right in the centre of town and 300m from the slopes (they have a transfer service). The layout's good, as is the bar and the prices at €385–777 per person per week for half-board.

For 2-star hotels, **Marmore** (0039 0166 949 057, info@marmore.com, www.hotelmarmore.com) is a decent small hotel that is close to the action. They offer half-board accommodation (€495–665 per

person per week), and will also rent rooms out per night if they're not fully booked. **Castelli** (0039 0166 949 183, info@aparthotel.it, www.castelli.ao.it) is an apart-hotel with 12 flats and two rooms, 300m from the slopes. A 4-person apartment costs €490–780 per week. **Petit Tibet** (0039 0166 948 974, info@petit-tibet.com) has some really cheap deals for apartments (from €530 for an apartment for 4 for the week) but it is incredibly inconvenient at the top of town and you can't easily access the town centre.

Eating out

On the mountain

The refuge **Guide del Cervinio**, right at the top of the Plateau Rosa, is a cute and small self-service restaurant where you can pick up a sandwich for about €5–6 or a main dish for €10–23. **Les Skieurs D'Antan** is a nice restaurant right at the bottom of the mountain, just above the main cable car where you can get pasta, fish, steak or raclette (€10–23). It's also open at night. The **Igloo**, on the lower part of the Ventina run serves the best burgers you could hope for, actually made with real meat. Enjoy it though, it'll cost you €10 and it doesn't even come with chips!

In town

The **Copa Pan** (see Bars and clubs) has a beautiful restaurant downstairs. The pizzas are a bargain in such gorgeous surroundings, at €6–12. The **Hotel Punta Maquignaz** serves steaks and fondues in comfortable surrounds, as long as you're not put off by all the bear skins and heads in the lobby. The **Capanna Alpina** has a great, atmospheric pizzeria on its top floor, overlooking the bar. In the basement is the cosy tavern, complete with pool table and candles. The **Maison de Saussure** (0166 948 249) is tiny, snug and traditional, and reservations are a must. The **Matterhorn** is an informal but welcoming place, and serves some of the best pizzas in town.

For a memorable night, try the **Cretaz Lodge**, just up the slopes from town, who will come into town on skidoos to pick you up. One again, the food is traditional and the atmosphere relaxing.

Bars and clubs

There are some great bars in Cervinia and all are a few minutes' walk from each other to save you getting chilly in-between beers. Facing the slopes are the Yeti and the Dragon pubs. The **Yeti** (0166 949 196, www.breuil-cervinia.com/Yeti) is a dark but cosy bar with loads of big screens showing sports, internet access and good value sandwiches, burgers and hot dogs. Between 5 and 6pm a jug of beer will cost you only €9. The **Dragon** (0166 948 085, hoteldragon@ aosanet.com) is like a big British pub so you'll feel right at home. The Dragon is open 10.30am–12 or 1am upstairs and 2.30am downstairs. Food is served 12–3pm and 7.30–9.30pm, and at 4–5pm a pint or a long drink is only €3, and a vodka Redbull €4. It's busy at après and then again from about 9.30pm. Thursdays tend to be theme nights.

Our favourite bar for après is the **Ymeletrob** (0166 949 145), a cute and cosy wine and cocktail bar at the end of the town centre that has chips, dips and more free snacks dotted around the bar. The prices are inflated because of the free snacks but it's worth it. The cocktail of the day tends to be a reasonable price. The **Copa Pan** (0166 940 084) has a stunning restaurant (see Eating out), a bar and a club. The bar is open 4pm–1am, and the club 10pm–3/4am. The

Copa Pan attracts a mix of seasonaires and tourists and has theme nights about once a month where they really go to town; for example, on Woodstock night they laid the floor with grass and tepees. The **Café des Guides** is like a big old hotel lounge with comfy, un-matching, leather chairs and a hotchpotch of patterns, pictures and memorabilia adorning the walls.

Out of town, past the cable car, towards the big apartment blocks at the top of town, there are a few shops and restaurants. There is also a fab bar and restaurant where an old cinema used to be, called the **Taverna di Gargantua** (0166 940 167), run by the welcoming Kiko. There's a massive screen that usually shows concerts and, instead of a pool table to entertain you, there is a hole to practise your putting.

Useful facts and phone numbers

Tourist office

T: 0039 0166 949 136
F: 0039 0166 944 399
E: breuil-cervinia@montecervinio.it
W: www.cervinia.it

Emergency services

- Police: 0166 944 311/ 948 103
- In a medial emergency call 118

Doctors

- Medical centre: 0166 94 01 75

Taxis and airport transfers

- Paolo Giannini: 0039 0166 62 220/0039 0335 565 3189, skitaxi@libero.it
- Pino Pession: 0039 0166 925 62/ 0039 0348 312 3036, pinopession@libero.it
- Riccardo Ferraris: 0039 0166 61 874/ 0039 0339 13 96 490, riccardoferraris@cheapnet.it
- Sergio Meynet: 0039 0166 92 723/0039 0333 23 74 523, sergiomeynet@libero.it

Getting there

By plane

Milan (170km) Fly to either Milano Malpensa or Milano Linate.
Turin (118km)
Geneva (180km)
Transfer details can be obtained from the Consortium-Consorzio per lo Sviluppo Turistico del Comprensorio del Cervino (0039 0166 949 136, info@breuil-cervinia.it). Alternatively call a taxi transfer (see above). Car rental services, minibuses and buses can be obtained from C.A.A.R.P. (0039 0112 472 072, info@caarp.it, www.caarp.it).

N.B. If you fly to Geneva you will have to come through the Mont Blanc Tunnel. If so, this will cost €30, and watch your speed as they have cameras all over the place, and if you're an ounce over 70km/hour, the Italian police will be waiting for you on the other side with an on-the-spot fine that they seem to make up depending on how they feel.

Cortina d'Ampezzo

It's beautiful, but only the Italians really fit in

On the slopes	
Snow reliability	✳ ✳ ✳
Parks	✳ ✳
Off-piste	✳ ✳

Off the slopes	
Après ski	✳
Nightlife	✳
Eating out	✳ ✳
Resort charm	✳ ✳ ✳ ◖

The resort

Cortina is one of the few resorts that we really didn't get a feel for. The town is beautiful and quaint, and the Dolomite scenery some of the most dramatic and stunning in Europe, so it's not resort charm that's a problem. It's more that it doesn't feel like a ski resort, and this is largely due to the Cortina regulars. The typical lady patron of Cortina would most likely be decked out in fur at all times, and be sporting large, dark Gucci sunglasses that covered her whole face. She would not be at all fussed if she didn't go out on the mountain during the day, and would probably only make the effort to get out early in order to secure a prime deckchair spot. Come evening time she would change into even more decadent finery and walk around town three times until she was sure that everyone had seen her, at which point she could happily retire to bed to prepare for the next tiring day. We're not trying to be cruel, everyone looked perfectly happy, and if this sounds like heaven to you, then pack your bags and trot to Cortina, but don't be surprised if you are looked down upon if you start jibbing around outside cafés in your baggy pants.

The mountains

Height: 1224–2939m

Ability	Rating
Expert	✳ ✳
Intermediate	✳ ✳ ✳
Beginner	✳ ✳ ✳ ✳

Getting about

The 115km of pistes in Cortina are a nightmare to get to – no wonder half the Cortina visitors don't bother trying. There are two main cable cars leaving Cortina town, from opposite ends of the town's fringes. It's so disjointed that you would be best off with a car, but the one-way system is so stressful and confusing that driving around is not fun. The Mandres cable car takes you up to the Faloria area, where you can find your way across to the few red runs under the

> "There are two main cable cars leaving Cortina town, from opposite ends of the town's fringes"

spectacular Cristallo. Just underneath here is the separate, inconvenient Mietres that only has about five runs anyway. From the other side of town is the cable car to Tofana, from which you can make your way over to the Socrepes area, the largest area full of cruisy blues. Cinque Torri and Passo Falzarego are two small areas that can only be accessed by car or bus, but they have the best freeride potential.

The park

Until recently this park was 'boarders only' but they seem to be becoming a little more skier-friendly. The park is located in the Faloria area, which you can get to by catching the cable car from the bottom of the resort. There are up to four kickers (depending on the amount of snow), rails and a small half pipe. You wouldn't catch the experts and pros hanging out here, but it's good for starting off in or just having a jib.

Off-piste and backcountry

We weren't particularly inspired by this mountain as a freeride destination (apart from the incredible views, which are hard to beat). There are places to check out, but the best bits aren't all that great, and are often inconvenient. A guide will be able to show you the areas worth visiting, which include a decent couloir at the top of Forcella Staunies (2930m), under Son Forca chair, or the narrow gorges of Bus Tofana and Canalino del Prete. Alternatively your guide could take you to the Cinque Torri or Passo Falzarego, respectable freeriding areas that can only be accessed by car or bus.

Instruction

Guide Alpine Scuola d'Alpinismo

This school can guide you round the pistes of the Sella Ronda or they can teach and/or guide you in off-piste and freeride.

T: 0039 0436 868 505
E: info@guidecortina.com
W: www.guidecortina.com

Lift passes	Cortina, San Vito di Cadore, Auronzo and Misurina	Dolomiti Superski
1 day	€31	€34
6 days	€153	€167
13 days	€266	€289
Prices will be slightly less out of season and slightly more at high season. There are discounts for children and seniors.		

Scuola Sci Snowboard Cortina
Private lessons are €35–42 per hour.
T: 0039 0436 2911
E: scuolascicortina@dolomiti.org
W: www.cortina.dolomiti.org/scuolascicortina

Other activities

Contact Cortina Adrenalin (www.adrenalincenter.it, cortina@adrenalincenter.it) for more information about the activities.
Bobsleighing: Have a go on the bobsleigh (December–February), and reach speeds of up to 75 miles an hour. If the mood takes you, you can throw yourself down the sheet ice without the aid of a bobsled, just on a crazy sledge.

"The handiest one can be reached by the first stage of the Mietres chairlift"

Ice skating and curling: The ice rink is open for skating, curling, and a crazy ice disco once a week.
Sledging: There are loads of sledging runs but most aren't too easy to get to. The handiest one can be reached by the first stage of the Mietres chairlift. This is 1km long, pisted, and reserved for sleds. You can also sledge from Rifugio Ra Stua (1668m), after an hour's walk from the car park. This 3km run has a vertical drop of 200m. The enthusiastic tobogganists should head to the Croda da Lago (2046m). The walk up is 3 hours, but you can contact the Croda da Lago refuge and see if they will get the motorsled out for you. A 4km run (550m vertical drop), starts out at the Rifugio Scoiattoli. The walk up is an hour and a half or you can take the chair from Bai de Dones, although you wind up 3.5km from where the chairlift sets off. Moonlight sledding is available too, and you get to wear a helmet with a light on it.
Snowrafting: This looks pretty cool; sit in a large rubber dinghy and fly down pretty steep snow/ice at 60 miles an hour.

Events

Cortina Winter Polo, **bobsleigh races** and the **Sleddog European Championships** are about as exciting as it gets.

Accommodation

There are two 5-star hotels: the **Cristallo** (0039 0436 881 111, info@cristallo.it, www.cristallo.it) and the **Miramonti** (0039 0436 4201, www.geturhotels .com, miramontimajestic@geturhotels.com). Both are beautiful big buildings but they are pretty inconvenient. The best hotel in town, in our opinion, is the 4 star **Ancora** (0039 0436 3261, www. hotelancoracortina.com, info@hotelancoracortina .com), a beautiful and traditional hotel that has won a number of awards, as well as a tribute in the *Hip Hotels Ski* book. The 2-star **Hotel Montana** (0039 0436 862 126, www.cortina-hotel.com, montana@ cortina-hotel.com) is right in the pedestrianised centre of town and is simple but cheap (€273–435 per person for 7 nights).

Eating out

On the mountain

There are lots of lovely mountain huts to stop off at for lunch, and the fur-clad contingent will head straight to them. The beautiful **Rifugio Tondi** (0436 5775) is one of the best places to lunch. You'll find it on the Tondi Normale piste (61) in the Faloria area. Under Cristallo, the **Rifugio Son Forca** (0436 866 192) has great big terraces with beautiful views and the Rio Gere (0436 3434) is a cute, family-run hut. On the other side of the valley, under Tofana, the **Pomedes** restaurant (0436 862 061) is one of the best places to stop for a bite to eat.

> # "Lots of lovely mountain huts to stop off at for lunch"

In town

Ra Stua restaurant (0436 868 341) do the standard pasta, risotto and meat dishes (main €9–18), and **La Botte** (0436 866 283) serves up Mexican for a change. For pizza, **Rotondo** on the main square is cosy, **Al Passetto** (0436 2254) is good, and there's a tiny little takeaway pizza place, **Al Due Forni**, opposite the cinema.

Michelin rates many restaurants around Cortina: **Tivoli** (0436 866 400) has a star and **El Toulá** (0436 3339), in a converted barn, has three Michelin forks. We liked **Restaurant Zoco** (0436 860 041), on the edge of town, as it's really cosy and serves good, smart food.

Bars and clubs

The après ski scene wasn't really our cup of tea, but there are a couple of fun places to go. The **Entoca** wine bar is the best; it's cosy and usually packed. For dancing the night away, head to the **Metro Club** or the **Limbo**.

Useful facts and phone numbers

Tourist office

T: 0039 0436 866 252
F: 0039 0436 867 448
E: cortina@dolomiti.org
W: www.cortina.dolomiti.org

Emergency services

- Police-public service: 113
- Police emergency services: 112
- Town police: 0436 866 200
- Alpine First Aid: 0436 2943

Doctors

- Doctor for tourists: 0436 883 111
- Croce Bianca Ambulance Aid: 0436 862 075

Getting there

By car

There is a route planner on Cortina's website that will help you to plan your route.

By plane

Venice (162km)
Treviso (168km) Ryanair.
On Saturdays and Sundays there is a transfer service from Venice and Treviso airports to Cortina for the guests of Cortina Hotels. Journey time is 2 hours.
Innsbruck (156km)

Courmayeur

Beautiful, picturesque,
and full of fur

On the slopes	
Snow reliability	✲ ✲ ✲
Parks	–
Off-piste	✲ ✲ ✲ ✤

Off the slopes	
Après ski	✲ ✲ ✲
Nightlife	✲ ✲ ✲
Eating out	✲ ✲ ✲ ✲
Resort charm	✲ ✲ ✲ ✲

The resort

Courmayeur is only 10 minutes away from the Mont Blanc Tunnel; a charming and picturesque village, with a maze of cobbled streets and some stylish and chic bars and restaurants. The slopes aren't extensive but

"The slopes aren't extensive but are good for cruising and posing"

are good for cruising and posing. It's a great place for people-watching too; there are some fantastic outfits walking around and most seem to have no qualms about decking themselves from head to toe in fur. If you want to parade around in the latest designer clothes, sip cocktails in classy bars and don't need a massive challenge on the slopes, this could be the resort for you.

The mountains

Height: 1210–2755m

Ability	Rating
Expert	✲ ✲ ✲
Intermediate	✲ ✲ ✲ ✲
Beginner	✲ ✲

Getting about

The slopes aren't the easiest to get to; the cable car on the edge of town takes you across the river to the mountains and most choose to take this lift down at the end of the day rather than to come down across the river and face the wait for the bus back to town. There are only 100km of slopes that are mostly cruisy runs, a few challenging pistes for the expert and no park, but there is some decent off-piste. Check out some of our favourite runs below and contact Società Guide Alpine for more information (see Instruction).

The park

We don't understand why Courmayeur doesn't have a park. There are a few areas that would be ideally suited to one. If you want to jump, get your shovel and start digging. There is a boardercross but it seems to get neglected.

Off-piste and backcountry

There's tons of good backcountry around Courmayeur. As well as loads of wicked tree riding, you will find routes to La Thuile, and to La Rosière and Chamonix in France.

The Valley Blanche Descent is one not to miss. It starts at Punta Helbronner (3462m) and ends in Chamonix (1037m); a 24km descent in the heart of the Mont Blanc Massif on the glaciers of the Colle del Gigante descending into the Valley of Chamonix. This is an amazing adventure across the Mar de Glace sea of ice that takes you through crevasses and ice tunnels. Don't do this one without a guide.

The Toula Glacier is a great place to go in the right conditions. From Helbronner point (3452m) you can get to the Toula pass (3450m) in a few minutes. Then you have to make your way up a metal staircase to get to the Toula Glacier, after which you have a 2000m descent back down to La Palud Courmayeur. You don't have to be a pro to do this, as long as you feel comfortable off-piste you should be fine, though it is recommended to take a guide.

We recommend guides from the Società Guide Alpine Courmayeur centre who can show you the routes we have described and many more as well as heliskiing and boarding. They're located in the centre of town and prices are pretty reasonable.

Lift passes	
1 day	€34
6 days	€175
13 days	€315

Instruction

Scuola Sci/ Snowboard, Courmayeur

This ski and snowboard school offers freeride, freestyle, tours and camps. Private lessons cost €30–42 per hour depending on the time of season and time of day. A 21-hour ski or snowboard camp costs €184.

T: 0039 0165 848 254
E: info@scuolascicourmayeur.it
W: www.scuolascicourmayeur.it

Società Guide Alpine Courmayeur

Skiers and snowboarders can discover more of the Courmayeur ski area through backcountry and freeride guides, ski-touring, heliskiing, mountaineering and ice-fall climbing. Guiding costs €64 –169 per person, depending on the location.

T: 0039 0165 842 064
E: info@guidecourmayeur.com
W: www.guidecourmayeur.com

Other activities

When not on the mountain, most people choose to wander round town in their best designer kit, elegantly sipping cocktails and looking gorgeous, but there are a few other things to entertain you.

Forum sports centre: Most of the sporting activities can be found at this huge sports centre (0165 844 096) with ice skating, ice hockey matches to watch, indoor tennis, squash, gym and climbing wall. It's across the river and contains the Planet bar (see Bars and clubs).

Ice-fall climbing This costs €157 per person in a group of 4 (see Società Guide Alpine details above).

Mountain guide museum: This is worth a look if you're interested in guiding and mountaineering in the olden days.

Paragliding, snow-biking and dog-sledding: Contact the tourist office for more details (see Useful facts and phone numbers).

Events

None worth mentioning.

Accommodation

There are some seriously swish and swanky hotels in Courmayeur, as you would expect, as well as a few cheaper options. The **Royal and Golf Hotel** (0039 0165 831 611, www.royalegolf.com, hotelroyalgolf@ventaglio.com) is smart and luxurious. There are 86 elegant rooms, all kitted out with internet connections, satellite tv and mini bar. There is also a fitness centre, gym, sauna, steam room and massage facilities. Rooms cost from €115 per person per night for half-board. It's exactly what you would expect of a smart hotel, but it's pretty impersonal. We would rather stay at the **Hotel Mont Blanc Perrier** (0039 0165 846 555), a traditional and elegant place with a welcoming and cosy atmosphere. All rooms have video recorder and mini bar. You will find the Hotel Mont Blanc on the left of the main square as you drive into town.

"A traditional and elegant place with a welcoming and cosy atmosphere"

Less than a minute's walk from the cable car is the retro-looking **Le Grand Chalet** (0039 0165 841 448, www.legrandchalet.it, into@legrandchalet.it). This apart-hotel consists of 33 apartments, including 13 studios, 17 one-bedroom flats and 3 two-bedroom flats. Prices start at €550 for a small studio. Also close to the lifts is the cosy **Hotel Courmayeur** (0039 0165 846 732, www.hotelcourmayeur.it, info@hotelcourmayeur.com), which is full of character. Rooms can only be rented for a full week, Sunday to Sunday, and start at €490 per person. Try to get a room with a balcony.

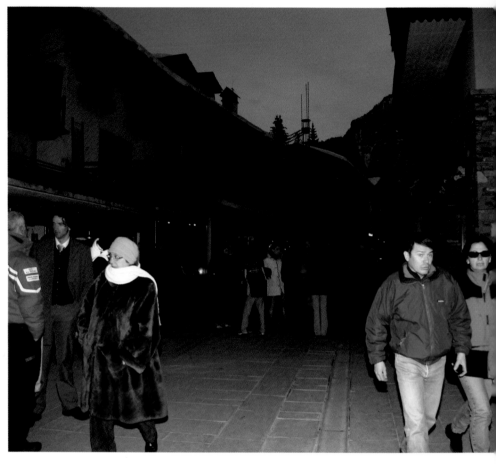

Eating out

On the mountain

There are loads of choices in Courmayeur when it comes to eating on the mountain; from snacks to delicious bites in rustic huts – the most well known of which is **Maison Vieille** (0165 809 399), infamous for its homemade pasta, wood-fired oven, friendly service and cosy atmosphere. For sunny terraces and snack bars, head over to the Val Veny side of the valley and try the **Grolla** (0165 869 095), **La Fodze** or **Zerotta** (0165 869 091).

In town

Cadran Solaire is a gorgeous, romantic and rustic restaurant. A main meal will cost you €14–22. **Pierre Alexis** is another smart restaurant that is definitely worth a try. It's renowned for being an expensive place but not everything will cost you a fortune; pasta dishes start at €10. The gastronomic menus will set you back €70/ €100 for a 2–4 course meal. The **Leone Rosso** is a small and charming restaurant that serves great regional specialities. Dishes include pastas, fish, meat and fondues and will cost you €10–20.

For a quick snack at après ski, head to the **Petit Bistrot**, where you can sit in a small, cosy and busy atmosphere tucking into a tasty crêpe. **Coquelicot** is one of the few places that still does beef fondues (€24), as well as cheese fondues and lots of fish. **Pizzeria du Tunnel** is a good value and cute snack bar that serves homemade pastas, pizzas, omelettes and steaks. They also do massive pizzas for sharing (€18) and heart-shaped pizzas on request!

Mont Frety, on the road that leads from the town to the gondola, is a good pizzeria that is less expensive than most of the other options and not at the expense of quality. A pizza will cost you €6.50–10 and meaty main meals €11–18. **Poppy's Bar** (see Bars and clubs), also serves great pizzas for lunch and at night; 7–10pm you can pay €10 for any wood-fired pizza and a beer.

Bars and clubs

The **Roma** is the best bar in town, especially for après ski. It's beautiful and cosy and there is a huge amount of food out for you to munch on whilst you drink. The **Café Della Posta** looks like a regular café but if you sneak through to the room at the back you will find a huge stone fireplace with a roaring fire, a few tables and some snug sofas and chairs. **Cadran Solaire** (see Eating out) has a gorgeous, but expensive bar attached. **Ziggy's** is the (only) place to go to check your E-mails. Down one of the winding backstreets, this dark, basement bar opens at 3pm. To wow the opposite sex on the dancefloor head to **Poppy's Bar** (also a good place to grab a pizza, see Eating out), a great bar/restaurant/club that is convenient, big, good value and fun. **Planet**, at the sports complex in La Villette across the river, is a huge open bar/club that has a big stage for live music and DJs; it also has pool and table football tables. It's open 11am–2am and

> "A huge open bar/club that has a big stage for live music and DJs"

looks very much like your student union bar with long wooden tables and a lived-in feel. It's inconvenient if you're staying in town but is a good night out and you can get a burger for under €4!

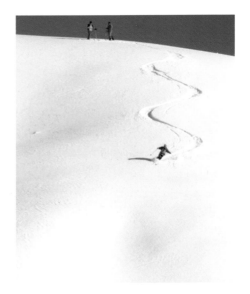

Useful facts and phone numbers

Tourist office

T:	0039 0165 842 060
F:	0039 0165 842 072
E:	aiat.montebianco@psw.it
W:	www.aiat-monte-bianco.com

Emergency services

- Police: 0165 890 720/ 0165 831 334
- Medical emergency: 118

Doctors

- Dr Bahren: 0165 860 088
- Dr Di Cesare: 340 979 5327
- Dr Mannu: 0165 809 853
- Dr Rocchio: 0165 841 113

Taxis

- P.le Monte Bianco Courmayeur: 0165 842 960
- Taxi Granato: 0165 844 283

Getting there

By car

Courmayeur is easy to get to from France as it is only 10 minutes' drive from the Mont Blanc Tunnel. Make sure you don't speed whilst you're in the tunnel – they'll catch you on the other side.

By plane

Geneva (100km)
Turin (150km)
Transfer from both airports takes around 2 hours.

Gressoney

Relax in this quiet, unspoilt
village and take advantage of
the heliskiing capital of Europe

On the slopes	
Snow reliability	❄ ❄ ❄
Parks	–
Off-piste	❄ ❄ ❄ ❄

Off the slopes	
Après ski	❄
Nightlife	❄
Eating out	❄ ❄
Resort charm	❄ ❄ ❄ ❄

The resort

Gressoney, in the Monterosa ski area, is a beautiful, quiet and unspoilt village; many of the local families have lived here for over 500 years. There's little to do in the evenings in this idyllic community, although this is probably for the best in order for you to keep your strength up for the next day on the mountain, as Gressoney has access to extensive backcountry terrain and some of the finest

"A long weekend of heliskiing and mountain exploration would be a first-rate trip"

heliskiing in Europe. Like its neighbours, Alagna and La Grave in France, Gressoney would not be the model resort for most. However, for the earnest skiers (Gressoney is less suitable for boarders) who value their time on the mountain more than in the pub, and would take pleasure in tranquil, yet spectacular surroundings, a long weekend of heliskiing and mountain exploration would be a first-rate trip.

When we were here we were unlucky with the weather, and unfortunately didn't experience the heliskiing first hand (we did get a detailed account

from one of the top boys in the mountain guiding school) but we're already planning our trip for next season.

Gressoney consists of two separate villages. Gressoney La Trinité is at the end of the valley where the lifts to the Monterosa ski area are located. Here you will find a number of convenient hotels, and a couple of local facilities. Gressoney St Jean is further from the lifts (it does have a few of its own, but the reason you're here is to experience the Monterosa area so we wouldn't bother too much with these) but is larger and has more hotels, restaurants and facilities. However, this part of town does extend over a few kilometres and the restaurants and hotels require a certain amount of travel between them. Although the bus service isn't bad, we wouldn't come here without a car.

The mountains

Height: 1200–3550m

Ability	Rating
Expert	❄ ❄ ❄ ❄
Intermediate	❄ ❄ ❄
Beginner	❄

Getting about

There are 200km of pistes in Monterosa, and a landscape that consists of almost endless off-piste. Snowboarders are advised to go elsewhere – there is a fair bit of traversing on most of the off-piste itineraries. The piste map is pretty shocking, but the signs on the mountain are good so just decide where you're headed and follow the signs. From anywhere on the mountain you can also be guaranteed stunning views, not least of the striking Monte Rosa glacier.

The cable car connecting Gressoney and Alagna is now firmly in place and the local enthusiasts are ecstatic at the amount of terrain this has opened up. On top of this, new plans are in order to enhance the available territory even further. In 2006 there are plans to install a lift in Alagna from Passo Salati to Cresta Rossa and demolish the old cable car from Bocchetta to Indren, extending off-piste opportunities enormously.

N.B. The Monterosa area tends to remain in good condition until the end of April and the later half of the season is usually the best time to visit.

The park

In between Gressoney and Alagna we found a small park which consisted of two rails, one of which was kinked, one table top over a 6m gap and a pretty wicked hip jump. There were also two fun boxes at the bottom. You wouldn't come here if riding the park was all you wanted to do, but it's still good for a change. We enjoyed it.

Off-piste and backcountry

Gressoney has fantastic access to massive backcountry areas, being right in the centre of the Monterosa area, which is renowned for its backcountry expeditions. There are a number of off-piste itineraries marked on the map – we had a great long run down from the **Punta Indren** on the way back from Alagna to Gressoney. These itineraries are fairly easy to explore without a guide if you are a confident off-piste rider.

Understandably, many people come to Gressoney and Alagna for the heliskiing on the Monte Rosa. We highly recommend the Guide Monterosa (see Instruction), who offer guiding, touring and heli-trips, with four different drop-offs. If you are splashing out on a heli-trip try the descent down the huge Alexandra couloir or the descent right down to Zermatt. This trip usually involves a helicopter flight to the Col du Lys (4270m) and descent towards the Swiss side of the Monte Rosa (Grenz glacier) to Furi, a hamlet of Zermatt.

"The cable car will take you to the Matterhorn with a descent to Frachey near Champoluc"

The cable car will take you to the Matterhorn with a descent to Frachey near Champoluc and from here you will return to Gressoney using the Monte Rosa lifts.

Heliskiing is by no means the only way to get the best out of the mountain; the day, weekend or week-long excursions planned by the Guide Monterosa, are a fantastic way to explore. We have a few recommendations. If couloirs are your thing, head to the Balma area, which can be reached from the Gressoney lift, or the Salza Valley, which has a huge area of piste and several couloirs. The Lost Valley and the Bettolina area in between Gressoney and Champoluc (which involves 1.5 hours with skins on) are two vast and astonishing areas that are worth a look.

If you would like to explore the off-piste but are lacking in confidence you can ask for a special package in which you spend three days with an instructor and three days with a guide (see Instruction).

To learn how to use your avalanche equipment, visit the Ortovox training ground at the Passo dei Salati.

Lift passes	
1 day	€32
6 days	€136/170 (depending on season)

Instruction

Guide Monterosa

This guiding association has been in existence for over ten years and they know the mountains better than anyone. They have 25 guides who speak a number of languages and can cater for any level of experience. They offer days for experienced riders such as a day tour of the Monte Rosa where you can ski over to Zermatt and back with the use of helicopters (€215 per person, see Off-piste and backcountry above), a day exploring the off-piste (€240/ €300 for a guide for the day) or a day's heliski (€180 per person). If you wish, they can arrange an airport to airport service, including your hotel, taxis, lift pass, skis/board, guiding – the lot.

T: 0039 0125 366 139
E: info@guidemonterosa.com
W: www.guidemonterosa.com

Scuola Sci Gressoney Monte Rosa
Lessons are offered in skiing, boarding, carving and freeriding. A 1-hour private lesson costs €31–45 depending on the number of people. Group lessons cost €130 for 12.5 hours.
T: 0039 0125 366 265
E: info@gressoneymonterosa.it
W: www.scuolascigressoney.it

Scuola Sci Gressoney St Jean
Prices are as above.
T: 0039 0125 355 291
W: www.scuolascigressoney.com

Other activities

There's not a huge amount to do in Gressoney, although there is a toboggan run in Gressoney St Jean and a popular cross-country skiing track (contact the tourist office).

Events

The acclaimed freeride event – the **Red Bull Snow Thrill** (www.redbullsnowthrill.com) – takes place in Gressoney. It is usually arranged for mid-March and the world's best big mountain skiers are invited. Once every two years the **Mezzalama Trophy** (www.trofeomezzalama.org) occurs; a 45km race from Cervinia to Gressoney La Trinite over snow, rock and ice at an average altitude of 4000m.

Accommodation

There are 23 hotels in Gressoney and 1800 beds. There should be something for most tastes, be it moderately priced, romantic or convenient.

Gressoney St Jean
Situated in a small hamlet is a top quality, moderately priced hotel, the 2-star **Hotel Villa Tedaldi** (0039 0125 355 123, villatedaldi@virgilio.it), that is more like a

stately home than a hotel. It's a charming building, grand and old fashioned, with eight large rooms that each have private bathroom, TV, phone and great view. The hotel offers only B&B accommodation, at €35–50 per person per night (assuming double room; there are reductions for 3rd/4th beds) and, to add to the quaintness, doesn't accept credit cards. The best thing about this place is that is allows short

> "Many of the rooms have separate lounges, hydromassage showers and a luxurious and romantic feel"

stays (which many hotels don't), which is perfect as Gressoney is the ideal place for a long weekend.

The stunning **Lyshaus** (0039 0125 356 643, info@lyshaus.com, www.lyshaus.com), has the most incredible rooms and suites – we have no idea why it has only a 3-star rating. Many of the rooms have separate lounges, hydromassage showers and a luxurious and romantic feel. And the bedrooms aren't the best feature of the hotel – this prize would have to go to the remarkable billiard room. Picture an upper class golf club with cigar-smoking aristocracy; there are wooden floors, a massive old billiard table, panelled walls lined with expensive old wines and a small wooden bar with racks of champagne glasses and dusty bottles of champagne. It also has a beautiful, candle-lit restaurant (Carducci) serving dishes such as fondues, risottos and a variety of meats. A main meal will cost you around €10–16. One night at the Lyshaus will cost €40–120 per person.

If you like to cater for yourself you could try the 4-star **Residenze des Sole** (0039 0125 357 400, reception@residenzadelsole.it, www.residenzadelsole.it) that has a number of facilities including a pool, sauna, gym, billiard room, beauty salon, cocktail bar and restaurant.

Gressoney La Trinité

If you like hopping out of bed straight on to the lifts you'll want to stay in this part of the resort. The 3-star **Hotel Jolanda Sport** (0039 0125 366 140, info@jolandasport.com, www.hoteljolandasport.com) is about as close to the slopes as you can get and is a lovely hotel. However, you can only book for the whole week and half-board accommodation is essential. The week will cost €310–600 per person. Also close to the slopes is the friendly **Hotel Dufour** (0039 0125 366 139), with a homely feel and a large, comfy bar area in which you can curl up with a book. The Dufour costs from €294 per week B&B and from €385 for half-board.

If you're on a budget there are a number of other options. In Issime, for example, you can stay at the friendly **Albergo Poste**, for around €60 per room per night. At the bottom of the valley in Pont St Martin is the lovely, spacious and welcoming **Crabun Hotel** (0039 0125 806 069, www.crabunhotel.it). From here you can reach a number of ski areas; it's around half an hour to Gressoney (30km), about the same to Champoluc, under an hour to Cervinia and only 10km from a small local area in Val di Champorcher.

Eating out

On the mountain

The **Bedemie** (0125 366 429), is a cute little restaurant with a big terrace, serving simple food such as slices of pizza, sandwiches, pasta, soup and lasagne. Our favourite restaurant is the **Morgenrot,** just below the Bedemie on the way back down into Gressoney. From the outside it looks like a rowdy bar with music playing and Carlsberg banners but inside it is a beautiful restaurant with great food (homemade pastas, and chunky chips), lots of character and it's pretty good value too (dishes cost €8–12). The **Gabiet** is a good, simple establishment with a terrace overlooking the snow park and the **Rifugio Guglielmina** (0163 914 44/0163 915 47, rifugioguglielmina@libero.it, www.rifugioguglielmina.it) has a traditional restaurant as well as accommodation, which can only be accessed off-piste. Finally the **Alpenhütte Lys** (0125 366 057), by the side of the chair from Gabiet to Passo Salati, has a stunning terrace with hand-built wooden loungers looking out on to the pistes and the mountains. We sat here with a pint (€3.50) as the lifts closed, watching the sun slowly fade, after a great run from the Punta Indren and we were in heaven.

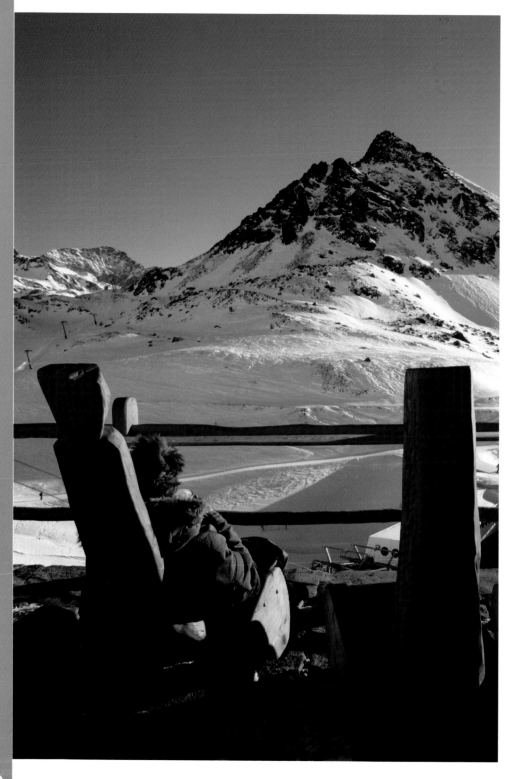

In town

In **St Jean** there are a few standard restaurants; the **Flora Alpina** has a big and bright restaurant with lots of plants. The **Genzianella** is cute, wooden and good value (if you can understand the Italian menu) and **Marmotte** at the Residenza del Sole looks smart but is, once again big and bright with little atmosphere. **Carducci** at the Lyshaus hotel is one of the finest restaurants in town (see Accommodation). Another is the **Nordkapp** (http://nordkapp.too.it) in the centre of the cobbled square. This charming restaurant has a great couple in charge, and the chefs met working at Mal Maison in Glasgow! It's pretty weird hearing an Italian speak English with a Glaswegian accent. They mix local specialities with their own culinary ideas and experiences and create beautiful food. There's also a cute bar downstairs with a little fire. In La Trinité there are only a handful of places to eat, most of them in the hotels. One great, atmospheric pizzeria is the **Walserchild**, where you can get a tasty pizza for only €5–8.

Bars and clubs

There isn't a huge choice of bars; a lot of the hotels claim to have bars but there is rarely anyone in them. In La Trinité there is pretty much only the **Schnee Blume**, opposite the Jolanda Sport hotel, that's a cosy bar, aimed at the local trade and a great place to sip a beer after a tiring day on the mountain. The bar at the **Dofour** is big and comfy. In St Jean you have the choice of the oldy worldy **Bierfall** in the centre of town (the cobbled bit) – a cute, and once again local place, and the **Sport Bar**, a small place with some kind of character and a small TV.

Useful facts and phone numbers

Tourist office

T: 0039 0125 366 1413 (La Trinité)/
     0039 0125 355 185 (St Jean)
F: 0039 0125 366 323
E: info@aiatmonterosawalser.it
W: www.aiatmonterosawalser.it

Emergency services

• Police: 0125 355 304
• In the case of medical emergency call 118.

Doctors

• Dr Silvio Boggio (338 115 88 66) visits
  Gressoney every day at various times.
• Dr Aldo Mignini (339 435 13 58) also visits
  Gressoney.
• During the day there is usually at least one
  doctor available, at any other time call 118.

Taxis

• 347 578 7132
• 0125 355 957

Getting there

By car

Take the A5 motorway from Turin to Aosta, exit at Pont-Saint-Martin and take the highway for the Valle di Gressoney.

By plane

Turin (100km) has the quickest and easiest access to Gressoney.
Milan (165km)

Selva in Val Gardena

A superb family holiday resort,
with stunning scenery, a
beautiful village and nightlife
if you want it

On the slopes	
Snow reliability	❄ ❄ ❄
Parks	❄
Off-piste	❄ ❄ ❄
Off the slopes	
Après ski	❄ ❄ ❄
Nightlife	❄ ❄ ❄
Eating out	❄ ❄ ❄
Resort charm	❄ ❄ ❄

The resort

Selva Gardena is just one of the villages within the Val Gardena valley. The alternative towns of Ortisei and S. Cristina are just as charming, but Selva has the best access to the slopes and the best selection of restaurants and bars. The Dolomite landscape is absolutely breathtaking and the extent of the slopes is equally as impressive. Intermediate cruisers will be in heaven with the far-reaching Sella Ronda circuit, that takes you on a spectacular journey round the Gruppo Sella – a magnificent limestone massif.

At first you will probably be confused by the language, no matter how good your skills are, as many locals still speak the age old dialect of Ladin. Fortunately all speak Italian and German as well and English is also pretty widespread. Road signs are also often expressed in the local dialect so expect to see signs for Wolkenstein (Selva) and Gröden (Val Gardena).

The mountains

Height: 1250–2520m

Ability	Rating
Expert	❄ ❄ ❄
Intermediate	❄ ❄ ❄ ❄ ❄
Beginner	❄ ❄ ❄ ❄

Getting about

The 510km of pistes will more than satisfy the adventurous intermediate, but the experts and beginners are also pretty well catered for. The serious experts should give heliskiing some serious thought or perhaps try the more demanding Porta Vescovo trail from Arabba.

N.B. The Sella Ronda circuit can take up to 6 hours depending on queues and how speedy you are, so don't crawl out of bed hungover at midday and decide to give it a shot; you might end up paying for a taxi back. You can set off clockwise or anticlockwise.

The park

There is a park in Selva that has a mediocre half pipe and a couple of hits that would be OK to learn some tricks or just have a jib, as well as a little park for kids by the euro chair. We also saw the remnants of a boardercross course which had been left to fade away. We did visit at the end of the season though, so it may have been a little better in its heyday. We're not massive fans of the freestyle scene here; Val Gardena is definitely more cruisy than crazy.

"Exploration requires a guide here, or you will get lost"

Off-piste and backcountry

Despite most of the terrain being fairly flat, there are some easily accessible bowls that would be great after a snowfall. Exploration requires a guide here, or you will get lost. Ask them to show you the Mezdi Valley, apparently the 'Grand Canyon' of the Dolomites, and a freerider's heaven with enough terrain for a whole day's riding in untracked snow (in good conditions).

Instruction

Ski and Boarders Factory

A 1-hour private lesson costs from €30 for one person (€7 for each additional person). Costs rise in high season. Six half-day courses start at €129.

T: 0039 0471 795 156
E: info@ski-factory.it
W: www.ski-factory.it

Ski and Snowboard School '2000'

A private lesson will cost from €30 and a group lesson from €29 for 1 day (3 hours), €77 for 3 days (9 hours) and €103 for 5 days (15 hours). Expect to pay more in high season. They can also offer you a package with equipment included.

T: 0039 0471 773125
E: snowboardvalgardena@val-gardena.com
W: http://www.snowboardvalgardena.com

Val Gardena Mountain Guide Association

This guiding school offers everything from guiding, touring, ice climbing, off-piste and freeride, to glacier hiking.

T: 0039 0471 794133
E: info@guidegardena.com
W: www.guidegardena.com

Other activities

Climbing: There are two climbing walls.
Horse-drawn sleighs: On the top station of the cableway Alpe di Siusi there are horse-drawn sleighs. Fares are approximately €28–45 for 1 hour.
Ice climbing and glacier hiking: Val Gardena Mountain Guide Association offer ice climbing and glacier hiking as well as many other exhausting activities. For contact details see Instruction.
Ice skating: There's an ice stadium.
Nativity: The biggest nativity in the world is exhibited in the Sport Centre Iman of S. Cristina. Each year new figures are added.
Night skiing: Every Tuesday, Thursday and Friday at 7.30pm Taxi Gardena (0335 560 6141, www.taxigardena.com) organise night skiing on floodlit slopes followed by après ski at Richy's Igloo. Transfer back to the hotel is included (at approx. 11pm).
Shooting: Facilities at the shooting centre.
Sleigh rides by night: Taxi Gardena (see Night skiing) organise sleigh rides by night. They take you to the Seiseralm, where you make an ascent by snowcat to the Dialer Lodge and then have dinner at 2145m. Depart at 7pm and return to your hotel at 11pm.
Swimming: There is an outdoor and indoor pool with wellness facilities.
Tennis: The massive tennis centre incorporates six tennis courts, two squash courts, billiards, bowling and a fitness centre.
Tobogganing: If tobogganing is your thing, there is a 6km sled run from the Rasciesa chair lift in Ortisei. The middle station allows you to go down the first part as many times as you like. You can hire sleds when you get there.

Events

There aren't too many New School events apart from a **Big Air Comp** that is usually held in late March. The **FIS World Cup (Super G and Downhill)** is also held in Val Gardena in December. The **Ski Jörring** event in February is a good one to watch. In this event 16 ski instructors, pulled by horses, compete against each other for the champion's title. If you see girls dressed up as witches don't be alarmed, it may just be the **Watch out for Witches** day; just one of the strange rituals and customs of Val Gardena.

Lift passes	Val Gardena (as far as Passo Sella and Passo Gardena)		Whole of the Dolomites	
	Low season	High season	Low season	High season
1 day	€31	€35	€34	€38
6 days	€158	€180	€171	€194
13 days	€275	€312	€296	€337

There are discounts for ski passes bought in December and for children and seniors. You can also buy tickets that will allow you 10 days out of 14 on the mountain so you can have a few chill-out days in town. The cards now have a chip in them for handsfree access to lifts – to get these free, book online on www.DolomitiSuperski.com

Accommodation

The 5-star **Alpenroyal Sporthotel** (0039 0471 795 555, www.alpenroyal.com, info@alpenroyal.com), on the outskirts of town, is a large and smart complex, although it does have a slight 80s tinge to it. There is a swimming pool and a games room with a pool table and table footie. It's not too handy for town but they do have a shuttle service. The lovely **Hotel Aaritz** (0039 0471 795 011, www.val-gardena .com/hotel/aaritz, aaritz@valgardena.it) has a

fantastic location in the centre of town and right opposite the lift. The pool, sauna and gym are another advantage.

We loved the beautiful **Hotel Freina** (0039 0471 795 110, www.hotelfreina.com, info@hotelfreina .com), a stunning chalet hotel just a couple of minutes from town and right next to the lifts. The rooms are huge (especially superior rooms and suites: 35–44m²) and the whirlpool and sauna are a great place to relax after a hard day on the slopes. Prices are €76–120 per person per day for half-board accommodation. **Hotel Laurin** (0039 0471 795 296, www.malleier.com, info@malleier.com) is the place to stay if you want to be in the centre of the action. Right in the centre of town, this hotel contains the popular après bar and restaurant Laurinkeller as well as a sauna, steam bath, Turkish bath, whirlpool and gym. Prices start from €72 per night but can be up to €130 depending on the type of room you are looking for.

Eating out

On the mountain

There are tons of cute and cosy huts dotted all over the Sella Ronda circuit, most of which are highly recommended. Our favourite was the **Baita Vallongian** (0471 794 071) that can be found on the route from Ciampino to Plan de Gralba. It is a stunning spot to sit and relax, either in the deckchairs or on the big wooden benches outside. The food is superb and it's the sort of place you could sit all afternoon – until the

continuous change of music from Tina Turner to Italian folk music takes its toll. Other favourites are the **Piz Setëur** (335 613 9112), especially for an après ski beer and the **Panorama** (0471 795 372) for its cosy and rustic atmosphere. For value, you can't beat the restaurant at the top of the cable car from Selva, where you can pick up a slice of pizza for €3.

In town

Pizzas, pasta and local dishes are the staple food of the restaurants in Selva. **L'Medel** (0471 795 235), on the outskirts of town, has loads of character and charm, and is well worth a very short taxi ride or drive. It has a really cute little bar and the restaurant serves hundreds of fantastic pizzas. Another stunning place to enjoy a pizza is the **Sun Valley** (0471 795 152, www.hotel sunvalley.it). Its classic wooden feel creates a superb, cosy atmosphere. For more casual surroundings, head to **Rino's** (0471 795 272), **Laurinkeller** (0471 795 004) for ribs, steaks and snacks or **La Bula** (0471 795 208), a pizzeria/club at the Hotel Stella. The restaurant at **Hotel**

Freina (0471 795 110) is really lovely and serves a huge range of tasty food.

Bars and clubs

One of the great things about Val Gardena compared to many other European resorts is the prices, so get drinking. For après, the liveliest haunt is the **Luislkeller**, which you may never leave. In fact, both the Luislkeller and **Laurinkeller** are kicking at all times of the evening – expect lots of beer swinging and dancing to the DJ's beats. Other options for après ski are the cosy **La Stua**, where you will often find live folk music, or the **Goalies Irish Pub** that also has live music to entertain the après crowd. Goalies has a proper pub feel and serves Guiness, Carling and Murphy's. The **Sissy's Alm** is open 4pm–2am and it's pretty good, but not crazy – probably better when you're a little drunk. It's all in pine and, at times, the music can be extremely odd. Those looking for a dance later on should boogie on to **La Bula**; the pizzeria-turned-club at the Hotel Stella.

Useful facts and phone numbers

Tourist office

T: 0039 0471 795 122
F: 0039 0471 794 245
E: selva@valgardena.it
W: www.valgardena.it

Emergency services

- In an emergency call 118
- Police: 113
- Avalanche information: 0471 271 177
- Medical Services Selva: 0471 794 266

Taxis

- Viaggi Gardena: 0471 795 150, info@ viaggigardena.com
- Senoner Gabriel: 0471 795 260
- Wienen Schmalzl M.: 0471 796 543
- Autosella: 0471 790 033, taxi-autosella@val-gardena.com

Getting there

By car

Val Gardena can be reached using the Brenner Motorway (A22) and take the Chiusa/Val Gardena exit. You should reach Selva after 20–30 minutes.

By plane

Bolzano (40km)
Innsbruck (120km)
Verona (190km)
Airport transfers can be arranged by bus or taxi (see above) or by helicopter! Check out www.elikos.it for more information.

Norway

Small, quiet resorts that
perk up at the weekend

Hemsedal

The best of Norway, with a great park, but the terrain is still pretty limited

HEMSEDAL

On the slopes	
Snow reliability	❄ ❄ ❄ ❄
Parks	❄ ❄ ❄ ❄
Off-piste	❄ ❄ ❄

Off the slopes	
Après ski	❄ ❄ ❄
Nightlife	❄ ❄
Eating out	❄
Resort charm	❄ ❄

The resort

Hemsedal is the best place for riding in Norway, but this still doesn't make it a real player in comparison to the resorts in France, Austria and Switzerland. The snow is really reliable but there's not a lot going on in the resort, with most visitors popping in for a weekend. The ski area is a few kilometres from the village centre but the free bus service isn't too bad.

The mountains

Height: 600–1920m

Ability	Rating
Expert	❄ ❄
Intermediate	❄ ❄
Beginner	❄ ❄ ❄

Getting about

Hemsedal has the highest alpine point of Scandinavia, at 1500m above sea level and a vertical drop of 810m. There are 40km of slopes with the longest slope at 6km. The terrain is limited, and not the best for cruisy intermediates but the beginners' slopes are pretty good and experts can amuse themselves on the eight black slopes, off-piste or in the fantastic park. Make sure you get wrapped up; it's cold.

The park

Hemsedal is very proud of its freestyle park, and rightly so. Each year money is pumped into expanding and developing it, ensuring that it is up there as one of the very best.

"The parks are groomed every day and the pipes are re-shaped two or three times a week"

In the main park they have catered for all standards of rider. They have a red line for advanced skiers and boarders, and a black line for the experts and pros. The 600m-long park contains two half pipes, jumps, table tops, quarter pipe, big air, boxes and rail slides.

More recently, Hemsedal built the Blue Park for beginner freestylers and those looking for a gentle jib. This has a blue line with the same sorts of jumps, table tops and rails as the main park, only smaller.

The parks are groomed every day and the pipes are re-shaped two or three times a week. On top of this, the elements are painted and outlined every day to make them visible.

Off-piste and backcountry

Off-piste conditions are usually pretty decent as Hemsedal gets a good share of snow. The top of the Totten summit (1450m) is the best place to head for freeriding, where you are more than likely to find some fresh snow, and fun cliff drops. There is also a popular couloir that is fairly steep and long, but it's not over-fierce. There's no shortage of trees and there are some good routes amongst them. You can also find some good off-piste just to the side of the pisted areas, from the top of Hamaren.

Lift passes	
1 day	NOK 310
6 days	NOK 1280

Instruction

Hemsedal Ski School

Group lessons for 5 days (90 mins per day) costs NOK 745. A course in the park, for 3 days (90 mins per day) is NOK 625. Private lessons cost NOK 670 for one person for 100 minutes, including video analysis. A personal trainer for 1–5 people costs NOK 995 for 3 hours, and NOK 1795 for 5 hours, both with video analysis.

T: 0047 32 05 50 67
W: www.skistar.co/English/hemsedal

Kruse Topptur

For more information, see the website.
T: 0047 41 41 96 82
E: info@topptur.no
W: www.topptur.com

Norske Opplevelser

One day a week there is a 6–8 hour guided mountain tour to one of Hemsedal's peaks. They also offer off-piste guiding, which costs NOK 1050 for 4 hours for 1 person. The 2nd person costs NOK 595, the 3rd NOK 450 and the 4th–10th NOK 495. A beginner's course (2.5 hours) costs NOK 295.

T: 0047 32 06 00 03
E: info@norskeopplevelser.no
W: www.norskeopplevelser.no

Other activities

Bowling, pool, darts and games: The activity centre, Experten Sportsbar, has four bowling lanes, pool, darts, games and a big TV for sports. Bowling costs NOK 45, and shoes are NOK 10 a pair.

Drive a pack of dogs: A great drive over 10km of frozen lakes and forest. Adults pay NOK 600, inclusive of snow shoes. Book at Hemsedal tourist office one day in advance (32 05 50 30).

Horse sleigh ride: Elvestad Fjellridning (90 88 45 45), Flaget Farm (91 51 70 82), Gjedokk Hestesenter (95 73 40 44) or Hemesedal Hestensenter (32 06 02 02) all offer sleigh rides. Most will take you through the forest and some provide food and drink round a camp fire. Usual cost is NOK 150 for an adult.

Ice climbing: Norske Opplevelser (32 06 00 03, info@norskeopplevelser.no, www.norskeopplevelser.no) offers ice climbing lessons for beginners (NOK 595 for 3 hours). Hemesedal tourist office (32 05 50 30, info@hemsedal.com) offers 2.5 day beginners' courses and instruction on more advanced ice waterfalls for those with experience. Cost is NOK 2500.

Kiteskiing: Wintersteiger Norge (33 11 77 73, post@kiteaction.no, www.kiteaction.no) will teach you how to fly a kite on your skis/board. Bring your own board/skis and helmet.

Night skiing: For 4 days a week the slopes of Hemsedalsløypa (red no.10), Såhaugløypa (black no. 8) and the children's and beginners' area are open for night skiing 5.30–9pm. Adults pay NOK 95 per night. Call Hemsedal Skisenter (32 05 53 00, skisenter@skihemsedal.no) for more information.

Paragliding: Oslo Paragliderklubb (www.opk.no) organise tandem flights (90 96 58 95, 92 81 95 45) for NOK 1000 and intensive courses (22 15 08 18, kurs@opk.no) for NOK 6900.

Snowmobile: You can either drive a snowmobile behind a guide on the mountain for NOK 350 for 45 mins (32 05 53 90, skiskolen@skihemsedal.no) or you can drive on race courses (32 06 02 02, hest@hemsedalhestesenter.no, www.hemsedalhestesenter.no). The race course below the ski centre on powerful mobiles costs NOK 200 for 15 minutes or you can drive on the big race track in Lykkja forest and over fields. This costs NOK 150–200 for 15 minutes and NOK 600 for 60 minutes.

Events

In mid February is the **SAAB Salomon Open Air**, with skiercross and down-hill competitions and a snowmobile show. At the end of March is a **Big Air competition** in the base area. The winner of this competition claims a 'Wild Card' to the Burton Spring Session. The **Hemsedal Freeride competition** takes place in early April. It is a two-day competition on the Mortenskaret and Katmandu slopes. Judges look for line, technique, control and intensity. There are telemark and alpine prizes. The after parties take place at the Hemsedal Café and Nattklubb.

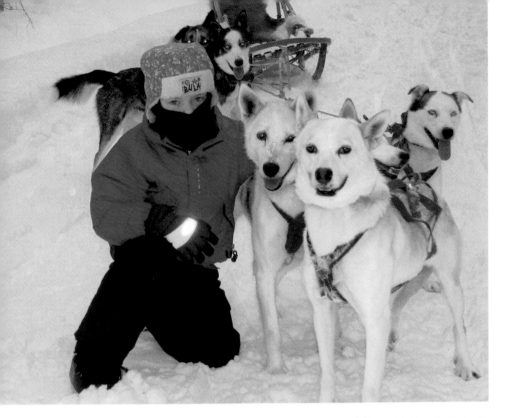

Accommodation

The best hotel around is the **Skarsnuten Hotel** (0047 32 06 17 00, booking@skarsnuten.dvgl.no, www.skarsnutenhotel.no). It has great modern, stylish architecture, and is made entirely out of rocks, steel, and lots of glass. There are 37 rooms (35 double and 2 suites) and a superb restaurant, fitness room and sauna. The only problem is that it is at 1000m altitude, on the slopes at Skarsnuten, so it's not too convenient

"It has great modern, stylish architecture, and is made entirely out of rocks, steel, and lots of glass"

for Hemsedal centre. In Hemsedal village, the **Norlandia Skogstad Hotel** (0047 32 05 50 00, service@skogstad.norlandia.no, www.norlandia.no/skogstad) is massive and has a good pool, sauna, jacuzzi, solarium as well as a few restaurants, bars and a nightclub. The **Hemsedal Hotel** (0047 32 05 54 00) is good too, but not actually in Hemsedal; it's 3km from the ski area and 6km from the village centre.

If you want to be right in the centre of the action, the **Hemsedal Café Skiers' Lodge** (0047 32 05 54 00) is in the same building as the very popular Hemsedal Café. There are four apartments for 4–6 people and four apartments for 7–9 people. Some apartments have a fireplace and balcony. **Hemsedal Fjellandsby** (0047 32 05 50 60) have a number of apartment blocks (Alpin, Staven, Tinden and Trotten) next to Hemsedal ski centre. Up on the slopes you can stay at **Harahorn Hyttegrend** (0047 32 06 23 80), next to Solheisen Ski Centre, or **Lykkja Feriesenter** (0047 32 06 18 20), well placed for cross-country skiing.

Tour operators organising holidays to Hemsedal include Crystal (0870 160 6040), Ski Norway (0207 917 6044), Neilson Ski (0870 333 3347) and Thomson (0870 606 1470).

Eating out

On the mountain

There is one self-service restaurant and a few huts, which are better for picking up a quick snack rather than relaxing over a nice lunch.

In town

There's not a huge choice of restaurants, many of them are in the hotels (see Accommodation); the **Bistro** at Skogstad Hotel is good. **Peppes** (32 05 50 00 or 22 22 55 55 for takeaway) is a popular pizzeria in town. The food at the **Hemsedal Café** (32 05 54 10) is pretty popular too; the burgers and breakfast are really good. The restaurant at the **Skarsnuten Hotel** on the slopes (see Accommodation) is very smart.

Bars and clubs

The best bar for après ski is the **Hemsedal Café** (32 05 54 10) that gets absolutely packed. The **Elgen Bar** at the Skogstad Hotel, the **Oxen** and the **Garasjen** are also popular bars. The **Experten Sportsbar** is good for games (bowling, darts, etc., see Activities) and for watching sports

Useful facts and phone numbers

Tourist office

T:	0047 32 05 50 30
F:	0047 32 05 50 31
E:	info@hemsedal.com
W:	www.hemsedal.com

Direct reservations

T:	0047 32 05 50 60
F:	0047 32 05 50 61
E:	booking@hemsedal.com

Emergency services

- Police: 32 05 55 11
- Ambulance: 113
- Emergency: 112
- Emergency at night time or weekends: 32 02 95 00
- Red Cross: 32 06 04 77

Doctors

- 31 40 89 00
- Night time or weekends: 32 06 07 88

Taxis

- 32 06 01 80

Getting there

By car

From Oslo take the E-16 to Sandvika, then the E-16 to Hønefoss, the R-7 to Gol and finally the R-52 to Hemsedal.

By plane

Oslo (220km) Ryanair flies to Oslo from Glasgow or London.
Lavik (290km)

Oppdal

A tiny resort, but it has a fairly lively scene at the weekends

On the slopes	
Snow reliability	✳ ✳ ✳ ✳
Parks	✳ ✳
Off-piste	✳ ✳
Off the slopes	
Après ski	✳ ✳
Nightlife	✳ ✳
Eating out	✳ ✳
Resort charm	✳ ✳

"The great snow conditions in Oppdal mean that you can find some decent freeriding"

The resort

Oppdal, located between the Dovrefjell mountain plateau and the Trollheimen mountain range, isn't well known, but it is Norway's largest downhill skiing area so deserves some credit. Norwegian resorts aren't huge and, as such, Oppdal only has a handful of bars, restaurants and hotels. The après ski and atmosphere is good at the weekends though. It's difficult to compare Scandinavian resorts to those in other areas of Europe, but unless you're coming for heliskiing, or happen to be passing, we'd probably recommend going elsewhere.

The mountains

Height: 550–1350m

Ability	Rating
Expert	✳ ✳
Intermediate	✳ ✳
Beginner	✳ ✳

Getting about

Snow reliability is great in Oppdal, but extent isn't. There are only eight blues, five greens, nine reds, and five blacks. There are three resort centres: Vangslia (0047 72 40 44 80), Stølen (0047 72 40 41 50) and Hovden (0047 72 40 41 92). Hovden is the best place for experts to head to, or check out the off-piste.

The park

There is a very small park in the Vangslia area, with a couple of kickers and the odd rail. There's also a half

pipe, but the resort doesn't seem to push the freestyle scene and the park does get neglected. Oppdal is all about downhill alpine, which is a little bit of a shame.

Off-piste and backcountry

The great snow conditions in Oppdal mean that you can find some decent freeriding. Stolen Valley is a popular place for getting some fresh tracks, but it does have a high avalanche risk and you will often find the patrollers will close the area before you get a chance to check it out. You can find some steeps and cliffs off the pisted areas and there's some decent tree riding too. Everything gets tracked out really quickly after a fresh snow fall, but on the whole it's not a bad mountain.

Lift passes	
1 day	NOK 280
6 days	NOK 1190

Instruction

The standard price for group lessons is £70–80 for 5 days, with 90 minutes each day and £65 for 100 minutes of private lessons.

Oppdal Skiskole Vangslia

For further information phone or E-mail.
T: 0047 72 40 44 85
E: oppdal.skiskole@oppdal-booking.no

Ski Akademit

For further information phone or E-mail.
T: 0047 72 40 41 70
E: skiakademi@opplev-oppdal.no

Other activities

Gymnasium: Access to gym and training equipment costs NOK 155. For more information contact Merete Nylende (72 40 16 09, merete.nylende@oppdal.kommune.no).

Oppdal Husky Resort: A half-day trip costs NOK 800 and a full day is NOK 1100. You can drive your own sled or simply be a passenger. For more information and booking contact Julie (95 92 96 08) or Øyvind (97 02 86 14, post@islandbreezecrew.com, www.islandbreezecrew.com).

Other sports: For information about kite skiing/boarding, ice climbing, sled rides and tandem hang-gliding contact the tourist office.

Accommodation

The **Quality Hotel Oppdal** (0047 72 40 07 00, post@oppdalbooking.no) has 75 rooms, including 20 rustic suites with four-poster beds, as well as a steakhouse, the Caledonian Bar and George's Pub and Bar. **Hotel Nor** has a nice bar and a lounge with a big fireplace.

> "Hotel Nor has a nice bar and a lounge with a big fireplace"

The **Vangslia Fjelltun** (0047 72 40 08 00, post@oppdalbooking.no) has top quality log apartments for 2–4 people, with private sauna, magnificent views, and the ever-useful dishwasher. Most have a balcony. They are 3km from the centre of town.

The cheapest accommodation in town is **Oppdal Vandrehjem** (0047 72 40 40 90, booking@sletvold-stolen.no), a partner of Norwegian Youth Hostels. There are 16 apartments, each with four beds, bathroom, mini kitchen and TV. Linen and towels can be rented. They are within walking distance of Oppdal centre.

Eating out

On the mountain

Generally, you'd only stop at a mountain hut to grab something to eat, not to spend any time there, but **Rockoss** (72 40 41 53) is good, especially for après ski.

In town

Pizzas, pasta and takeaways can be found at **Møllen's** and steaks at **Perrongen Steakhouse** at Quality Hotel Oppdal (72 40 07 00). The hotel restaurant at the **Quality Hotel** has good fish dishes. **Oppdalsporten** (72 40 06 40), 10km north of the centre, serves good, homemade food.

Useful facts and phone numbers

Tourist office

T: 0047 72 40 04 70
F: 0047 72 40 04 80
E: post@oppdal.com
W: www.oppdal.com

Direct reservations

W: www.oppdal-booking.no

Emergency services

- Police/Mountain rescue: 112
- Ambulance: 113

Doctors

- Medical centre: 72 42 11 00

Taxis

- 72 42 12 05

Bars and clubs

The **Rockoss** on the mountain is a good place to start, and back in town the **Loftet** (99 64 29 05) and the **Opp & Ne** après ski bar (93 86 80 00) get packed out later on at the weekend.

Getting there

By car

National road no. 70 comes from Kristiansund in the west of Norway and joins the E6, which runs through the centre of Oppdal.

By plane

Trondheim (150km) You can book a bus by calling 23 00 27 30, see www.nsb.no.
Oslo (320km) Book a bus by calling 81 54 44 44.

Sweden

Small resorts that are fun, friendly
and full of party people

WELCOME TO FIS ALPINE WORLD SKI CHAMPIONSHIPS

Åre

By far the best Swedish resort, with great riding, park, events and nightlife

On the slopes

On the slopes	
Snow reliability	❄ ❄ ❄
Parks	❄ ❄ ❄ ❄
Off-piste	❄ ❄ ❄

Off the slopes	
Après ski	❄ ❄ ❄
Nightlife	❄ ❄ ❄ ❄ ❄
Eating out	❄ ❄
Resort charm	❄ ❄ ❄

The resort

Åre is awesome. It's popular with everyone, from families and couples to groups of young party people. There aren't too many Brits around but the Swedes are fun, speak good English and know how to party. The centre of town has a great atmosphere and it's a charming and beautiful place, made up of stylish wooden buildings. Some awesome talent has originated in this area too, such as Jon Olsson (see Events), which gives the resort an even better profile and may be one of the reasons that many of the Scandinavian jetset head here for their holidays.

N.B. There are only two cash points in town which have massive queues at weekends and only one pay phone (by the supermarket in the centre of town). The phone doesn't take coins and phone cards are hard to come by.

The mountains

Height: 380–1270m

Ability	Rating
Expert	❄ ❄ ❄
Intermediate	❄ ❄ ❄ ❄
Beginner	❄ ❄ ❄ ❄

Getting about

Åre has around 100km of groomed runs, which are split over four areas: Åre and Åre Björnen (a fairly big area with the main slopes and off-piste) and Duved and Tegerfjäll (connected, but not massive). The variety of riding is good and should suit most. Darkness shrouds the resort for most of the days in early winter; the best time to come is March or later.

The park

We expected Åre's Land Park to rock as so many of the world's best riders grew up here, and we weren't disappointed by this crazy park. Everything is well set up, with the kickers all in a line like a slopestyle course. The jumps were in tip top condition and there were hits for all abilities. There are also some big-ass hip jumps and quarter pipes and a wicked half pipe, all well maintained by the shapers. The ideas tank is pretty good too, with locals designing their own rails and bringing them to the park. There's a boardercross, but it's not as popular as the rest of the park.

Off-piste and backcountry

Åre is a pretty good freeriding destination. There are steeps, wind lips and cornices to play on that are pretty obvious from the pistes or you can explore more unchartered terrain. One popular local adventure is to hitch a ride with a piste basher or skidoo to the top of Åreskutan and go exploring. There is some amazing backcountry terrain that you can reach from here (and a 1000m vertical drop) but it is very easy to get lost, so watch out or check it out with a mountain guide first. If everything goes to plan you will come out at the bottom of the resort.

As in Riksgransen, the heliskiing is mind-blowing, but it's not cheap. It's sometimes a good idea to get a group of three or four of you together and do a deal with your heli guide.

Lift passes	
1 day	1515 SEK
6 days	305 SEK

Instruction

Skidåkarna
T: 0046 (0)771 840 000
W: www.skistar.com

Other activities

Contact Åre tourist information for more information on any of these activities (0046 (0)647 177 20).

Gyms: A few of the hotels have gyms that are open to the public including Hotell Årevidden (6km east of Åre). Åre also has a training centre.

Horse riding: Try horseback riding on an Icelandic horse. One hour or half-day trips are available and a half-day ride will cost around 500 SEK per person.

Ice fishing: There are good ice fishing grounds at Åresjön, Fröåtjärn in Åre Björnen, Greningen above Duved and Hensjön in Edsåsdalen. A fishing permit is required and can be bought at tourist information or at an agent in any of the villages. Fishing permits cost 50 SEK per day.

Indoor climbing: Indoor climbing is available in the sports hall in Duvedshallen (book though the tourist office) or at the Lokalen in Åre. At Ristafallet you can climb the frozen waterfall.

Reindeer sledge: Drive a sledge driven by reindeer; you can even catch and harness them yourself if you like. A 1-hour trip costs 400 SEK and a half-day 700 SEK. Husky sleds are also an option.

Snowmobiling: This can be combined with ice fishing or dinner. Choose between a 1.5-hour trip, a 3-hour trip or a whole day trip. A short trip costs 375 SEK with two people on the snowmobile.

Tobogganning: A toboggan course runs from Hotel Fjällgården down to the square. You can toboggan at night on Wednesdays 6–9pm. For 60 SEK you can rent a toboggan, and spend 3 hours on the track.

Events

In 2005 Jon Olsson held his first ever event here, the **Jon Olsson Invitational** (www.jonolssoninvitational .com), to which he invited 16 of the world's best New School freeskiers too. Cash was obviously up for grabs, but so were some pretty blinding diamond rings. I was very honoured to be invited by Jon to MC his event, which was an amazing experience. The arena was built on the lower slopes, just by the bottom of the resort so it was easy enough for the 7000 spectators to see the crazy jumps. These monstrosities included 24-m tables with perfect kicks

"The Jon Olsson Invitational . . . is the best event I have ever seen"

and the longest landings. I witnessed tricks I never thought were possible. In the end it was Josh Bibby from Canada who took away the most sparkly diamond ring, with Jacob Wester in second place and the new wonder boy Mr T.J. Shiller in third. This is the best event I have ever seen and I would recommend anyone to make a special trip to see the 2006 Jon Olsson Invitational. This is obviously the coolest event but there are a few others. In early March the **SAAB/ Salomon Crossmax** series comes to Åre, and in April 20 of the world's best snowboarding girls compete in the **Candy Jam** weekend. There is a big end of season finale in April, when the elite New School riders, photographers and film-makers all meet up in Åre, with sessions, DJs and great après ski in the square.

Accommodation

The **Holiday Club** (0046 (0)647 120 00, info@ holidayclub.se, www.holidayclub.se) is one of the best hotels in town, and a short 5-minute walk from the town centre and the lifts. It is a huge complex that has everything including a great restaurant and bar, games room, free internet, a bowling alley, spa and sauna world and an awesome water world complete with a horizon pool with views of the mountains and a waterslide! All rooms have TV, mini-bar, internet and views of the peak or lake. Prices are 6340–12560 SEK for one week, Sunday to Sunday.

If you would prefer to stay in the centre of the resort the **Åregården** (0046 (0)647 502 65, www. diplomathotel.com) is the best and most popular. It's a beautiful and stylish place, with good rooms and friendly staff. The breakfasts are worth getting up for and the smart restaurant is popular in the evenings. Prices are 4725–9485 SEK for one week, Sunday to Sunday.

Eating out

On the mountain

Buustamons (0647 531 75, bokning@buustamons
fjallgard.se), a hut in the woods with an outdoor heated
tub, is the best restaurant, and you can book a meal
at night too. Give them a call and they will arrange to
pick you up on a skidoo.

In town

The **Karolinen** is one of the best restaurants in town,
a cosy and intimate place with good traditional food.
Broken attracts a younger crowd for burgers and
steaks and has plasma screens playing the latest ski
and snowboard movies. The hotel restaurants (see
Accommodation) are good too and the burger huts in
the centre of town serve fantastic fast food.

Bars and clubs

The après ski rocks on from 4pm and most people head
straight to the **Diplomat** where they have live bands.
This gets really crowded and it's great fun but not the

"Most people head straight to the Diplomat where they have live bands"

place for a quiet drink. You can also pick up snacks; the
burgers and chips taste superb after a few beers. Around
10–11pm the night really starts. The **Bygget Club** is
one of the best clubs ever, and it's the place to rub
shoulders with the Scandy jetset. It's absolutely massive,
and includes a restaurant serving great sushi, and loads
of rooms playing different types of music: live bands,
60s and 70s music, techno, hip hop… The atmosphere
is great and mega-crazy. It's definitely worth putting up
with the long queues and extortionate drinks' prices to
get in. Another club is the **Country Club**, which has live
bands and is worth checking out.

Useful facts and phone numbers

Tourist office

T: 0046 (0)647 177 20
E: info@areresort.com
W: www.skistar.com
Direct reservations
T: 0046 (0)771 840 000
E: reservations@areresort.se

Emergency services

• Police station in Järpen (22km from Åre):
    0647 105 55 or 112 in an emergency

Doctor

• Hälsocentralen: 0647 166 00

Getting there

By plane

Östersund (100km) There are regular bus
services from Östersund to Åre.
From Stockholm you can reach Östersund by air
or you can take the sleeper train, which brings
you almost right into Åre.

Riksgransen

Heliski in the Midnight Sun, but don't expect much from the resort - it's all in one hotel

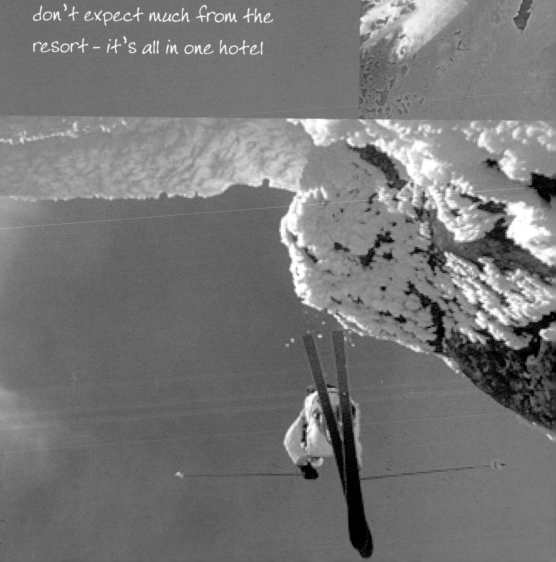

On the slopes	
Snow reliability	✴✴✴✴
Parks	✴✴✴
Off-piste	✴✴✴✴✳
Off the slopes	
Après ski	✴
Nightlife	✴
Eating out	✴
Resort charm	✴

The resort

Riksgransen is in Lapland, 300km north of the Arctic Circle and most visitors are there for the seemingly endless heliskiing. If you can, take your trip in May, when the sun never sets, and hit the mountain at midnight. The mountains are more majestic than most resorts in Scandinavia, with the jagged landscape you would expect to see in the Swiss or French Alps.

Back in resort, there is simply the Riksgransen Hotel, which contains the shops, restaurants, bars and nightclub. This is the resort; there is nothing else.

The famous ice hotel (and the world's biggest igloo) is in Jukkasjärvi, about half an hour from Kiruna, the closest airport to Riksgransen. We definitely recommend a little stop off on the way there or the way back, for a quick drink in the Absolut Ice Bar, and maybe a night stop for the full experience.

The mountains

Height: 520–910m

Ability	Rating
Expert	✴✴✴✴✴
Intermediate	✴✴✴
Beginner	✴

Getting about

The ski season doesn't actually start when the winter does; nothing happens in the first winter months as Riksgransen is in complete darkness. Only in

"The hours of sunshine gradually increase until midsummer's day, when the sun never goes down"

February are there sufficient daylight hours to kick off the season. The hours of sunshine gradually increase until midsummer's day, when the sun never goes down. It's pretty difficult to sleep when the sun's pouring through the window but there is another alternative – you can get your skis or board out and head up the mountain to ride the powder at midnight. At these times, lifts are open 10pm–1am; check with the tourist office for exact dates.

On piste there are 34 descents, but if you are looking for cruisy pistes you should really be elsewhere.

The park

The freestyle scene in Riksgransen is bigger than we expected. A lot of the terrain on the mountain is like a natural fun park and you find that most of the dedicated freestylers are up on the hill each day spending hours building huge gap jumps and crazy hips. The likes of Jon Olsson (X Games gold medallist) is often up there working hard and helping all the up-and-coming rippers. There's a selection of rails that are moved around to different spots and they do build a slopestyle for the King of the Hill event, however it's difficult to predict what's going to be shaped and what's not. This didn't really bother us too much as there's always a group of riders playing on something and they make you feel welcome to join in! There is a half pipe and a quarter pipe that are used for the Swedish Snowboard Cup and for all the freestyle camps that are held here.

Off-piste and backcountry

When the conditions are right (the weather is a tad unpredictable), this crazy mountain can become a freerider's heaven. The whole mountain is geared towards freeride and there are loads of really accessible steeps, cliffs and shoots. They even hold the Scandinavian Big Mountain Champs here.

A well known route to explore is called Lilla Ölturen, or 'The Little Trip for a Beer' (there's a nice place for a beer at the end). You start from the summit of Riksgransen and head down to the bottom of the Norweigian Björnfjell railway station. You should definitely take a guide, not just for safety, but because they can show you the best spots to find untracked powder. If you embark on a half-hour trek from the top lift station you can get to the fantastic Mörkhåla snow bowl. There are also some marked trails on the map: Branten, Ravinen and Gränsängarna.

To get the most out of these amazing mountains you definitely need a guide and a helicopter. The heliskiing here is out of this world and you are dropped off in areas that look like man has never touched them. We were very fortunate on the day we went heliskiing as we had been in Riksgransen for five days and the weather had been awful, but the day we went up in the heli, we flew above the clouds into perfect sunny blue skies to get one of the best powder days we have ever experienced. Our guide was Krister from Alpine Madness and his avalanche-trained dog kept up with us down some steep faces in 2 metres of powder. Superb.

Lift passes	
1 day	NOK 32.50
6 days	NOK 148

Instruction

Book instruction, off-piste guiding, and heliski trips at the Riksgransen Hotel (0046 (0)980 400 80).

Other activities

All activities can be booked at the hotel (0980 400 80). **Driving dog sleds and ice climbing:** Both of these are fun options at Riksgranen.

Snowmobiles and ice fishing: You can either rent snowmobiles and go off on your own or combine the outing with ice fishing in a frozen mountain lake.

Spa: If your bones are aching, visit the spa, which has massage, treatment pools, sauna, Tai Chi, yoga, Qi gong, facials and body treatments. They also offer Lappish Zen, a unique treatment that involves cleansing, deep relaxation, hot stone massage, birch oils and stones from the Torneträsk river bank. The hotel offers good ski and spa packages.

Events

At the **Scandinavian Big Mountain Championships** (SBMC) the best freeriders fight it out to become national champion. It is one of the oldest extreme competitions in the world, and has now reached its 15th year. The **King of the Hill** is a slopestyle event for skiers and snowboarders who battle it down a course full of kickers, rails and quarter pipes. This was one of the first events to push New School skiing and attracts the world's best.

Getting there

By car

From Kiruna, take the Nordkalott Highway (E-10) for about 3 hours.

By plane

Kiruna (130km) Domestic flights from Stockholm fly to Kiruna.
Stockholm (1500km) Fly to Kiruna or take the 18-hour overnight train.

Accommodation

The one and only **Hotel Riksgransen** (0046 (0)980 400 80) isn't anything amazingly special, but it's comfortable and cosy, and you're handy for everything. The hotel has apartments and rooms; a double room (Saturday to Saturday) costs €438–713 and a 4-bed apartment €818–1340.

Eating out

In town

Restaurant **Lapplandia** is the smartest restaurant in the Riksgransen Hotel, and has won awards for food and service. There is also **Café Lappis**, a pizzeria with a wood-fired, Italian stone-oven. For a quick hot dog or burger, head to the **Katterjaure Café** or the **Nordalskiosken**.

Bars and clubs

Grönan is a fairly decent après ski bar and club; it's a casual place, but can get pretty nuts. They often have live music at après, and the place kicks off properly about 11pm.

Useful facts and phone numbers

Tourist office

T: 0046 (0)980 400 80
F: 0046 (0)980 431 25
E: info@riksgransen.nu
W: www.riksgransen.nu

Emergency services

• Call 112

Doctors

There is a ski doctor in the hotel during the winter season.

Sälen

The ski-through McDonald's
and the world's biggest snowman
are the most entertaining
things about Sälen

On the slopes	
Snow reliability	❄ ❄ ❄ ❄
Parks	❄ ❄
Off-piste	❄ ❄

Off the slopes	
Après ski	❄ ❄
Nightlife	❄
Eating out	❄ ❄
Resort charm	❄ ❄

The resort

Sälen is definitely a resort for families; there is little excitement for the accomplished skier, boarder or drinker. The pistes are short and any decent rider will be down after a few turns, and bored within a day or so. The après ski is also limited, but if you do go, the best areas in which to base yourself are Högfjället and Tandådalen. Even here though, there is little community feel with accommodation mostly in the form of cabins, scattered over a fairly large area.

> "Sälen is definitely a resort for families; there is little excitement for the accomplished skier, boarder or drinker"

The mountains

Height: 557–860m

Ability	Rating
Expert	❄ ❄
Intermediate	❄ ❄ ❄
Beginner	❄ ❄ ❄

Getting about

Four separate areas make up the slopes of Sälen, comprising 108 slopes and 77 lifts. Lindvallen and Högfjället are connected by a lift and have a total of 56 pistes. These slopes are really best for beginners and low intermediates, as there are almost no challenges. The maximum vertical drop in this area is 303m and the longest piste only 2.5km. Hundfjället is a family resort with wide gentle slopes and this area is connected to Tandådalen, which contains steeper and more challenging pistes, including the Väggen, or wall, that has a 45 degree angle in parts.

The park

The park at Tandådalen isn't bad but it could be a little more loved by the guys who shape it. It consists of two half pipes, two hip jumps, and a couple of table tops. We hope that the freestyle scenes in Åre and Riksgransen rub off on Sälen at some point.

Off-piste and backcountry

There is very little off-piste to get excited about. The snow's good, but finding some powder just off the piste is about as much as you can hope for. Head to the reds and blacks and play on the sides of them. If you want decent off-piste, go elsewhere.

Instruction

Sälen Ski and Snowboard School

For bookings, call the number below or book on the internet.
T: 0046 (0)771 84 00 00
W: www.skistar.com/salen

Other activities

Contact the tourist office for further information.

Bowling, billiards, table tennis, a pool, a Jacuzzi, sauna, solarium and gym: You will find all these activities at Lindvallen.

Snowmobile safaris and dogsledding: Go to Högfjället for these options.

Snowman castle: On the Lindvallen-Högfjället Mountain, children will enjoy the Snögubbeborg (snowman) castle, between the Kalle and Oskar pistes.

Tobogganing: This is allowed near Kråken, Gustav Express and Illern on Lindvallen-Högfjället, and on Stora Backen at Tandådalen.

Accommodation

If you fancy a really nice chalet/apartment in Lindvallen, check out the **Timmerbyn** on the tourist office's website. The 8-bed chalets are the most spacious with 100m² of space (ten people also have 100m², four have 46m²). All apartments have private saunas, drying cupboards, a dishwasher, and some have fireplaces.

In Högfjället, the **Högfjällshotellet** (0046 (0)280 870 00/(0)280 871 00, www.salen-hotell.se, info@salen-hotell.se) is the best place to stay. As well as a mini-spa, the hotel contains a few restaurants and a wine bar, piano bar and the infamous Vinterträdgården (see Bars and clubs).

Hundfajallet is mega-quiet, so unless you are looking to hide yourself away from society, don't stay here.

Eating out

On the mountain

At Lindvallen you have the choice of the ski-through **McDonald's**, the popular restaurant at **Snögubben** by the big snowman or **Wärdhaus**, popular for lunch as well as après ski. For great food, in a rustic, cosy atmosphere, try the **Rådhauser** at Högfjället.

"Great food, in a rustic, cosy atmosphere"

Useful facts and phone numbers

Tourist office

T:	0046 (0)280 187 00
F:	0046 (0)280 187 15
E:	info@salen.se
W:	www.salen.se

Emergency services

- Police Sälen: 0280 204 20
- Police (emergency): 112
- Ambulance (emergency): 112
- Medical center/doctor: 0280 498 498

Taxis

- 0280 200 00
- 0280 204 00

Getting there

By plane

Mora (100km) Transfer takes around 1 hour.
Oslo (270km)

In town

There are few restaurants around. In Högfjället, the **Högfjällshotellet** has a gourmet restaurant, as well as a sea food bar and Bistro Julie, which serves traditional food and a great breakfast. Across the street is **Kalas**, serving pizza and pasta, and they also do takeaway.

In Lindvallen try the **Waldhaus**, **Bistro 303** or grab a Big Mac from Ronald.

In Tandådalen the **Wärdhaus** serves good food and has a lively atmosphere. There is also the **Fjällis Bar and Bistro**, **Ski Burger** and a takeaway pizza place for a quick bite.

Bars and clubs

The **Vinterträdgården** in Högfjället is probably the best après ski in the area. Later on, head to the **HC club**. Tandådalen has great après at the **Wärdshus**, with good live music and food. If you ever leave you could follow this with a trip to **Fjällis Nattklubb**. The **Lindvallen Wärdhaus** is good too, and at Hundfjället, **Ahléns** is the closest you'll get to après, with occasional live music.

✚ Switzerland

You'd be hard pushed to find a bad resort
in Switzerland, Swiss Tourism have their
finger on the button

Arosa

A good, intermediate mountain,
and a great town for everyone –
from families to party people

On the slopes	
Snow reliability	❄ ❄ ❄ ❄
Parks	❄
Off-piste	❄ ❄

Off the slopes	
Après ski	❄ ❄
Nightlife	❄ ❄ ❄
Eating out	❄ ❄ ❄
Resort charm	❄ ❄ ❄

"Arosa has a reputation for being poncey, but we didn't find this at all. It seems to attract all sorts of people"

The resort

We had a superb time in Arosa; it has a certain charm that we really fell for. The town is quite pretty, but it's the atmosphere that we loved: the people, the restaurants, the bars, everything. Most of the action is around the Obersee/Untersee area so this is the region we deal with. Arosa has a reputation for being poncey, but we didn't find this at all. It seems to attract all sorts of people – there were loads of families, a few fur coats, some trendies and some party people (Arosa has a great night scene if you know where to look). The mountain's not bad either; it's a wide, open area, perfect for blue and red run riders but not challenging enough for the expert.

The mountains

Height: 1800–2653m

Ability	Rating
Expert	❄
Intermediate	❄ ❄ ❄
Beginner	❄ ❄ ❄

Getting about

Arosa's 100km of pistes are great for beginner and intermediate riders. There are lots of gentle slopes to get you started and then you'll be cruising all over the mountain. If you are a good intermediate or expert you will be entertained for a couple of days but the terrain may start to wear a little thin after that. The tiny park

and freeride mountain might amuse you for an hour or so, but there are few serious challenges. Get used to sharing the mountain with walkers; there are loads of them wandering about.

The park

We turned up in Arosa around the end of March 2005 so the park may have been different earlier in the season, but it did look like it had been left to fade away. It could be OK for beginner freestylers but even then there's not much choice of what to do. There are two very small table tops and one very small rail. With a bit of work they could make it half decent, even though it's located in a fairly small area near to the Sit hütte restaurant, at the top of the Tschuggen-Ost chairlift.

On the plus side, Arosa does have a massive half pipe. They hold big competitions here, like the world junior half pipe championships, but we're not too sure how often it's shaped for the public.

Off-piste and backcountry

When we were researching Arosa, the snow was really wet and heavy and every face that looked half decent had slid. It looked like avalanche central. However, with the right conditions, there did seem to be some easily accessible and good spots for freeriding. A favourite place of the locals is towards the resort Lenzerheide by the Hornli area, where you can often find fresh tracks. It really did look dodgy for avalanching though, so do take a guide.

Lift passes	
1 day	CHF55
6 days	CHF256
13 days	CHF400

You can also get a beginners' pass that just lets you on to the easier runs; perfect for a first timer. This costs CHF35 for one day and CHF161 for 6 days.

Instruction and equipment

ABC

Private lessons cost from CHF130 for 2 hours and group lessons are CHF40–50 for a half day; 5 full days costs CHF240 for snowboarders and CHF360 for skiers.

T: 0041 (0)81 356 56 60
E: abcschneesportschule@spin.ch
W: www.abcarosa.ch

Bananas

Bananas is a great snowboard school for budding freestylers. A 2-hour group lesson costs CHF40 and a 5-day package costs CHF435, including lift passes.

T: 0041 (0)81 377 11 50
E: bananas@sssa.ch
W: www.sssssa.ch

Swiss Ski and Snowboard School

Private lessons cost from CHF140 for 2 hours, or CHF350 for a whole day (6 hours). There is also a Mickey Mouse club for kids.

T: 0041 (0)81 377 11 50
E: fun@sssa.ch
W: www.sssssa.ch

Ski Shop Beck

This located at the bottom of the cable car and chairlift. It's the perfect location for picking up your hire equipment and you can even leave it in the hut outside the shop when you come down from the slopes so you don't have to lug it around town. You can also pick up the essentials like socks, glasses, goggles, etc. The staff are very friendly and helpful.

T: 0041 (0)81 377 34 48
W: www.skishopbeck.ch

Other activities

Balloon trips: At weekends these trips are available over Arosa, the Grisons alps or in the low lying hills, with prices staring at CHF350 (081 391 37 14).

Ice skating: You can ice skate on the open air rink (081 377 17 45) until 5pm (night skating on Mondays and Wednesdays) and on the natural ice rink at Inner Arosa (081 377 29 30). Adults pay CHF4.50 for skating, CHF6 for skate rental and CHF4 for ice hockey stick rental. You can rent the whole ice rink for CHF160 per hour if you fancy your own ice hockey match, or you can learn how to curl for CHF48 per hour.

Paragliding: This costs CHF180 per person per flight. Call Jogi Engewald (079 449 88 13). You can buy a gift certificate at the Swiss Ski and Snowboard school by the bottom of the cable car.

Sleigh rides: By the station you will find horses and sleighs all ready to take you for a ride. The Prätschli-Maran round trip for 2 people costs CHF80 and longer circuits can cost up to CHF160.

Tobogganing: There are a number of toboggan runs in Arosa, with a variety of lengths, and one that is floodlit (Prätschli-Scheiterböden-Obersee). You can take the bus from Postplatz.

Events

At the end of March/beginning of April is the World Junior Half Pipe Championships and rumour has it that they could be holding the World Half Pipe Championships in the future. Arosa has another claim to fame in the world of the half pipe, as it is the home of snowboarder Gian Simmen, the World Half Pipe Champion for three years running (2000–3) who became the half pipe Olympic winner in Nagano in 1998.

As well as events on the mountain, Arosa seems to hold a fair number of music events, from rock concerts, to popular DJs and hip hop events.

Accommodation

If money was no object, there would be no question of where we would stay in Arosa; the **Hotel Eden** (0041 (0)81 378 71 00, info@edenarosa.ch, www.edenarosa.ch) is by far the best place in town. From the outside the hotel looks fairly standard, but take a look inside and you will find yourself at the cutting edge of interior design (check out www.designhotels .com). The bar is gorgeous; the lighting, chairs and atmosphere is perfect and one of the best clubs in town, the Kitchen Club, resides in the hotel's basement (see Bars and clubs). The rooms don't let you down either; individually designed, some are more mental than others. The Garden Eden room has a tree above the bed and rocks and gorges around the whirlpool. For an interesting Valentines Day why not book yourself into the Lilly Tiger room, complete with velvet, fur, a cage bed and an open bathroom. Prices start at CHF85 per person per night for a classic kitchen room and extend to CHF210 for a 50m² design apartment. In high season, add another CHF45. Not cheap, but an experience.

Another smart and more classic hotel is the **Hotel Cristallo** (0041 (0)81 377 22 61, www.crisalloarosa.ch,

cristalloarosa@swissonline.ch) on the main road. It has a lovely smart restaurant and you can hire DVD players and films for a quiet night in. Prices start at CHF120 per person per night. The large **Post Hotel** (0041 (0)81 378 50 00, mail@posthotel-arosa.ch, www.posthotel-arosa.ch) is in a good location, has a spa and has tons of different restaurants in the same building including a pizzeria, the Mexicalito Mexican, and a classic eatery. It's pretty 70s, but in an endearing way. Prices start at CHF119 per person per day.

If you want to be the first on the mountain you could stay at the simple but friendly **Hotel Vetter** (0041 (0)81 377 17 02, hotelvetter@swissonline.ch, www.arosa.ch/hotels/vetter), which will cost you from CHF150 per night for 2 people, B&B only. If you're looking for a bargain, your best bet is probably to get an apartment. The tourist office has a good selection on the website. We rented an apartment in Haus Bristol and loved it; we had a great view and a great location.

Eating out

On the mountain

Our favourite bar on the mountain on a sunny day is the very accessible bar on the **Brüggerstuba** (081 378 84 25) at the top of the cable car from Obersee. This is a great place to sit and have beers after a hard day on the mountain. If you're peckish, they also cook up a tasty hot dog. In bad weather, a big umbrella type cover keeps you out of the snow. The **Sit hütte** (079 407 89 38), at the top of the 'park' is the place to sit back and look cool. There are big, loungy cushions on the snow and a palm tree with sofas round it. There's also table football and good snack food. At **Tschuggenhütte** (081 378 84 45), by the colourful tented Mickey Mouse club, there is raclette bar, snack bar, ice cream hut, massive terrace and huge double loungers to relax on. If you're a bit knackered, take a good book and chill out here. The restaurant at the top of the **Weisshorngipfel** (081 378 84 02) lacks atmosphere inside but has amazing views from the outside. Surprisingly the food isn't *too* expensive. As well as traditional dishes, they serve the simpler sausage and chips or spag bol.

In town

There are some great restaurants around town. In the centre you will see the pizzeria **Grottino** (081 377 17 17), a really cosy and friendly place, and a great choice. Owned by the same people is the restaurant below it: **Schnüggel** (081 377 17 17). It's a small, romantic restaurant, decorated by chickens and a trough in the centre. Order one of the special meat spits, where you can choose two sauces and three side dishes to accompany it. Above the pizzeria is a raclette/fondu restaurant: **Alpträumli** (081 377 06 06), also under the same ownership. The cheese fondue is absolutely superb and the raclettes good, although you don't have the satisfaction of melting the cheese yourself which

is a shame; they do it in the kitchen and bring it out to you.

For some Mexican nosh, head to **Mexicalito/ Boomerang Bar** (081 378 50 00) – a strange mix between Australian and Mexican cuisine, with Kangeroo burgers and fajitas on offer. The decorations are also slightly confused but interesting. The food, atmosphere and service are all fantastic. If Australian/ Mexican doesn't take your fancy, how about a good Thai? Head to **Chilli's** (081 377 13 66) at the top end of town. For a smart meal, try the Italian in the Casino building, the traditional **Le Bistro** restaurant in the **Crisallo**, (081 378 68 68) or the funky restaurants at the **Hotel Eden** (081 378 71 00), where you can choose between a fondue at the **Roggenmoser** or an Italian at **Sapori**.

Bars and clubs

One of the best bars in town is **LOS Café Bar**, which is great for a game of Pacman or table footie and après ski beers, and it's not too busy then as it isn't near the slopes. Later at night it's heaving and fun. The other good places for après ski are the **Sitting Bull**, although it's never too busy, and **Bellini's** café bar (also not for raving, more for a chilled out glass of wine). The **Boomerang** Bar (see Eating out) is also great for a few games and tequilas. The **Casino** building may have you reaching for your poker chips but hold your horses, there's no blackjack, roulette or that kind of thing, just a few slot machines. There is a really nice smart bar though, and **Nuts Club** for dancing later on.

Our absolute favourite bar is the **Eden Bar** in the Hotel Eden, a smart place where it's great to chill out and chat in the midst of candlelight and sushi. On one night there was a massive bed adorned with Egyptian sheets, and a glam crowd smoking a sheesha pipe. We could stay here for hours. Downstairs is the unique **Kitchen Club** which still looks just like an old kitchen with a couple of bars put in. The drinks are really expensive but it has a great atmosphere and music, and the Wednesday night hip hop nights are superb.

Useful facts and phone numbers

Tourist office

T: 0041 (0)81 378 70 20
F: 0041 (0)81 378 70 21
E: arosa@arosa.ch
W: www.arosa.ch

Emergency services

- Police: 117 or 081 377 19 38/ 081 378 67 17
- If you have an accident on the piste call 081 378 84 05

Doctors

- Drs V Meyer and M Walkmeister: 081 377 27 28
- Dr M Röthlisberger: 081 377 14 64

Taxis

- Taxi Keller: 081 377 35 35
- Taxi Obersee: 081 377 11 33

Getting there

By car

The road to Arosa is pretty dreadful. It takes almost an hour from Chur on a windy and narrow road and accidents are not uncommon. Best avoided if possible.

By plane

Zurich (163km)
Friedrichshafen (around 170km) for Ryanair flights.
Transfer from Zurich and Friedrichshafen will take around 1.5 hours. Your best bet is to avoid the awful road and take the efficient and beautiful train up to Arosa from Chur.
Milano (217km)

Champéry

Beautiful Swiss 'chocolate box'
resort, with extensive terrain
and an amazing snowpark

On the slopes	
Snow reliability	❄ ❄ ❄
Parks	❄ ❄ ❄ ❄ ❄
Off-piste	❄ ❄ ❄

Off the slopes	
Après ski	❄ ❄ ❄
Nightlife	❄ ❄ ❄
Eating out	❄ ❄ ❄ ❄
Resort charm	❄ ❄ ❄ ❄ ❄

The resort

Champéry is an undiscovered gem. The resort itself is a charming place, full of ultra-friendly people. There are a number of great places to stay, some fantastic restaurants to check out, good access to the Portes de Soleil circuit (the largest internationally connected ski area in the world), and one of the finest snowparks in which we have had the pleasure of riding. We had not heard of Champéry until recently, but it has now soared into our shortlist of favourite places to visit.

The mountains

Height: 975–2275m

Ability	Rating
Expert	❄ ❄ ❄ ❄
Intermediate	❄ ❄ ❄ ❄
Beginner	❄

Getting about

The slopes have a lot going for them. Intermediates and experts will have a whale of a time, whether exploring the 650km of pistes in the Portes de Soleil, tackling the more challenging steep and mogully Swiss wall or attacking the massive kickers in the incredible super-park. However, Champéry is not suited to beginners; there are very few gentle enough slopes for your first venture on to skis or board. The other disadvantage is the inability to ride back into the centre of town; you can come all the way back down into Grand Paradis (and pop into the charming Fire and Ice après ski bar in the Auberge de Grand Paradis), but to get straight to the centre of Champéry you will have to take the cable car down and then possibly a bus if you're not staying near the lift.

The park

At the end of 2004 one of the best parks in Europe was formed in Le Crosets area. The park is high and has the biggest selection of kickers we have ever seen. It kicks ass. There are different-sized kickers for all standards of riders ranging from small table tops to 30m gap jumps. There are four hip jumps, at a variety of heights, ten rails, including a massive rainbow rail and a couple of flat-downs. A big bonus, which we enjoyed filming on, was the gap jump to a big snow block to drop off, then a quarter pipe with a rail on top to finish off. A jibber's paradise. When we were there we saw the likes of world-famous pro boarders Travis Rice and Roman Dimarchi filming for their latest flick. If parks are your thing, check this place out, it's arguably the best park in Europe. At least visit the website www.superpark.ch – if your French isn't up to scratch, you'll have to settle for the pictures.

Off-piste and backcountry

Champéry's highlights on the mountain are the access to the Portes de Soleil, the freestyle park and the scenery – the off-piste isn't amazing. This is primarily due to the sun killing the lovely powder, so if there is an area that you spot and want to ride, make sure you check it out first thing. Les Crosets and Chavanette are good places to look. Also at Chavanette is the legendary Swiss wall: a marked black run that gets the best moguls on the mountain. This is a pretty steep face and can be amazing after a big snowfall. The Swiss wall does have a fierce reputation, but don't be intimidated by the hype, its not over-challenging. You may want to seek out some spots in Avoriaz, Chatel and Morzine for the off-piste.

Lift passes	
1 day	CHF54
6 days	CHF258
There are discounts for children, teenagers, students and the over 60s.	

Instruction

Freeride Co.

Snowboard, ski, freestyle and telemark. Private lessons (1–2 people) cost CHF60 per hour (discounts for 3–6 hours), and semi-private lessons (3–5 people) cost CHF150 for 2 hours.

T: 0041 (0)24 479 20 29/ 0041 (0)24 479 10 00
W: www.skichampery.com

Swiss Ski School

Ski, snowboard, telemark, racing, freeride and heliskiing. A 2-hour private lesson costs CHF120 for 1–2 people and CHF160 for 3–4. Group lessons cost CHF170 for 5 half days and CHF45 per day.

T: 0041 (0)24 479 16 15
E: ess@champery.ch
W: www.esschampery.ch

Other activities

Unless other contact details are given, call the tourist office for more information (024 479 20 20).

Night skiing: This takes place twice a week and is actually really good fun; 5km of ski runs are open until 10pm.

Paragliding: Tandem flights, training flights or initiation courses can all be arranged.

Snow-kiting: To try your hand at this call 079 409 22 75.

Sports centre: The Champéry **palladium** (024 479 15 11) has pool, fitness and curling rink.

Tobogganing: This takes place on the Grand Paradis. Rent your toboggan from Berra Sports (024 479 13 90), or Borgeat Sports (024 479 16 17).

Trampolining: There are two bungee **trampolines** and one normal trampoline to play around on.

Events

In the first week of February is the **Chavanette Session**; a race which takes place on the densely moguled Chavanette piste, also known as the Swiss wall. As part of this festival is the **Derby**, a great competition in which teams of three race to finish the 5km course from Pas de Chavanette (2180m) to Grand-Paradis (1055m). There is also **The Wall**, an individual race on the Chavanette. The **Nokia Snow Park Tour** is also in February and worth a look (www.snowparktour.com).

At the end of the season is the **Champéry Snow Mix**, with a big air ski/snowboard comp, a waterslide or a snowskate contest. The après ski and party scene is great, with a number of good DJs.

Accommodation

The rustic and charming chalet-hotel **Auberge de Grand-Paradis** (0041 (0)24 479 11 67, rhondsworld @aol.com, www.grandparadis.ch) gets a huge thumbs up from us. It's right on the slopes and the only hotel in Champéry that boasts ski-in, ski-out accommodation. This does mean that it's a 20 minute walk into the centre of town, but avoiding the après-ski jostle to catch the cable car and bus more than makes up for this. Paul and Rhonda, the new British proprietors, will welcome you into one of their ten spacious bedrooms (which share five bathrooms), and it's fantastic value at CHF110 per room per night. If you require half board, you will pay an extra CHF32.50 per head for a four-course meal. The food is superb, as both Paul and Rhonda are excellent chefs. One of the highlights is raclette night (usually Thursday), when Rhonda stands in front of the fire in the cosy, rustic dining room, dishing out melted cheese to the drooling guests.

In town, the newly refurbished **Beau-Sejour** (0041 (0)24 479 58 58, www.bo-sejour.com, info@bo-sejour.com) is a great option, with some beautiful rooms and a games room with PlayStations. A room will cost CHF140–240 for a double with B&B. The **Hotel Suisse** (0041 (0)24 479 07 07, www.champery .com/hotelsuisse, gthotelsuisse@bluewin.ch) is right in the centre of town and has charming rooms. It also contains the Bar des Guides and Les Mines D'Or (see Bars and clubs). A double room costs CHF240–260.

Eating out

On the mountain

Restaurant Coquoz (024 479 12 55) at Planachaux is one of the best places to stop for a bite to eat. **Les Marmottes** (079 691 07 00) is a cosy alpine chalet towards Chavanette and Ripaille. On the French side, Avoriaz has some great places to stop for lunch (see Avoriaz chapter, page 122).

In town

The best restaurant in town is, without a doubt, **Mitchell's** (024 479 20 10, mitchells_champery@ hotmail.com). The menu is beautifully composed. For lunch choose between a homemade burger, grilled sandwich (big or small), wrap, beef or fish noodle wok, or delicious salad. In the evening you will have a really tough time choosing between the mouth-watering dishes. The king prawns are absolutely fantastic, as are most things on the menu (we tried as many as we could). To top it off, you enjoy these delicacies in equally sumptuous Midsummer Night's Dream-style surroundings. Tree trunks grow through the restaurant, and the lighting is perfect, with well placed spot lights and candles. If you go to Champéry, you must eat here at least once.

Another good restaurant is **Café Centre**, open all day. It's very cool and on two levels. The top floor serves only their gourmet menu (CHF28–48), but downstairs serves just as delicious dishes, such as Thai green curry, Indonesian stew, fish and Cajun Chicken. The **Auberge de Grand Paradis** (just at the bottom of the slopes at Grand Paradis) serves lunch – choose from burgers, spag bol, steak and ale pie, chilli, etc. Similar fare is on offer for dinner – if you plan to visit on the popular raclette night (see Accommodation), make sure you book. The **Gueullhi** (024 479 35 55, info@legueullhi.ch) café-restaurant, by the cable car station is a decent place to stop for lunch or dinner. The menu and food is fantastic but the service a bit slow at peak times. For a good pizza, try the **Farinet**, a restaurant 7pm–1am, with fondues, steaks and salads and pizzas, and a club 11pm–4am (see Bars and clubs).

Bars and clubs

Champéry isn't massively into its boozing, but the bars there are, are good. In the Hotel Suisse is the **Bar des Guides**, a bar full of locals enjoying après ski, and the **Mines D'Or**, a wicked bar, with cavernous hideaways – a great place at all times of night for a cosy pint and live music. **Mitchell's** restaurant (see Eating out) also has a great bar, with massive comfy sofas and a gorgeous atmosphere. With such welcoming hosts as Kina and John, it's no wonder that this is a popular meeting point for the Champéry community. After hours, you will find the locals at **Le Farinet** and the riders at **La Cravasse**.

Useful facts and phone numbers

Tourist office

T:	024 479 20 20
F:	024 479 20 21
E:	info@champery.ch
W:	www.champery.ch

Emergency services

- Police: 024 479 09 18
- Ambulance/ mountain rescue: 144
- Medical centre: 024 479 15 16
- Hospital de Monthey: 024 473 17 31
- Hospital d'Aigle: 024 468 86 88

Taxis

- Serge Rey-Bellet: 0041 (0)79 430 15 15
- Closillon Tours: 0041 (0)79 622 22 24 (for 1–4 people: Lausanne CHF160, Geneva CHF300, Zurich CHF540).

Getting there

By car

From Geneva take the Lake Geneva motorway past Lausanne to Monthey and follow signs to Champéry.

By plane

Lausanne (62km)
Geneva (126km) Transfer around 1.5 hours.
Zurich (250km)

Crans Montana

Sunny cruising on the slopes
and a town you'll want to
come back to

On the slopes	
Snow reliability	❄ ❄ ❄
Parks	❄ ❄ ❄
Off-piste	❄ ❄ ❄

Off the slopes	
Après ski	❄ ❄
Nightlife	❄ ❄ ❄
Eating out	❄ ❄ ❄
Resort charm	❄ ❄ ❄

The resort

The two resort centres of Crans and Montana have a definite charm about them; the town doesn't have the 'chocolate box' feel that a number of Swiss resorts possess but the mountains are stunning, and the resort has a certain character and warmth. Crans is full of Paris-style boutiques, and has some top-class restaurants and hotels. Most of the good bars and clubs are in Crans too, although there are a couple in Montana, as well as the massive Casino. It's not too British either; we make up only 3.5 per cent of visitors to Crans Montana. The slopes are dominated by fur-clad skiers searching for a nice restaurant before cruising back down to town for a massage. However, the area does have more to offer.

The mountains

Height: 1500–3000m

Ability	Rating
Expert	❄ ❄
Intermediate	❄ ❄ ❄ ❄
Beginner	❄ ❄ ❄

Getting about

The Crans Montana mountains have some truly stunning views. They are, however, geared to the cruisy intermediate with a preference for pretty paths through the trees rather than steep and challenging terrain. Saying this, there are a few slopes for the expert skier/boarder and there are a number of options for the enthusiastic powder hounds, and these areas rarely get tracked out as few Crans Montana regulars are interested in exploring the surrounding backcountry.

The park

The Aminona Snowpark is a decent size, with a good range of jumps and rails for all standards of rider. There are several small kickers in different lines, according to the level of the rider and a reasonable range of rails, including a rainbow rail and C-rail. There's a fairly easy skier/boardercross course and two huge big-air jumps in the centre of the park, which are very well looked after. New in for last winter were a steel-made quarter pipe and a 6m long box slide. The shapers and designers are enthusiastic and do a great job. There is also a snack bar and BBQ hang-out spot. Check out www.evilplayers.ch/snowpark/.

Off-piste and backcountry

There aren't loads of backcountry areas to explore in Crans Montana, but there is a lot of really easily accessible off-piste to be had. Just off the side of the pisted runs are some super sweet faces. There are a couple of narrow couloirs (experts only) and a steep face by the Bella-Lui area. We recommend that you only do this with a guide or knowledgeable local. Some easier spots can be found beneath La Tza and Chetseron. Beware of the sun; most of the mountain is exposed to the sun and the snow can get very heavy by lunchtime, resulting in some nasty slides.

Lift passes	
1 day	CHF55
6 days	CHF268
13 days	CHF455

Instruction

Crans Montana official guide office

These are the guys to call if you want to explore Crans Montana's off-piste potential. They can take you ski touring, off-piste skiing, on avalanche courses, and heliskiing. They also offer semi-private lessons (min. 4 people, max. 6) in ice climbing and freeride.

T: 0041 (0)27 481 14 80
E: info@essmontana.ch
W: www.essmontana.ch

Ecole Swiss de Ski de Crans

One week of group skiing lessons (15 hours) costs CHF170 and snowboarding lessons (12 hours) cost CHF200. Alternatively you can pay CHF40/45 (pm/am) for one half day. Private lessons cost CHF60–90 per hour depending on the number of people.

T: 0041 (0)27 485 93 70

E: esscrans@quick-soft.ch

W: www.cranskischool.ch

Ecole Swiss de Ski de Montana

One week of group lessons (18 hours) costs CHF185 or you can pay CHF35/50 (pm/am) for one half day. Private lessons cost CHF60 for one person per hour; add CHF10 for each extra person.

T: 0041 (0)27 481 14 80

E: info@essmontana.ch

W: www.essmontana.ch

Ski and Sky

Ski and Sky will teach you skiing, boarding, snowbiking and telemarking. Their hourly rate is CHF60 for private lessons for one; add CHF10 for each extra person. They also organise tandem paragliding.

T: 0041 (0)27 480 42 50

E: info@skiandsky.ch

W: www.skiandsky.ch

Stoked

Private lessons in skiing or boarding cost CHF60–90 per hour and group lessons (max. 6 people) cost CHF45/60 (pm/am) and CHF110 for a whole day.

T: 0041 (0)27 480 24 21

E: crans-montana@stoked.ch

W: www.stoked.ch

Swiss Mountain Sports

Swiss Mountain Sports can organise all-in-one packages including accommodation, activities, transport and meals. Activities include ski and snowboard lessons (1 week of group lessons – 20 hrs – costs CHF215 and private lessons are CHF60–90 per hour), tandem paragliding, paintball, telemarking, free ride, heliski and sledging.

T: 0041 (0)27 480 44 66

E: info@swiss-mountain-sports.ch

W: www.swiss-mountain-sports.ch

Other activities

Casino: This is most definitely worth checking out (see Bars and clubs).

Curling: There are a few curling rinks, on which you can have lessons (027 485 04 04).

Hot air ballooning: Flights can be arranged by the Club Aérostatique de Crans-Montana (079 206 84 35/ 079 332 02 93) at a cost of CHF300 per person.

Ice climbing and snow-kiting: Adrenatur offer these activities, as well as riding a snow monster (a kind of scooter).

Ice skating: There are two ice skating rinks – the Ycoor in Montana (027 481 30 55) and Sporting in Crans (027 485 97 95). An adult pass is CHF5 and a 20-minute lesson is CHF28.

Indoor bowling: Another great way to while away an evening (027 481 50 50, barlebowling@netplus.ch). There are four lanes, and the cost for one adult is CHF9.

Internet cafes: There are a number of places to check your E-mails and surf the web – Avalanche (which also has a wireless hotspot), Café 'Au Garage', Club 360, Restaurant Le Farinet and Bar Number Two, Hotel Olympic, and the New Pub.

Night skiing: This takes place on Friday nights, 7–10pm, and costs CHF15.

Paintballing: This can be arranged with Paralook (079 606 46 28, www.paintball-center.ch, paralook@ netplus.ch) and costs CHF30 for 1 hour, including 100 shots, clothing and equipment.

Paragliding: Tandem paragliding flights can be booked with Ski and Sky (see Instruction), or Paralook for CHF140 (see above).

Shopping: For shopoholics with cash to splash, there are some seriously chic boutiques to mosey around. Not the place to pick up the slope fashions though – it's more Prada and Chanel than Oakley.

Squash: There are two squash courts (027 481 16 15, www.leregent.ch) which cost CHF10 for half an hour.

Swimming: A number of hotels have swimming pools available to the public – Hotel Aïda-Castel (Montana, CHF15), Alpina and Savoy (Crans, CHF15), Hôtel Etrier (Crans, CHF15) and Hôtel de la Forêt (Montana, CHF9).

Tennis: Crans Montana has the largest tennis centre in the Swiss Alps (027 481 50 14) with five indoor

courts and six outdoor courts. Court hire costs CHF28–38 and CHF85 for a private lesson.

Tobogganing: There is a 6km toboggan run from Petit Mt-Bonvin (2400m) to Aminona (1500m). Sledges can be hired for CHF9/13 (2hrs/4hrs) and one trip on the Télécabine will cost you CHF16.

Wellness centres: There are a number of centres offering treatments, swimming pools, etc. The Centre de santé et beauté Mességué-Phytotherm at Hôtel Crans Ambassador (027 485 48 48, www.crans-ambassador.ch, info@crans-ambassodor.ch) has a pool, sauna, hammam, solarium, and a number of beauty treatments and slimming treatments. Other centres offering similar treatments include Dabliu Beauty Farm (next to Hotel du Golf, 027 480 34 81, www.dabliu.com, dabliu.crans@bluewin.ch), Centre thérapeutique 'Medica' (027 480 40 41, medica@bluewin.ch) and Centre de 'Bien-être' (027 481 26 12, www.club-hotel-valaisia.ch, valaisia@datacomm.ch).

Events

Crans Montana have a number of good events, from the **Crans Montana Snowgames** (www.cransmontanasnowgames.ch) in late February which combines a big-air jam session, a water slide contest and a sumo contest, to **Caprices**, the music festival (www.capricesfestival.ch) in which 60 concerts are scheduled over nine days. In February 2005 Texas played on the slopes and there was a huge marquee packed with spectators.

"The Crans Montana Snowgames combines a big-air jam session, a water slide contest and a sumo contest"

Accommodation

Crans

If price isn't an issue, the best place to stay is the **Hostellerie du Pas de L'Ours** (0041 (0)27 485 93 33, www.relaischateaux.fr/pasdelours, pasdelours@relaischateaux.fr) which has nine suites, including junior suites, that are all individually decorated and absolutely stunning. Each suite has a fireplace, mini bar and Jacuzzi and will set you back CHF370–850 for the room per night, depending on the time of season and the type of suite (the most expensive is a 4-person suite). There is one restaurant in the hotel and another beside the main building, Bistrot des Ours, which is equally as stunning, and equally as expensive.

The larger **Hôtel de l'Etrier** (0041 (0)27 485 44 00, hotel.etrier@bluewin.ch, www.hoteletrier.ch) next door shares the newly built spa, massage and pool complex. It's slightly less expensive; a room will cost CHF100–490 depending on room and time of season. The **Hotel Alpha** (0041 (0)27 484 24 00, www.hotel_alpha.ch, hotelalpha@bluewin.ch) is a great hotel within a few minutes' walk of Crans centre and about 10 minutes' walk from the lifts. It's pretty 60s looking from the outside but the staff are mega friendly, the rooms comfortable and spacious with stunning views and the restaurant has a really cosy, alpine feel. There is an outdoor swimming pool in the summer. We highly recommend it.

Montana

Montana has some more reasonable hotels. **Hôtel Olympic** (0041 (0)27 481 29 85, hotel-olympic@bluewin.ch, www.amadeus-holidays.ch) is a simple hotel in the centre of Montana, right next to loads of the bars and the casino and only 300m from the slopes for only CHF65 per person per night for B&B. **Hotel Mirabeau** (0041 (0)27 480 21 51, www.hotelmirabeau.ch, contact@hotelmirabeau.ch) is well placed, pretty nice and not too expensive with a double room costing CHF210–550 per night depending on whether you want a bath or shower, and on the time of season.

Slightly more off the beaten track is the **Grand Hôtel du Parc** (0041 (0)27 481 41 01, www.parc-hotel.ch, hotel.parc@bluewin.ch). It's a big ugly building on the outside but inside it's really nice, the staff are friendly and the views are incredible. The prices are always changing so it's best to check with the hotel. The Bella-Lui (0041 (0)27 481 31 14, www.bellalui.ch, info@bellalui.ch) is in a quiet area in the trees but it's not too far from everything. Again it's not beautiful, but the views are. B&B accommodation costs CHF55–100 per person per night depending on the type of room.

The 4-star Alpina and Savoy (0041 (0)27 485 09 00, www.alpinasavoy.ch, info@alpinasavoy.ch) is bang in-between Crans and Montana, but close to the lifts, and it's pretty retro inside. There's a spa centre, a pool and comfy rooms that will cost from CHF200 per person per night.

You can book your accommodation directly on the Crans Montana website (www.crans-montana.ch) and they give you cheaper prices for booking earlier (December). Crans Montana are perfectly happy for you to book for 3 or 4 days and not the whole week.

Eating out

On the mountain
We had a great meal at the Plumachit (027 481 25 32) tucked away in the trees on the path to Aminona

with a huge terrace and stunning views. The service can take a while on busy, sunny days, but once you've managed to get your order in, the food arrives pretty quickly. The run down is a very flat path so it attracts a lot of walkers too. Other favourites of ours with outdoor bars and terraces are the restaurant at Merbé, at the first stop of the gondola from Crans Montana, and the Amadeus (027 481 24 95), above Montana.

In town
In Crans, Le Chalet (027 481 05 05) is a stunning restaurant in the centre of town that serves a fantastic raclette and other tasty treats. If raclette is your cup of tea you may also want to try La Dent Blanche (027 481 11 79), whose cheese is like no others. Raphaele (027 480 31 50) is the best pizzeria in town, opposite the post office. It has a beautiful interior and a large wine cellar. A pizza will cost you CHF13–19. Hotel Alpha (see Accommodation) has a good rustic restaurant in its basement. Tapas ex La Channe (027 481 30 11) is one of our favourite restaurants in town. It serves fantastic Mexican food in a romantic, candlelit atmosphere. Alternatively, you can also sit at or near the bar and have some tapas, which is great if you get sick of big meals. For gourmet cuisine you should head to

the **Bistrot des Ours** at the Hostellerie du Pas de L'Ours (027 485 93 33) and get your favourite credit card ready.

In Montana the **Farinet** (027 481 36 15) is a lovely pine-clad restaurant serving traditional food including raclettes, fondues and the like. The **Mayen** (027 481 29 85, www.amadeus-holidays.ch), under the Hotel Olympic, is similarly traditional and has an alpine feel. Rostis are their tasty specialities. At the end of town, the **Micheal Angelo Pizzeria** (027 481 09 19) is simple and cheery, with checked tablecloths. You can get a pizza for CHF14–18. The **Gerber**, on your left as you come into Montana from Crans, has a large terrace

that gets the sun at lunchtime and is also beautiful inside. A great place for lunch or dinner. There is also a café area and patisserie.

Bars and clubs

In Crans, If you're looking for somewhere nice to take your grandpa, head to **Bar 1900**, a nice enough place that does a good club sandwich and chips for CHF12.50. If you're looking for somewhere a bit more lively head to **Le Pub** (also known as George and Dragon) – the busiest bar, open 4pm–2am. **Tapas ex La Channe** (see Eating out) also has a cosy bar where you can snack on some tapas as you drink. From 11pm there are a number of lively options to choose from: **Punch Bar**, **Absolut**, **Le Baroque** and the very funky **Leo's Bar**. The best thing about all the bars in Crans is that they are only a few steps away from each other.

Most of the good bars are in Crans but there are a couple in Montana that are worth checking out. The **Amadeus** bar has concerts on Sundays and a jam session every Thursday (days may change). It's open 4.30pm–1am. The **Grange** is a bar to stay away from – it's pretty dingy, amazingly smoky and full of old locals. When the bars close, head to the **Number Two** bar/club under the restaurant Mayen. One of the best places to while away an evening in Montana is the **Casino** (027 485 90 40, www.casinocm.ch, info@casinocm.ch) with roulette, blackjack and slot machines as well as a great restaurant and a bar open 3pm–3am. Remember to take your passport.

Useful facts and phone numbers

Tourist office

T:	0041 (0)27 485 04 04
F:	0041 (0)27 485 04 60/61
E:	information@crans-montana.ch
W:	www.crans-montana.ch

Direct reservations

T:	0041 (0)27 485 04 44
F:	0041 (0)27 485 04 60

Weather and snow information: www.mycma.ch

Emergency services

- Police municipale: 027 481 81 81
- Police cantonale: 027 486 65 60
- Medical centre: 027 480 40 40
- Medical emergency: 144

Doctors

- Dr Bonvin Louis: 027 481 35 35
- Dr Kunz Ariane: 027 481 32 32
- Dr Vouilloz Patrick: 027 481 42 74

Taxis

- Emery, Jean: 027 481 19 19
- Morard, Jaques: 027 481 53 65
- Pott, César: 027 481 13 13
- Pott, Michel: 027 481 71 71
- Taxi Philippe: 079 422 29 85
- Taxi Sylvio: 079 400 75 45

Getting there

By plane

Geneva (180km)
Milan (260km)
Zurich (300km)

Davos

Great mountains, weird
'city style' resort

On the slopes	
Snow reliability	❄ ❄ ❄ ❄
Parks	❄ ❄ ❄ ❄
Off-piste	❄ ❄ ❄ ❄
Off the slopes	
Après ski	❄ ❄ ❄
Nightlife	❄ ❄ ❄ ❄
Eating out	❄ ❄ ❄ ❄
Resort charm	❄ ❄

The resort

There's no doubt about it, Davos is a bizarre place. On the plus side the mountains are incredible. There are five main mountains in the Davos-Klösters area which present stacks of opportunities for all sorts of riding, from unlimited on-piste opportunities to masses of freeriding and the best pipes around. Travelling from, to and between the mountains can be a bit of a laborious task though and you really have to make use of the mountains to make it worthwhile. You certainly wouldn't visit Davos to experience resort charm. It's not ugly at all, but its city feel doesn't create a particularly endearing atmosphere. There are loads of restaurants, bars and clubs as well as the kind of designer shops, museums and other facilities that you expect in a large town or city but it's almost eerie in the way that it is fairly rare to see people moseying around town. We couldn't quite figure it out; let us know what you think.

The mountains

Height: 1124–2844m

Ability	Rating
Expert	❄ ❄ ❄ ❄ ❄
Intermediate	❄ ❄ ❄ ❄ ❄
Beginner	❄ ❄ ❄

Getting about

There are 103 pistes (310km) in the Davos-Klösters region, with 54 lifts to serve them. There are four different mountains to be accessed from Davos, each with their own clientele. **Parsenn**, accessible from Davos Dorf (also reachable from Klösters) is the best mountain for cruising around on well-groomed slopes and checking out the stunning scenery. The restaurants are great, there's some fantastic off-piste and it's generally a great place. The only run back down, though, is to the outskirts of Dorf and if you don't know where you are, it can be a bit confusing.

From the centre of Davos Platz, you can get to **Jakobshorn** mountain, home of the park, fun restaurants and good, wide pistes. **Rinerhorn** and **Pischa** both take a bit of travelling to get to from Dorf or Platz but are both good for cruising around in the sun. You can get to some wicked off-piste from Pischa.

"Jackobshorn is the main hangout spot for the freestylers"

The park

Jackobshorn is the main hangout spot for the freestylers. It has two superb pipes; one super pipe is located in the village in the Bolgen area and is floodlit for night-time riding, the other is at the top of Jatz with the park. There are a lot of world-class riders who hang out in the area, including Danny Costandache, who organises the SB Jam, sponsored by O'Neill and these guys make sure that the pipes are always perfectly shaped. There's a good range of kickers, from small table tops to big booters and plenty of rails to jib. The Rinerhorn and Pischa mountains each have a park and there's supposed to be a pipe at Parsenn, but they need the right conditions in order to build it. Davos rocks for freestyle.

"The Weissfluh, a north-facing slope, is one of the most famous off-piste runs"

Off-piste and backcountry

The off-piste on Pischa is fantastic, but not for the lazy. If you are prepared to hike for 2 hours you can drop down the back of the mountain and have access to everything: cliffs, bowls and couloirs. From there you end up in the middle of nowhere though so you have to have a car or hitch back. Parsenn has some of the best off-piste; you can pretty much access powder from every lift. There's not much hiking involved and plenty to do. The Totalphorn area, between the Meierhoftäli and Totalp chairlifts, is superb, but does get sketchy if the snow isn't great and bad accidents have been known to happen in these conditions. Don't let that put you off: on a perfect powder day it's definitely worth checking out. If the visibility is bad, there are loads of tree runs to play in and you always find good snow here.

The Weissfluh, a north-facing slope, is one of the most famous off-piste runs. It's around a 500m drop with a 15-minute hike out. Definitely take a guide with you for this one. We recommend contacting Lukas Dürr at Swiss Freeride (www.swissfreeride.ch). There is also the option of taking a guided tour to Austria – the terrain isn't too challenging (although there is some hiking and walking involved) but the scenery is incredible. The expense is a drawback though as you need different lift passes for each area. Don't forget your passport if you do give it a go.

There is an avalanche training centre at the top of the Carjöl lift (Fuxägufer) on the **Jackobshorn**. Here you can practise using your avalanche equipment under realistic conditions. For further information and group reservations contact Fun Mountain Holidays (081 414 90 20).

Lift passes	
1 day	CHF61
6 days	CHF279
14 days	CHF496

Children and teenagers get reductions. You can order your pass in advance on the internet at www.davosklosters.ch.

Instruction

Ski School 'New Trend'

Lessons can include off-piste and there are freeride camps that offer video coaching.
T: 0041 (0)81 413 20 40
E: info@newtrenddavos.ch
W: www.newtrenddavos.ch

Snow and You

Reto Cahenzli is a local ski teacher who offers carving, guiding and powder skiing.
T: 0041 (0)79 636 70 30
E: snowdesign1@bluewin.ch

Swiss Snowsport-School Davos

This school offers the usual lessons including off-piste and telemarking and freestyle boarding.
T: 0041 (0)81 416 24 54
E: info@ssd.ch
W: www.ssd.ch

Top Secret Snowboard School

Freestyle, freeride and off-piste courses are available and include video coaching.
T: 0041 (0)81 413 20 40
E: info@topsecretdavos.ch
W: www.topsecretdavos.ch

Other activities

Remember to get a guest card from your hotel as it entitles you to a number of discounts on activities as well as unrestricted use of the Landschaft Davos public transport network.

Non-sporting activities

Casino: This is located at the Hotel Europe in Davos Platz, offering blackjack, American roulette and 70 slot machines. Remember to take your passport for ID.

Cinema: Four or five films are shown daily. Call 0900 900 123 for information about the programme or check out www.kino.ch or www.diesewoche.ch.

Museums: There is a choice of visiting a cultural museum, a doll museum, a folk museum, a winter sports museum, a mining museum or a museum of medicine. Don't exhaust yourself with all that culture.

Wellness centres:

Arabella Sheraton Hotel Seehof (081 416 12 12) has a sauna, steam bath, whirlpool, exercise room, beauty farm and solarium and offers massage.

Bad Alvaneu (081 420 44 00) has a sulphur bath, steam bath, solarium and sauna, and offers various therapies, massage, and exercise facilities.

Bad Serneus (081 422 14 44) has a 34-degree sulphur bath, an aqua gym, sauna and solarium, and offers mud packs and medical care.

Bristol Wellness (081 416 31 33) has a sauna, steam bath, whirlpool and solarium, and offers massage and shiatsu.

Turmhotel Victoria (081 417 53 00) has sauna, steam bath, whirlpool, solarium, health club and beauty parlour.

Waldhotel Bellevue (081 415 37 47) has steam grotto, whirlpool, sauna, steam bath and brine bath, and offers massage.

Sporting activities

Hang-gliding and paragliding: Choose from tandem flights, passenger flights or a weekly course over Jackobshorn or Parsenn from a number of schools: Luftchaft Paragliding School (079 623 19 70, info@luftchraft.ch, www.luftchraft.ch); Flugcenter Grischa (081 422 20 70); Paragliding Davos (079 236 39 49, www.paragliding-davos.ch).

Horse riding: Lessons and treks can be booked for both beginners and advanced riders. Call either Hans Lenz (081 413 19 55) or Andreas Stiffler (081 416 46 82).

Ice skating: Europe's largest natural ice rink (over 18000 m²), an outdoor ice rink and an ice stadium are all top venues for ice hockey, ice skating, speed skating, curling, and Bavarian curling. Admission for skaters is CHF4 for adults with guest card and it's CHF25 for a 20-minute lesson (081 415 36 00).

Sports complex and gymnasium: This is open to the public for a range of activities including athletics, football, handball, volleyball, basketball, streetball, etc. If you're staying in Davos you can use the facilities free of charge but you should make a reservation (081 415 36 00, sportzentrum@davos.ch).

Swimming: The public pool is in Davos Platz (081 413 64 63) and has a sauna and solarium. The Hotel Sonnenberg in Davos Dorf (081 417 59 00) and the

"The Spengler Cup Ice Hockey Tournament is the most important ice hockey event on the international calendar"

Waldhotel Bellevue in Davos Platz (081 415 37 47) also have public indoor swimming pools.

Tennis and squash: Phone to book courts on 081 413 31 31.

Tobogganing: There are toboggan runs on Schatzalp, Rinerhorn, Madrisa and Parsenn (totalling 22km of runs).

Swissraft (081 911 52 50) offer a range of activities to try, from **balloon trips** to **canyoning** and **hydrospeeding**.

Events

The **Spengler Cup Ice Hockey Tournament** is the most important ice hockey event on the international calendar, and is held annually in Davos between Christmas and New Year (www.spenglercup.ch). The **O'Neill Snowboard Jam** is also held at New Year in Davos on the Bolgen area at Jakobshorn. It has become one of the major events on the freestyle snowboarding calendar. The qualifying heats are open to all, and the best up-and-coming boarders can challenge the pros at the Grand Show Finale which should not be missed.

For further information regarding events in Davos comtact the tourist office (see Useful facts and phone numbers, or E-mail events@davos.ch).

Accommodation

There are 71 hotels in Davos, with a total of 24000 guest beds and there is something for any budget. In Davos Platz, **Hotel Europe** (0041 (0)81 415 41 41, www.europe-davos.ch) is a great place to stay – just to be near all the action. With restaurants, bars and a casino in the one place, who'd want to go anywhere else? It's a 4-star hotel and one night's B&B costs CHF105–220. The **Alte Post** (0041 (0)81 414 90 20, www.fun-mountain.ch) is really handy for Jacobshorn and is cosy and attractive. It will cost CHF150–210 for one night's B&B.

In Davos Dorf, **Hotel Parsenn** (0041 (0)81 416 32 32, www.hotelparsenn.ch) is an attractive, 3-star hotel, right opposite to the Parsenn railway so in a perfect position for the slopes. It will cost CHF560–980 for 7 nights' half-board and CHF80–140 for one night's B&B. The **Snowboarders'**

Palace (0041 (0)81 414 90 20) provides the cheapest, dormitory style accommodation and is handy for the Schatzalp funicular.

Eating out

On the mountain

The restaurant at the **Höhenweg**, just up the Parsennbahn train from Davos Dorf, has a massive terrace and bar and it's a great place to chill out with some top nosh. Also on Parsenn, **Bruhin's** is a fancy restaurant right at the top of the Gipfelbahn cable car. It has stunning views but there is no terrace which is a bit of a shame on a sunny day. The **Gruobenalp** is a traditional chalet-style restaurant, just down from Gotschnagrat; perfect on a sunny day as the terrace has a gorgeous view. The **Alta Schwendi** (081 332 13 24, www.freeridelodge.ch, freeridelodge@E-mail.ch) is the best mountain restaurant in which to hang out due to the great music and atmosphere. It's located at Chesetta, just above the Schifer. There's a massive terrace, great traditional food, a cosy chalet inside and really friendly staff. If you just fancy grabbing a good burger, the restaurant on the **Weissfluhjoch** has the best in town.

On Jackobshorn, the **Bolgen Plaza** is where the après ski dancing is to be found and **Jatzhütte's**, near to the terrain park, is pretty funky and madly themed with fake palm trees and other paraphernalia.

In town

There is a great variety of cuisine in Davos if you know where to look. **Tab Tim Siam** in Davos Dorf is a really popular and friendly Thai restaurant, full of only slightly tacky, brightly coloured decorations. **Bistro Angelo** is a simple but cool restaurant. In Davos Platz there are lots more opportunities to track down a decent meal. If you have a taste for some oriental cuisine you will not be disappointed with **Zum Goldenen Drachen** in the Hotel Bahnhof-Terminus (081 414 97 97). Hotel Europe (081 415 41 41) also has a stylish Chinese eatery, **Zauberberg,** and the same building houses another restaurant, **Scala,** which serves some good value and tasty dishes until midnight. If you're peckish in the early hours of the morning try **After Hours** (081 413 63 76), for 24-hour takeaway munchies including pizzas, sandwiches and hot dogs. If you're too lazy to move from your room, **Hotel Albana** (081 413 58 41) deliver pizzas to your door.

Bars and clubs

If you pick the right bars and clubs you can have a great night out in Davos. The crowd is young and there is a good mix of tourists and locals around. **Bolgenschanze** is the snowboard hangout. It has great deals on pitchers and shooters and plays a range of music: hip hop, rock and the like. It's a big place, gets pretty busy, and has a young, hip atmosphere. **Chämi Bar** is one of the most popular bars in Davos Platz and tends to be pretty hectic and jam-packed. **Ex Bar** is a good late-night bar, especially if you have the munchies as you can eat

"The crowd is young and there is a good mix of tourists and locals around"

until 6am. The **Hotel Europe** is right in the centre of the action and comprises a number of restaurants and cafés (see Accommodation), the casino, a comfy and chilled out piano bar, **Toxic,** where the top people tinkle out their tunes, and the two main clubs: **Cabanna Club** and **Cava** (081 413 23 57).

Useful facts and phone numbers

Tourist office

T: 0041 (0)81 415 21 21
F: 0041 (0)81 415 21 00
E: info@davos.ch
W: www.davos.ch/ www.davosklosters.ch

Weather information

T: 081 415 21 33/162
• Snow and avalanche report – 187

Emergency services

• Fire brigade: 118
• Police (emergency): 117
• Local police: 081 414 33 11
• Cantonal police: 081 413 76 22
• Rescue and ambulance: 144
• Hospital: 081 414 88 88

Doctors

There are nearly 30 doctors and dentists in Davos
    so I shall name only a few.
• Dr med. P Flurry (081 413 71 28)
    Promenade 33A, Davos Platz
• Dr med. B Knöpfli (081 415 70 70)
    Scalettastrasse 5, Davos Platz
• Dr med. R Stocker (081 416 61 62)
    Bahnhofstrasse 15, Davos Dorf
• Dentist – Dr med. Dent. A Bader
    (081 413 34 30) Promenade 41, Davos Platz

Taxis

• Angelo's Taxi: 081 416 73 73 or 079 416 59 05
• Express Taxi: 081 410 11 11

Getting there

By car

It takes about 12 to 13 hours to get to Davos from Calais, so it's probably easier to fly unless you're going to take a few days over the drive.

By plane

Zurich (150km) is the easiest place to fly to and it takes under 3 hours to get from the airport to Davos by train or car. You can get the train straight to Davos Dorf or Platz but you will have to change trains a couple of times. For CHF20 per bag you can send your luggage to the appropriate station from Zurich airport. For more info contact the railway on 0041 (0)81 288 32 50, www.rhb.ch, davos-platz@rhb.ch.

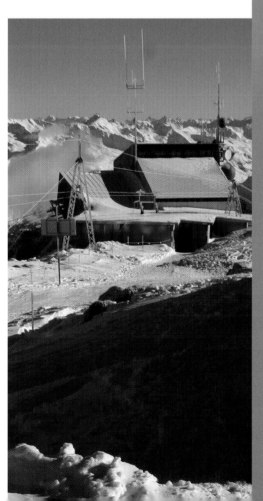

Flims

A freestylers' mountain and
a pretty Swiss resort, spoilt
by a constant flow of traffic

On the slopes	
Snow reliability	✸ ✸ ✸
Parks	✸ ✸ ✸ ✸ ✸
Off-piste	✸ ✸ ✸
Off the slopes	
Après ski	✸ ✸ ✸
Nightlife	✸ ✹
Eating out	✸ ✸
Resort charm	✸ ✸

The resort

The Flims-Laax-Falera mountains are fantastic. They are particularly perfect for the budding freestyler, and there's some good off-piste into the bargain that you can find with or without guidance. It's a little flat, but you'll forgive that when you see the park. The town, however, is not for the fun-crazed freestyler; there are a couple of very cool après ski bars but little to entertain you later on. It is quite attractive in the way that all the buildings have an appealing, chalet-style look, but the resort is hugely disadvantaged by the endless traffic that runs through the centre of the town at all hours of the day. Also many of the interiors of hotels and restaurants look like they need bringing into the 21st century. Obviously this may appeal to some but we personally need more going on in a resort. If you want to ride these mountains we suggest you stay in Laax Murschetg (see Laax Murschetg chapter, page 366); it has easier access to the park, and the best bars and places to stay.

The mountains

Height: 1100–3018m

Ability	Rating
Expert	✸ ✸ ✸
Intermediate	✸ ✸ ✸ ✸
Beginner	✸ ✸ ✸ ✹

Getting about

Flims is located at the far end of the Alpenarena (which combines Flims, Laax and Falera), providing access to 220km of slopes. The mountain is pretty flat so it's great for cruisy intermediates, though there is a fair bit of fresh powder that you can see from many of the pistes. The park is located at Crap Sogn Gion and there are some freeride routes marked on the piste map. As the mountains in the Alpenarena are the same, the details on the park and the off-piste can be found in the Laax Murschetg chapter, page 366.

Lift passes	
1 day	CHF61
6 days	CHF301
13 days	CHF443

You can get a park and pipe pass for CHF38 per day. Teens and children get a discount.

Instruction

Mountain Fantasy
These are the best mountain guides in town for skiers, boarders and anyone else who wants to explore.
T: 0041(0)81 936 70 77
E: bergsport@mountain-fantasy.ch
W: www.mountain-fantasty.ch

Ski Schule
Five days in ski school will cost CHF300.
T: 0041 (0)81 927 71 71
W: www.laax.com/skischule

Snowboarding School
Five days will cost around CHF460.
T: 0041(0)81 927 71 55
W: www.laax.com/fahrschule

Other activities

Curling: There is a curling stadium in Flims (081 911 19 50) with four rinks and a heated spectator stand. You can pay to rent the stadium or for lessons.
Full-moon skiing: In January, February and March you can ski under the full moon; contact the tourist office for more details and exact dates.

Golf: There is an indoor driving range at the Park Waldhaus Hotel (081 928 48 48) if you can't stand a week away from your golf clubs.

Helicopters: These can be hired for pleasure trips or as a taxi (081 911 52 50).

Ice skating: There are two ice skating rinks; the natural rink can be skated on from December until February and the other until the end of March.

Paragliding or delta flying: Training and trial days paragliding or delta flying can be arranged by a few companies including Swissraft (081 911 52 50) and X-Dream Fly (081 921 28 47).

Sports centre: The sports centre (081 920 91 91) has an ice rink, fitness room, basement shooting range, solarium, table tennis, outdoor ice rink, Bavarian curling and an interestingly named 'Vibra bed'.

Tobogganing: There is a 3km tobogganing run from Foppa to Flims (081 927 70 78).

Wellness centres: There are loads of wellness centres to check out with the best two being La Mira at the Hotel Adula (081 928 28 28) with an outdoor hot tub, and Delight at the Park Hotel Waldhaus (081 928 48 48).

Events

The best events are in the park; these are detailed in the Laax Murschetg chapter, page 366.

Accommodation

Waldhaus

The **Park Hotel Waldhaus** (0041 (0)81 928 48 48, www.parkhotel-waldhaus.ch, info@parkhotelwaldhaus.ch) was awarded Hotel of the Year in 2004 by Gault-Millau, a very prestigious Swiss award. It was awarded on the completion of the Delight spa and beauty wellness centre which is stunning and needs to be seen. The 'water world' area is made up of three different pools with a total of 355m^2 of water. The hotel (that's really more like a self-contained village) is massive, with acres of long corridors. It is pretty impersonal, despite being impressive. We would prefer to stay in the beautiful **Hotel Adula** (0041 (0)81 928 28 28, www.adula.ch, info@adula.ch), a more friendly and cosy kind of luxury. The spa (La Mira) has a gym, pool and outdoor spa and the restaurants are the best in town (see Eating out). The spa facilities in both the Park Hotel and the Adula are open to the public.

For a slightly less expensive alternative try the pleasant and comfortable **Arvenhotel Waldeck** (0041

(0)81 928 14 14, www.waldeck.ch, info@waldeck.ch) or **Hotel Garni National** (0041 (0)81 928 14 74, www.national-flims.ch, info@national-flims.ch) – both owned by the same company.

Flims Dorf

The best hotels are in Waldhaus but there are some in Dorf that are worth a look, and they do have the advantage of being closer to the lift station. The cosy and friendly **Meiler Hotel Prau da Monis** (0041 (0)81 920 93 93, www.meiler-pdm.ch, hotel@meiler-pdm.ch) is in a fantastic position for the slopes and après ski bars (it is attached to the Stenna Bar). Most rooms have a balcony or terrace and will cost you CHF144–290 per room per night for B&B. They also offer half-board accommodation.

If you're not into late-night partying (and if you are, you really shouldn't be in Flims in the first place), and enjoy the tranquillity of isolation, one of the best places to stay is the **Fidazerhof** in the nearby town of Fidaz (0041 (0)81 911 35 03, www.fidazerhof.ch, info@

> "The spa facilities in both the Park Hotel and the Adula are open to the public"

fidazerhof.ch). It is a short bus ride from the town and slopes (the buses run every half hour during the day) and has a spectacular view from the terrace. It's really friendly, has great rooms and restaurant and a wellness suite that offers a large variety of treatments.

Eating out

On the mountain
If you're hitting the park and pipe you will be eating and drinking at the popular bars at Crap Sogn Gion: **Rock Bar** and **Café No Name** (081 927 73 44). These bars are just above the half pipe and they are great places to hang out. For a cheeky beer, hit the terrace of Café No Name right at the top of the park and for a great cheeseburger head upstairs to the café **Gastro-Zentrum** (081 927 73 73). There are tons of deckchairs and comfy outdoor seating at the Rock Bar

so you'll always be able to find a place to relax with a beer. There's even a free games room in the basement with an Xbox and table football. The restaurant at **Foppa** (081 911 16 50) is a good place for lunch, just above Flims, and can be reached by foot as well as by skiing or boarding. If you like small, family-run chalet-restaurants, turn off the route from Startgels to Flims to **Runcahöhe** (081 911 15 88).

In town
Most of the decent restaurants in Flims are in hotels and take a little searching for. In Waldhaus, the **Hotel Adula** (081 928 28 28, info@adula.ch) has two of the best restaurants in town. **La Clav** is a small and smart Italian restaurant that serves top quality pasta and risotto (no pizza). The cream of the crop is the **Barga**, a very beautiful and quaint French restaurant; perfect for a smart celebration. There are two restaurants in the Hotel

Bellevue, the most atmospheric of which is the **Caverna-Keller** (081 911 31 31, info@bellevueflims.ch), a 425-year-old cavernous basement perfect for a romantic candlelit dinner. If you tire of the traditional cuisine, try the fantastic **Little China Restaurant** (081 928 48 27). If you fancy a pizza, you can head to the **Pomodoro** (081 911 10 62) in Waldhaus for a wood-fired pizza or the cheery **Pizzeria Veneziana** (081 911 01 03) in Flims Dorf.

A 5-minute drive away in Fidaz is the **Fidazerhof Hotel** that has a pleasant restaurant with stunning views from the terrace. For something unusual you can take a trip up the slopes to the **Startgels Alpenrose** (081 911 58 48); when you book they will arrange to come and pick you up in a piste basher from outside the Legna Bar on the slopes. Every Tuesday and Thursday evening, the **Foppa** restaurant (see Eating out on the mountain) is open; enjoy a raclette or fondue and then a sledge ride back to town.

Bars and clubs

The best bars are the après ski bars in Flims Dorf. The **Legna Bar** is right on the slopes in Flims Dorf and has a great après ski vibe. Stylish and simple, it's a great place to get drunk. Moving on down a few stairs you will come to the **Iglu**, a small dome that is very cool and cosy. If you're still standing, the **Stenna Bar** isn't too bad, but it does need a revamp to keep up with the times. There's a bar outside too but the scenery's not great as you're overlooking the main road. The **Livingroom** is a good nearby bar that has a lounge fireplace, and good food all day.

After hitting these bars you're probably best to go for a good meal and collapse into bed as there's not too much going on in Flims later on. If you want to hear some top class DJs in action you should take a taxi to Laax Murschetg where you can find the über-cool **Riders Palace** lobby bar and club complete with neon lighting (see Laax Murschetg chapter, page 366).

Useful facts and phone numbers

Tourist office

T: 0041 (0)81 920 92 00
E: tourismus@alpenarena.ch
W: www.alpenarena.ch

Emergency services

- Police: In an emergency call 117, if not call 081 928 29 40/ 081 911 11 64
- In an emergency on the mountain call the SOS central office on 081 972 70 01
- Hospital in Chur: 081 256 61 11
- Fire: 118

Doctors

- Dr B Durschei: 081 911 26 66
- Dr A Lötscher: 081 911 10 55
- Dr Michel: 081 911 12 07
- Dr P Reiser: 081 911 13 13

Taxis

- Taxi Mario: 081 941 22 22

Getting there

By car

Don't try to drive from Geneva via Andermatt; we did and it became a 4-hour detour – halfway along the road it stopped; it's only completely open in summer. You best bet is to fly to Zurich or Friedrichshafen. From there you can hire a car or catch a bus.

By plane

Zurich (150km)
Friedrichshafen (140km) for Ryanair flights.

Klösters

Infiltrate the Klösters scene
and you'll completely fall in love
with this beautiful place

On the slopes	
Snow reliability	✳ ✳ ✳
Parks	–
Off-piste	✳ ✳ ✳ ✳ ⅃

Off the slopes	
Après ski	✳ ✳ ✳
Nightlife	✳ ✳
Eating out	✳ ✳ ✳ ✳ ⅃
Resort charm	✳ ✳ ✳ ✳

The resort

Klösters has a distinguished reputation as the choice of the rich, royal and famous. Whilst this is not an unfair statement, and it obviously attracts an opulent clientele, there are few signs of full-on pretentiousness. The striking characteristic of Klösters is the returning population and although it can appear a bit cliquey, if you are willing to put in the effort you can infiltrate the scene pretty easily and a new world will open up. Klösters is also an ideal place for young families – there are mountains dedicated for family use and the facilities are fantastic. In fact, the mountains have something for everyone; you are unlikely to be disappointed. We loved this place; it has a lot going for it.

The mountains

Height: 1124–2844m

Ability	Rating
Expert	✳ ✳ ✳ ✳ ⅃
Intermediate	✳ ✳ ✳ ✳
Beginner	✳ ✳ ✳ ✳

Getting about

There are two mountains that can be accessed from Klösters: Parsenn, a large ski area connected to Davos, and Madrisa, a smaller, family-orientated zone that has some fantastic off-piste potential.

The Parsenn mountain has to be one of the most beautiful areas in the world. The acres of pistes are always well groomed and it is the perfect place for intermediates to cruise around. The runs back down from Parsenn to Klösters and the surrounding areas are not the easiest runs (beginners might be advised to catch the lift back down), but they are great. The long run to Klösters Dorf through the trees is beautiful and a great way to finish the day. Alternatively you could embark on the 12km-long run down to Küblis. You'll need to catch the train back to Klösters, but the transport system is superb so it shouldn't pose too much of a problem. The only niggle we have is that the mountain can only be accessed from the Gotschnabahn lift from Klösters which can mean really big queues in busy holiday periods.

"You can make your way up to the top of Madrisa by catching the Madrisabahn bubble lift which is an experience in itself"

Madrisa is a smaller mountain, but has a lot to offer and it has the added benefit of being far quieter than Parsenn. You can make your way up to the top of Madrisa by catching the Madrisabahn bubble lift which is an experience in itself – a real trip back to Old School bubbles, and the quaintness of the whole thing more than makes up for its lack of speed. There are plans to replace it though, which is probably for the best. Madrisa could almost be classed as a separate resort as there are locally based ski and snowboard schools, a great restaurant, different play areas for the kids and a super cool bar to hang out in – the Igloo Bar which can't be missed in its big glass dome. Madrisa is filled with T-bar lifts which can be a little hard for beginners but if that doesn't bother you, you can take full advantage of this superb area. There's something for everyone; for starters it's perfect for learning to ride using the magic carpet and special beginners' lifts, there are also some great groomed slopes for carving and loads of untracked areas for freeriding. In our opinion, Madrisa is the perfect area for young families. Mum and dad can be happy leaving their child in the care centre and can go off for a bit of on- or off-piste action (for children 2–6 years old it costs CHF10 for the first hour and CHF5 after that. There is also a room for you to supervise your own child that is free of charge).

There are three mountain regions of Davos (Jakobshorn, Rinerhorn and Pischa) that are fairly easily accessible from Klösters (see Davos chapter, page 344).

The park

Klösters doesn't have a park but the idea is far from being written off. The local fans of Madrisa Mountain want one and there is plenty of space available. Klösters would really benefit from a park so keep your fingers crossed and watch this space… Failing that, you can always go over to Jackobshorn mountain in Davos which has a great park and is known for its world-class pipes.

Off-piste and backcountry

The off-piste in Klösters is fantastic, one of the reasons being that you can almost always find good snow, even if there has been no snow for a month, due to the large numbers of north-facing slopes and countless tree runs. Disadvantages include more often than not having to catch a bus, train or taxi from wherever you end up as few of the runs actually end up in Klösters. We were shown the ropes by Chris Southwell, a professional snowboarder sponsored by Oakley, and Lukas Dürr, a local and well respected mountain guide. On a sunny day Madrisa is the place to hit the backcountry. From the top of the mountain is the long run down to San Antonian that is superb. A 5–10-minute walk takes you to a big open powder field. It's not too hard (although there are some steeps if you fancy it) and can be done with the whole family if you feel confident. However, it should be done with a guide so you don't get lost. Once in San Antonian there is a beautiful restaurant to sample and then you'll need to take a taxi back.

On Parsenn you can pretty much access powder from every lift. There's not much hiking involved and plenty

to do. The Totalphorn area, between the Meierhoftäli and Totalp chairlifts, is superb but does get sketchy if the snow isn't great and bad accidents have been known to happen in these conditions. Don't let that put you off completely; on a perfect powder day it's definitely worth checking out. If the visibility is bad, there are loads of tree runs to do and you always find good snow there. The Weissfluh, a north-facing slope is one of Klösters' most famous off-piste runs. It's around a 500m drop with a 15-minute hike out. You should take a guide with you for this one. We recommend contacting Lukas Dürr at Swiss Freeride (www.swissfreeride.ch). There is also the option of taking a guided tour to Austria – the terrain isn't too challenging (although there is some hiking and walking involved) but the scenery is incredible. The expense is a drawback though as you need different lift passes for each area. Don't forget your passport if you do give it a go.

We had a chat to Romano Pajarola, the head of the SOS mountain rescue team for Klösters, about the avalanche risks here. They take good care of their mountain and so have very few unexpected avalanches. He explained that the serious accidents almost always happen when people ignore or go against the advice of the mountain rescue team and take a trip down a closed area for example. The other killer happens when people are out of control and hit trees or rocks with no helmet on. It is so important to wear helmets and to listen to the advice of those whose job it is to make sure you're as safe as possible on the mountain.

Lift passes	
1 day	CHF61
6 days	CHF279
13 days	CHF476
Discounts are available for children, teenagers, seniors, groups and early birds.	

Instruction

Bananas Swiss Snowboard School Klösters

Bananas is a very well respected snowboard school offering private lessons, group instruction and guiding.
T: 0041 (0)81 422 66 60
E: klosters@bananas.net
W: www.bananas.ch

Boardriding

T: 0041 (0)81 420 26 62
E: office@boardriding.ch
W: www.boardriding.ch

Swiss Ski and Snowboard School Klösters

A 3-day course (Mon–Wed) costs CHF195 for skiing
or boarding. A 5-day ski course is CHF435.
T: 0041 (0)81 410 28 28
E: info@sssk.ch
W: www.sssk.ch

Swiss Ski and Snowboard School Saas

Costs are similar to those above but may not be
identical. Contact the school for more information.
T: 0041 (0)81 420 22 33
E: ssssaas@bluewin.ch
W: www.sss-saas.ch

Other activities

Paragliding and delta-gliding: Contact the tourist
office about taxi flights, lessons and test days.

Shopping: There isn't too much in the way of shopping
in Klösters, even though it's a great place to wander
round. They are hoping to attract more shops though
with the opening of the new bridge and tunnel that will
almost free Klösters of traffic by allowing the Davos
traffic to bypass the town, restoring the quiet charm
of the resort.

Sports centre: The sports centre has artificial ice rinks
for skating and ice hockey, skating lessons, curling for
beginners and ice stick shooting (Bavarian curling).

Swimming: There are five public indoor swimming
pools in local hotels.

Tennis and badminton: There are several courts (you
can get in for 1 hour a day free with the guest card).

Tobogganing: There are a number of runs: 8.6km from
Saaseralp (Madrisa) to Saas, 3.5km from Gotschnagrat
to Klösters, 2.5km from Melcheti to Aeuja and 2.5km
from Alpenrösli to Klösters Platz.

Events

Klösters doesn't have too many fixtures organised in town. There are often events for the disabled though and in mid-March the popular and highly entertaining **Wild Girls on Snow** charity spectacle. Celebrities, models and the local stars are invited for a 3-day event involving lots of dressing up, larking around and looking gorgeous. Each year the event is run for different charities and follows different themes, for example one of the latest was 'What Not to Wear Skiing'. The event includes a ski race with past and present racers from the Swiss National Ski Team so there's loads to watch on the mountain but at night the partying tends to happen behind closed doors.

    The Mardens Club is a 75-year-old traditional ski club, president of which is Jeremy Palmer-Tomkinson. They hold a fab event during which lords, ladies and other high-society types bash it out on the slopes for cups and trophies and generally let their hair down a tad. And they do a pretty good job of it. Contact the tourist office for more information about the events in Klösters.

"The pool and wellness area has to be seen to be believed and contains sauna, steam bath, solarium, beauty salon and fitness area"

Accommodation

Klösters isn't huge on the whole tour operator thing, you're better off booking directly with hotels and organising your own transfer. Renting apartments is also popular in Klösters; there are 6600 beds in rented and privately owned flats and houses and 1900 in hotels. Contact the tourist office for specific information about renting.

The 4-star hotel **Alpina** (T: 0041 (8)1 410 24 24, F: 0041 (0)81 410 24 25, www.alpina-klosters.ch, hotel@alpina-klosters.ch) has everything that anyone would want from a hotel. It has the most amazing location in town and it is absolutely stunning. The pool and wellness area has to be seen to be believed and contains sauna, steam bath, solarium, beauty salon and fitness area. The rooms are beautiful and if you want to splash out there are some great suites available with dressing rooms and the works. Call the number above to request a brochure and price list for the various types of rooms and dates, etc.

Hotel Rustico (0041 (0)81 410 22 88, www.rustico hotel.com, www.rusticohotel.com) has 11 rooms (10 rooms and 1 junior suite) and is a 3-star hotel. All of the rooms have a really cosy, alpine feel. The guys who run the hotel, Al and Renee Thöny, are the nicest people you could meet and will bend over backwards to make sure that your stay is enjoyable. As an added bonus the restaurant is superb; a real treat (see Eating out).

The **Hotel Vereina** (0041 (0)81 410 27 27, www.vereinahotel.ch, klosters@vereinahotel.ch) is a top quality 4-star establishment. It was rebuilt fairly recently and is a majestic and splendid building. Everything about the hotel is superb, from the gourmet restaurant to the amazing views, to the wellness area and spa. If you want to splash some serious cash, ask for the queen's or president's suite with their balconies, fire places, office areas, etc.

Silverpina (0041 (0)81 422 14 68, www.silva pina.ch, hotel@silvapina.ch) in Klösters Dorf is a family-run hotel and it's a great place for families to stay. Breakfast and dinner are provided so it's more like a chalet than a hotel. It's not as pricey as elsewhere, but it's probably not for those who want to be out on the town every night because it's pretty far away. It has a lovely feel though.

Eating out

On the mountain

On Madrisa, the **Saaseralp** restaurant is a superb place, with really tasty traditional Swiss food (we recommend the homemade rosti) and the best team of staff, headed up by the friendly manager, Mike Benz. It's a large place and has all the facilities you need, including a separate restaurant for large parties, usually dominated with ski school groups, and rooms where kids can play around, supervised by you or their staff. It also has the funky and popular **Igloo Bar** outside in a big glass dome. Try a whisky-filled egg from the chickens on the bar. If you're on Madrisa, eat here.

Bruhin's (081 417 66 44) is a fairly fancy restaurant right at the top of the Weissfluhgipfel on Parsenn, at the top of the Gipfelbahn cable car. It's a smart restaurant with stunning views but there is no terrace which is a bit of a shame on a sunny day. If you do fancy some posh nosh, book a table by the window so you can get the best views.

If you're looking for a traditional, chalet-style restaurant, the **Gruobenalp**, just down from Gotschnagrat on the other side to Klösters, is perfect, especially on a sunny day as the terrace has a gorgeous view. The **Alta Schwendi** (081 332 13 24, www.freeride lodge.ch, freeridelodge@E-mail.ch) is the best mountain restaurant for hanging out in due to the great music and atmosphere. It's located at Chesetta, just above the Schifer. There's a massive terrace, great food, a cosy chalet feel inside and really friendly staff. Be careful though, it's pretty easy to end up staying all afternoon; in fact you can even stay overnight if you like! Below the Schifer, on the way back to Klösters Dorf is the **Serneuser Schwendi** which has recently changed hands and is now run by locals, so is serving some great traditional Swiss cuisine. If you just fancy grabbing a good burger, the restaurant on the **Weissfluhjoch** has the best in town. Basically, there are loads of great places to eat and if you stop in at any of them, we don't think you'll be disappointed.

In town

Hotel Rustico (081 410 22 88, www.rusticohotel.com, www.rusticohotel.com) has a superb restaurant. It manages to create a really stylish and luxurious atmosphere whilst remaining cosy and friendly. The staff are so charming and the unusual cuisine falls under a Euro-Asian theme with Japanese, Asian and international specialiites. The dishes are divine and we seriously recommend trying it. It's open for lunch and dinner but is very popular in the evening so it's a good idea to book a little in advance. In addition to the main restaurant is a cosy Stübli for fondues and raclettes and above is a gorgeous hotel (see Accommodation).

The **Alpenrösli** (081 422 13 57) is a beautiful restaurant. You have to walk up to it (which can take about half an hour from Klösters Platz but it's well worth it – or taxi if you can't be bothered) and then you toboggan back down after a few cheeky drinks. We accept no responsibility for drunken tobogganing. The excellent rosti dishes are their speciality.

The **Chesa Grischuna** (081 422 22 22) is a chic restaurant with a very smart bar attached. The funky and stylish hotel attached is featured in *Hip Hotels*, along with only a handful of others throughout Europe.

There are also loads of pizzerias around where you can get a pizza for about CHF18. If you are feeling lazy, the following restaurants offer a takeaway option: **Pizzeria Grottino Al Berto** in Klösters Dorf (081 423 21 20), **Alte Post** in Platz (081 422 17 16), and **Pizza Fellini** also in Platz (081 422 22 11).

Attention, gourmands. Klösters has a glowing reputation for gourmet food and in the summer they arrange an event which encorporates a Cirque de Soleil-type circus (not actually Cirque de Soleil), and a gourmet meal whereby each of the best chefs from the region cooks a different course.

The tourist office also provides a great gastro-guide which gives a good summary of all of the restaurants in town and shows you exactly where they all are.

Bars and clubs

The **Brasserie**, in the super smart Vereina Hotel, is probably the best bar in Klösters. Its friendly staff, headed up by Claudia, are great. There's often live music, DJs, pianos, and lots more.For a classy place it's quite surprising the carnage that goes on! **Chesa** is another really smart bar that once again is great fun. The beers in these bars can be pretty expensive, approximately CHF8.50 for a pint – much cheaper beverages can be found in the local bars such as the **Bistro**, next to the train station, or the **Rusli** bar in the centre of town. Later on, the most famous and prestigious club to be seen at is the **Casa Antica**, where William, Harry and those boys hang out. Have a boogy, chill with the cool kids, but try to work it so that it's someone else's round when you get there – a bottle of Heineken costs a whopping CHF18 and it's more for spirits and mixers.

Useful facts and phone numbers

Tourist office

T: 0041 (0)81 410 20 20
F: 0041 (0)81 410 20 10
E: info@klosters.ch
W: www.klosters.ch

Emergency services

- European emergency number: 112
- Fire brigade: 118
- Police: 117
- Ambulance: 144/081 422 17 13
- Medical care: 081 422 49 49
- Police station: 081 423 36 80

Getting there

By car

It takes about 12 to 13 hours to get to Klösters from Calais, so it's probably easier to fly unless you're going to take a few days over it.

By plane

Zurich (140km) is the easiest place to fly to and it takes under 3 hours to get from there to Klösters by train or car. For more info contact the railway on 0041 (0)81 288 32 50, www.rhb.ch, davos-platz@rhb.ch.

Laax
Murschetg

Partying freestylers look
no further

On the slopes	
Snow reliability	✳ ✳ ✳
Parks	✳ ✳ ✳ ✳ ✳
Off-piste	✳ ✳ ✳
Off the slopes	
Après ski	✳ ✳ ✳
Nightlife	✳ ✳ ✳
Eating out	✳ ✳
Resort charm	✳ ✳

"The other side of the park had some of the best rails we had ever seen"

The resort

Laax was relatively undiscovered by the Brits until the British Championships moved here in 2005, bringing it on to the map. Laax itself is a small town with several separate areas, and Laax Murschetg contains all of the important bits – i.e. lifts, bars and clubs. Laax is a sanctuary for the avid freestyler: the park is second to none in Europe, you can stay here pretty cheaply (although drinks will set you back a fair bit) and the nightlife is cool (as long as you are). You should have second thoughts if you spend much of your time moseying around town (although Flims is a short bus ride if needs be – see Flims chapter, page 352) or if you get bored going to the same restaurants and bars every night. If these things don't bother you, you should definitely give it a whirl.

The mountains

Height: 1000–3000m

Ability	Rating
Expert	✳ ✳ ✳
Intermediate	✳ ✳ ✳ ✳
Beginner	✳ ✳ ✳ ✳

Getting about

Laax is at the centre of the Alpenarena, providing good access to its 220km of slopes. From Laax Murschetg it is a quick cable car ride to Crap Sogn Gion and you'll be in the park in a matter of minutes. The mountain is pretty flat so it's great for cruisy intermediates, though there is a fair bit of fresh powder to be had, which you can see from many of the pistes, and there are some freeride routes marked on the piste map.

The park

This is one of our favourite parks in Europe. We were there for the Orange British Ski and Board Championships so everything was shaped perfectly, but we got the impression that the guys looking after it were pretty keen and park-proud. There are two different areas to the park, on either side of the café/bar/hostel at Crap Sogn Gion. The riders loved the slopestyle area at the Brits; it consisted of a selection of rails, including 10-metre down rails, a C-rail, and a fun wall ride. You could hit three different kickers on the way down, with a choice of sizes at each hit. In total there are six jumps (5–25m tables). The other side of the park had some of the best rails we had ever seen. There's an S-rail, C-rail, rollercoaster, and big gap jumps to a 5-metre high rail. There are also six straight boxes, one 4-frame rail, one kinked box, and four rainbow rails. To finish it off there are two super pipes (one 80m and one 140m) which were in mint condition, with the big pipe being one of the best we rode all winter. Good work, lads!

Off-piste and backcountry

Most of the Alpenarena's off-piste terrain is pretty accessible and not bad at all considering the shallow gradients of the mountain. Like many other resorts, they now provide 40km of unprepared but marked and avalanche-controlled slopes for freeriders to play on. These runs lead from the summits of the three main peaks: Vorab Pign (2897m), La Siala (2810m), above Laax, and Cassons (2675m). Cassons has been recommended, not just for the marked run there, but also for the off-piste terrain surrounding it (which would require a guide). If you do want to hire a guide for a day or so they can show you more of the area contact Mountain Fantasy (see Instruction). From Cassons, they can take you into the backcountry to Seghesgkecier or down to Bargis. Alternatively, you can start your trip from the Vorab Gletscher (3018m), above Falera, and skin (hike) to the Bündner Vorab (3028m), from which you can expect a great ride down a big open valley, ending up in Alp Ruschein (1774m). These expeditions should only be undertaken with a qualified guide.

Lift passes

1 day	CHF61
6 days	CHF301
13 days	CHF443

You can also buy just a park and pipe ticket for CHF38 if that's all you're interested in or a beginner's ticket for the same price that gives you access to all the beginners' areas.

Instruction

Mountain Fantasy

These are the best mountain guides in town for skiers, boarders and anyone else who wants to explore. The office is located in Flims.
T: 0041 (0)81 936 70 77
E: bergsport@mountain-fantasy.ch
W: www.mountain-fantasty.ch

Ski Schule

Five days in ski school will cost CHF300.
T: 0041 (0)81 927 71 71
W: www.laax.com/skischule

Snowboarding School

Five days will cost around CHF460.
T: 0041(0)81 927 71 55
W: www.laax.com/fahrschule

Other activities

There isn't too much to do in Laax Murschteg. If you need other activities, such as paragliding and sledging, Flims is your best bet (see Flims chapter, page 352).
Full-moon skiing: In January, February and March there is full moon skiing (weather dependant) on Crap Sogn Gion (081 927 70 00); from 8pm you can take the gondola lift up and take a guided moonlit tour down.
Ice skating and curling: You can ice skate and do Bavarian curling on Laax lake (081 921 51 53).
Wellness centre, pool and tennis: The Hotel Signina (081 927 90 00) in Laax Murschteg has a wellness suite, Laguna pool and tennis courts that are open to the public. Hotel Laaxerhof (081 920 82 00) has a public pool and sauna. If you don't mind catching the bus to Flims the wellness centres at the Park Hotel and Adula are well worth a look (see Flims chapter, page 352).

Events

The superb and well maintained park means that there are a crazy number of events that take place in Laax. Most of the after parties take place later on in the Riders Palace so if you're competing, or watching, this is the place to book into.

> "Most of the after parties take place later on in the Riders Palace so if you're competing, or watching, this is the place to book into"

To start the season there is the **Ski and Snowboard Open** in October (when the snowpark is moved on to the Vorab glacier) with DJs, new equipment to be tested and the Burton Team demo. The **Snow Groove Party** in November is another freestyle party which is repeated in early December when the Monster Pipe is re-opened.

In January the **Burton European Open** takes place. In total 600 athletes compete – pros, amateurs and juniors – in the super pipe and slope style. In one bizarre but great competition, Microsoft Xbox and Laax team together to fund the **Amped Champ**. This unique contest looks for champion snowboarders, both real and virtual. The qualifiers are in early February and the best real and virtual boarders will battle it out in the Amped Champ finals in early April. For more information, check out www.amped champ.ch. In late February the **Iceripper contest** is held in the Monster Pipe.

In early March the **FIS Freestyle World Cup** (skier cross and ski half pipe) takes place. In mid–late March the **Orange British Ski/Snowboard Championships** kicks off, a must for British boarders and skiers. This competition attracts both pros and up-and-coming riders, all trying to make a name for themselves. It consists of skier and boardercross, slopestyle, big air and half pipe. There are cash prizes for the top three in each category, but the title is the main trophy. The Brits moved to Laax in 2005 and it was a big success; in terms of weather, organisation and the night scene. Well done to the organisers, Stu Brass, Spencer Claridge and Jenny Ahnell for all the hard work they put into such a wicked competition. Check it out on www.orangebrits.com.

"The coolest
place to stay
is the Riders
Palace"

Accommodation

The coolest place to stay is the **Riders Palace** (0041
(0)81 927 97 00, www.riderspalace.ch), a funky, glass,
neon-lit hotel/bar/club, full of ultra-cool clientele.
Rooms vary from basic dorms to stylish multimedia
rooms and suites with DVD player, games consoles, sky
and projector screens. One night's stay and a 1-day ski
pass will cost you CHF65–185 per person, depending
on the type of room. They do deals for weekends and
for 4–7 days, all including lift pass. For example, 7 nights
and 7 days of ski passes will cost you CHF401 per
person for a basic dorm, CHF506 for a 3-bed multimedia

room, CHF611 for a double and CHF1241 for a suite. It's the best place to stay if you are going to be partying every night as it's all in the building, but it's not the place to get a quiet night's sleep.

If you really want to be the first to hit the park you can stay in the **Mountain Hostel** on Crap Sogn Gion (0041 (0)81 927 73 73), at 2228m. Five nights in a room with 4 beds, including a 6-day lift ticket, dinner, breakfast and sauna, will cost from CHF425 per person. The **Laaxerhof** (0041 (0)81 920 82 00) is a pretty smart hotel with an elegant restaurant and good pool and sauna. Prices are CHF155–255 per person for half-board accommodation, depending on the type

of room (lowest price is for 6 people in a room). The **Hotel Signina Sport Golf** (0041 (0)81 927 90 00) is another great traditional hotel with a wellness suite and tennis courts that are open to the public. Prices are CHF120–180 per person per night.

Eating out

On the mountain

If you're hitting the park and pipe you will be eating and drinking at the popular bars at Crap Sogn Gion: **Rock bar** and **Café No Name** (081 927 73 44). These bars are just above the half pipe and they are great places to hang out. For a cheeky beer, hit the terrace right at the top of the park and for a great cheeseburger, head up to the café. There are tons of deckchairs and comfy outdoor seating so you'll always be able to find a place to relax with a beer.

At **Plaun**, the old chairlift station has been converted into a bar with deckchairs outside in good weather; and they barbeque sausages and serve good soup.

On the way back down to Laax there are two superb restaurants: **Tegia Curnius** (081 927 99 30) and **Tegia Larnags** (081 927 99 10), both with cosy, traditional atmospheres, sizeable sun terraces and local foods.

In town

There are very few restaurants in Laax Murschetg, although you can eat in most of the hotels. Restaurant **Muhbarack** (081 927 99 40, muhbarack@laax.com), above the Crap Bar, serves great pasta and local specialities, including fondues and raclettes.

"There are tons of deckchairs and comfy outdoor seating so you'll always be able to find a place to relax with a beer"

Pizzeria Cristallina (081 921 22 52, casaselva@ kns.ch) is a fantastic pizzeria at the bottom of Laax Murschetg on the main road. It cooks superb pizzas on a big open wood fire and also does takeaways.

If you need something a little more gourmet, you should take a short bus ride to Flims where you will find a few really good restaurants such as La Clav and Barga at the Hotel Adula and the Little China if you're bored with local food (see Flims chapter, page 352).

Bars and clubs

There are only a handful of bars in Laax; in fact 'handful' is being generous. For après ski, head to the Crap Bar at the bottom of the slopes, built with 24 tons of granite. For a change, you could come down into Flims Dorf and have some beers in the Legana and Iglu bar (see Flims chapter, page 352) and then catch a bus back to Laax. After this, you should head to the neon-lit Riders Palace Lobby Bar, kitted out with leather sofas, internet and a huge bar. Unfortunately the huge bar rarely has enough staff on a busy night but apart from that, it's wicked. Downstairs is the massive (and expensive) Ministry-of-Sound-run Palace Club where the cool kids hang out. Later on the music ranges from hip-hop to trance and house. If you prefer rock and pop try the Casa Veglia club.

Useful facts and phone numbers

Tourist office

T: 0041 (0)81 920 81 81
E: tourismus@alpenarena.ch
W: www.alpenarena.ch

Emergency services

- Police: In an emergency call 117, if not call 081 928 29 40/ 081 911 11 64
- In an emergency on the mountain call the SOS central office on 081 972 70 01
- Hospital in Chur: 081 256 61 11
- Fire: 118

Doctors

- Dr P Schneller: 081 921 48 48
- District nurse: 081 921 55 05

Taxis

- Taxi Mario: 081 941 22 22

Getting there

By plane

Zurich (150km)
Friedrichshafen (140km) for Ryanair flights.

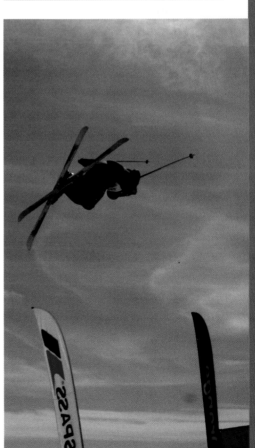

Saas Fee

A magical place – the ultimate
summer resort

On the slopes	
Snow reliability	✼ ✼ ✼ ✼ ✼
Parks	✼ ✼ ✼ ✼
Off-piste	✼ ✼ ✼ ✼
Off the slopes	
Après ski	✼ ✼ ✼ ✼
Nightlife	✼ ✼ ✼ ✼
Eating out	✼ ✼ ✼ ✼
Resort charm	✼ ✼ ✼ ✼ ✼

The resort

The village of Saas Fee does not feel, as many do, like a functional resort built purely to support the winter sports; it is a magical place that you can easily fall in love with. The unique atmosphere is traditional and romantic, and the entire town is surrounded by 13 imposing, 4000-metre peaks, including the highest mountain in Switzerland, the Dom (4545 metres above sea level).The traffic-free town and the chalet-style buildings contribute to the relaxing pace of this charming glacier village. And it manages to provide a varied and rich nightlife. There is, however, an argument that Saas Fee is a better summer resort, as in the winter the village is in the shade of the mountains for 23 hours of the day and becomes very cold.

The mountains

Height: 1800–3600m

Ability	Rating
Expert	✼ ✼ ✼
Intermediate	✼ ✼ ✼ ✼
Beginner	✼ ✼ ✼ ✼ ✼

Getting about

Take two Alpin Express cable cars to Felskinn at 3000m. From here you can either enjoy some long, sweeping red runs back to town or take the highest underground funicular in the world, the Metro Alpin to the Mittelallalin glacier (3500m). When visibility is good you can apparently see the lights of Milan. We couldn't,

"It is a magical place that you can easily fall in love with"

but maybe your eyesight's better than ours. It will take you around 40 minutes to reach the top.

Winter

There are 100km of marked pistes in Saas Fee in the winter, most designed for the beginner/intermediate skier or boarder. The 32 runs comprise 13 blue trails, 14 red and 5 black. Saas Fee has a great reputation for maintaining the runs in tip top condition, allowing the intermediate riders a great base from which to push themselves to the next level and, unknown to many, there is a lot more ground worth exploring. Mogul buffs should head to the unprepared mogul piste under the Längfluh chairlift.

Summer

The glacier provides 20km of ski slopes for summer skiing, geared to high standard riding. It is best to get out early, as the glacier closes some time between 12pm (at high summer) and 2pm. The runs are pretty good but if you're not doing slalom training or hitting the park, you may end up twiddling your thumbs. If you are hitting the park, you will not be disappointed. Get used to the T-bars and draglifts; chairlifts are difficult to manoeuvre and so are not practical with the moving glacier.

The park

There is a park in the winter, but it is far better maintained in the summer. Saas Fee was one of the first resorts to put real money in to develop the park and skier/boarder cross. It is, therefore, renowned for hosting many of the major competitions such as the Rip Curl Challenge and the World Cup Half Pipe events. Professionals often train here in the summer, and ski and board manufacturers are regularly spotted testing their products.

The park is changed regularly but always consists of a super half pipe, three big kickers ranging from 6m to 12m gaps and a huge range of rails. There are plenty

> " From the top of the Alpin Express you can find the Morenia, great if you like the steeps, and it's hardly ever touched"

of table-top jumps for learning and practising new tricks, before stepping it up to the bigger ones. The atmosphere in the park is superb; a DJ often plays at the bottom and photographers and cameramen are frequently spotted filming for the latest movies.

Off-piste and backcountry

It is wise to be cautious when exploring the off-piste around a glacier due to the crevasses and concealed dangers. However, this does not mean that there aren't any off-piste opportunities to be had, quite the contrary. There are three pistes that are marked as yellow or off-piste runs but, having spoken with locals, we managed to find a few more. The absence of glacier on the Plattjen makes it a great place to find fresh tracks through the trees. You also have the benefit that the trees shelter the snow, so it often stays in good condition all day. Be warned though, this area can be quite challenging!

The Maste 4 is another good area to keep you out of the way of crevasse dangers. It is a relatively easy powder run – a perfect place for cruising. From the top of the Alpin Express you can find the Morenia, great if you like the steeps, and it's hardly ever touched. It is very important only to attempt this after a good snowfall and, even then, it must be done early in the morning. The Hannig, at the other side of town to the Alpin Express (used for hill-walking in the summer), is another great place for an early morning hike. There is a lift from the bottom of the resort but they won't let you on with your board or skis so it is a bit of a trek. If you fancy a backcountry adventure, set off

early from Brittania Hutte and enjoy the legendary, 1.5-hour freeride down to Saas Almagell. This is pretty challenging, especially at the beginning, and is only recommended with a guide.

Lift passes	Summer	Winter
1 day	CHF60	CHF60
7 days	CHF328	CHF335
14 days	CHF520	CHF530

Instruction

Eskimos Snowboard School

This is a well-known school. Taster courses are run on Sundays for 2 hours for CHF35. Courses teach basic to freestyle/carving, 3 days costs CHF115 and a week (10 hours) is CHF165. Private instruction costs CHF70 for 1 hour, for one to two people.
T: 0041 (0)27 957 49 04
E: info@eskimos.ch
W: www.eskimos.ch

Saas Fee Ski and Snowboard School

This school comes highly recommended by locals. Not that there is a huge amount of choice. All instructors speak a variety of languages.

Ski lessons

Class instruction: 1 day CHF48 for 3 hours, 1 week CHF179 for 15 hours. Private instruction is available; prices vary. For example, one or two people for 1 hour will cost CHF60.

Snowboard lessons

Class instruction: 1 day CHF45, 1 week CHF165. Private instruction is available, one or two people for 1 hour will cost CHF60.
T: 0041 (0)27 957 23 48
E: info@skischule-saas-fee.ch
W: www.skischule-saas-fee.ch

British Freeski Camps

These run for 3 or 4 weeks in the summer every year through the whole of July, and are organised by Warren Smith. You can sign up for the whole time or any one week. On the camp, you have the choice of hitting the park, perfecting the skier cross course or getting your carving up to scratch. The top professional skiers in Britain gather together for these camps, some coaching and others training, so it's a great place to introduce yourself to the British ski scene.

T: 0044 (0)1525 374757
E: admin@snowsportsynergy.com
W: www.britishfreeskicamps.com

Popcorn shop

For **buying or renting** snowboards or freestyle skis we can highly recommend this shop, located right in the centre of town near the clock tower. They always have the latest equipment and clothing and are also happy to offer their expert advice.

Other activities

Always ask if there is a discount with a guest card, obtainable from your hotel or apartment landlord.

Winter and summer

Bobsleigh: The Feeblitz Bobsleigh is a 900m long toboggan run. Great fun for all the family. It can be adapted to suit the adrenaline junkie – although not 'officially' recommended, it has been known not to apply the brakes and keep your eyes closed. We didn't tell you to do it though (CHF5.30 with guest card, CHF6 without).

Ice grotto: Visit the Allain Ice Pavilion – the biggest ice grotto in the world. It can be accessed from the Metro Alpin top station hall at 3500m above sea level.

Mountain climbing: The mountain climbing schools offer a number of activities for keen climbers, or those who fancy giving it a go. Rock and ice climbing, canyoning, glacier trekking and mountaineering are available for both beginners and advanced climbers. For a James Bond-type activity, the 'Alpine Gorge' is an opportunity to be seized. This is a mountain descent from Saas Fee to Saas Grund, where you make your way down with the aid of a guide, fixed steel ropes, ladders, three Tyroliennes and a suspension bridge. It costs CHF100 to do the full canyon and CHF70 for half. A final option is to conquer one of the three Via Ferratas (secured climbing routes). The Mittaghorn is fairly easy and good for families, the Jägihorn is pretty difficult and should be undertaken with a guide and the Via Ferrata del Lago is recommended as a 2-day tour.

For further information contact Active Dreams (027 957 14 44, www.weissmies.ch, weissmies@rhone.ch) or Bergführerbüro Mountain Life (027 957 44 64, www.mountainlife.ch, info@mountainlife.ch).

Tennis and badminton: There are two indoor tennis courts and four indoor badminton courts available.

Wellness centre: If you're looking for a good way to while away a bad weather day look no further than the Beilen Wellness Centre. There is a huge swimming pool as well as a sauna, solarium, whirlpool, steam bath, solar sun bathing, fitness room, table tennis and table football. It costs CHF12 to use the swimming pool with a guest card (CHF13 without). The 5-star Hotel Ferienart contains the Paradisa wellness centre and non residents can pay for a day's spa package. We'd love to tell you what it was like but we couldn't afford it.

Summer only

Adventure forest: This opened in 2004. You can swing from tree to tree and walk across hanging bridges. There are a couple of routes to choose from and depending on which you prefer it will cost CHF22–28.
Crazy golf: A fantastic way to pass an hour or so! Not a course to be sniffed at, it really is quite difficult and should be taken very seriously. Costs CHF4 with guest card (CHF4.50 without).

Golf: A 9-hole alpine golf course can be found just behind the Kalbermatten sports field.
Hiking: There's loads of hiking to be had in and around Saas Fee. Contact the tourist office for all the details.
Mountain biking: Bikers will be in their element in the summer, as there are around 70km of trails. The marked trails suit a range of abilities. Contact the tourist office for a detailed mountain bike map.
Sports: The Kalbermatten sports ground offers football, basketball, volleyball, a mini skate ramp for skateboarding and in-line skating and tennis courts. Pit-Pat (a weird combination of snooker and crazy golf) is located nearby, at the Hotel Waldesruh.

Winter only

Heliskiing and snow touring: These are definitely worth checking out later on in the season.

Husky tours: These run several times a week from 4.30am. It costs CHF40 per adult and can be booked at the tourist office.

Ice skating: The natural ice rink is open all day from mid-December to the end of February and costs CHF4. Snow bowling on the rink costs CHF20 an hour.

Sledge run: A 5km sledge run can be found at Hannig. On Tuesdays and Thursdays (6–9pm) sledging by night is an experience not to be missed. A single run costs CHF18. Sledge rental is CHF5 and head torch rental CHF3. There is also an 11km run in the nearby town of Saas Grund – the longest in Europe.

Snow shoe trekking: This is organised daily. Contact the tourist office if the idea of expelling huge amounts of energy to walk around in big shoes rocks your boat.

Snow tubing and air boarding: This looks mightily more fun. It costs CHF8 and occurs several times a week.

Events

Saas Fee is a very popular venue for a wide variety of events because the height of the glacier pretty much guarantees snow all year round. The **FIS World Cup** has been held in Saas Fee for many years with disciplines for skiers and boarders in the half pipe and skier-boardercross. The Dutch and British Championships have also been held here over the years. The **Saas Fee Ride** takes place every summer, usually at the end of July, and many of the best freestyle skiers and boarders in the world turn up for the event. If you fancy your chances at entering the competition or if you just want to improve your style, why not book on to the **British Freeski Camps** (www.britishfreeskicamps.com) which take place in the few weeks running up to the Saas Fee Ride.

Accommodation

There are a variety of packages available to suit all budgets and it is a good idea to contact the tourist office with your particular requirements. Renting an apartment is often a good option; you will pay anything from £250 a week but the quality of accommodation is generally a lot better than a hotel

at the equivalent cost. Another thing to bear in mind is that the north end of the village is a bit of a hike from the lifts so always make sure you check the location before you book.

For a funky, unique, well placed and friendly hotel call the **Dom Hotel** (0041 (0)27 957 51 01, relax@uniquedom.com, www.uniquedom.com). Its mad décor and the fact the rooms contain PlayStations and Minidisc and CD players, as well as everything you would expect, really do make this the ultimate choice. The rooms are minimalist and funky with wooden floors, and the balconies have stunning views. The hotel also contains the hugely popular Popcorn bar that the nightlife of Saas Fee is centred around and the Living Room, a stylish chill-out bar. We have stayed here many times and we love it! It will cost you CHF108–169 for a single person, depending on the

> "It has a beautiful location sitting above a deep creek and contains a charming restaurant"

season. For two people the prices are CHF216–338.

If being near the slopes is of utmost importance to you, check out **La Gorge** Apart-Hotel. It has a beautiful location sitting above a deep creek and contains a charming restaurant. It is only 100m from the lifts and is also close to all the facilities of the town. The rooms are fairly basic but contain a little kitchen so you can save money on food. Depending on the season it will cost CHF190–260 per night for two people.

For a luxury apartment at a decent price check out the 5-star **Shangri-La Apartments** (contact Pamela Andermatten on 0041 (0)27 958 15 15, zum.lerch@rhone.ch, www.rhone.ch/zumlerch). The apartments are huge (47–83m²) and contain Sky TV, a DVD player, an internet connection, a coffee machine, a dishwasher, a washing machine, a massive balcony and there is a sauna and whirlpool room for the use of guests. A two-room apartment will cost CHF560–1120 for the night. Larger apartments are also available. When you divide the cost between the number of people sharing this massive luxury apartment, it doesn't look quite so much!

If price is no object and you enjoy fancy hotels, it has to be the 5-star **Hotel Ferienart** (0041 (0)27 958 19 00, info@ferienart.ch, www.ferienart.ch). It has all the charm and splendour that you would expect at this price with six restaurants, a piano bar, dance hall and beauty spa. We can't bring ourselves to print the costs – if you need to know, you can't afford it.

Eating out

On the mountain
The world's highest **revolving restaurant** is at the top lift station on the Mittelallain glacier. It spins all the way round about once an hour. The views are stunning, the food is tasty and we thought it was pretty good value too. Definitely worth doing at least once. And it's been featured in a James Bond film. Best to book if you want a table by the window – call 027 957 17 71.

Other restaurants worth checking out are the popular, rustic **Gletschergrotte**, halfway down from Speilboden (worth booking – 027 957 21 60) and the more trendy hangout, **Popcorn Plaza** at Längfluh (027 957 17 71) which has dramatic views that can be enjoyed from comfy deckchairs on the huge terrace.

In town
La Ferme is a superb restaurant in the centre of town. It has a traditional, rustic and charming atmosphere and all the staff don the traditional dress. It's not cheap, but is good value as the food is fantastic. There are lots more traditional Swiss restaurants along the main street and it's worth exploring if your budget can take it.

The **Bodmen** restaurant (027 957 20 75) takes 10 to 15 minutes to walk to along a beautiful woodland path and is well worth the trip. It's a beautiful place to sit at lunchtime in the summer as the huge terrace has marvellous views and little goats scuttle in between the tables. In the evening it's not too formal and has great food, from fondues to fillet steak. If you wish, you can request the special table next to a glass panel with views into a barn so you can see lots of chickens and other farmyard animals strutting their stuff whilst you eat. Not advisable to ask for this table if you fancy tucking into a chicken dish. To find the restaurant, walk past the Alpin Express lift station, in the opposite direction to town, and you will see a sign pointing you towards the Bodmen.

The **Fletschhorn** restaurant (027 957 21 31) is highly recommended by gourmands and is highly expensive. **Boccalino's** is a great pizza restaurant on the main street serving pizzas, pasta and risottos. Probably the best value in town, this is a great place to eat if you're on a restricted budget.

Bars and clubs

Saas Fee has a very good night scene. The laws have also recently changed so that there is no specific time at which a bar should close; if it's busy they will open until it's time to hit the slopes again. Dangerous stuff.

The **Popcorn** bar is definitely at the centre of the action with good après ski, a variety of nights with European DJs and live bands, and the odd 'Diva Night' when they play all the classic cheesy music and dressing up is optional. It's not cheap here though, a pint will set you back CHF9, and a cocktail CHF14. The younger crowd tend to hang out at the **Happy Bar**, at the north end of town, where the drinks are cheaper, especially during happy hour.

If you are in the 25+ category you might favour **The Living Room** in the Dom Hotel, which is more of a chill-out bar with sofas and candles. If the mood takes you later on, you can always head downstairs to the Popcorn for a drunken boogie. **Poison** nightclub is popular and good fun. Again, it's more for the 25+ age group. Opposite the Popcorn is the **Alpen bar**, which has live music in the winter and on quieter nights is a great place to have a cosy beer and a game of darts.

The **Metropol** is a typical American diner with a number of pool tables and table football along with an 80s-style dance floor. You can also have a delicious (but overpriced) burger to soak up the alcohol. If you intend to do your partying indoors, watch out for the 'hush police' who parade the streets after 10pm and can collar you into a fine of about CHF120 if they think you're making too much noise.

Useful facts and phone numbers

Tourist office

T:	0041 (0)27 958 18 58
F:	0041 (0)27 958 18 60
E:	to@saas-fee.ch
W:	www.saas-fee.ch or www.saastal.ch

Direct reservations

T:	0041 (0)27 958 18 68
F:	0041 (0)27 958 18 70
E:	saas-fee.ch. Online booking at www.saas-fee.ch

Weather information

T:	0900 57 30 70 (CHF1.49/min)

Emergency services

- Police: 117
- Police station (by the car park): 027 957 10 26
- Ambulance: 114
- Breakdown service: 140

Doctors

- Stefan and Stephanie Kuonen, Saas Fee: 027 957 58 59
- Medical Centre, Saas Grund: 027 957 11 55
- Pharmacy, Saas Fee: 027 957 26 18
- Dentist, St Imseng: 027 957 20 52

Electro-taxis

- Ambros: 079 439 10 29
- Taxi Anselm: 079 220 21 37
- Bolero: 027 958 11 35
- Center Reisen: 027 958 11 33
- Imseng 027 957 33 44

Getting there

By car

From Calais, it will take around 10 hours to drive to Saas Fee. Enter Switzerland above Lausanne and from there follow signs for Sion, and then Brig, where you are signed to Saas Fee.

The village itself is car-free, so you will have to leave your car in the car park (open air or covered).

The car park prices decrease the longer you are staying and are cheaper if you have a guest card, which can be obtained from your hotel or apartment owner on arrival. (Winter: 1 day CHF14, 1 week CHF74, 2 weeks CHF 123 with guest card. Summer: 1 day CHF11, 1 week CHF56, 2 weeks CHF98 with guest card.)

There are free phones in the unloading areas to call your hotel for a free lift or to call a taxi (free phone numbers are by the phone).

The recommended price for all taxis from the car park to your hotel/apartment is CHF18–28 (plus luggage and waiting time).

By plane

Geneva (234km) Transfer from Geneva is approximately 3 hours by car. If transfer is by train, change in Brig (or Visp) for the postbus, which takes you right to Saas Fee. There are hourly connections from Brig from 6:15 to 20:15 and from Visp from 6.30 to 20:30. Reservations may be necessary with the post bus (0041 (0)27 958 11 45).

Zurich (246km) There are regular transfers to Brig or Visp. The transfer is approximately 3 hours.

St Moritz

A fantastically glitzy, glam-
and exclusive resort, with
incredible freeriding terrain

On the slopes	
Snow reliability	❅ ❅ ❅ ❅
Parks	❅ ❅
Off-piste	❅ ❅ ❅ ❅
Off the slopes	
Après ski	❅ ❅ ❅
Nightlife	❅ ❅ ❅ ❅
Eating out	❅ ❅ ❅ ❅
Resort charm	❅ ❅ ❅ ❅

The resort

St Moritz is absolutely fabulous: stunning mountains, fantastic freeriding and striking resort. Set over the beautiful Lake San Murezzan, St Moritz Dorf is one of the most famous and exclusive resorts in Europe; it has more 5- and 4-star hotels than you could shake a hat at, top-class bars and restaurants, Versace and Louis Vuitton shops a plenty, and is populated by fur-clad guests and small poodles. And if you need any more evidence of exclusivity, St Moritz is host to the Cartier Polo World Cup on Snow. It was the upper crust Brits who established the style of the resort, and they're never too far away. Amazingly though, it's not too pretentious; you'd be mad not to love it.

The mountains

Height: 1327–4354m

Ability	Rating
Expert	❅ ❅ ❅ ❅
Intermediate	❅ ❅ ❅ ❅
Beginner	❅ ❅ ❅

Getting about

From Dorf a funicular takes you up to the sunny slopes of Corviglia. From St Moritz Bad you can get a gondola up to these slopes and there is the advantage that you can ride back down into town. However, if you place value on nightlife and shopping, we would still recommend staying in Dorf. The other slopes on

"St Moritz is host to the Cartier Polo World Cup on Snow"

Corvatsch are a bus or car ride away which is worth it if you like cruisy reds or the snow park. The best time to check out this mountain is for the Snow Night Parties each Friday, during which 5km of pistes are floodlit. The parties carry on until 2am and are more focused on drinking than riding. Diavolezza is also considered to be part of the St Moritz ski area but it's a half hour drive away. The avant-garde lift system and 350km of pistes are impressive, but it is a shame that the areas aren't linked.

The park

The Mellowpark on the Furtschellas area, has a half pipe and a couple of jumps, rails and a hip, but it can be neglected on occasion. Rumour has it that they are pumping more money into it in the years to come to attract more freestylers, so watch this space…

Off-piste and backcountry

The off-piste possibilities in St Moritz are great, but not obvious, so it's a good place to invest in a guide if you want to make the most of the area. The powder hounds should head straight to the peaks of Piz Nair (3057m) or Piz Corvatsch. There are some tricky spots, but the snow usually stays in good nik. Get there early after snow fall if you're after fresh tracks. Some steep and deep can also be found opposite the Marguns lift.

Lift passes	
1 day	CHF56–69
6 days	CHF262–332
13 days	CHF437–549

Instruction

Board School St Moritz Suvretta

Private instruction costs CHF330 per day; a class costs CHF47 per half day and CHF210 for 6 half days.
T: 0041 (0)81 836 36 00

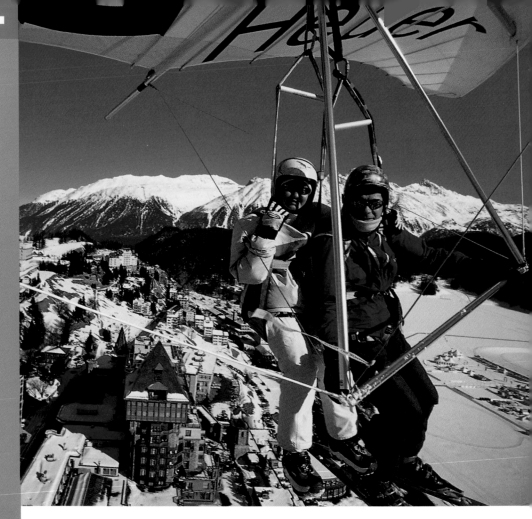

Suvretta Snowsports School

Private instruction costs CHF330 per day.
T: 0041 (0)81 836 36 00
W: www.suvrettasnowsports.ch

Swiss Ski School

Private instruction costs CHF320 per day; a class costs CHF70 per day.
T: 0041 (0)81 830 01 01
W: www.skischool.ch

Other activities

Bobsled: Pros can get up to speeds of 85mph on the natural bobsled run. The races and the championships are great to watch and if you fancy it, you can have a taxi ride driven by a pro or you can have a go yourself with instructions. The bobsled run has seen the Swiss European Championships, Bobsled World Championships, and two Olympic Winter Games. Call 081 830 02 00, or check out www.olympia-bobrun.ch. The 100-year-old unique **Cresta Run** (www.cresta-run.com) is another chance to reach speeds of 85 mph – but only if you're a bloke. Though male chauvinism is on the out in the UK, the British clientele of St Moritz have managed to keep a firm grip on it. To race down sheet ice, grabbing hold of a 'skeleton' sled, the male gent will fork out around £200 for five rides over a season. Bargain! Events on the Cresta Run to look out for include the Heaton Gold Cup, Curzon Cup, Grand National and Gunter Sachs Challenge Cup.

Casino: The casino in St Moritz Bad is definitely worth a look (081 837 54 54, www.casinostmoritz.ch).

Curling: Rink rental at the Curling Centre (081 833 45 88) costs CHF25 per person for 2 hours. A 45-minute lesson is CHF50–100. Group instruction costs CHF20–25 per person. Events held here include the Jackson Cup and the St Moritz Grand Prix.

Horse-drawn sleigh ride: Take a romantic horse-drawn sleigh ride over the frozen lake and through the Staz forest. You can find the sleighs in St Moritz Bad, next to the church. A half-hour ride for 1–4 people costs CHF55 and CHF95 for an hour.

Horse riding: Indoor horse riding (081 833 57 33) costs CHF60 and group trail riding CHF60 per hour.

Ice skating and hockey: Open air ice skating, hockey and curling takes place on the Ice Arena; CHF5.50 for adults (CHF3.50 for kids) and CHF5 for ice skate rental (081 833 50 30).

Medical centre: For some pampering, head to the Medical Therapy Centre, Heilbad St Moritz (081 833 30 62), where you can take a mineral or aromatic bath,

> "Take a romantic horse-drawn sleigh ride over the frozen lake and through the Staz forest"

beauty treatment, mud bath or pack, massage, physical therapy and a solarium. Massages costs from CHF54 and carbonic acid mineral baths from CHF35.

Museums: If you like your museums you can head to either the Engadin Museum, Segatini Museum, Mili

Weber's House or Albana's Hunting Museum.

Paragliding and hang-gliding: These take place every hour 10am–4pm, from Corviglia mountain top. It costs CHF230.

Shopping: A favourite activity of visitors to St Moritz – bring your best credit card with you.

Sledging: If the boblsed runs all sound a bit too much for you, there is some normal sledging (a 2.5km run) from Muottas to Punt Muragl. Sledges can be rented from the bottom of the Muottas Muragl funicular. It is open every day 9.30am–4pm.

Snow night parties: These Friday night parties on Corvatsch are a great place to go for riding, drinking and partying. Have a bite to eat at the charming Alpetta Hut and a few beers at the Hossa Bar.

Tennis and squash: Courts can be found in the Corviglia Tennis Centre in St. Moritz Bad (081 833 15 00). One hour of tennis costs CHF49 and 45 minutes of squash CHF19.

Events

To get the latest on the hundreds of events that take place in St Mortiz you're best to check out the website www.stmoritz.ch. Whereas our event section normally details the coolest ski and board events in the park or on the big mountain, the events in St Moritz take a rather unique slant. Whilst St Moritz has embraced a couple of alpine ski events, ambassadors were more inclined simply to bring the traditional British high society events to the St Moritz frozen lake.

In mid-January, is the **Concours Hippique**, an international equestrian jumping tournament on snow (www.stmoritz-concours.ch). This annual event sees more than 100 horses competing in 15 tests, including ski jöring (with a riderless horse pulling a skier). The last week in January sees the amazing **Polo on Snow** (www.polostmoritz.com), in which around 60 polo horses and 24 of the world's best polo players take part. In 2006, the 22nd Cartier Polo World Cup on Snow is set to take place on 26–29 January.

Cricket on Ice (www.cricket-on-ice.com) has been played on the lake since '89 and **Winter Golf** since '78. Red golf balls and white greens are an amazing sight at the Winter Golf Tournament in Silvaplana (www.silvaplana.ch). **White Turf Horse Races** take place the first three Sundays in Febuary (www.whiteturf.ch).

There are short-distance, flat, trotting and ski jöring events and each winter the prize money totals a whopping CHF500,000. At the end of February international **greyhound races** are held, with traditions dating back to the 1930s.

The **gourmet festival** in the first week in February (www.stmoritz.ch/gourmetfestival) is yet another long-standing tradition, in which the best chefs from all over the world inspire young talented chefs from St Moritz hotel kitchens. The Grand Gourmet Finale once again takes place on the St Moritz frozen lake.

Accommodation

We would definitely want to stay in St Moritz Dorf; St Moritz Bad is not half as much fun and you won't want to walk up to the Dorf area. Only stay in St Moritz Bad if you don't care about the atmosphere and nightlife and would prefer the benefit of being able to ride back to town.

There is a huge range of 5- and 4-star hotels to choose from. On the whole, the 5-star hotels were a tad too grand for us. For example, on walking into the distinguished and impressive **Badrutts Palace** (0041 (0)81 837 10 00, reservations@badruttspalace.com, www.badruttspalace.com), there are two people swinging the revolving door for you which is, in our opinion, slightly excessive. The **Kulm hotel** (0041 (0)81 836 80 00, info@kulmhotel-stmoritz.ch, www.kulmhotel-stmoritz.ch) is another imposing one; remarkable to look at, but again we didn't feel too comfortable here.

We much preferred the smart, comfortable and friendly 4 stars in the centre of town. The **Schweizerhof** (0041 (0)81 837 07 07, reservation@schweizerhof.stmoritz.ch, www.schweizerhofstmoritz.ch) is one of the best, with amazing staff, a beautiful dining room, and a relaxation room on the top floor where you can chill out in your dressing gown after a nice sauna and read a magazine, looking out at the beautiful river through the glass windows. It has one of the best locations, one of the best restaurants and three of the best bars in town. Now who could ask for any more? Smart, luxurious, and you are allowed to open the door yourself. The **Steffani** (0041 (0)81 836 96 96, info@steffani.ch, www.steffani.ch), across the road, is another great option and the 4-star **Crystal** (0041

(0)81 836 26 26, stay@crystalhotel.ch, www.crystal hotel.ch) is superb, and is as close to the funicular as you can get.

Most of the less expensive hotels aren't in the best locations and still aren't cheap. The 3-star **Hotel Arte** (0041 (0)81 837 58 58, info@hotel-arte.ch, www.hotel-arte.ch) is one of the most inexpensive, yet central, hotels but don't expect a bargain. You can also contact the tourist office (0041 (0)81 837 33 99), who are incredibly helpful, and will be happy to help you find a hotel or apartment to suit your budget.

Eating out

On Corviglia

If your parched mouth will sip nothing but champagne alongside a soupçon of caviar, and you managed to squash your platinum credit card into your white fur-lined ski suit without spoiling the lining, swish your way over to the **Marmite** restaurant (081 833 63 55), where your palate and wallet are in for an exquisite shock. **Paradiso** (081 842 63 03) and **Trutz Lodge** (081 833 70 30) are both charming, traditional and have beautiful views.

On Corvatsch

The **Hossa Bar** (081 828 96 44) is a heated tent with music and a packed terrace. This place is great on the Snow nights, when it's open until late. The **Hahnensee** (081 833 36 34), on the run back down to St Moritz Bad, is great for lunch, après and evening meals. The **Alpetta** (081 828 86 30) is charming and rustic.

In town

Secondo (081 834 99 90) is one of our favourite restaurants, and a break from the swanky white tableclothed eateries. It is stylish and colourful, with a busy atmosphere and a wide range of food, from tapas and Mexican to pasta and local dishes. On a bad weather day we'd be very happy to sit there all day with a bottle of wine. **California bar** is good for a quick burger or snack, as is **Bobby's Bar** (081 834 42 83), with hot dogs, burgers and chicken nuggets. You should also pop into the renowned **Hanselmanns** at tea time; it's part of the St Moritz history and everyone goes there at least once.

Of the smart places to eat, the **Acla** (081 837 07 07) at the Schweizerhof is superb. The **Grissini** (081 836 26 66) at the Crystal is another smart open restaurant, and it's not extortionate – the most expensive main you can get is CHF52. **Cascade** brasserie (081 833 02 01) serves pasta, meat, salads and risotto, and a main dish will cost CHF 24–41. If you are peckish for a pizza in smart surroundings, head to the **Chesa Veglia** (081 837 28 00), a beautiful, cosy pizzeria (pizza around CHF30). For a night of pure indulgence, take a 5-minute taxi to **Jöhri's Talvo** in Chamfér (081 833 44 55). In a converted hay barn, you will find a beautiful, cosy, candlelit restaurant on two levels. If you are planning a romantic night, ask for one of the two tables on the separate balcony. It is definitely recommended to book, especially in high season. If caviar, foie gras and lobster with black truffles make your mouth water, you're in the right place. If not, there are other mouth-watering meat and fish dishes to choose from. To give you an idea of price, a fancy steak will cost you CHF88 and the six-course menu CHF230. Add on a couple of bottles of wine and you'll need a stiff drink to face the bill.

"If caviar, foie gras and lobster with black truffles make your mouth water, you're in the right place"

Bars and clubs

Après ski is good at the outdoor **Roo Bar** (081 837 50 50) in the main square in good weather. There are loads of bars to choose from, with varying degrees of exclusivity. Our cocktail for a good night includes a stop in **Bobby's Bar** (081 834 42 83), set into the shopping centre. It is done in a British-pub style, with a comfy 'outdoor' area indoors and pool tables. After that, head to the **Cava bar** in the Steffani (081 836 96 96), a cavernous bar with a relaxed and friendly feel, and then over the road to the Schweizerhof Hotel, where you will often find live music in the packed and great fun **Stübli bar**, live jazz in the **Piano bar** and the country-style **Muli bar** (081 837 07 07). If you're still going, head to the bar/club **Diamond**, opposite the Kulm hotel, or the **Vivai** (081 833 69 39) back at the Steffani. At the **Bailando Dancing Bar** (081 834 47 40) you can Latino dance

the night away. If you have infinite cash, and popped your jacket and tie into your ski or board bag, you could head to the **Kings Club** at Badrutts Palace, or to the **Casino** down in St Moritz Bad.

Useful facts and phone numbers

Tourist office

T: 0041 (0)81 837 33 33
F: 0041 (0)81 937 33 77
E: information@stmoritz.ch
W: www.stmoritz.ch

Direct reservations

T: 0041 (0)81 837 33 99
E: reservation@stmoritz.ch

Emergency services

- Police: 117
- Medical emergency: 144
- Heli-rescue:1414

Doctors

- Dr P R Berry: 081 833 79 79
- Dr P Hasler: 081 833 83 83
- Dr F Kuthan: 081 833 18 48
- Dr C Riederer: 081 833 30 30
- Dr P F Signotell: 081 833 69 43
- Dr P O Steiner: 081 833 17 77

Taxis

- Cattaneo Taxi: 081 833 69 69
- Erich's Taxi: 081 833 35 55
- Taxi Alessandro: 081 833 70 49
- Taxi Angelo: 081 833 13 93
- Taxi Bären: 081 833 72 72

Getting there

By plane

Zurich (200km) Transfer will take you 3 hours by car, 4 by bus.
Basel (290km) Transfer takes 4 hours by car.
Munich (360km) Transfer takes 4 hours by car.

Verbier

Some of the most extreme
riding in Europe, attached to
a stylish, hip resort

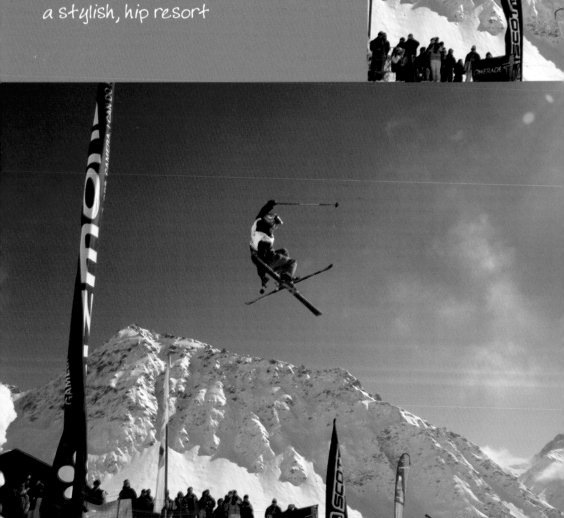

On the slopes	
Snow reliability	❄ ❄ ❄ ❄
Parks	❄ ❄ ❄
Off-piste	❄ ❄ ❄ ❄ ❄

Off the slopes	
Après ski	❄ ❄ ❄ ❄
Nightlife	❄ ❄ ❄ ❄
Eating out	❄ ❄ ❄ ❄
Resort charm	❄ ❄ ❄

"The Verbier Ride Slopestyle event is held here and attracts the world's best New School skiers"

The resort

Verbier is a fantastically fashionable resort and has an equally fierce mountain. If you're a keen freeriding skier or boarder you won't get bored, with the mountain or the nightlife, even if you're there for the season. You might tire of the prices though, and the hecticness of the place. It's a beautiful, but sprawling resort, with lots of cute chalets, but few people are moseying around enjoying the view – everyone's on a mission. Nothing wrong with this though – just get lots of sleep before you arrive.

The mountains

Height: 1500–3330m

Ability	Rating
Expert	❄ ❄ ❄ ❄ ❄
Intermediate	❄ ❄ ❄ ❄
Beginner	❄ ❄

Getting about

Verbier is at the far side of the Quatre Vallées, connecting 412km of pistes. The skiing area of the Quatre Vallés links the ski runs of Verbier, La Tzoumaz, Nendaz, Veysonnaz, and Val de Bagnes/Entremont. The Mont Fort Glacier keeps the area pretty snow sure.

The park

The park, located on Mont Fort, has been around for a while now, and has a good team of shapers working on it. The terrain is a little strange and the run-ins to some of the kickers are somewhat flat which makes it hard to get the speed to clear the gaps. However, it does have a few good kickers at the top of the park and a good selection of rails including a C-rail, wall ride and up-flat-up. This last rail is a favourite of the British pros, who while away hours sliding up it, and then reversing and coming back down. There is also a great big hip jump located at the bottom of the park. It's not the best place for learning freestyle, but advanced riders will enjoy it. The Verbier Ride Slopestyle event is held here and attracts the world's best New School skiers. To see this park being ridden at its best, check this event out on www.verbierride.com.

Off-piste and backcountry

Verbier is the freeriding capital of Europe. It is a test for even the world's best big-mountain riders; Seth Morrison has said that this is his favourite area as there is so much challenging terrain. The Bec des Rosses face (home of the O'Neill Xtreme event, see Events) is one of the hardest faces in the world and should only be attempted by the seriously good riders, with a guide. Mont Gele is the home of the Verbier Ride event, and once again has extreme terrain and some massive cliffs. There is a cable car up there but it's rarely open so you usually have a 40-minute hike.

The back of the Mont Fort is another favourite. On a powder day this is the perfect spot to find amazing steeps, gullies and cliff drops. Getting out is quite hairy though, as there is a long traverse along the side of the dam on the way. Its difficulty varies depending on whereabouts you go, though we would not recommend it to anyone who wasn't a competent rider. For those who don't mind a steep climb, check out the Stairway to Heaven. It starts near the Col de Gentianes and takes you right over into the next valley. This place is known for its incredible snow conditions and you won't see many other riders around. If you need shelter from the weather, head across the valley to Bruson, the perfect place to ride through the trees.

Verbier also provides marked ski routes that are not groomed or patrolled. They are great for riders wanting to improve their off-piste riding. A couple of good routes are the Vallon s'Arby and Col des Mines. You can get to these areas from the Lac des Vaux.

Verbier is not only one of the best places for freeriding, but also one of the most dangerous. We highly recommend that you always carry the right equipment; avalanche transceiver, shovel, probe, helmet, back protector, etc. Also, if you are venturing into the unknown, take a qualified mountain guide to ensure that you get the best out of Verbier's incredible terrain.

We would like to thank Warren Smith, Chris Southwell and Nick Southwell, our fellow British freeriding buddies and close friends, for showing us round and helping with our research.

Lift passes	Quatre Vallées	Verbier
1 day	CHF61	CHF53
6 days	CHF314	CHF272
13 days	CHF559	CHF485
There are discounts for children, young people, families and groups.		

Instruction

Adrenaline Ski and Snowboard School
A Swiss school; recommended.
T: 0041 (0)27 771 74 59
E: info@adrenaline-verbier.ch
W: www.adrenaline-verbier.ch

European SnowSport
This is another good British-run school.
T: 0041 (0)27 771 62 22
E: info@europeansnowsport.com
W: www.europeansnowsport.com

La Fantastique
T: 0041 (0)27 771 41 41
E: lafantastique@verbier.ch
W: www.lafantastique.com

La Maison du Sport
The Maison du Sport is the official Swiss school and good, though Old School.
T: 0041 (0)27 775 33 63
E: info@maisondusport.ch
W: www.maisondusport.ch

Warren Smith Ski Academy
Run by one of Britain's top performance coaches, this is the perfect school to bring your skiing to the next level.
T: 0044 (0)1525 374757 (UK office)
  0041 (0)79 359 65 66 (Swiss office)
E: admin@snowsportsynergy.com
W: www.warrensmith-skiacademy.com

Other activities

Adventure trail: There is an adventure trail open in both winter and summer with a climbing wall in the summer and ice climbing in winter. Call La Maison du Sport on 027 775 33 63.

Heliskiing/boarding and off-piste: For off-piste guiding or heliskiing/boarding call La Maison du Sport on 027 775 33 63 or La Fantastique on 027 771 41 41.

Horse riding; In Le Châble horse riding treks and lessons are available on request (027 776 12 00).

Paragliding: Call the paragliding centre (027 771 68 18) for an introduction to paragliding, lessons, licence courses and tandem flights. Other paragliding schools are Fly Time (079 606 12 64, www.fly-time.ch, info@fly-time.ch), Verbier Summits (079 313 56 77), L'Envol (079 679 94 52) or Max biplace (027 771 55 55). A tandem flight will cost CHF100–250 (10–45 mins). It will cost you around CHF240 to learn how to fly solo.

Sports centre: At the Sports Centre (027 771 66 01, www.verbier-sport.ch, info@verbier-sport.ch) you can enter the pool for CHF8 (with access to whirlpools), or CHF20 (with access to sauna and steam bath). As well as ice hockey events you can go ice skating yourself for CHF7 (equipment extra), squash is CHF15 for 30 minutes and tennis is CHF10/20 for an hour (upper/lower courts respectively). You can get a 7-day holiday package for CHF40 including pool and ice skating. There are also six artificial curling rinks at the multi-sports centre.

Tobogganning: Take a sled down the 10km toboggan run from Savoleyres-Tzoumaz (call Téléverbier on 027 775 25 11).

Events

24 Heures Freeride, in mid-December, is a 24-hour charity event to launch the winter season. Participants ski in teams of four, accumulate as many kilometres as they can and convert them into francs. It's also a chance to party for 24 hours with live concerts and DJs set up at Médran

The **Verbier Ride** in February (www.verbierride.com) is Europe's leading New School skiing event. Top skiers compete in three disciplines: Big Mountain Freeride (from the awe-inspiring Mont Gelé), Skier-X and Big Air in the snow park at La Chaux. The event was started

in 2000 by British freeski pioneer Warren Smith and it's now a world-recognised event. It attracts the biggest names from around the globe and the skiercross and slopestyle are X-games qualifiers. On top of this, the Big Mountain event has just recently become a part of the widely acclaimed World Tour. If there is one competition you are going to see this year, check out the Verbier Ride. Over the last couple of years Warren has extended the series by adding two more events. In July on the glacier of Saas Fee is the Saas Fee Ride (see Saas Fee chapter, page 374 and www.saasfeeride.com) and a new addition is the London Ride (www.thelondonride.com), held at the Daily Mail Ski and Show in October; an indoor big air event.

The **O'Neill Xtreme** usually takes place mid–late March (www.xtreme-snowboard.com). Launched in 1996, this competition brings together the finest freeriders (two-thirds snowboarders, one-third skiers) to compete at Bec des Rosses, opposite Col des

Gentianes, on gradients between 45 and 55 degrees, with couloirs and cliff drops. The **Ultime Session**, at the end of April, is a great finish to the winter season. There is a speed skiing race at Le Mont Fort, big air, waterslide concert, equipment testing and loads more going on in bars and clubs later on.

Accommodation

Verbier has a huge number of guest beds: over 15000. The only 5-star hotel is **Le Chalet d'Adrien** (0041 (0)27 771 62 00, www.chalet-adrien.com, info@chalet-adrien.com), right next door to the Savoleyres lift, but a little walk from the centre of town. For a smart hotel it's very homely, cosy and welcoming, but it does come at a seriously hefty price. Expect to pay CHF450–1030 per room/suite per night, and add another CHF40 per person for breakfast and another CHF85 per person for half board. The balconies overlooking the valley are well worth requesting and the view from the outside terrace is absolutely stunning. You should also take advantage of the gym, sauna and hot tub, as well as the indoor swimming pool (planned to open for the 05/06 season). The other super smart hotel is the 4-star **Rosalp** in the centre of town (0041 (0)27 771 63 23, www.rosalp.ch, rosalp@relaischateaux.com).

> # "It has one of the best locations, bang in the centre of town, only a few minutes' walk from the main cable car"

It has a gorgeous restaurant, but we found the staff a little surly.

If we could stay in any hotel in town, we would choose to stay in the 3-star **Farinet** hotel (0041 (0)27 771 6626, www.hotelfarinet.com, farinet@axiom.ch). It has one of the best locations, bang in the centre of town, only a few minutes' walk from the main cable car. It has recently had a complete revamp and the interior is amazing. All rooms have plasma screen TVs, iPods, free wireless internet, a DVD player, and there is a DVD library downstairs from which you can help yourself. There's even a menu of pillows for you to choose from! There are 16 rooms (all with underfloor heating and south-facing balconies – the ones on the first floor have a massive terrace) and four fantastic apartments. A double room costs CHF200–375 per room per night and an apartment CHF460–795. The staff are also top quality. Not only is it the best place to stay, it's also the best place to enjoy après ski and late-night dancing (see Bars and clubs) and to eat (see Eating out). We can't imagine anyone being disappointed with this hotel.

The **Bunker** at the Sports Centre (0041 (0)27 771 66 02, sleep@thebunker.ch, www.thebunker.ch) is really cheap, dormitory accommodation for individuals and groups, 800m from the village square. It has 128 beds starting at CHF49 for half-board accommodation (breakfast and three-course dinner) including entrance to the swimming pool, whirlpool and ice rink. Remember to bring your own sleeping bag! It's a great budget option, but not great accommodation; as it's an old nuclear fall out centre, there are no windows

and it's not particularly pleasant. A better option, for not too much more money, is the **Summer House** next door, which has much more pleasant dormitory accommodation.

Eating out

On the mountain

One of the best mountain restaurants is the **Cabane du Mont Fort**, which serves local Swiss specialities (as well as the odd hot dog) on a beautiful sun terrace with great views of the valley. **Chez Dany**, slightly off the beaten track, is a cosy, friendly chalet, again with a great terrace for bathing in the rays. For a quicker, and less expensive, burger and chips, head to the less attractive **Les Attelas** or **Les Ruinettes** restaurants.

In town

Verbier has loads of restaurants offering a wide variety of food, for a wide variety of budgets. If you've too much cash on your hands, you could palm some of it off on the very expensive, very smart and Michelin-starred **Restaurant Pierroz** in the Hotel Rosalp. Slightly less expensive, but in a similar budget category, is the more cosy and Swiss **Le Caveau**. Enjoy local specialities in the less formal, and more comfortable surroundings. **Au Vieux Verbier** serves more innovative and unusual food; it's a really fun and good restaurant, but once again prepare yourself for the bill.

Our favourite restaurant in town is the **Farinet**, the centrally located local hangout. In the relaxing, cosy and romantic lounge bar, choose from one of the mouth-watering platters – sushi, Indian, Mexican or Thai, or a simple snack of bread and hummus. We'd be quite happy to eat here every night. For an inexpensive, but superb meal, head to the **Fer à Cheval** in the centre of town. Enjoy a pizza or local dish, and the very friendly service. The Fer à Cheval has a great little terrace for eating in the sun at lunchtime, if you're not on the mountain. You can also enjoy a great meal downstairs at the **Pub Mont Fort**, whose food is much smarter than the usual pub grub, or failing that, head to the beautifully cosy **Al Capone's**, towards the Savoleyres lift. It has fantastic pizzas, made in the open, wood-fired oven, and you will be welcomed with a smile every time. **Offshore**, by the Medran lift, has a great surfy atmosphere inside, and it serves the best breakfasts in

town (that you pay CHF20 for). It's great for an informal lunch or dinner, and is a local hangout spot. For a swift burger, at any time until 1am, head to **Harold's** in the centre of town (also an internet café). For something a bit different call **Chez Dany's** mountain restaurant (027 771 25 24); you get a skidoo up there and can toboggan back down.

Bars and clubs

Après ski in Verbier is difficult to beat. To start the fun, stop off at the **1936** bar on the mountain, basically a big tent on the piste and a great place for a beer in the sun and a little something from the barbeque. When down the mountain, head straight to the **Farinet** for the rousing live music. Feel free to stomp on the bar in ski/board boots if the mood takes you. If the music gets a bit much and you actually want to talk to the people you're with, either head inside to the Farinet's beautiful and leather-sofa clad lounge bar or sit outside in the sunshine next door at the **Central T Bar** that's very London inside. The massive **Pub Mont Fort**, open until 1.30am, is popular at all times of the evening; it plays great music, has a great atmosphere and is a staple part of the Verbier scene – no night is complete without a beer here.

There are a few clubs to choose from that are open until 4am. Most popular is the **Casbah**, under the Farinet, which has a number of rooms playing different music, from rock, to pop, to hip hop. **Tara's** (Taratata) is a big club full of party people, jiving away to the usual commercial sounds. The rich and famous should head to the **King's** bar and the **Farm Club**, ridiculously exclusive and expensive, but fun nevertheless.

Useful facts and phone numbers

Tourist office

T: 0041 (0)27 775 38 88
F: 0041 (0)27 775 38 89
E: info@verbier.ch
W: www.verbier.ch

Emergency services

- Police: 117 in an emergency or 775 63 20 (Police cantonale)/775 35 45 (Police municipale)
- In a medical emergency call 144 for an ambulance
- Pharmacy: 771 66 22/ 771 23 30

Taxis

- Bruchez: 079 221 06 66
- Carron Vincent: 776 28 29
- May Taxis Excursions (24h): 771 77 71
- Taxi Edelweiss: 079 460 67 60

Getting there

By train

From Martigny, change to the Martigny-Le Châble line then from Le Châble to Verbier by bus or cable car.

By plane

Geneva (170km) Transfer costs CHF58 and takes around 3 hours.
Zürich (300km) Transfer costs CHF94 and takes around 4.5 hours.
For a timetable and more information contact CFF on 0900 300 300 or www.cff.ch.

Zermatt

Awesome skiing/boarding,
nightlife and food - love it

On the slopes	
Snow reliability	❄ ❄ ❄ ❄ ❄
Parks	❄ ❄ ❄
Off-piste	❄ ❄ ❄ ❄
Off the slopes	
Après ski	❄ ❄ ❄ ❄
Nightlife	❄ ❄ ❄ ❄
Eating out	❄ ❄ ❄
Resort charm	❄ ❄ ❄ ❄

The mountains

Height: 1620–3899m

Ability	Rating
Expert	❄ ❄ ❄ ❄
Intermediate	❄ ❄ ❄ ❄
Beginner	❄ ❄

The resort

Zermatt is a beautiful resort that has a not unjustified reputation for being expensive and elitist. Although it is a little poncey, the mountains (both in respect of scenic value and the ski and board action) are absolutely amazing. The 38, 4000-metre peaks surrounding Zermatt, make for impressive views, not least due to the trademark of Zermatt – the 4478m high Matterhorn.

In case you're interested in a bit of history, the Matterhorn was first conquered on 14 July 1865 by climber Edward Whymper and six others, only three of whom returned alive. The cemetery in the central area of town is where many climbers who were not as triumphant as Whymper have been laid to rest.

Zermatt is a car-free town but there are loads of electric cars and buses whizzing round so it's not quite as relaxed as you might imagine. To get your bearings, the main road is from the station to the church and if you turn towards the river at the church and cross over it, you will find another buzzing street with plenty more bars and restaurants.

One tiny grumble we have with Zermatt is the icy pathways in town. We saw four people, young and old, fall on their backs after slipping on the ice. There is no need for that in a resort that has taken enough of our money to be able to afford a good gritting service or under-floor heating.

Getting about

There are 394km of marked runs and acres of backcountry terrain. In total there are 132 runs and 73 lifts. There is a pretty good diversity of runs with something for everyone, except perhaps for the complete beginner. In Zermatt alone there are 18 black and yellow pistes (70.5km), 33 red pistes (106km), 19 blue pistes (17.5km); if you include the runs from Zermatt to Cervinia in Italy (mostly red pistes) you get the total of 394km of marked runs.

The slopes are well-groomed and there are many long, scenic runs, perfect for cruising. It used to be a big grumble that you could not always ride back to the resort but this can be moaned at no longer as they have now installed snow cannons all the way to the bottom so it doesn't matter if it has been a little short on snow. However, it may still be icy so perhaps still not best for the more nervous rider.

The lift systems in general are not great; on sunny days and weekends there are usually pretty nasty queues to get on to crammed gondolas that will leave you hot, flustered and unable to move. This would be a pretty big setback but, luckily for Zermatt, the memories of the horrendous lift journeys are soon forgotten.

Zermatt consists of three separate areas, two of which are well linked.

The **Sunnegga** area (including Blauherd and Rothorn) is reached by the underground funicular which is located about 5 minutes' walk from the station.

The **Gornergrat** area (including Hohtälli and Stockhorn) is linked to the Sunnegga area by a 125-person cable car linking Gant to Hohtälli. Gornergrat can be reached directly from Zermatt by trains (Gornergrat-Monte Rosa railway, GGB) that leave every 24 minutes and take 30–40 minutes. The views from this train are definitely worth a look if you're not in a hurry. The red runs from Gornergrat and Hothälli to Gant are beautiful.

The **Klein Matterhorn** area (including Trockener Steg and Schwarzsee) is the highest region and includes the glacial area used for summer skiing. There are tenuous links to the other regions but you really need to head back down to the main valley in order to get to a different mountain. The Klein Matterhorn also gives you access to Cervinia in Italy (see Cervinia chapter, page 256) – for which you need to buy an international pass or pay a daily supplement on your lift pass. The Klein Matterhorn glacier (now called the Matterhorn Glacier Paradise) is the highest summer ski area in the Alps. It consists of 36km^2 of pistes, six in total, and is at a height of 2900–3900m. There are also six drag lifts and a cable car. The glacier is open until 2pm depending on snow conditions.

Park

There are two parks in Zermatt, as well as a separate pipe at the Gornergrat which has a bar in the shape of an igloo and is much enjoyed by the locals. The Gravity Park is above the Trockener Steg in the Klein Matterhorn area and the other slightly lower down, used more in the winter as it can get very cold at the top. The parks contain some great rails from easy wide 5m rails to some 8m kinks. Unfortunately the jumps are not the best, but the couple of table tops are always in good condition.

Off-piste and backcountry

The glacier does limit the extent to which you can freely explore the backcountry terrain on the mountain tops but we found a number of areas, only really known to the locals (until now – sorry, locals), that raise the level of the off-piste opportunities in Zermatt.

At the top of the **Höhtalli** lift is an amazing area for freeride. This always has great snow, and you can get fresh tracks three or four days after a snowfall which is unheard of in most resorts nowadays. The best moguls around can be found on the slopes between Höhtalli and Gant, at **Triftji**, where the Triftji bump bash is held each year, organised by the local pros. Above the Höhtalli and Triftji areas is the **Stockhorn** region, which has been designated as a freeride area. The runs are marked, but not prepared, and not checked at the end of the day. However, the Stockhorn area often doesn't open until around February.

The **Rothorn** area has a fantastic diversity of terrain and there are loads of amazing and challenging faces to ride. There are rumours that there will be a big-mountain freeride competition here next winter, an ideal venue for such an event. We were also informed of a hidden valley in the Rothorn area, but we do suggest that you hire a guide or local who knows it well if you are going to check it out.

A guide is definitely recommended if you want a full day of adventure on the **Schwarzsee** tour. It is a good 1.5-hour hike round the back of the glacier and 3–4 hours of non-stop riding back down.

Zermatt is also famous for its extensive **heliskiing** opportunities with trips up to the **Monte Rosa** at 4250m (a fantastic run down through stunning glacial scenery to Furi), the Alphubeljoch at 3728m and up to the Plateau Rosa at 3479m. Trips cost from CHF450.

Instruction

Independent Swiss Snowboard Instructors

Private instruction for one to two people, including video analysis, costs CHF160 for 2 hours, CHF 220 for 3 hours and CHF 360 for a full day (5 hours). A full day's guiding costs CHF360 for 1–4 people.

T: 0041 (0)27 967 70 67
E: info@issi.ch
W: www.issi.ch

Lift passes	International pass (inc. Cervinia)	Zermatt only	Summer
1 day	CHF74	CHF66	CHF110
7 days	CHF416	CHF368	CHF332
14 days	CHF660	CHF586	CHF528
Season pass	CHF1122	CHF1320	CHF690
Children aged nine or younger receive free lift passes and 16 or under pay only 50 per cent.			

Stoked AG Ski and Snowboard School
T: 0041 (0)27 967 70 20
E: info@stoked.ch
W: www.stoked.ch

Summit Ski School
Call Paul for information on 0041 (0)79 616 74 53

The Swiss Ski and Snowboard School
T: 0041 (0)27 966 24 66
E: info@skischulezermatt.ch
W: www.skischulezermatt.ch

Other activities

Bowling: Contact the tourist office for information about the bowling alley.
Cinema: This is located at Vernissage (see Bars and clubs).

Climbing: There are both outdoor and indoor walls. Alternatively, the Gorge Adventure is a dynamic secured climbing route in the Gorner Gorge (contact the Alpin Centre for more information on 027 966 24 60).
Fitness centre: Contact the tourist office for more information.
Heliskiing: Extensive heliskiing is available in the area (see Backcountry and off-piste).
Ice grotto: The grotto at the Klein Matterhorn Glacier is the highest glacier palace in the Alps at 3810m. It contains various sculptures and information about glaciers, geology and climbing. Special events can be held in the ice grotto. It is open in both summer and winter.
Ice skating and curling: There are both natural and artificial skating rinks and a curling rink. Contact Obere Matten sports arene on 027 967 36 73.

Moonlit skiing/boarding: This can be arranged from the Rothorn area.

Night in an igloo: The igloos on Gornergrat are decorated with artistic sculptures by a local Inuit, and can be rented for the night (see Accommodation).

Night skiing/boarding: This requires headlamps and takes place from Schwarzsee.

Paragliding: Contact the Air-Born Flight School on 027 967 67 44.

Saunas, solariums and massages: These are on offer at a number of hotels at various prices. Hotel Arca (027 967 15 44), Hotel Christiania (027 966 80 00) and Mont Cervin (027 966 88 88) are good places to start looking.

Sledding: There are 2.5km of sledding runs. Sledding can also be done at night, with a number of additional options such as a party at a mountain hut or a fondue party.

Squash: Call the Hotel Alex on 027 966 70 70.

Swimming: There are indoor swimming pools at various hotels including Hotel Christiania (Roger Moore's hotel of choice! – call 027 966 80 00) and Hotel Eden (027 967 26 55).

Tennis: Both indoor and outdoor courts are available.

Torchlit skiing: Ski at night by the light of flaming torches, then move on to a fondue party.

Winter hiking: There are 30km of prepared paths.

Summer only

Climbing: Contact the tourist office for more information.

Golf: There is a 9-hole golf course at Zermatt-Randa (027 968 10 75, www.golfclubmatterhorn.ch) and also a mini golf course.

Hiking: There are 400km of marked hiking paths.

Mountain biking: There are 80km of mountain bike trails.

Sports field: Football, volleyball, basketball, tennis and unihockey can all be played here. Contact Obere Matten sports arena on 027 967 36 73.

Events

The **Triftji Bump Bash** mogul competition is held every year on the infamous mogul runs. Rumours that there is to be a freeride competition on the Rothorn are also rife.

Accommodation

In 1838 the local surgeon opened the first guest house that could accommodate three people, called the Hotel Mont Cervie (which was later changed to Monte Rosa). Zermatt can now accommodate 14000 guests in 112 hotels (6800 beds) and around 2000 holiday apartments. There are three 5-star hotels, thirty-six 4-star, and forty-five 3-star. The other twenty-eight hotels are 2-star or less.

You should take care when choosing the location of your hotel/apartment as the resort does sprawl a fairly long way. The best location is probably near the Gornergrat and Sunnegga railways, as here you are close to two of the lifts and the main street. You will need to take a bus to the Klein Matterhorn lift from here unless your hotel offers a free shuttle.

On a budget there are few decent places to stay. Some say that you should stay down in Täsch where you leave your car, but the train journey every day won't be much fun. There is a **youth hostel** in Zermatt, located about 400m from the main lifts in the centre of town. This is fairly cheap and offers half-board accommodation.

For an average priced hotel in a good location, we recommend the **Admiral Hotel** (0041 (0)27 966 90 00, info@hotel-admiral.ch, www.hotel-admiral.ch). This is a very friendly, 3-star hotel, with lots of character and charm (and a health and spa room). The rooms are cosy, and all of the 20 double rooms have fantastic views of the Matterhorn from their balconies. There are also four single rooms. In the summer a double room will cost CHF115–135 per person per night. This price is for bed and breakfast only; if you would like full board you will pay an extra CHF40 per night for a four-course dinner on five nights and a gala dinner on one night. The hotel is located right next to the Sunnegga-Rothorn lifts, and 5 minutes' walk from the centre of town. The bus stop for the Klein Matterhorn is a few seconds' walk away.

For sheer luxury, book yourself into the stunning, 5-star **Mont Cervin** (0041 (0)27 966 88 88, www.seiler hotels.ch/montcervin) in the centre of town. A double room could cost you CHF287–890 per room per night, for half board, depending on the time of season and standard of room.

For a bizarre experience, stay in an igloo village below the Gornergrat, at 2700m! There are romantic suites for two people, or group igloos sleeping six. There is also a whirlpool to relax in whilst enjoying the awe-inspiring views above Zermatt. You can find more information on the igloo village at www.ggb.ch.

Eating out

On the mountain

There are 38 restaurants on the mountain, with nearly every one having a reputation for serving excellent food. It is also difficult not to have beautiful scenery on the mountains of Zermatt, even the couple of ugly concrete restaurants have stunning views. At Findeln, below Sunnegga, are several busy, rustic and atmospheric restaurants (that are not cheap). Of these, **Chez Vrony** (027 967 25 52, www.chezvrony.ch) is the most widely esteemed. Between Furi and Zermatt are another variety of options including **Simi** (027 967 26 95) and **Zum See** (027 967 20 45, www.zumsee.ch), which are both fantastic. Also at Furi, the **Farmerhaus** (027 967 39 96) is a beautiful, traditional rustic chalet with a big log fire inside. Outside you will find a large terrace with a

bar and pizza hut. This place really comes into its own after 4pm for après ski when the live music starts. The food ranges from pizzas and crepes to pastas and steak. To get to this cluster of restaurants you need to take the red run from Schwarzsee to Furi. This is a very scenic run through the trees and there are cannons to make sure that there is always decent snow cover.

Further down the mountain is **Hennu Stadl**, another great place for loud live music during après ski. The hotel restaurant at **Schwarzsee** (027 967 22 63), right at the foot of the Matterhorn, has a massive terrace with incredible views of the Matterhorn and glacier. Booking is recommended.

In town

There is no doubt that Zermatt is an expensive place to eat. If you are on a strict budget then you should maybe hit the supermarkets (or even McDonald's – not that this is particularly cheap). However, as there are around 100 restaurants in Zermatt with a huge range of cuisines, it would be rude not to indulge a little.

Grampis is right in the centre of town; you can't miss it for the sparkling fairy lights. It has a funky bar/club downstairs and serves good pizzas and pastas upstairs at decent prices. **The Brown Cow Snack Bar** in the Hotel Post (again you can't miss it in the town centre) is another option. It serves good burgers and sandwiches and always has a busy, fun atmosphere.

Hotel Abana Real (www.hotelabanareal.com) contains two restaurants: **Rua Thai** (027 966 61 81) and **Fuji** (027 966 61 71), a Japanese restaurant where teppanyaki dishes are prepared in front of your very eyes. These restaurants are located on the river; turn at the church on the main street, and cross the river. Walk along this side of the river and you will come to the Hotel Abana Real. **Hotel Beausutie** is popular for the all-you-can-eat grill. And for something very different, **Restaurant Rifflealp** is a 5-star hotel and restaurant that produces pizzas in the shape of the Matterhorn – 10 points for originality go to them.

The 5-star restaurants have posh nosh if you fancy it. Try **Prato Borni** in the 5-star Zermatterhof (027 966 66 00, www.zermatterhof.ch) and **Mont Cervin** (027 966 88 88, www.seilerhotels.ch/montcervin). These restaurants are no doubt a gourmet treat but the same as other 5-star restaurants that you would find anywhere around the world. For superb food in very

smart but cosy surroundings, we highly recommend **Le Mazot** (027 966 06 06, le.mazot@reconline.ch, www.lemazotzermatt.ch). This restaurant has been owned by a lovely guy called Roger for the last 12 years, and he is there evening after evening to welcome customers, oversee the running of the open kitchen, and generally ensure that every aspect of the food and service is carried out to the highest level. The owner's pride in the restaurant and dedication to service is what makes it really stand out above the rest and is the reason that 70 per cent of guests return year after year. The cuisine is dominated by lamb, the restaurant's speciality, and we can't speak highly enough of the mixed lamb plate for main course, which includes leg of lamb followed by lamb fillet, both of which are divine. The 'surf and turf' is also excellent. To complement these dishes is a menu of 150 different European wines (CHF40–150), but you can't go wrong with the local house wines chosen by the owner; a fendant (white) and dole (red). You should book a few days in advance, unless you are flexible about what time you eat, and expect to pay CHF70–100 per person for two courses and wine.

Bars and clubs

Zermatt has 44 bars and a buzzing, year-round nightlife. After some tough nights of research, here our some of our favourites.

For a good après ski scene, try **Papperla** (027 967 40 40, info@papperla-pub.ch) where the club downstairs is becoming ever more popular with the workers. **The Country Bar** (027 967 15 96, www.elite-zermatt.ch) offers the Internet, karaoke and a game of pool. If you fancy drinking and eating with the seasonaires, **The North Wall** bar hosts the Natives' party each year as well as numerous fancy dress nights (Facstnacht). Sunday and Tuesday are the nights to be with the locals, whilst Saturdays are more touristy. For great snack food to accompany your beers, **The Pipe** (079 758 53 24, www.gozermatt.com/thepipe) is open from 4.30pm every day and has a great surfy-type atmosphere and the friendliest staff. For getting drunk quickly, **Z'Alt Hischi** (027 967 42 62, www.rhone.ch/hischi) pours the biggest measures ever. For drunken partying later in the evening, **Hotel Post** has loads of bars and restaurants to check out, but the main partying tends to occur in a cave-type club at the bottom of the building called the **Broken Bar**. Everyone should go to **Vernissage**. (027 967 66 36, www.vernissage-zermatt .com). This mega trendy bar needs to be seen. Its bizarre décor really works, with chandeliers made out of chains, loads of candles, and comfy sofas. It serves food at night and downstairs you will come across an art gallery and cinema! You can take your drinks downstairs for the film and later on the chairs move away, a DJ gets on stage and it turns into a club. Awesome stuff.

For the more discerning drinker who desires more than just getting hammered, **Pink** at Hotel Post (027 967 19 31, www.hotelpost.ch) has live jazz music every night and a great atmosphere. It's also in the same building as the cheesy parties, so when you're done being civilised you can join in the carnage. **Elsie's** bar (027 967 24 31, www.elsiebar.ch), opposite the church on the main street, is tiny but atmospheric. It tends to attract the 25+ age group, who have enough cash to splash out on a decent bottle of plonk. Elsie's also serves as a restaurant that apparently has fresh oysters every day.

Useful facts and phone numbers

Tourist office

- T: 0041 (0)27 966 81 00
- F: 0041 (0)27 966 81 01
- E: zermatt@wallis.ch
- W: www.zermatt.ch
- Mountain Guide's Office: 027 966 24 60
- Avalanche situation: 187 (excluding foreign mobile phones)

Emergency services

- Fire brigade: 118
- Police: 117
- Ambulance/rescue service: 144
- Police station: 027 966 22 22 (community police), 027 966 69 20 (cantonal police)

Doctors

- Dr med. Ch. Bannwart: 027 967 11 88
- Dr med. J Bieler und Dr med. P Brönnimann: 027 967 44 77
- Dr med. E Julen: 027 967 67 17
- Dr med. N Lutz: 027 967 19 16
- Dr med. D Stoessel: 027 967 79 79
- Dr Hermann Steffen (dentist): 027 967 34 67
- Hospital in Visp: 027 948 21 11
- Hospital in Brig: 027 922 33 33

Electric taxis

- Bolero: 027 967 60 60
- Imboden: 027 967 77 77
- Schaller: 027 967 12 12
- Dorsaz: 027 967 30 30

Getting there

By car

The drive time from Calais is 10 hours (1070km). From Geneva, take the N1/N9 via Sion to Sierre. Then take the E62 to Visp, where you will turn and head towards Zermatt via Stalden.

Cars have to be left in a car park in Täsch in open-air or covered car parks. A shuttle train runs from the car park to Zermatt every 20 minutes and this will set you back CHF15.60 for a return (www.mgbahn.ch). (N.B. If you would prefer a taxi to pick you up from the car park there are a number of options – try Taxi Eden on 027 967 64 44 or Taxi Schaller on 027 967 12 12.)

By plane

Geneva (244km) Transfer by bus (around 4–5 hours) or train (4 hours, see www.rail.ch), or car (3.5 hours).

Zurich (248km) Transfer is 5 hours by train (faster access is planned for 2007 – when it should take 3 hours), 3.5 hours by car.

Sion (80km) Transfer is 2 hours by train, and just over an hour by car. Although this is the closest airport, it is pretty dodgy and often closed. You will pay more to fly to Sion and then may well be directed back to Geneva!

Milan (234km) Transfer is nearly 4 hours by train, 3 by car.

You can take trolleys on to the train up to Zermatt and wheel them off the other end which can save a lot of hassle if you carry as much rubbish round with you as we do. Your hotel should arrange an electric car to pick you up from the station, just give them a call on the free phones at Zermatt station. If not, taxis are available (see above).

Ski and snowboard banter for dummies

Backcountry

Some people use the terms off-piste and backcountry interchangeably, but backcountry really refers to riders heading out into the really remote and untouched areas of the mountain.

Backcountry kicker

You will sometimes see skiers and boarders building their own jumps in the backcountry. This enables you to hand pick your location, size and landing, and many people will session these kickers for hours.

Big booter

A massive jump that really stands out from the rest.

Box

Budding freestylers will practise sliding on boxes in the park before progressing to rails.

Cornice

A big chunk of snow (caused by wind and such like) that is dangerously balanced on the side of the mountain. Look out for cornices in the backcountry; whilst it may seem enjoyable to jump off them, they are very unstable and have a tendency to break and cause an avalanche that could sweep you away in the process.

Couloir

A gully in the mountain. Couloirs range from little more than a narrow run that many people could have a bash at, to steep and tight shoots only to be attempted by experts.

Drop-off

This involves riding off a cliff on your board or skis.

FIS standards

The FIS (Fédération Internationale de Ski) organise world-class events so if something is to FIS standards it means it's pretty damn good.

Freeride

Freeriding has been attributed to many different kinds of riding – when we use the word 'freeride', we are referring to backcountry, big-mountain and off-piste riding.

Freestyle

Freestyle can mean anything from skiers in the moguls to skiers and snowboarders hitting the jumps in the park. Sometimes freestyle is related too closely to the park; many freestyle riders enjoy jibbing off natural hits all over the mountain.

Freshies

You can get freshies if you are the first person up the mountain first thing after a fresh snowfall, as they refer to the first tracks in fresh powder.

Gap jump

This is when a rider has to clear a gap from the take-off to the landing.

Half pipe

Take a big pipe, cut it in half and put snow in it – voilà. Variations are a quarter pipe (take a big pipe, cut it in half, and cut that half in half so that you just have one wall to hit) and a super pipe (take a really really big pipe, cut it in half and put snow in it). These pipes have massive walls and are used in all the world-class comps.

Hip

A hip is the same as a spine.

Hit

A jump.

Hook

To hook is to throw yourself off something, a cliff, for example. If somebody refers to you as a 'hooker' it's not necessarily a compliment, as hookers will throw themselves off anything, but without any element of control or style.

Jibbing

This is when riders play around on the pistes or in the park. In the park you might jib on rails or fun-boxes whilst on the piste you might be doing nose or tail presses or playing on natural hits wherever you might spot them.

Line

As well as being a top brand of ski, the term 'line' also refers to the route you take down the mountain. In big-mountain competitions, judges rate the line a competitor chooses, as well as their technique, style, etc.

Mogul field or bumps

A slope covered in natural or manmade bumps.

New School

This is a term that has emerged fairly recently in the skiing world, referring to the new movement in freestyle skiing. Skiing has gone through a huge change in the past decade, and the gap between skiing and boarding has seriously closed in. There is no longer the rift between skiers and boarders that there used to be, and there is no real difference in the image, or desires of freestyle skiers and boarders. As always, it will take probably another decade or so for the new style of skiing to be recognised by everyone – some resorts are still seriously Old School, only allowing snowboarders into their parks and other guidebooks out there will have separate sections of the book for skiers and boarders, or deal exclusively with one or the other. We are the first to acknowledge that the new generation of rider, whether skier or boarder, is after the same thing.

Off-piste

This is the natural terrain, outside the marked areas of the piste.

Pisteurs/ski patrol/ ski monitors

These are the lifeguards of the mountain. They will come and help you if you've injured yourself on the slopes and they know everything there is to know about the mountain and weather conditions. These are the people to consult before you venture off-piste as they will inform you how safe it is and which areas should be avoided.

Powder

Good, light, deep snow.

Rails

These are just like hand rails that you see in the street and you'll mainly find them in parks. Skiers and snowboarders use them to slide down, or up, and they come in many different shapes and sizes, such as a rainbow rail, kinked rails (flat-down, up-flat-up, Y-down, etc.), C-rail, S-rail or rollercoaster rail. If you want to start learning rails, most parks provide a fun box on which to learn and practise.

Rider

We use the term 'ride' or 'rider' to refer to both skiers and boarders. We don't differentiate between them; we all ride the same mountain.

Sessioning

This means hitting a jump or rail once, walking back up and repeating this process for as long as you fancy.

Shapers

These are the people who maintain and look after the park. Some resorts leave their parks to fade away once they have been built, whilst others employ a number of shapers, who take huge pride in their work and are a great asset to the resort.

Skiing switch

This means skiing backwards.

Slopestyle

A course of jumps, rail slides and other obstacles.

Spine

A jump shaped like a spine, where you can land on either side of the landing.

Step up

A type of jump where you land at a higher point than where you took off.

Table top

A jump with a platform that you must clear to reach the landing. Table tops are less intimidating than gap jumps and small ones are suitable for learning on.

Wall ride

A steep wall, found in the park, for boarders and skiers to ride up and jib around on.

Index

Page refs for (rated) facilities are in **bold** for 5 star rating; ordinary type for 4 star rating. Resorts: (And) =Andorra (Aus) =Austria (Fr) =France (It) = Italy (Nor) =Norway (Swe) =Sweden (Sz) =Switzerland

413